COPYRIGHT LEGISLATION & COMMENTARY

2022 Edition

The Honourable Roger T. Hughes, Q.C.
Susan Peacock

 LexisNexis

Copyright Legislation & Commentary, 2022 Edition

© LexisNexis Canada Inc. 2022

April 2022

Library and Archives Canada Cataloguing in Publication

Copyright legislation and commentary / Roger T. Hughes.

Annual.

2004/2005 ed.—

Continues: Copyright Act . . . consolidation.

ISSN 1717-2829

ISBN 978-0-433-51873-0 (2022 edition)

1. Canada. Copyright Act. 2. Copyright—Canada.

3. Design, Industrial—Canada. I. Hughes, Roger T., 1941–

KE2794.54.A2   2004/05–346.7104'82'02632   C2005-301336-0

KF2994.C66   2004/05–

Published by LexisNexis Canada, a member of the LexisNexis Group

LexisNexis Canada Inc.

111 Gordon Baker Road, Suite 900

Toronto, Ontario

M2H 3R1

Customer Service

Telephone: (905) 479-2665 • Fax: (905) 479-2826

Toll-Free Phone: 1-800-668-6481 • Toll-Free Fax: 1-800-461-3275

Email: customerservice@lexisnexis.ca

Web Site: www.lexisnexis.ca

Printed and bound in Canada.

(4/2022–Pub.8007)

Order Today!
Take Advantage of Our 30-Day Risk-Free* Examination!

---

5 Ways to Order

☽ Phone: 1-800-387-0899

🖹 Fax: 1-800-461-3275

✉ Email: customerservice@lexisnexis.ca

🖱 Online: www.lexisnexis.ca/store

👤 Contact: Account Executive

Multiple Copy Discounts

Number of Copies	You Save
10 to 24	5%
25 to 49	10%
50 to 99	15%
100 or more	20%

* Pre-payment required for first-time purchasers. Purchasers will be placed on standing order to receive future editions automatically on 30-day risk-free examination terms. New editions are published regularly as required. Price and other details are subject to change without notice.

ABOUT THE EDITORS

The Honourable Roger T. Hughes, Q.C. was a judge of the Federal Court of Canada until his retirement in September 2016. He is an author of several texts in the litigation and intellectual property field, including *Federal Court of Canada Service*; *Canadian Federal Courts Practice*; *Hughes & Woodley on Patents, Second Edition*; *Hughes on Trade Marks, Second Edition*; *Hughes on Copyright & Industrial Design, Second Edition*; *Patent Legislation & Commentary* (annual edition); *Trademarks Act & Commentary* (annual edition); *Halsbury's Laws of Canada — Trademarks, Passing Off and Unfair Competition*; *Halsbury's Laws of Canada — Patents, Trade Secrets and Industrial Designs*; *Canadian Forms & Precedents — Intellectual Property*; and *Canadian Forms & Precedents — Licensing*. He has published numerous papers and is a frequent speaker on diverse topics, including court practice and procedure; patent, trademark and copyright law; and media and entertainment law. As counsel, Mr. Hughes has appeared in all levels of court, including the Supreme Court of Canada, in a large number of cases, and mainly in the intellectual property field.

Susan Peacock practised law in the areas of copyright and broadcasting regulation. From 1989 until 2008, she was Vice President of Copyright Collective of Canada and The Canadian Motion Picture Distributors Association (now The Motion Picture Association — Canada), a trade association of the major international motion picture distribution companies. Until 1989 she was in-house counsel for various companies in the business of television production, distribution, financing and broadcasting. From 1988 to 1996 she was Chair of the Board of YTV Canada Inc. She served on Statistics Canada's National Advisory Committee on Cultural Statistics and the Program Advisory Committee of Ryerson University's School of Radio and Television Arts. Ms. Peacock is a graduate of Osgoode Hall Law School and a member of the Law Society of Ontario.

LEGISLATIVE CURRENCY

The legislation reproduced in this consolidation is current to

Canada Gazette, Part I, Vol. 155, No. 50, December 11, 2021 and Part II, Vol. 155, No. 25, December 8, 2021.

GENERAL TABLE OF CONTENTS

INDUSTRIAL DESIGN

INTEGRATED CIRCUIT TOPOGRAPHY

GENERAL TABLE OF CONTENTS

2021 YEAR IN REVIEW

JURISPRUDENCE

Protected Subject-Matter

A work includes its title when the title is original and distinctive, but the title is not a separate work and copying the title of a work constitutes infringement only when the title is determined to be a substantial part of the work itself.[1]

An author who publishes what they claim to be a nonfiction historical account cannot later claim the account is actually fictional to avoid the principle that there is no copyright in facts. It is not necessary to determine whether facts are actually true; the author's plausible assertions that the facts and events in question are true is sufficient to find that they are not protected by copyright.[2]

The use of brief excerpts of news reports in political "attack ads" was infringement of copyright in the news reports: facts and ideas are not protected by copyright, but the taking was of the broadcaster's style of material, which came from some of their most popular and widely recognized programs.[3]

A work is only protected by copyright if it is original, but that test has been satisfied with respect to such mundane works as a quotation form, a standard form contract and a warranty certificate.[4]

Ownership of a Cinematographic Work

Although the statement of claim stated that the individual plaintiff had assigned his copyright to the corporate plaintiff, the individual plaintiff was found to be the owner of copyright in the cinematographic work because his name appeared on the work as the maker of the work.[5] This is not the only decision where "author",

---

[1] *Winkler v. Hendley*, [2021] F.C.J. No. 497, 2021 FC 498 (F.C.) at paras. 147 and 151.

[2] *Winkler v. Hendley*, [2021] F.C.J. No. 497, 2021 FC 498 (F.C.) at paras. 53-111.

[3] *Canadian Broadcasting Corp. v. Conservative Party of Canada*, [2021] F.C.J. No. 417, 2021 FC 425 (F.C.) at paras. 37-66.

[4] *Patterned Concrete Mississauga Inc. v. Bomanite Toronto Ltd.*, [2021] F.C.J. No. 308, 2021 FC 314 (F.C.) at paras. 20-36.

[5] *Wiseau Studio, LLC v. Harper*, [2020] O.J. No. 1909, 2020 ONSC 2504 (Ont. S.C.J.) at paras. 155, 156. A motion to vary that decision was dismissed, *Wiseau Studio, LLC v. Harper*, [2020] O.J. No. 3137, 2020 ONSC 3920 (Ont. S.C.J.); an appeal from that decision was dismissed for failure to post security for costs of the trial and the appeal, *Wiseau Studio, LLC v. Harper*, [2021] O.J. No. 3974, 2021 ONCA 532 (Ont. C.A.). An application for leave to appeal the order to post security, [2021] O.J. No. 198, 2021 ONCA 31 (Ont. C.A.), has been filed with the Supreme Court of Canada, [2021] S.C.C.A. No. 464, SCC #39765 (S.C.C.). A new action for damages for fraudulent misrepresentation was stayed as an abuse of process, *Wiseau Studio, LLC v. Harper*, [2021] O.J. No. 7067, 2021 ONSC 8324 (Ont. S.C.J.).

"owner" and "maker" have been equated or confused with respect to cinematographic works.[6] Although the Act defines "maker" in relation to a cinematographic work,[7] the first owner of copyright in a cinematographic work, as with all works, is its author, not its maker.[8] The Act refers to makers of cinematographic works only with respect to subsistence of copyright.[9]

Reproduction

Psychometric tests were found to have been reproduced when the defendant's version produced almost identical results to those of the plaintiff's version, even if the questionnaires and the algorithms were different.[10]

Communication to the Public by Telecommunication

The provision of technological means such as caches, where information is temporarily stored, does not, by that act alone, make the provider of communication liable for copyright infringement, so long as such technology is a normal part of the communication technology[11] and the only remedy available against the provider of an information location tool is an injunction.[12] However, the Federal Court of Appeal distinguished between content-neutral search engines and a website operator who hosted and distributed infringing add-ons that targeted infringing content in a user-friendly and reliable way, thus providing unauthorized access to copyrighted material.[13]

Making Available

The so-called "making available right" provides that communication of a work or other subject-matter to the public by telecommunication includes making it available to the public by telecommunication in a way that allows a member of the

---

[6] In addition to *Wiseau*, see *Bell Canada v. L3D Distributing Inc. (c.o.b. INL3D)*, [2021] F.C.J. No. 867, 2021 FC 832 (F.C.) at para. 47; *Canadian Broadcasting Corp. v. Conservative Party of Canada*, [2021] F.C.J. No. 417, 2021 FC 425 (F.C.) at paras. 32 and 33, which was following *Interbox Promotion Corp. v. 9012-4314 Québec Inc (Hippo Club)*, [2003] F.C.J. No. 1581, 2003 FC 1254 (F.C.) at paras. 19 and 24.

[7] *Copyright Act*, R.S.C. 1985, c. C-42, s. 2, definition of "maker". A sound recording may also have a maker, but a sound recording is not a work.

[8] *Copyright Act*, R.S.C. 1985, c. C-42, subs. 13(1).

[9] *Copyright Act*, R.S.C. 1985, c. C-42, para. 5(1)(b).

[10] *Arc En Ciel RH c. Services Swissnova inc.*, [2021] J.Q. no 3112, 2021 QCCS 1187 at paras. 65-73.

[11] *Canadian Assn. of Internet Providers v. Society of Composers, Authors and Music Publishers of Canada*, [2004] S.C.J. No. 44, [2004] 2 S.C.R. 427 at paras. 113-119.

[12] *Copyright Act*, R.S.C. 1985, c. C-42, s. 41.27.

[13] *Bell Canada v. L3D Distributing Inc. (c.o.b. INL3D)*, [2021] F.C.J. No. 867, 2021 FC 832 (F.C.) at paras. 64 and 65. See also *Bell Canada v. Lackman*, [2018] F.C.J. No. 176, 2018 FCA 42 (F.C.A.) at paras. 23-37.

public to have access to it from a place and at a time individually chosen by that member of the public.[14]

The Copyright Board found that the act of making a work available to the public was a separate communication to the public by telecommunication regardless of whether any subsequent transmission occurred and regardless of whether any subsequent transmission was a download or a stream.[15] The Federal Court of Appeal quashed the Board's decision,[16] holding that the Board had failed to follow a determination of the Supreme Court of Canada. The Supreme Court of Canada had said that the principle of technological neutrality requires the *Copyright Act* to be interpreted so as to avoid imposing "an additional layer of protections and fees based solely on the method of delivery of the work to the end user".[17] Although the Supreme Court of Canada decision preceded the coming into force of the making available right, the Federal Court of Appeal held that the making available provision does not create a new exclusive right and that the act of making available is merely a "preparatory act".[18] In 2021, the Supreme Court of Canada granted leave to appeal the Federal Court of Canada's decision.[19] Also in 2021, the Federal Court said that the Federal Court of Appeal had "merely found that the making available provisions did not create a new exclusive right in the context of setting tariffs".[20]

Default judgment and statutory damages of more than $29 million were awarded where the defendants, by dealing in pre-loaded set-top boxes containing software or configured for accessing unauthorized television content, made the plaintiffs' works available in a way that allowed the users of the pre-loaded set-top boxes to access

[14] *Copyright Act*, R.S.C. 1985, c. C-42, subs. 2.4(1.1) with respect to works, para. 15(1.1)(*d*) with respect to sound recordings of performers' performances, and para. 18(1.1)(*a*) with respect to sound recordings.

[15] Online Music Services (CSI: 2011-2013); SOCAN (2011-2013); SODRAC (2010-2013) — Scope of section 2.4(1.1) of the Copyright Act — Making Available (August 25, 2017) Copyright Board Decision at paras. 12 and 16.

[16] *Entertainment Software Assn. v. Society of Composers, Authors and Music Publishers of Canada*, [2020] F.C.J. No. 671, 2020 FCA 100 (F.C.A.).

[17] *Entertainment Software Association v. Society of Composers, Authors and Music Publishers of Canada*, [2012] 2 SCR 231, 2012 SCC 34 (S.C.C.) at para. 9.

[18] *Entertainment Software Assn v. Society of Composers, Authors and Music Publishers of Canada*, [2020] F.C.J. No. 671, 2020 FCA 100 (F.C.A.) at para. 96.

[19] *Society of Composers, Authors and Music Publishers of Canada v. Entertainment Software Association*, [2020] S.C.C.A. No. 392, [2020] C.S.C.R. no 392 (S.C.C.), April 22, 2021.

[20] *Warner Bros. Entertainment Inc. v. White (c.o.b. Beast IPTV)*, [2021] F.C.J. No. 38, 2021 FC 53 (F.C.) at paras. 99-104.

those works by telecommunication from a place and a time individually chosen by the user.[21]

The *Radiocommunication Act* prohibits interference with, or obstruction of, any radiocommunication as well as decoding encrypted programming signals and dealing in equipment or devices for such purposes without lawful excuse.[22] The Federal Court has determined that such activity is also an infringement of the making available right, as well as an authorization of infringement.[23]

Authorization

Although a person does not authorize a use protected by copyright merely by authorizing the use of equipment that could be used to infringe, defendants were found to have infringed by authorizing the communication of the plaintiffs' works to the public by telecommunication when they dealt in pre-loaded set-top boxes that had been modified to allow access to the plaintiffs' works and offered instruction and technical support to infringing customers.[24]

Fair Dealing

Although they declined to assess the university's fair dealing guidelines, the Supreme Court of Canada did say that they did not endorse the reasoning of the courts below in assessing the guidelines, particularly with respect to their analysis of the "purpose of the dealing" factor in the fairness analysis.[25]

Fair dealing for the purpose of news reporting (if the source and, if available, the author, performer, maker or broadcaster is mentioned) is not an infringement of copyright. The source must be identified or identifiable by a reasonably informed consumer and was therefore satisfied when the source's logo was displayed or when the source was a core program featuring well-known television personalities associated with the source.[26]

The requirement to mention the source, when claiming fair dealing for the purpose of news reporting, was satisfied when the source was referred to and a link to the source was provided, but the requirement to mention the author was not satisfied

---

[21] *Bell Canada v. L3D Distributing Inc. (c.o.b. INL3D)*, [2021] F.C.J. No. 867, 2021 FC 832 (F.C.) at paras. 56-65.

[22] *Radiocommunication Act*, R.S.C. 1985, c. R-2, paras. 9(1)(*b*) and (*c*) and para. 10(1)(*b*).

[23] *Bell Canada v. L3D Distributing Inc. (c.o.b. INL3D)*, [2021] F.C.J. No. 867, 2021 FC 832 (F.C.) at paras. 56-70. See also declarations 2, 3 and 5 at para. 90.

[24] *Bell Canada v. L3D Distributing Inc. (c.o.b. INL3D)*, [2021] F.C.J. No. 867, 2021 FC 832 (F.C.) at paras. 66-70.

[25] *York University v. Canadian Copyright Licensing Agency (Access Copyright)*, [2021] S.C.J. No. 32, 2021 SCC 32 (S.C.C.) at paras. 97-107.

[26] *York University v. Canadian Copyright Licensing Agency (Access Copyright)*, [2021] S.C.J. No. 32, 2021 SCC 32 (S.C.C.) at paras. 85 and 86.

when the author's name was ascertainable only by accessing the source.[27]

A business that sold reports about users' interaction with crowd-sourced content that was reproduced on its website was found to be dealing with that content for the purpose of research.[28]

Where the use of news reports in political "attack ads" was intended to inform and persuade, but was not intended to train, to discipline or to pass on knowledge other than for the transitory period of an election campaign, the use was not for the purpose of education,[29] but that use was for the purpose of criticism.[30] As to whether that use was fair:

- The purpose of the criticism was to secure votes in a political campaign, a legitimate political purpose that pointed to fairness.[31]

- When the product of the dealing was viewed two million times over six days, and "retweeted" and "liked" hundreds of times without knowing how many times the tweets were viewed, the respondents failed to satisfy the court that the character of the dealing was fair.[32]

- Where the nature of the work that was copied was news or news-like content produced by a public broadcaster, it favoured a fairness conclusion.[33]

The purpose of the dealing was not fair when it was commercial with no benefit to the copyright owner and no associated broader public interest.[34]

The reduced quality and resolution of photographs posted on the Internet was not analogous to use of only portions of a song and did not establish that the amount of

---

[27] *Stross v. Trend Hunter Inc.*, [2021] F.C.J. No. 1017, 2021 FC 955 (F.C.) at paras. 16-19, finding that there was a palpable but not overriding error on this point in *Stross v. Trend Hunter Inc.*, [2020] F.C.J. No. 225, 2020 FC 201 (F.C.) at para. 31.

[28] *Stross v. Trend Hunter Inc.*, [2021] F.C.J. No. 1017, 2021 FC 955 (F.C.), affg *Stross v. Trend Hunter Inc.*, [2020] F.C.J. No. 225, 2020 FC 201 (F.C.) at paras. 22-30.

[29] *Canadian Broadcasting Corp. v. Conservative Party of Canada*, [2021] F.C.J. No. 417, 2021 FC 425 (F.C.) at para. 84.

[30] *Canadian Broadcasting Corp. v. Conservative Party of Canada*, [2021] F.C.J. No. 417, 2021 FC 425 (F.C.) at paras. 71-87.

[31] *Canadian Broadcasting Corp. v. Conservative Party of Canada*, [2021] F.C.J. No. 417, 2021 FC 425 (F.C.) at paras. 89-91.

[32] *Canadian Broadcasting Corp. v. Conservative Party of Canada*, [2021] F.C.J. No. 417, 2021 FC 425 (F.C.) at paras. 92-95.

[33] *Canadian Broadcasting Corp. v. Conservative Party of Canada*, [2021] F.C.J. No. 417, 2021 FC 425 (F.C.) at paras. 104, 105.

[34] *Stross v. Trend Hunter Inc.*, [2021] F.C.J. No. 1017, 2021 FC 955 (F.C.) at paras. 26-30, affg [2020] F.C.J. No. 225, 2020 FC 201 (F.C.) at paras. 32-41.

the dealing in the photographs was less than if the quality had been better.[35]

Registration

Unlike a certificate of registration issued by the Canadian Register of Copyrights, a certificate issued by the United States Copyright Office is not *prima facie* proof of the subsistence of copyright or of the identity of the owner.[36] However, if the U.S. certificate satisfies the requirements of the *Canada Evidence Act*,[37] it may be admissible as evidence.[38]

Evidence

On a motion for default judgment, a plaintiff must provide evidence that is sufficiently clear, convincing and cogent to satisfy the balance of probabilities test. This test was satisfied, even though the infringement happened entirely within the defendant's premises.[39] The plaintiff used technology to determine, each time a copy of its software was opened, whether that copy was licensed. If it was not, technology enabled the plaintiff to identify the time, date and location of each unauthorized use and to identify the device used and the associated email address. The plaintiff used that information to identify the defendant, who admitted the unlicensed use in an email to the plaintiff.

Although the onus is on the plaintiff to prove infringement, it was inferred, in the absence of evidence to the contrary, that once infringement had been established, the defendant's subsequent versions of infringing computer software continued to infringe; the defendant could not rely on the plaintiff's onus and a general allegation that they had continued to modify the software.[40]

Remedies

Collection of Royalties by Collective Societies

In case of default, a collective society may collect the royalties in an approved tariff (or the royalties fixed by the Board in a court of competent jurisdiction),[41] but this

---

[35] *Stross v. Trend Hunter Inc.*, [2021] F.C.J. No. 1017, 2021 FC 955 (F.C.) at paras. 32-34, affg [2020] F.C.J. No. 225, 2020 FC 201 (F.C.) at paras. 45-47.

[36] *Lickerish, Ltd. v. Airg Inc.*, [2020] F.C.J. No. 1252, 2020 FC 1128 (F.C.) at paras. 39-40.

[37] R.S.C. 1985, c. C-5.

[38] *Lickerish, Ltd. v. Airg Inc.*, [2020] F.C.J. No. 1252, 2020 FC 1128 (F.C.) at paras. 18-38.

[39] *Trimble Solutions Corp. v. Quantum Dynamics Inc.*, [2021] F.C.J. No. 55, 2021 FC 63 (F.C.).

[40] *Ark Innovation Technology Inc. v. Matidor Technologies Inc.*, [2021] F.C.J. No. 1973, 2021 FC 1336 (F.C.) at paras. 41-52.

[41] *Copyright Act*, R.S.C. 1985, c. C-42, s. 73.

remedy is not available against a user who is not a licensee.[42] A person who has not paid or offered to pay the royalties in an approved tariff is not a licensee and may be liable for infringement for unauthorized use,[43] but an infringement action can only be brought by someone with an interest in the relevant copyrights,[44] and a collective society may not have such an interest.

Common Law

In addition to the statutory causes of action available under the *Copyright Act*, the common law cause of inducement is available under certain circumstances.[45]

Equitable Remedies

The Federal Court made an order transferring control of the infrastructure of a defendant's IPTV service to independent supervising solicitors. The purpose of the order was not to collect evidence (as with an Anton Piller Order), but to prevent the defendants from transferring ownership or control of their service outside the court's jurisdiction.[46]

The *Telecommunications Act* prohibits a Canadian carrier, including an ISP, from controlling the content or influencing the meaning or purpose of telecommunications carried by it,[47] but it does not displace the Federal Court's equitable powers of injunction, including the power to impose a site-blocking order.[48] Furthermore, compliance with a site-blocking order does not amount to controlling or influencing and, therefore, does not require the CRTC's approval and does not offend net neutrality.[49] A site-blocking order does not infringe the ISPs' right to freedom of expression, as ISPs do not engage in expressive activity.[50] Given the strong *prima*

---

[42] *York University v. Canadian Copyright Licensing Agency (Access Copyright)*, [2021] S.C.J. No. 32, 2021 SCC 32 (S.C.C.) at paras. 20-76.

[43] *York University v. Canadian Copyright Licensing Agency (Access Copyright)*, [2021] S.C.J. No. 32, 2021 SCC 32 (S.C.C) at para. 34.

[44] *Copyright Act*, R.S.C. 1985, c. C-42, subs. 41.23(1).

[45] *Bell Canada v. L3D Distributing Inc. (c.o.b. INL3D)*, [2021] F.C.J. No. 867, 2021 FC 832 (F.C.) at paras. 71-77.

[46] *Warner Bros. Entertainment Inc. v. White (c.o.b. Beast IPTV)*, [2021] F.C.J. No. 38, 2021 FC 53 (F.C.).

[47] *Telecommunications Act*, S.C. 1993, c. 38, s. 36.

[48] *Teksavvy Solutions Inc. v. Bell Media Inc.*, [2021] F.C.J. No. 486, 2021 FCA 100 (F.C.A.) at paras. 33-38. An application has been made to the Supreme Court of Canada for leave to appeal this decision (SCC #39876).

[49] *Teksavvy Solutions Inc. v. Bell Media Inc.*, [2021] F.C.J. No. 486, 2021 FCA 100 (F.C.A.) at paras. 33-37. An application has been made to the Supreme Court of Canada for leave to appeal this decision (SCC #39876).

[50] *Teksavvy Solutions Inc. v. Bell Media Inc.*, [2021] F.C.J. No. 486, 2021 FCA 100 (F.C.A.) at para. 50. An application has been made to the Supreme Court of Canada for leave to appeal this decision (SCC #39876).

facie case of ongoing infringement and the restrictions and safeguards in the order, concerns about freedom of expression did not tip the balance against granting the order.[51]

The Federal Court rejected a defendant's argument that no injunction should be awarded because the infringing behaviour had ceased.[52]

Reverse Class Action

In 2019, the Federal Court refused to certify a class of defendants in a proposed "reverse class action" against a number of alleged copyright infringers.[53] On appeal, the Federal Court of Appeal (FCA) set aside the Federal Court's decision and sent the matter back to be reconsidered.[54] The FCA found that the Federal Court had erred in the application of the test of whether a reasonable cause of action was disclosed in the application. The FCA noted that if the trial division's reasoning prevailed, the plaintiff could be without any remedy for infringement. The FCA acknowledged that the proposed respondents had raised a number of substantive concerns about the legality and administrative viability of the class proceeding, but said that it was premature to conclude that they would be fatal to the certification application.

Damages

The Federal Court declined to award damages under both the *Copyright Act* and the *Radiocommunication Act*.[55]

In addition to damages, a successful plaintiff may be awarded that part of the infringer's profits that resulted from the infringement. Profits were not awarded where marketing materials infringed and there was no evidence that profits resulted from the infringement.[56]

Punitive Damages

Punitive damages were awarded against defendants who chose to operate in an industry that inherently and blatantly disregards copyright owners' rights —

---

[51] *Teksavvy Solutions Inc. v. Bell Media Inc.*, [2021] F.C.J. No. 486, 2021 FCA 100 (F.C.A.) at paras. 46-59. An application has been made to the Supreme Court of Canada for leave to appeal this decision (SCC #39876).

[52] *Patterned Concrete Mississauga Inc. v. Bomanite Toronto Ltd.*, [2021] F.C.J. No. 308, 2021 FC 314 (F.C.) at para. 50.

[53] *Voltage Pictures, LLC v. Salna*, [2019] F.C.J. No. 1533, 2019 FC 1412 (F.C.).

[54] *Salna v. Voltage Pictures, LLC*, [2021] F.C.J. No. 943, 2021 FCA 176 (F.C.A.). An application has been made to the Supreme Court of Canada for leave to appeal (SCC #39895).

[55] *Bell Canada v. L3D Distributing Inc. (c.o.b. INL3D)*, [2021] F.C.J. No. 867, 2021 FC 832 (F.C.) at para. 93.

[56] *Constellation Brands US Operations Inc. c. Société de vin internationale ltée*, [2021] Q.J. No. 14386, 2021 QCCA 1664 (Que. C.A.) at paras. 31-60, affg [2019] Q.J. No. 7355, 2019 QCCS 3610 (Que. S.C.).

egregious conduct warranting denunciation and the additional sanction of punitive damages.[57]

Statutory Damages

Conduct of the parties is a factor considered when setting the level of statutory damages. The conduct of the parties includes behaviour consistent with the actions of a "copyright troll", such as aggressive threatening of litigation and pressing for early settlement.[58]

Network service providers who fail to perform their statutory obligations with respect to notices of claimed infringement may be liable for statutory damages of from $5,000 to $10,000, or such other amount as may be fixed by regulation.[59] Although a claim for such damages can be dealt with by motion in conjunction with an application for a disclosure order, if the disclosure issue is settled and only the damage claim remains, the statutory damages claim must be addressed through a separate action.[60]

Statutory damages were awarded in the middle of the range ($10,000 per work), even though the defendants' conduct was so egregious that it warranted punitive damages. The court declined to set the rate at $20,000, the amount claimed by the plaintiffs, because the plaintiffs had already obtained judgment of $5,000,000 in another similar action and intended to pursue default judgments in other similar actions, and had admitted that their decline in business was only partly the result of infringement. Damages in this action totalled $29,300,000.[61]

A factor to be considered in determining the level of statutory damages is the good or bad faith of the defendants. The defendants exhibited bad faith when they knowingly and deliberately authorized and induced unlawful communication of the plaintiffs' works, ignored the court's process by failing to respond to the court or the plaintiffs, and by causing, and continuing to cause, serious and enduring harm to the plaintiffs by authorizing growing and potentially unlimited infringement by third parties.[62]

Another factor is the conduct of the parties before and during the proceedings. Where the plaintiffs expended significant resources to investigate the defendants'

---

[57] *Bell Canada v. L3D Distributing Inc. (c.o.b. INL3D)*, [2021] F.C.J. No. 867, 2021 FC 832 (F.C.) at paras. 107-109.

[58] *August Image, LLC v. airG Inc.*, [2021] F.C.J. No. 280, 2021 FC 272 (F.C.) at paras. 22 and 23.

[59] *Copyright Act*, R.S.C. 1985, c. C-42, subss. 41.26(3) and (4). There are no such regulations.

[60] *TBV Productions, LLC v. Doe*, [2021] F.C.J. No. 208, 2021 FC 181 (F.C.).

[61] *Bell Canada v. L3D Distributing Inc. (c.o.b. INL3D)*, [2021] F.C.J. No. 867, 2021 FC 832 (F.C.) at paras. 105 and 106.

[62] *Bell Canada v. L3D Distributing Inc. (c.o.b. INL3D)*, [2021] F.C.J. No. 867, 2021 FC 832 (F.C.) at paras. 101 and 102.

infringing activities and the defendants did not respond in any manner, despite being served and notified of their default, the parties' conduct favoured the plaintiffs.[63]

Another factor, the need to deter infringement, was underscored by the fact that the defendants were engaged in a growing commercial infringement industry dealing in pre-loaded set-top boxes where the number of defendants impleaded in the matter had reached about 175 and the number of works particularized in the action (2,930) was but a subset of the total infringement.[64]

LEGISLATION

The Governor in Council has made regulations setting various timelines, including deadlines for the completion of any matter before the Copyright Board or any procedural step in any such matter.[65] These regulations are applicable to matters pending on the day when they came into force[66] — December 4, 2020.[67] These regulations prevail over regulations made by the Board with respect to its procedures.[68]

Approval of Proposed Tariffs

The new regulations provide that the Board must make a decision with respect to the approval of a proposed tariff within 12 months of the deadline fixed by the Copyright Board, or by a case manager for presentation of submissions to the Board, if the Board holds a hearing about that proposed tariff.[69] An extension of that deadline does not change the date when the Board's decision is due.[70] If the Board does not hold such a hearing, the Board must make a decision before the beginning of the effective period of the proposed tariff.[71] Any such time period may only be extended in exceptional circumstances by a direction or order that justifies the

---

[63] *Bell Canada v. L3D Distributing Inc. (c.o.b. INL3D)*, [2021] F.C.J. No. 867, 2021 FC 832 (F.C.) at para. 103.

[64] *Bell Canada v. L3D Distributing Inc. (c.o.b. INL3D)*, [2021] F.C.J. No. 867, 2021 FC 832 (F.C.) at para. 104.

[65] *Time Limits in Respect of Matters Before the Copyright Board Regulations*, SOR/2020-264. The authority for this regulatory authority is *Copyright Act*, R.S.C. 1985, c. C-42, subs. 66.91(2).

[66] *Time Limits in Respect of Matters Before the Copyright Board Regulations*, SOR/2020-264, s. 7.

[67] *Time Limits in Respect of Matters Before the Copyright Board Regulations*, SOR/2020-264, s. 12.

[68] *Copyright Act*, R.S.C. 1985, c. C-42, subs. 66.91(3).

[69] *Time Limits in Respect of Matters Before the Copyright Board Regulations*, SOR/2020-264, subs. 2(*a*).

[70] *Time Limits in Respect of Matters Before the Copyright Board Regulations*, SOR/2020-264, s. 4.

[71] *Time Limits in Respect of Matters Before the Copyright Board Regulations*, SOR/2020-264, subs. 2(*b*).

extension, and the Board must publish a notice of any such direction or order.[72] The Board must notify the collective society that filed the proposed tariff as to whether the Board will hold a written or oral hearing in respect of the proposed tariff within three months of the day on which the Board publishes the proposed tariff.[73]

Copyright Board Arbitrations

The new regulations provide that in an arbitration proceeding in which the Board fixes royalty rates or their related terms or conditions, the Board must make a decision within 12 months of the deadline fixed by the Board or by a case manager for presentation of submissions to the Board.[74] An extension of that deadline does not change the date when the Board's decision is due.[75]

Copyright Board

In certain circumstances, and subject to certain conditions, it is not an infringement of copyright in a computer program to make a single modified or converted reproduction if the reproduction is essential for the compatibility of the program with a particular computer.[76] However, the Copyright Board found that this exemption from liability does not apply to reproduction of electronic music files because such files are not computer programs,[77] as defined.[78]

The reproduction of music included in television programs copied for inclusion in CBC's archive of television broadcasts was fair dealing with the musical works. Although the entire works were copied, other factors were satisfied: reproduction was for the purpose of private study, research and education and it was fair: the purpose was cultural and archival; the volume of copying was small; there was no alternative; the works were intended for broadcast to the public; and the reproduc-

---

[72] *Time Limits in Respect of Matters Before the Copyright Board Regulations*, SOR/2020-264, s. 6.

[73] *Time Limits in Respect of Matters Before the Copyright Board Regulations*, SOR/2020-264, s. 5.

[74] *Time Limits in Respect of Matters Before the Copyright Board Regulations*, SOR/2020-264, s. 3.

[75] *Time Limits in Respect of Matters Before the Copyright Board Regulations*, SOR/2020-264, s. 4.

[76] *Copyright Act*, R.S.C. 1985, c. C-42, subs. 30.6(*a*).

[77] *SODRAC 2003 Inc. v. Canadian Broadcast Corp.*, [2021] C.B.D. No. 1 at paras. 298-302.

[78] *Copyright Act*, R.S.C. 1985, c. C-42, s. 2 defines "computer program" as "a set of instructions or statements, expressed, fixed, embodied or stored in any manner, that is to be used directly or indirectly in a computer in order to bring about a specific result".

tions did not compete with the musical works.[79] Furthermore, the use was fair even if copies are kept indefinitely.[80]

A digital network service provider does not infringe copyright merely by providing the means for the telecommunication or reproduction of a work or other subject-matter through a digital network.[81] The Copyright Board held that this exemption from infringement is not limited to activities of intermediaries and the telecommunication need not occur over a "long" distance, and that it applied to the making of "transition copies" for the purpose of efficiently moving files between servers connected through a private digital network.[82]

The Board may find that uses that are not exempt from liability are nonetheless of no economic value.[83]

---

[79] *SODRAC 2003 Inc. v. Canadian Broadcast Corp.*, [2021] C.B.D. No. 1 at paras. 225-229.

[80] *SODRAC 2003 Inc. v. Canadian Broadcast Corp.*, [2021] C.B.D. No. 1 at paras. 239-243.

[81] *Copyright Act*, R.S.C. 1985, c. C-42, s. 31.1(1).

[82] *SODRAC 2003 Inc. v. Canadian Broadcast Corp.*, [2021] C.B.D. No. 1 at paras. 284-297.

[83] *SODRAC 2003 Inc. v. Canadian Broadcast Corp.*, [2021] C.B.D. No. 1 at paras. 274-277 and 283.

COMMENTARY: COPYRIGHT

INTRODUCTION

These notes are intended to be a brief overview of the *Copyright Act*.[1] Readers are cautioned that many details have been omitted and many circumstances have not been considered. Other resources include the following:

- For a more detailed legal text that is updated several times a year, see *Hughes on Copyright & Industrial Design, Second Edition* (LexisNexis Canada Inc.).

- For forms and precedents, see *Canadian Forms & Precedents—Intellectual Property* (LexisNexis Canada Inc.).

- For commentary and case digests respecting the *Federal Courts Act* and Rules, see *Canadian Federal Courts Practice* (annual publication) (LexisNexis Canada Inc.).

- For encyclopedic treatment of the law, see *Halsbury's Laws of Canada—Copyright* (LexisNexis Canada Inc.).

Canada draws from two sources for its copyright laws. The British source goes back to the time of Queen Anne, when publishers were given rights to prevent unauthorized copying, hence "copyright". The other source is the European continent, particularly France, where protection was given to the works of authors. "Droit d'auteur", literally, "right of the author", is the French translation of "copyright".

The Canadian *Copyright Act* was enacted initially in 1924; it was first proposed in 1921 and is therefore sometimes called the 1921 Act. It was modelled substantially on the British *Copyright Act* of 1911.

Many of the most significant amendments to the *Copyright Act* have been necessary so that Canada could adhere to international treaties which create reciprocal rights between countries: Canadian copyright owners acquire rights in other treaty countries and nationals of treaty countries acquire rights in Canada.

Canada adheres to the Berne Convention, the Rome Convention, the Agreement on Trade-Related Aspects of Intellectual Property Rights (TRIPS Agreement), the WIPO Copyright Treaty (WCT), and the WIPO Performances and Phonograms Treaty (WPPT).

Amendments to the *Copyright Act* have also been negotiated in trade agreements such as the 1989 Free Trade Agreement (FTA) between Canada and the United States, the 1992 North American Free Trade Agreement (NAFTA) and the 2020 Canada–United States–Mexico Agreement (CUSMA).

---

[1] R.S.C. 1985, c. C-42.

Occasionally, circumstances demonstrate the need for an amendment, often in response to new technology.

Recent amendments restrict the content of notices of infringement under the "notice and notice" regime (in force December 13, 2018); and relate to collective administration of copyright and the Copyright Board of Canada (in force April 1, 2019). Amendments to the *Bankruptcy and Insolvency Act*[2] and the *Companies' Creditors Arrangement Act*[3] that protect user rights in intellectual property when the licensor becomes insolvent came into force November 1, 2019.

ADMINISTRATION OF THE COPYRIGHT ACT

Under the *Constitution Act, 1982*,[4] copyright is the responsibility of the federal government.

Although nominally assigned to the Minister of Industry (section 2, definition of "Minister"), in fact, copyright is handled jointly with the Minister of Canadian Heritage. The Copyright Office is attached to the Patent Office (section 46). Much useful information, including a searchable database of copyright registrations, is available on the Canadian Intellectual Property Office's website.

WORKS AND OTHER SUBJECT-MATTER

Copyright applies to original literary, dramatic, musical and artistic *works* and protects the author's form of expression, not facts or ideas. Performers' performances, sound recordings and communication signals, collectively referred to as "other subject-matter", are also protected, but copyright in other subject-matter is more limited than copyright in works and is sometimes referred to as "neighbouring rights".

Works

Copyright subsists in "every *original* literary, dramatic, musical and artistic work".

"Original" means that a work must have originated with the author, not be copied, and must be the product of the exercise of skill and judgment that is more than trivial.

Copyright may exist in an unfinished work as long as it is sufficiently developed and beyond the state of being merely an idea.

Various categories of works are defined in section 2 of the Act:

1. *Literary Work includes* (*i.e.*, is not restricted to) books, pamphlets and other writings, tables, computer programs.

2. *Dramatic Work includes* recitation, choreography, music if fixed in writing, movies (cinematographic works) and dramatic-musical works.

---

[2] R.S.C. 1985, c. B-3.

[3] R.S.C. 1985, c. C-36.

[4] Schedule B to the *Canada Act 1982* (U.K.), 1982, c. 11.

14

3. *Musical Work means* (not "includes") any work of music or musical composition with or without words. Until 1993, a musical work had to be "graphically produced or reproduced", by definition.

4. *Artistic Work includes* paintings, drawings, maps, charts, plans, photographs, engravings, sculpture, crafts and architectural works such as buildings, sculptures and models. This definition was revised in 1993. The previous definition required that architectural works have "artistic character" which one court interpreted as "panache".

5. *Collective Work and Compilation* are each defined in section 2. Further, the definition of "every original literary, dramatic, musical and artistic work" includes "compilations" thereof. The differences between collective works and compilations are small; either may be comprised of other works. Whether or not there is copyright in the parts, the compilation or collection has its own copyright if its selection and arrangement or other attributes are sufficiently original. The author of a collective work or compilation is the person who compiled or collected and arranged the contents so as to create the new work, even though copyright in elements of the content may be owned by someone else. A compilation may consist of data.

Additional subcategories of works, such as "computer program", are defined in section 2 of the Act. Care must be taken to make sure that all relevant definitions are considered when reading the Act.

Other Subject-Matter

A number of treaties have extended more limited copyrights (sometimes called "neighbouring rights") to subject-matter other than works: performers' performances (sections 15 to 17); sound recordings (section 18), and communication signals (section 21).

Copyright in performers' performances and sound recordings does not include the right to perform performances or recordings in public or to communicate them to the public by telecommunication, but owners of copyright in performers' performances and sound recordings have a right to remuneration when their performances or recordings are performed in public or communicated to the public by telecommunication in the circumstances set out in sections 19 and 20.

REGISTRATION AND MARKING

Eligible works and other subject-matter are protected by copyright automatically when they are created. There is no need to register copyright or to affix any copyright notice, as Canada adheres to the Berne Convention which stipulates that such things are unnecessary.

If a name is indicated in the usual way as author, performer, maker or broadcaster on a work or other protected subject-matter, the person named is presumed to be the author, performer, maker or broadcaster (paragraph 34.1(2)(*a*). In the absence of any other indication, the publisher or owner is presumed to be the owner if its name is so indicated (paragraph 34.1(2)(*b*)). Many copyright owners mark their work with a notice such as "Copyright 2018 Smith & Co." or simply "© 2019 Smith & Co.", 2019 being the year of first publication.

Copyright may be registered in Canada by completing a simple form and filing it with the Canadian Intellectual Property Office indicating the type of work (*e.g.*, literary, musical, *etc.*) or other subject-matter (*e.g.*, sound recording), its title, the name and citizenship of the author, maker or performer, as the case may be, the name of the owner and the place of first publication, if any (section 55). No copy of the actual work or other subject-matter should be filed, and none will be accepted, which could make it difficult to prove that a particular work is the one that is registered. Registration serves as presumptive notice of copyright and is *prima facie* proof of the subsistence of copyright and other particulars, which may be rebutted at trial. The courts are skeptical of registrations secured shortly before actions are begun or during the course of an action.

TERM OF COPYRIGHT

The term during which copyright subsists in Canada will depend, among other things, on the type of subject-matter in question, on whether the identity of the author or authors is known, and on whether there are joint authors. The term of copyright in Canada is independent of the term granted in other countries to the same work.

The term of copyright begins when the work or other subject-matter is created.

The term of copyright was extended for some subject-matter on July 1, 2020 when the legislation implementing the Canada–United States–Mexico Agreement came into effect.[5]

1. *For most works*, copyright ends 50 years after the end of the calendar year in which the author died (section 6).

2. Where there are *joint* authors, that is, where the work of one cannot be separated from the work of the other, the term ends 50 years after the end of the calendar year of the death of the *last* of the authors to die (section 9).

3. Where there are *joint authors and the identity of all of them is unknown* copyright subsists until the end of 75 years after the end of the year in which the work was made, unless the work is published before the copyright expires. In that case, copyright subsists until the earlier of (a) the end of 75 years after the end of the year of first publication of the work; or (b) 100 years after the end of the year in which the work was made, unless the identity of one or more of the authors becomes commonly known during the term, in which case the term in section 6 applies (section 6.2).

---

[5] *Canada–United States–Mexico Agreement Implementation Act*, S.C. 2020, c. 1.

4. Where *the identity of the author of a work is unknown*, and remains unknown for the term, copyright subsists until the end of 75 years after the end of the year in which the work was made, unless the work is published before the copyright expires. In that case, copyright subsists until the earlier of (a) the end of 75 years after the end of the year of first publication of the work; or (b) 100 years after the end of the year in which the work was made (section 6.1).

5. *Posthumous works* — There is no special treatment for works first published, performed in public or communicated to the public posthumously after December 31, 1998. However, if, a work was first published, performed in public or communicated to the public posthumously and before December 31, 1998, copyright in that work subsists until 50 years after the end of the year in which the work was published, performed in public or communicated to the public by telecommunication, whichever happened first. If a work had not been published, performed in public or communicated to the public by December 31, 1998, and its author died on or before that date, one of two transitional provisions applies. If the author died during the 50 years before December 31, 1998, copyright subsists until the date that is 50 years from the end of the year of that death. If the author died more than 50 years before December 31, 1998, copyright ended on December 31, 2003 (section 7).

6. A *cinematographic work* which has a dramatic character has the same term of protection as any other "dramatic work" (section 6). A cinematographic work that lacks a dramatic character is protected until 70 years after the end of the year it was made, unless it is published within that period, in which case its copyright subsists until the earlier of (a) the end of 75 years after the end of the year in which the first publication occurred; and (b) 100 years after the end of the year in which the work was made (section 11.1).

7. In the case of *Crown copyright*, the term ends 50 years after the end of the year of first publication (section 12).

8. *Moral rights* in a work or performer's performance subsist for the same term as copyright in that work (section 14.2) or performance (section 17.2).

9. Copyright in a *performer's performance* that is *not fixed* in a sound recording expires 50 years after the end of the year in which the performance occurs. Copyright in a performer's performance that is *fixed* in a sound recording before copyright in the performance expires, expires 70 years after the end of the year in which the first such fixation occurs. If the performance is fixed in a sound recording that is *published* before the copyright in the performance expires, copyright in the performance continues until the earlier of the end of 75 years after the end of the calendar year in which the first publication of the sound recording occurs and the end of 100 years after the end of the calendar year in which the first

fixation in a sound recording occurs (subsection 23(1)).

10. Copyright in a *sound recording* ends 50 years after the end of the year in which the first fixation of the sound recording occurs, unless the sound recording *is published* before the copyright in the recording expires. In that case, copyright in the recording continues until the earlier of the end of 75 years after the end of the calendar year in which the first publication of the sound recording occurs and the end of 100 years after the end of the calendar year in which the sound recording was first fixed (subsection 23(1.1)).

11. The rights to *equitable remuneration for the performance* in public or communication to the public by telecommunication of a performer's performance or a sound recording conferred by section 19 have the same term as that performance and the recording respectively (subsection 23(2).

12. Copyright in a *communication signal* ends 50 years after the end of the year of broadcast (subsection 23(1.2)).

AUTHORS AND OTHER FIRST OWNERS OF COPYRIGHT

Depending on the type of subject-matter, the first owner of copyright is usually its creator — author (in the case of a work), maker (in the case of a sound recording), performer (in the case of a performer's performance) or broadcaster (in the case of a communication signal):

1. A work's *author* is ordinarily the first owner of copyright in that work (subsection 13(1)), but see below regarding employers. "Author" is not defined in the Act, but as the term of copyright protection refers to the life of the author, and as only natural persons have a lifetime, presumably an author must be a natural person. Jurisprudence indicates that the author is the person who creates an original work — gives it originality and expression. An author is not someone who gives suggestions to the person who actually creates the work or who merely writes down something dictated by another.

2. Employers are the first owners of copyright in works (but not other subject-matter) created by their employees in the course of their employment, but if the work is a contribution to a periodical, the rights to publish, other than in a periodical, remain with the author (subsection 13(3)). Even when an employer is the first owner of copyright, moral rights remain with the author.

3. Where any work is, or has been, prepared or published by or under the direction or control of Her Majesty or any government department, the copyright belongs to Her Majesty, subject to any agreement with the author (section 12).

4. Its *maker* is the first owner of copyright in a sound recording (section 24).

18

The "maker" of a sound recording is defined in sections 2 and 2.11 of the Act and is the person, whether a natural person or a body corporate, who makes the arrangements for the sound recording to be produced. ("Maker" is a term also associated with cinematographic works, but it relates to subsistence of copyright in such works, not ownership. See paragraph 5(1)(*b*).)

5. *Performer* is the first owner of copyright in a performer's performance (section 24). "Performer" is not defined in the Act.

6. *Broadcaster* is the first owner of copyright in a communication signal (section 24) and is defined in section 2 of the Act as a body which broadcasts a communication segment but excludes someone who primarily retransmits communication signals.

ASSIGNMENT, LICENCE AND REVERSION

An interest in copyright, including an exclusive licence or rights to remuneration, but excluding moral rights, may be assigned, but only in writing (subsection 13(4)). Various forms of writing, such as a bill of sale, may be sufficient. The assignment may be in whole or in part (subsections 13(4) and (5) and section 25). An assignment of copyright is not an assignment of moral right; moral rights may not be assigned, but may be waived (subsections 14.1(2) and (3)).

A non-exclusive licence need not necessarily be in writing: it may be given orally; implied through custom of the trade; or inferred from the conduct of the parties. A freelance engagement to produce a work protected by copyright implies a permission or consent or licence permitting the engager to use the material in the way that the parties contemplated it being used at the time of the engagement.

Although it is not an assignment in the usual sense, when a work is prepared or published by or under the direction or control of Her Majesty or any government department, the copyright in the work belongs to Her Majesty (subject to any agreement with the author) (section 12).

Where the author is the first owner of copyright in a work, copyright reverts to the author's estate 25 years after the author's death (section 14) regardless of any arrangement made during the author's lifetime. This provision does not apply to the assignment of the copyright in a collective work or a licence to publish a work or part of a work as part of a collective work, nor does it apply to subject-matter other than works.

RIGHTS CONFERRED BY COPYRIGHT

Copyright in a work means the sole right to produce or reproduce a work in any material form, to perform a work in public, or to publish an unpublished work, and to authorize any such acts. The other particular rights set out in the paragraphs of subsection 3(1) are "simply illustrative":

- to produce, reproduce, perform or publish any translation;
- to create a novel from a dramatic work;

- to create a dramatic work from a non-dramatic work;
- to make a "contrivance" that may be used to mechanically reproduce or perform a literary, dramatic or musical work;
- to make a movie of a novel;
- to communicate the work to the public by telecommunication, which includes the right to make it available to the public by telecommunication in a way that allows a member of the public to have access from a place and at a time chosen by that member of the public;
- to exhibit an artistic work in public (other than for the purpose of sale or hire);
- to rent out certain computer programs;
- to rent out a sound recording of a musical work; and
- in the case of work in the form of a tangible object, to transfer ownership of the object for the first time.

Copyright in a performer's performance includes the right to "fix" (*i.e.*, record) the performance, to rent a sound recording of it, to make a sound recording of it available to the public by telecommunication in a way that allows a member of the public to have access from a place and at a time chosen by that member of the public; and, if it is fixed in a sound recording that is a tangible object, to transfer ownership of the object for the first time (section 15).

Copyright in a sound recording includes the right to publish it for the first time, to reproduce it, to rent it out to make it available to the public by telecommunication in a way that allows a member of the public to have access from a place and at a time chosen by that member of the public; and, if it is a tangible object, to transfer ownership of the object for the first time (section 18).

Copyright in a communication signal includes the right to record it, to reproduce any recording of it, to rebroadcast it, or to perform a television communication signal in public on payment of an entrance fee (section 21).

RIGHTS CONFERRED BY MORAL RIGHTS

Canadian copyright law has been influenced by the European traditions, which include a concept that the author of a work, or the performer in the case of certain performer's performances, has the inalienable right to the "moral rights" attaching to that work or performance. These rights include the right to integrity of the work or performance, that is, the right not to have the work or performance distorted, and the right of attribution, that is, the right to be associated with the work as its author by name or under a pseudonym and the right to remain anonymous (sections 14.1, 14.2, 17.1, 17.2).

Moral rights cannot be assigned, and are not assigned when copyright is assigned (subsections 14.1(3) and 17.1(3)). However, moral rights can be waived in whole or in part, and a waiver in favour of an owner or licensee of copyright may be invoked

20

by any person authorized by the owner or licensee, unless the waiver stipulates otherwise (subsections 14.1(2), and (4) and 17.1(2) and (4)). Moral rights do not subsist in sound recordings, communication signals or ineligible performers' performances.

INFRINGEMENT OF COPYRIGHT

Primary infringement occurs when someone, without the consent of the copyright owner, does something that only the owner has the right to do. Thus, for instance, it is an infringement to reproduce a substantial part of a magazine article or perform a substantial part of a musical work in public, or to authorize somebody to do so without the consent of the copyright owner.

With respect to what constitutes a "substantial" part, the test is not quantity but quality. The question of whether there has been substantial copying focuses on whether the copied features constitute a substantial part of the *plaintiff's* work, not the *defendant's*. But if the differences are so great that the defendant's work, viewed as a whole, is not an imitation, but rather a new and original work, then there is no infringement.

As to what constitutes "authorization", simply to provide the means, such as rental of a theatre or provision of a photocopier does not constitute authorization; there must be a relationship such as employer/employee or clear direction to someone else or the alleged infringer must have sanctioned, approved or countenanced the protected activity. Authorization may arise from a passive situation, such as failure to perform a duty of control. Although a person does not authorize a use protected by copyright merely by authorizing the use of equipment that could be used to infringe, communication of works to the public is authorized by dealing in pre-loaded set-top boxes that have been modified to allow access to the plaintiffs' works and offering instruction and technical support to infringing customers.

Secondary infringement occurs when someone deals with an infringing copy of a work or other subject-matter commercially, such as by selling, renting or distributing it, or imports or exports an infringing copy for such purposes, if that person knew, or ought to have known, that they were dealing with an infringing copy (subsection 27(2)). In dealing with imported goods, whether or not the importer knew that the copy or fixation infringed is irrelevant with respect to acts of secondary infringement committed by someone other than the importer (subsection 27(3)).

Subject to narrow limitations, copies of a work or other subject-matter in which copyright subsists may not be imported or exported if they were made without the consent of the owner of the copyright in the country where they were made; and they infringe copyright or would infringe copyright if they had been made in Canada by the person who made them (section 44.01).

It is an infringement of copyright to deal with a "lesson" in certain specified ways, including to sell or rent it; or to distribute it or communicate it to the public, except as specifically permitted (subsection 27(2.2)). A "lesson" is defined in subsection

21

30.01(1) as a lesson, test or examination in which a work or other subject-matter is used pursuant to a limitation or exception in the *Copyright Act*.

It is an infringement of copyright for any person to provide a service, by means of the Internet or another digital network, to enable copyright infringement. This provision applies only if an actual infringement occurs as a result of the use of that service (subsection 27(2.3)).

It is an infringement of copyright to make or possess a "plate" (as defined in section 2) that has been specifically designed or adapted for the purpose of making infringing copies of work or other subject-matter (subsection 27(4)).

Copyright is infringed by anyone who, for profit, permits a place of entertainment to be used for the performance in public of a work, a performer's performance, a sound recording, or a communication signal without the consent of the owner of the copyright (subsection 27(5)). A performance may be for profit if an admission fee is charged, whether or not a net profit is realized.

It is an infringement of copyright in a book for any person to import copies of it without the consent of the copyright owner if the importer did not have the right to make copies of it in Canada (subsection 27.1(1)). Likewise, it is an infringement to deal with imported copies in any of the ways listed in subsection 27.1(2), including selling or distributing them, if the person dealing in the copies knew or should have known that the importer did not have the right to make copies of the book in Canada. These provisions apply only where there is an exclusive distributor of the book in the part of Canada or the sector of the market in which the acts occurred. No exclusive distributor, copyright owner or exclusive licensee is entitled to a remedy for infringement under these importation provisions unless notice has been given as prescribed (subsection 27.1(5)).

INFRINGEMENT OF MORAL RIGHTS

Generally, any act or omission that is contrary to any moral right — either the right to integrity or the right of attribution — that is done or omitted, without the consent of the author of a work or the performer of a performer's performance, is an infringement of that right (section 28.1). The moral right to integrity is infringed only if the work or performance is, to the prejudice of the honour or reputation of its author or performer, distorted or mutilated or otherwise modified or used for promotion in association with a product, service, cause or institution (subsection 28.2(1)). In the case of a painting, sculpture or engraving, such prejudice is deemed to have occurred in respect of any distortion, mutilation or other modification of the work (subsection 28.2(2)).

A change in the location of a work, the physical means by which a work is exposed or the physical structure containing the work, or steps taken in good faith to restore or preserve the work, do not constitute a distortion, mutilation or other modification of the work (subsection 28.2(3)).

USERS' RIGHTS — FAIR DEALING AND OTHER EXEMPTIONS FROM LIABILITY FOR INFRINGEMENT

Copyright is a balance between the rights of the author who created the subject-matter and the rights of the public to use that subject-matter. The *Copyright Act* includes a number of exemptions from liability for infringement for uses that would otherwise infringe the rights of the copyright owner. Such exemptions have been called "users' rights". Many of these exemptions include complex terms and conditions that must be reviewed carefully.

"Fair dealing" is not an infringement of copyright, but the use must be fair and for one of the specified purposes (sections 29 to 29.2):

- for the purpose of research, private study, education, parody or satire;

- for the purpose of criticism or review (if the source and, if available and applicable, the author, performer, maker or broadcaster are mentioned); or

- for the purpose of news reporting (if the source and, if available, the author, performer, maker or broadcaster are mentioned).

Parody has two elements: the evocation of an existing work while exhibiting noticeable differences, and the expression of mockery or humour.

Factors which can be used in assessing whether a dealing is fair include: (1) the purpose of the dealing; (2) the character of the dealing; (3) the amount of the dealing; (4) alternatives to the dealing; (5) the nature of the work; and (6) the effect of the dealing on the work.

A number of activities are exempt from liability for infringement when done by individuals for their personal non-commercial use: inclusion in non-commercial user-generated content (section 29.21), reproduction of certain subject-matter for private purposes (section 29.22), time-shifting (section 29.23) and the making of backup copies (section 29.24). The exemptions in sections 29.22 to 29.24 are not available if it is necessary to circumvent a technological protection measure (as defined) in order to carry out the activity.

Specific exemptions are provided for the benefit of educational instructions (sections 29.4 to 30.04); libraries, archives and museums (sections 30.1 to 30.21); reprography machines in educational institutions, libraries, archives and museums (section 30.3); libraries, archives and museums in educational institutions (section 30.4); and the Librarian and Archivist of Canada (section 30.5).

Other specific exemptions include:

- Reproduction of computer programs for the purpose of backup or interoperability (sections 30.6 and 30.61).

- Reproduction for the purpose of encryption research (section 30.62).

- Reproduction for the purpose of security of a computer, computer system or computer network (section 30.63).

- Incidental use (section 30.7).

- Temporary reproductions for technological processes (section 30.71).

- Ephemeral recordings made to facilitate broadcasting (sections 30.8 and 30.9).

- Provision of services relating to operating the Internet or other digital network, including caching and hosting services (section 31.1).

- Certain acts for the benefit of perceptually disabled persons (sections 32 and 32.01).

- Certain acts required by law (section 32.1).

A number of other miscellaneous exemptions are included in section 32.2 relating to an author's ongoing right to use his or her mould; agricultural fairs and religious or charitable organizations; reproduction of public buildings and sculptures; report of a public lecture or political address; public recitation; and non-commercial use of a photograph or portrait by the person who commissioned it.

The *Copyright Act* includes certain exemptions for which royalties must be paid (sometimes referred to as "compulsory licences") such as retransmission of works on terrestrial radio or television signals (section 31), making, by an educational institution, of a single copy of a work or other subject-matter at the time of its communication to the public by telecommunication and performance of that copy for students (section 29.7), and private copying of musical works, sound recordings of musical works, and the performers' performances of musical works as embodied on sound recordings (sections 79 to 86). Note that this private copying regime differs from the royalty-free exemption in section 29.22 of the Act, which allows reproduction of certain subject-matter for a private purpose if the source copy was legally obtained. Section 29.22 explicitly applies only where sections 79 to 86 do not, for example, to literary or cinematographic works or to copying onto an imbedded memory.

Subject to certain limitations, the Act exempts some uses of designs applied to a useful article and reproduced in a quantity of 50 or more and exempts certain acts having to do with useful or functional articles or that are topographies or intended to generate a topography (sections 64, 64.1, 64.2). See also the *Industrial Design Act*.[6]

PROCEEDINGS FOR INFRINGEMENT

A civil action for infringement of copyright or moral rights can be commenced in the Federal Court or an appropriate provincial court (section 41.24). The proceeding may be by way of an action or by application in a summary way (subsection 34(4)).

In such civil proceedings, copyright is presumed to subsist and the first owner of copyright, whether author, performer, maker or broadcaster is presumed to be the

---

[6] R.S.C. 1985, c. I-9.

owner of the copyright (section 34.1). Registration of copyright affords a number of other presumptions.

No civil action may be commenced more than three years from the date when the plaintiff knew or ought to have known of the alleged infringement (section 41).

Infringers may be anonymous, but Internet service providers cannot disclose the names and addresses of their customers without a valid subpoena, warrant or order. In issuing such an order (a Norwich Order), the courts should exercise caution to ensure that privacy rights are invaded in the most minimal way and that the judicial process is not used to support a business model intended to coerce innocent individuals to make payments to avoid being sued.

A digital network service provider who receives a notice of claimed infringement in the proper form (section 41.25) must forward the notice to the electronic location identified in the notice and must retain records that will identify the person to whom the location belongs for at least six months, or for one year if the claimant commences proceedings relating to the claimed infringement before the end of those six months. The service provider may not charge a fee for the performance of these obligations unless and until maximum fees are set by regulation (section 41.26). However, a service provider is entitled to the reasonable costs of the steps that are necessary to comply with a Norwich Order that are above and beyond the statutory obligations under section 41.26, including the costs of discerning a person's identity from the records that it is required to retain.

Such service providers include providers of the means for connecting to a digital network, hosts and providers of "information location tools" (commonly referred to as "search engines") (subsection 41.25(1)).

Customs officers may detain copies of a work or other subject-matter that they suspect infringe copyright and share information relating to the detained goods with rights owners so as to assist them in pursuing legal remedies (sections 44.01 to 44.1). A copyright owner may file a "request for assistance" (RFA) and if the RFA is accepted, a customs officer may provide information about detained copies to the owner, but only for the purpose of pursuing remedies under the *Copyright Act*, and may allow inspection of the copies by the owner, importer, exporter and consignee of the copies. Copies may be detained for no more than 20 working days unless the copyright owner commences an action. In that case, the copies are detained until the proceedings are disposed of, settled or abandoned, a court directs otherwise, or the copyright owner consents.

Section 44.12 provides that a copyright owner may apply to the court for an order requiring the Minister to detain copies that are about to be imported into Canada, or have been imported into Canada but have not been released, if the copies were made without the consent of the person who is owner of the copyright in the country where they were made, or were made elsewhere than in a country to which the *Copyright Act* extends and the copies would infringe copyright if they were made in Canada by the importer and the importer knows or should have known this. Such copies may be detained for 10 working days unless an action is commenced. If the plaintiff is successful, the court may order that the detained copies be destroyed or delivered up.

The *Copyright Act* also provides for criminal proceedings against infringers, those who deal unlawfully with infringing copies, and those who deal unlawfully with technological protection measures or rights management information (sections 42 and 43).

REMEDIES FOR INFRINGEMENT

Remedies for copyright infringement and infringement of moral rights are extensive and include:

1. *An injunction*, which is the *only* remedy if the infringer can prove that he/she/it had no reasonable basis for knowing that copyright subsisted or was infringed (section 39).

2. *A wide injunction*, which extends beyond those specific works infringed presumably if the court perceives that broad scale infringement is likely (section 39.1).

3. *Damages and profits*: Both damages and profits may be granted although either one or the other is more usual. In proving profits, all a plaintiff has to do is prove the value of sales; the defendant has to prove all proper deductions (section 35).

4. *Statutory damages*: A copyright owner may, at any time before final judgment, elect an award of statutory damages instead of "damages and profits" (section 38.1). Statutory damages for infringement for *non-commercial* purposes range from $100 to $5,000 with respect to all infringements of all works or other subject-matter in the proceedings. If the infringement is for *commercial* purposes, statutory damages range from $500 to $20,000 for all infringements of each work or other subject-matter, infringed by any one infringer or by any two or more infringers who are jointly and severally liable, but may be reduced in a variety of circumstances, including when the total award would otherwise be grossly out of proportion to the infringement.

5. *All other usual remedies* (subsection 34(1)), which would include interest, punitive and/or exemplary damages, delivery up and costs.

An unrepentant continuing offender may be found in contempt of court, the consequences of which may include a term of imprisonment.

Third Party Orders

Where it is necessary to ensure an injunction's effectiveness, the court can make an order enjoining conduct of third parties anywhere in the world.

A Norwich Order, also known as a disclosure order, requires a third party to disclose the identity of an unknown infringer.

Where the defendants made obvious efforts to remain anonymous and to avoid legal action by rights holders, and ignored injunctions, third parties who provided networking services to the defendants were ordered to block access to websites and Internet services operated by those defendants.

It is customary for the applicants to pay the reasonable cost of implementation of third party orders.

Technological Protection Measures and Rights Management Information

The *Copyright Act* provides protection for technological protection measures (TPMs) used by copyright owners (1) to control access to certain kinds of protected subject-matter ("access control TPMs"); and (2) to restrict the doing of any act that only the owners of such copyrights have the right to do ("use control TPMs") (sections 41 and 41.1).

The *Copyright Act* prohibits the circumvention (defined in section 41) of access control TPMs, but not use control TPMs; it also prohibits certain dealing in a service, technology, device, or component for the purpose of circumvention of either access or use control TPMs (paragraphs 41.1(1)(b) and (c)).

An owner of copyright in eligible subject-matter whose access control TPMs have been circumvented or in respect of which subject-matter a TPM has been or could be circumvented is entitled to remedies otherwise available for infringement, (subsections 41.1(2) and 41.1(4)), subject to certain limitations (subsection 41.1(3) and sections 41.19 and 41.2).

There are a number of exemptions from liability for circumventing or otherwise dealing with TPMs for various purposes (sections 41.11 to 41.2) and other limitations may be imposed through regulation (section 41.21).

The *Copyright Act* also addresses rights management information (RMI) in electronic form as defined in subsection 41.22(4). The owner of copyright in the associated content has a cause of action against anyone who knowingly removes RMI without the consent of the owner of copyright in the protected subject-matter if that person knows or should have known that the removal or alteration will facilitate or conceal any infringement of the owner's copyright or adversely affect the owner's right to remuneration under section 19 of the Act. The copyright owner is entitled to all remedies otherwise available for copyright infringement (subsection 41.22(1)). The copyright owner also has a cause of action against those who deal in that content in certain specified ways and who knew or should have known that RMI had been removed or altered contrary to the Act (subsection 41.22(3)).

An injunction may be the only remedy available against the provider of an information location tool unless the tool is designed and has been used to enable infringement (section 41.27).

The *Copyright Act* also provides for criminal proceedings against those who deal unlawfully with technological protection measures or rights management information (subsections 42(3.1) to (3.4)).

27

COLLECTIVE ADMINISTRATION OF COPYRIGHT

Copyright Board (Sections 66 to 66.91)

The Copyright Board consists of not more than five members: a Chair, who is or has been a judge; a Vice-chair; and full-time or part-time members, each of whom may serve for a term up to five years and may be reappointed once (section 66). The Board has the general powers of a superior court of record and its decisions may be made an order of the Federal Court or any superior court, and are enforceable as such (section 66.7).

The most significant powers of the Board are:

- the power to vary and approve proposed tariffs filed by collective societies (subsection 70(1)) with respect to rights administered under section 3 (copyright in works), section 15 (copyright in performers' performances), section 18 (copyright in sound recordings), section 19 (right to remuneration for the performance in public or certain communications to the public of published sound recordings and performer's performances) and section 21 (copyright in communication signals)

- the power to vary and approve proposed tariffs establishing royalties under compulsory licences referred to in subsection 29.7(2) or (3) (copying and use by educational institutions) or in paragraph 31(2)(d) (the retransmission of works on distant signals) (subsection 70(1))

- on application by a collective society or a user, where they are unable to agree, the power to fix royalty rates or terms and conditions, or both, of certain licences (subsection 71(2))

- the power to examine licence agreements at the request of the Commissioner of Competition and alter royalties therein (subsection 76.1(1))

- the power to vary and approve tariffs with respect to levies payable by manufacturers and importers of blank audio recording media (subsection 83(8))

- the power to grant licences, upon application, where copyright owners cannot be found (section 77)

- the power to determine compensation for acts done before certain rights were recognized by the Act (section 78)

The Board may vary certain of its decisions on application, if a material change in circumstances has occurred since the decision was made (section 66.52 and subsection 66.7(4)). The Board may make regulations with respect to its own procedure (section 66.6).

Royalty and levy rates and any related terms and conditions fixed by the Board must be fair and equitable, in consideration of fair market value, the public interest, any regulations made by the Governor in Council issuing policy directions and establishing criteria for the Board, and any other criterion that the Board considers appropriate (section 66.501). All matters before the Board must be dealt with informally and expeditiously (section 66.502): any person or entity may authorize any other to represent them before the Board (section 66.503) and a case manager may be assigned to any matter before the Board (section 66.504).

In establishing royalties and rendering its decisions, the Board must have regard to any regulations made by the Governor in Council issuing policy directions and establishing criteria for the Board (subsection 66.91(1)). The Governor in Council has made regulations setting various timelines, including deadlines for the completion of any matter before the Board or any procedural step in any such matter (subsection 66.91(2)).[7] Such regulations prevail over regulations made by the Board with respect to its procedures (subsection 66.91(3)).

Collective Administration of Copyright (Sections 67 to 76)

"Collective society" is defined in section 2 of the *Copyright Act*. A collective society administers copyrights or remuneration rights in a repertoire of subject-matter on behalf of more than one author, performer, sound recording maker or broadcaster, either by operating a licensing scheme for classes of uses or by carrying on the business of collecting and distributing royalties or levies payable under the *Copyright Act*. A collective society represents "those who, by assignment, grant of licence, appointment of it as their agent or otherwise, authorize it to act on their behalf". If a copyright owner is entitled to royalties under a compulsory licence but is not affiliated with a collective society, the Board may designate a collective who must pay royalties to that claimant, subject to the same conditions as any other claimant that it represents, and this is the claimant's only remedy (section 75).

Collective societies that administer compulsory licences or the private copying levy may not enter into agreements and must proceed by filing a proposed tariff (subsection 67(2) and section 83, respectively), although the Board must have regard to agreements between collective societies and retransmitters.[8]

Collective societies, other than those that administer compulsory licences or the private copying levy, may file a proposed tariff with the Copyright Board (subsection 67(1)) or may administer their repertoires by entering into agreements (subsection 67(3)). If an agreement is reached, and if it is filed with the Board within 15 days, the criminal prosecution provisions of section 45 of the *Competition Act*[9] do not apply, but if the Commissioner of Competition considers the agreement to be contrary to public interest, he or she may ask the Board to examine the agreement (section 76), and the Board may alter the royalties and any related terms and conditions (section 76.1). If a collective society and prospective users are unable to

---

[7] Time Limits in Respect of Matters Before the Copyright Board Regulations, SOR/2020-264.

[8] Retransmission Royalties Criteria Regulations, SOR/91-690, s. 2(c).

[9] R.S.C. 1985, c. C-34.

reach an agreement, the Board may be asked to fix the royalties or any related terms or conditions or both (subsection 71(1)).

Sections 68 to 70.1 set out the procedure for approval of a tariff. The provisions relating to arbitration by the Board are in sections 71 and 71.1.

Section 72 constrains the Board with respect to royalty rates for certain users with respect to remuneration for the performance in public or communication to the public of music.

A collective society may collect the royalties in an approved tariff or the royalties fixed by the Board and, in case of default, the collective may recover them in a court of competent jurisdiction (section 73), but this remedy is not available against a user who is not a licensee. Someone who is not a licensee may be liable for infringement, but remedies for infringement are only available to someone with an interest in the copyright. A collective may apply to a court of competent jurisdiction for an order enforcing any terms and conditions of an approved tariff or terms and conditions fixed by the Board (section 73.1). Copyright owners' remedies are restricted when their rights are collectively administered (sections 73.2, 73.3, 73.4, 73.5).

COPYRIGHT ACT

31

TERM OF COPYRIGHT

OWNERSHIP OF COPYRIGHT

MORAL RIGHTS

PART II   COPYRIGHT IN PERFORMERS' PERFORMANCES, SOUND RECORDINGS AND COMMUNICATION SIGNALS AND MORAL RIGHTS IN PERFORMERS' PERFORMANCES

PERFORMERS' RIGHTS

COPYRIGHT

COPYRIGHT

33

TERM OF RIGHTS

OWNERSHIP OF COPYRIGHT

PERFORMERS' RIGHTS — WTO COUNTRIES

PART III   INFRINGEMENT OF COPYRIGHT AND MORAL RIGHTS AND EXCEPTIONS TO INFRINGEMENT

INFRINGEMENT OF COPYRIGHT

GENERAL

PARALLEL IMPORTATION OF BOOKS

MORAL RIGHTS INFRINGEMENT

EXCEPTIONS

FAIR DEALING

NON-COMMERCIAL USER-GENERATED CONTENT

REPRODUCTION FOR PRIVATE PURPOSES

FIXING SIGNALS AND RECORDING PROGRAMS FOR LATER LISTENING OR VIEWING

BACKUP COPIES

ACTS UNDERTAKEN WITHOUT MOTIVE OF GAIN

EDUCATIONAL INSTITUTIONS

LIBRARIES, ARCHIVES AND MUSEUMS

37

COMPENSATION FOR ACTS DONE BEFORE RECOGNITION OF COPYRIGHT OR MORAL RIGHTS

PART IV   REMEDIES

CIVIL REMEDIES

INFRINGEMENT OF COPYRIGHT AND MORAL RIGHTS

TECHNOLOGICAL PROTECTION MEASURES AND RIGHTS MANAGEMENT INFORMATION

FEES

PART VI   MISCELLANEOUS PROVISIONS

SUBSTITUTED RIGHT

CLERICAL ERRORS

REGULATIONS

INDUSTRIAL DESIGNS AND TOPOGRAPHIES

PART VII   COPYRIGHT BOARD

PART VII.1 COLLECTIVE ADMINISTRATION OF COPYRIGHT

COLLECTIVE SOCIETIES

TARIFFS

PROPOSED TARIFFS

EFFECTS OF AGREEMENT

CLAIM BY COPYRIGHT OWNER — PARTICULAR ROYALTIES

EXAMINATION OF AGREEMENTS

PART VII.2 CERTAIN APPLICATIONS TO BOARD

OWNERS WHO CANNOT BE LOCATED

COMPENSATION FOR ACTS DONE BEFORE RECOGNITION OF COPYRIGHT OR MORAL RIGHTS

PART VIII PRIVATE COPYING

INTERPRETATION

COPYING FOR PRIVATE USE

RIGHT OF REMUNERATION

LEVY ON BLANK AUDIO RECORDING MEDIA

DISTRIBUTION OF LEVIES PAID

EXEMPTION FROM LEVY

REGULATIONS

CIVIL REMEDIES

PART IX   GENERAL PROVISIONS

TRANSITIONAL PROVISIONS

SCHEDULE

COPYRIGHT ACT

(R.S.C. 1985, c. C-42)

Note: For your convenience, where the Act refers to another piece of legislation not otherwise reproduced in this publication, the cite and/or text of that other piece of legislation is reproduced after the referencing section.

Amendments: R.S.C. 1985, c. 10 (1st Supp.), s. 1; R.S.C. 1985, c. 1 (3rd Supp.), s. 13; R.S.C. 1985, c. 41 (3rd Supp.), ss. 116, 117; R.S.C. 1985, c. 10 (4th Supp.), ss. 1-16; S.C. 1988, c. 65, ss. 61-65, 149, 150 proclaimed in force February 13, 1989; S.C. 1990, c. 37, s. 33 proclaimed in force May 1, 1993; S.C. 1992, c. 1, ss. 47-52 in force February 28, 1992; S.C. 1993, c. 15, ss. 2-10 proclaimed in force June 9, 1993, s. 11 in force January 15, 1994; S.C. 1993, c. 23 proclaimed in force August 31, 1993; S.C. 1993, c. 44, ss. 52-80 proclaimed in force January 1, 1994; S.C. 1994, c. 47, ss. 56-59 proclaimed in force January 1, 1996; S.C. 1995, c. 1, s. 62(1)(g) in force March 29, 1995; S.C. 1997, c. 24, ss. 62 and 63 deemed in force June 30, 1996, and balance of sections in force as follows: s. 1(1) to (4), s. 1(5) insofar as it enacts the definitions "broadcaster", "collective society", "commercially available", "communication signal", "copyright", "country", "perceptual disability", "premises", "Rome Convention country", "sculpture" and "sound recording", s. 2 insofar as it enacts ss. 2.11-2.5 and 2.7, ss. 3-5, 8, 9, 10(2), 11-14, s. 15 insofar as it enacts s. 27, ss. 16, 17, s. 18(1) insofar as it enacts ss. 29-29.5, 29.8, 30 and 30.4-30.7, ss. 18(2), 19, s. 20(1) insofar as it enacts ss. 34(1)-(3), 34.1-38 and 39, ss. 21-28, 35-44, s. 45 insofar as it enacts ss. 67.1(3)-(5), 68-68.2, ss. 46-49, s. 50 insofar as it enacts ss. 71-78 and 89-92, ss. 51, 52, 53.1, 54, 55-58, 59 and 60 in force September 1, 1997; s. 45 insofar as it enacts ss. 67, 67.1(1) and (2) in force January 1, 1998; ss. 29-34 in force October 1, 1997; s. 58.1 in force March 12, 1998; s. 50 insofar as it enacts ss. 79-88 and s. 53 in force March 19, 1998; s. 10(1) in force July 1, 1998; s. 6 in force December 31, 1998; s. 7, s. 18(1) insofar as it enacts ss. 29.6, 29.7 and 29.9, and s. 54.1 in force January 1, 1999; s. 18(1) insofar as it enacts ss. 30.1-30.3 in force September 1, 1999; s. 1(5) insofar as it enacts the definitions "defendant" and "plaintiff", s. 18(1) insofar as it enacts ss. 30.8 and 30.9, s. 20(1) insofar as it enacts ss. 34(4)-(7), 38.1, 38.2 and 39.1, and ss. 20(3) and (4) in force October 1, 1999; s. 20(2) repealed before coming into force by S.C. 2008, c. 20, s. 3; S.C. 1997, c. 36, s. 205 in force January 1, 1998; S.C. 1999, c. 2, ss. 45, 46 in force March 18, 1999; S.C. 1999, c. 17, s. 119 in force November 1, 1999; S.C. 1999, c. 31, ss. 59-62 in force June 17, 1999; S.C. 2001, c. 34, ss. 34-35 in force December 18, 2001; S.C. 2001, c. 27, ss. 235-241 in force June 28, 2002; S.C. 2002, c. 26 in force March 21, 2003; S.C. 2003, c. 22, ss. 154, 224 (z.20) and 225(s) in force April 1, 2005; S.C. 2004, c. 11, s. 21 in force April 22, 2004, ss. 25 and 26 in force May 21, 2004; S.C. 2005, c. 38, ss. 139(b), 142(d), 145(2)(j) in force December 12, 2005; S.C. 2012, c. 20 in force November 7, 2012 except ss. 2(1), 5, 9(3), (4), 11(2), (4), (5), 12(2), 14, 15(2), (4), 16 and 50 in force August 13, 2014, ss. 41.25, 41.26 and 41.27(3), as enacted by s. 47, in force January

2, 2015; S.C. 2014, c. 20, s. 366(E), in force June 17, 2019; S.C. 2014, c. 32, ss. 1, 3 and 4 in force December 9, 2014, ss. 2, 5 and 6 in force January 1, 2015; S.C. 2015, c. 36, ss. 81, 82 in force June 23, 2015; S.C. 2016, c. 4, ss. 1-4 in force June 22, 2016; S.C. 2017, c. 9, s. 55 in force June 19, 2017; S.C. 2018, c. 27, ss. 243-246 in force December 13, 2018, ss. 280-301 in force April 1, 2019; S.C. 2020, c. 1, ss. 23-34 in force July 1, 2020.

SHORT TITLE

Note: S.C. 1997, c. 24, s. 57 provides that, for greater certainty, the amendments to the *Copyright Act* that eliminate references to "British subject" and "Her Majesty's Realms and Territories" do not affect any copyright or moral rights subsisting in Canada immediately before the coming into force of those amendments.

1. Short title — This Act may be cited as the *Copyright Act*.

INTERPRETATION

2. Definitions — In this Act,

architectural work means any building or structure or any model of a building or structure;
[S.C. 1993, c. 44, s. 53(2).]

artistic work includes paintings, drawings, maps, charts, plans, photographs, engravings, sculptures, works of artistic craftsmanship; architectural works, and compilations of artistic works;
[S.C. 1993, c. 44, s. 53(2).]

Berne Convention country means a country that is a party to the Convention for the Protection of Literary and Artistic Works concluded at Berne on September 9, 1986, or any one of its revisions, including the Paris Act of 1971;
[S.C. 1993, c. 44, s. 53(2).]

Board means the Copyright Board established under subsection 66(1);
[R.S.C. 1985, c. 10 (4th Supp.), s. 1(3).]

book means a volume or a part or division of a volume, in printed form, but does not include

(*a*) a pamphlet,

(*b*) a newspaper, review, magazine or other periodical,

(*c*) a map, chart, plan or sheet music where the map, chart, plan or sheet music is separately published, and

(*d*) an instruction or repair manual that accompanies a product or that is supplied as an accessory to a service;
[S.C. 1997, c. 24, s. 1(2).]

broadcaster means a body that, in the course of operating a broadcasting undertaking, broadcasts a communication signal in accordance with the law of the country in which the broadcasting undertaking is carried on, but excludes a body whose primary activity in relation to communication signals is their retransmission;

[S.C. 1997, c. 24, s. 1(5).]

Canada–United States–Mexico Agreement has the meaning assigned by the definition Agreement in section 2 of the *Canada–United States–Mexico Agreement Implementation Act;*

[S.C. 2020, c. 1, s. 23]

choreographic work includes any work of choreography, whether or not it has any story line;

[R.S.C. 1985, c. 10 (4th Supp.), s. 1(3).]

cinematographic work includes any work expressed by any process analogous to cinematography, whether or not accompanied by a soundtrack;

[S.C. 1993, c. 44, s. 53(2); S.C. 1997, c. 24, s. 1(2).]

collective society means a society, association or corporation that carries on the business of collective administration of copyright or of the remuneration right conferred by section 19 or 81 for the benefit of those who, by assignment, grant of licence, appointment of it as their agent or otherwise, authorize it to act on their behalf in relation to that collective administration, and

(*a*) operates a licensing scheme, applicable in relation to a repertoire of works, performer's performances, sound recordings or communication signals of more than one author, performer, sound recording maker or broadcaster, pursuant to which the society, association or corporation sets out classes of uses that it agrees to authorize under this Act, and the royalties and terms and conditions on which it agrees to authorize those classes of uses, or

(*b*) carries on the business of collecting and distributing royalties or levies payable under this Act in relation to a repertoire of works, performer's performances, sound recordings or communication signals of more than one author, performer, sound recording maker or broadcaster;

[S.C. 1997, c. 24, s. 1(5); S.C. 2018, c. 27, s. 280.]

collective work means

(*a*) an encyclopaedia, dictionary, year book or similar work,

(*b*) a newspaper, review, magazine or similar periodical, and

(*c*) any work written in distinct parts by different authors, or in which works or parts of works of different authors are incorporated;

commercially available means, in relation to a work or other subject matter

(*a*) available on the Canadian market within a reasonable time and for a reasonable price and may be located with reasonable effort, or (*b*)   for which a licence to reproduce, perform in public or communicate to the public by telecommunication is available from a collective society within a reasonable time and for a reasonable price and may be located with reasonable effort;

[S.C. 1997, c. 24, s. 1(5).]

communication signal means radio waves transmitted through space without any artificial guide, for reception by the public;

[S.C. 1997, c. 24, s. 1(5).]

compilation means

(*a*)   a work resulting from the selection or arrangement of literary, dramatic, musical or artistic works or of parts thereof, or

(*b*)   a work resulting from the selection or arrangement of data;

[S.C. 1993, c. 44, s. 53(2).]

computer program means a set of instructions or statements, expressed, fixed, embodied or stored in any manner, that is to be used directly or indirectly in a computer in order to bring about a specific result;

[R.S.C. 1985, c. 10 (4th Supp.), s. 1(3).]

Note: Section 24 of R.S.C. 1985, c. 10 (4th Supp.), states, "Subsection 1(2), the definition 'computer program' in subsection 1(3) and section 5 apply in respect of a computer program that was made prior to the day on which those provisions come into force but where, by virtue only of subsections 1(2) and (3) and this section, copyright subsists in a computer program that was made prior to May 27, 1987, nothing done in respect of the computer program before May 27, 1987 shall be construed to constitute an infringement of the copyright."

copyright means the rights described in

(*a*)   section 3, in the case of a work,

(*b*)   sections 15 and 26, in the case of a performer's performance,

(*c*)   section 18, in the case of a sound recording, or

(*d*)   section 21, in the case of a communication signal;

[S.C. 1997, c. 24, s. 1(5).]

country includes any territory;

[S.C. 1997, c. 24, s. 1(5).]

defendant includes a respondent to an application;

[S.C. 1997, c. 24, s. 1(5).]

delivery [Repealed by S.C. 1997, c. 24, s. 1(1).]

dramatic work includes

(*a*)   any piece for recitation, choreographic work or mime, the scenic arrangement or acting form of which is fixed in writing or otherwise,

(*b*) any cinematographic work, and

[S.C. 1997, c. 24, s. 1(4).]

(*c*) any compilation of dramatic works;

[S.C. 1993, c. 44, s. 53(2).]

educational institution means

(*a*) a non-profit institution licensed or recognized by or under an Act of Parliament or the legislature of a province to provide pre-school, elementary, secondary or post-secondary education,

(*b*) a non-profit institution that is directed or controlled by a board of education regulated by or under an Act of the legislature of a province and that provides continuing, professional or vocational education or training,

(*c*) a department or agency of any order of government, or any non-profit body, that controls or supervises education or training referred to in paragraph (*a*) or (*b*), or

(*d*) any other non-profit institution prescribed by regulation;

[S.C. 1997, c. 24, ss. 1(5) and 62(1).]

engravings includes etchings, lithographs, woodcuts, prints and other similar works, not being photographs;

every original literary, dramatic, musical and artistic work includes every original production in the literary, scientific or artistic domain, whatever may be the mode or form of its expression, such as compilations, books, pamphlets and other writings, lectures, dramatic or dramatico-musical works, musical works, translations, illustrations, sketches and plastic works relative to geography, topography, architecture or science;

[S.C. 1993, c. 44, s. 53(2).]

exclusive distributor means, in relation to a book, a person who

(*a*) has, before or after the coming into force of this definition, been appointed in writing, by the owner or exclusive licensee of the copyright in the book in Canada, as

(i) the only distributor of the book in Canada or any part of Canada, or

(ii) the only distributor of the book in Canada or any part of Canada in respect of a particular sector of the market, and

(*b*) meets the criteria established by regulations made under section 2.6,

and, for greater certainty, if there are no regulations made under section 2.6, then no person qualifies under this definition as an "exclusive distributor";

[S.C. 1997, c. 24, ss. 1(5) and 62(1).]

Note: S.C. 1997, c. 24, s. 62(2) provides that notwithstanding the coming into force provisions of subsection (1) of section 62, the definition "exclusive distributor" referred to in paragraph (1)(*a*) shall be read as follows during the period beginning on June 30, 1996 and ending on the day that is sixty days after the day on which S.C. 1997, c. 24 is assented to (Royal Assent - April 25/97):

exclusive distributor means in relation to a book, a person who has, before or after the coming into force of this definition, been appointed in writing, by the owner or exclusive licensee of the copyright in the book in Canada, as

(*a*)   the only distributor of the book in Canada or any part of Canada, or

(*b*)   the only distributor of the book in Canada or any part of Canada in respect of a particular sector of the market.

See also S.C. 1997, c. 24, s. 63.

Her Majesty's Realms and Territories [Repealed by S.C. 1997, c. 24, s. 1(1).]

Note: See also Transitional Provisions (section 57) of S.C. 1997, c. 24.

infringing means

(*a*)   in relation to a work in which copyright subsists, any copy, including any colorable imitation, made or dealt with in contravention of this Act,

(*b*)   in relation to a performer's performance in respect of which copyright subsists, any fixation or copy of a fixation of it made or dealt with in contravention of this Act,

(*c*)   in relation to a sound recording in respect of which copyright subsists, any copy of it made or dealt with in contravention of this Act, or

(*d*)   in relation to a communication signal in respect of which copyright subsists, any fixation or copy of a fixation of it made or dealt with in contravention of this Act.

The definition includes a copy that is imported in the circumstances set out in paragraph 27(2)(e) and section 27.1 but does not otherwise include a copy made with the consent of the owner of the copyright in the country where the copy was made;

[S.C. 1994, c. 47, s. 56(1); S.C. 1997, c. 24, s. 1(2).]

lecture includes address, speech and sermon;

legal representatives includes heirs, executors, administrators, successors and assigns, or agents or attorneys who are thereunto duly authorized in writing;

library, archive or museum means

(*a*)   an institution, whether or not incorporated, that is not established or conducted for profit or that does not form a part of, or is not administered

COPYRIGHT ACT

or directly or indirectly controlled by, a body that is established or conducted for profit, in which is held and maintained a collection of documents and other materials that is open to the public or to researchers, or

(*b*) any other non-profit institution prescribed by regulation;

[S.C. 1997, c. 24, ss. 1(5) and 62.]

literary work includes tables, computer programs, and compilations of literary works;

[S.C. 1993, c. 44, s. 53(2).]

Note: Section 24 of R.S.C. 1985, c. 10 (4th Supp.), states, "Subsection 1(2), the definition 'computer program' in subsection 1(3) and section 5 apply in respect of a computer program that was made prior to the day on which those provisions come into force but where, by virtue only of subsections 1(2) and (3) and this section, copyright subsists in a computer program that was made prior to May 27, 1987, nothing done in respect of the computer program before May 27, 1987 shall be construed to constitute an infringement of the copyright."

maker means

(*a*) in relation to a cinematographic work, the person by whom the arrangements necessary for the making of the work are undertaken, or

(*b*) in relation to a sound recording, the person by whom the arrangements necessary for the first fixation of the sounds are undertaken;

[S.C. 1993, c. 44, s. 53(3); S.C. 1997, c. 24, s. 1(2).]

Minister, except in sections 44 to 44.12, means the Minister of Industry;

[S.C. 1993, c. 44, s. 53(2); S.C. 1995, c. 1, s. 62; S.C. 2014, c. 32, s. 2.]

moral rights means the rights described in subsection 14.1(1) and 17.1(1);

[S.C. 1993, c. 44, s. 53(2); S.C. 2012, c. 20, s. 2(1).]

musical work means any work of music or musical composition, with or without words and includes any compilation thereof;

[S.C. 1993, c. 44, s. 53(2).]

perceptual disability means a disability that prevents or inhibits a person from reading or hearing a literary, musical, dramatic or artistic work in its original format, and includes such a disability resulting from

(*a*) severe or total impairment of sight or hearing or the inability to focus or move one's eyes,

(*b*) the inability to hold or manipulate a book, or

(*c*) an impairment relating to comprehension;

[S.C. 1997, c. 24, s. 1(5).]

performance means any acoustic or visual representation of a work, performer's

performance, sound recording or communication signal, including a representation made by means of any mechanical instrument, radio receiving set or television receiving set;
[S.C. 1994, c. 47, s. 56(1); S.C. 1997, c. 24, s. 1(2).]

performer's performance means any of the following when done by a performer:

(a) a performance of an artistic work, dramatic work or musical work, whether or not the work was previously fixed in any material form, and whether or not the work's term of copyright protection under this Act has expired,

(b) a recitation or reading of a literary work, whether or not the work's term of copyright protection under this Act has expired, or

(c) an improvisation of a dramatic work, musical work or literary work, whether or not the improvised work is based on a pre-existing work;
[S.C. 1994, c. 47, s. 56(3); S.C. 1997, c. 24, s. 1(2).]

photograph includes photo-lithograph and any work expressed by any process analogous to photography;
[S.C. 1993, c. 44, s. 53(2).]

plaintiff includes an applicant;
[S.C. 1997, c. 24, s. 1(5).]

plate includes

(a) any stereotype or other plate, stone, block, mould, matrix, transfer or negative used or intended to be used for printing or reproducing copies of any work, and

(b) any matrix or other appliance used or intended to be used for making or reproducing sound recordings, performer's performances or communication signals;
[S.C. 1997, c. 24, s. 1(2).]

premises means, in relation to an educational institution, a place where education or training referred to in the definition "educational institution" is provided, controlled or supervised by the educational institution;
[S.C. 1997, c. 24, s. 1(5).]

receiving device [Repealed by S.C. 1993, c. 44, s. 79(1).]

Rome Convention country means a country that is a party to the International Convention for the Protection of Performers, Producers of Phonograms and Broadcasting Organisations, done at Rome on October 26, 1961;
[S.C. 1997, c. 24, s. 1(5).]

sculpture includes a cast or model;
[S.C. 1997, c. 24, s. 1(5).]

sound recording means a recording, fixed in any material form, consisting of

sounds, whether or not of a performance of a work, but excludes any soundtrack of a cinematographic work where it accompanies the cinematographic work;
[S.C. 1997, c. 24, s. 1(5).]

telecommunication means any transmission of signs, signals, writing, images or sounds or intelligence of any nature by wire, radio, visual, optical or other electromagnetic system;
[S.C. 1988, c. 65, s. 61.]

treaty country means a Berne Convention country, UCC country, WCT country or WTO Member;
[S.C. 1994, c. 47, s. 56(3); S.C. 2012, c. 20, s. 2(1).]

UCC country means a country that is a party to the Universal Copyright Convention, adopted on September 6, 1952 in Geneva, Switzerland, or to that Convention as revised in Paris, France on July 24, 1971;
[S.C. 1994, c. 47, s. 56(3).]

WCT country means a country that is a party to the WIPO Copyright Treaty, adopted in Geneva on December 20, 1996;

work includes the title thereof when such title is original and distinctive;

work of joint authorship means a work produced by the collaboration of two or more authors in which the contribution of one author is not distinct from the contribution of the other author or authors;

work of sculpture [Repealed by S.C. 1997, c. 24, s. 1(1).]

WPPT country means a country that is a party to the WIPO Performances and Phonograms Treaty, adopted in Geneva on December 20, 1996;

WTO Member means a member of the World Trade Organization as defined in subsection 2(1) of the *World Trade Organization Agreement Implementation Act.**
[S.C. 1994, c. 47, s. 56(3); S.C. 2012, c. 20, s. 2(2).]

---

*World Trade Organization Agreement Implementation Act, **S.C. 1994, c. 47**

2. *Definitions* — (1) In this Act,

Agreement **means the Agreement Establishing the World Trade Organization, including**

(*a*) **the agreements set out in Annexes 1A, 1B, 1C, 2 and 3 to that Agreement, and**

(*b*) **the agreements set out in Annex 4 to that Agreement that have been accepted by Canada,**

all forming an integral part of the Final Act Embodying The Results Of The

Uruguay Round Of Multilateral Trade Negotiations, signed at Marrakesh on April 15, 1994;

. . .

World Trade Organization **means the World Trade Organization established by Article I of the Agreement;**

WTO Member **means a Member of the World Trade Organization.**

2.1. Compilations — (1) A compilation containing two or more of the categories of literary, dramatic, musical or artistic works shall be deemed to be a compilation of the category making up the most substantial part of the compilation.

(2) *Idem* — The mere fact that a work is included in a compilation does not increase, decrease or otherwise affect the protection conferred by this Act in respect of the copyright in the work or the moral rights in respect of the work.
[S.C. 1993, c. 44, s. 54.]

2.11. Definition of *maker* — For greater certainty, the arrangements referred to in paragraph (*b*) of the definition *maker* in section 2, as that term is used in section 19 and in the definition *eligible maker* in section 79, include arrangements for entering into contracts with performers, financial arrangements and technical arrangements required for the first fixation of the sounds for a sound recording.
[S.C. 1997, c. 24, s. 2.]

2.2. Definition of *publication* — (1) For the purposes of this Act, *publication* means

(*a*)   in relation to works,

  (i)   making copies of a work available to the public,

  (ii)   the construction of an architectural work, and

  (iii)   the incorporation of an artistic work into an architectural work, and

(*b*)   in relation to sound recordings, making copies of a sound recording available to the public,

but does not include

(*c*)   the performance in public, or the communication to the public by telecommunication, of a literary, dramatic, musical or artistic work or a sound recording, or

(*d*)   the exhibition in public of an artistic work.

(2) *Issue of photographs and engravings* — For the purpose of subsection (1), the issue of photographs and engravings of sculptures and architectural works is not deemed to be publication of those works.

COPYRIGHT ACT

(3) *Where no consent of copyright owner* — For the purposes of this Act, other than in respect of infringement of copyright, a work or other subject-matter is not deemed to be published or performed in public or communicated to the public by telecommunication if that act is done without the consent of the owner of the copyright.

(4) *Unpublished works* — Where, in the case of an unpublished work, the making of the work is extended over a considerable period, the conditions of this Act conferring copyright are deemed to have been complied with if the author was, during any substantial part of that period, a subject or citizen of, or a person ordinarily resident in, a country to which this Act extends.

[S.C. 1997, c. 24, s. 2.]

2.3. Telecommunication — A person who communicates a work or other subject-matter to the public by telecommunication does not by that act alone perform it in public, nor by that act alone is deemed to authorize its performance in public.

[S.C. 1997, c. 24, s. 2.]

2.4. Communication to the public by telecommunication — (1) For the purposes of communication to the public by telecommunication,

(*a*) persons who occupy apartments, hotel rooms or dwelling units situated in the same building are part of the public, and a communication intended to be received exclusively by such persons is a communication to the public;

(*b*) a person whose only act in respect of the communication of a work or other subject-matter to the public consists of providing the means of telecommunication necessary for another person to so communicate the work or other subject-matter does not communicate that work or other subject-matter to the public; and

(*c*) where a person, as part of

  (i) a network, within the meaning of the *Broadcasting Act,** whose operations result in the communication of works or other subject-matter to the public, or

  (ii) any programming undertaking whose operations result in the communication of works or other subject-matter to the public,

transmits by telecommunication a work or other subject-matter that is communicated to the public by another person who is not a retransmitter of a signal within the meaning of subsection 31(1), the transmission and communication of that work or other subject-matter by those persons constitute a single communication to the public for which those persons are jointly and severally liable.

(1.1) *Communication to the public by telecommunication* — For the purposes of this Act, communication of a work or other subject-matter to the public by telecommunication includes making it available to the public by telecommunication in a way that allows a member of the public to have access to it from a place and at a time individually chosen by that member of the public.

(2) *Regulations* — The Governor in Council may make regulations defining "programming undertaking" for the purpose of paragraph (1)(*c*).

(3) *Exception* — A work is not communicated in the manner described in paragraph (1)(*c*) or 3(1)(*f*) where a signal carrying the work is retransmitted to a person who is a retransmitter within the meaning of subsection 31(1).
[S.C. 1997, c. 24, s. 2; S.C. 2002, c. 26, s. 1; S.C. 2012, c. 20, s. 3.]

---

* *Broadcasting Act*, S.C. **1991, c. 11**

network includes any operation where control over all or any part of the programs or program schedules of one or more broadcasting undertakings is delegated to another undertaking or person;

2.5. What constitutes rental — (1) For the purposes of paragraphs 3(1)(*h*) and (*i*), 15(1)(*c*) and 18(1)(*c*), an arrangement, whatever its form, constitutes a rental of a computer program or sound recording if, and only if,

(*a*)   it is in substance a rental, having regard to all the circumstances; and

(*b*)   it is entered into with motive of gain in relation to the overall operations of the person who rents out the computer program or sound recording, as the case may be.

(2) *Motive of gain* — For the purpose of paragraph (1)(*b*), a person who rents out a computer program or sound recording with the intention of recovering no more than the costs, including overhead, associated with the rental operations does not by that act alone have a motive of gain in relation to the rental operations.
[S.C. 1997, c. 24, s. 2.]

2.6. Exclusive distributor — The Governor in Council may make regulations establishing distribution criteria for the purpose of paragraph (*b*) of the definition *exclusive distributor* in section 2.
[S.C. 1997, c. 24, ss. 2 and 62(1).]

2.7. Exclusive licence — For the purposes of this Act, an exclusive licence is an authorization to do any act that is subject to copyright to the exclusion of all others including the copyright owner, whether the authorization is granted by the owner or an exclusive licensee claiming under the owner.
[S.C. 1997, c. 24, s. 2.]

PART I
COPYRIGHT AND MORAL RIGHTS IN WORKS

[S.C. 1997, c. 24, s. 2.]

COPYRIGHT

3. Copyright in works — (1) For the purposes of this Act, *copyright*, in relation to a work, means the sole right to produce or reproduce the work or any substantial part thereof in any material form whatever, to perform the work or any substantial part thereof in public or, if the work is unpublished, to publish the work or any substantial part thereof, and includes the sole right

(*a*)   to produce, reproduce, perform or publish any translation of the work,

(*b*)   in the case of a dramatic work, to convert it into a novel or other non-dramatic work,

(*c*)   in the case of a novel or other non-dramatic work, or of an artistic work, to convert it into a dramatic work, by way of performance in public or otherwise,

(*d*)   in the case of a literary, dramatic or musical work, to make any sound recording, cinematograph film or other contrivance by means of which the work may be mechanically reproduced or performed,

[S.C. 1997, c. 24, s. 3(2).]

(*e*)   in the case of any literary, dramatic, musical or artistic work, to reproduce, adapt and publicly present the work as a cinematographic work,

[S.C. 1993, c. 44, s. 55(1); 1997, c. 24, s. 3(2).]

(*f*)   in the case of any literary, dramatic, musical or artistic work, to communicate the work to the public by telecommunication,

[S.C. 1988, c. 65, s. 62(1).]

(*g*)   to present at a public exhibition, for a purpose other than sale or hire, an artistic work created after June 7, 1988, other than a map, chart or plan,

[S.C. 1993, c. 44, s. 55(2).]

(*h*)   in the case of a computer program that can be reproduced in the ordinary course of its use, other than by a reproduction during its execution in conjunction with a machine, device or computer, to rent out the computer program,

[S.C. 1993, c. 44, s. 55(2); S.C. 2012, c. 20, s. 4.]

(*i*)   in the case of a musical work, to rent out a sound recording in which the work is embodied, and

[S.C. 1997, c. 24, s. 3(3); S.C. 2012, c. 20, s. 4.]

(*j*)   in the case of a work that is in the form of a tangible object, to sell or

63

otherwise transfer ownership of the tangible object, as long as that ownership has never previously been transferred in or outside Canada with the authorization of the copyright owner,

[S.C. 2012, c. 20, s. 4.]

and to authorize any such acts.

(1.1) *Simultaneous fixing* — A work that is communicated in the manner described in paragraph (1)(*f*) is fixed even if it is fixed simultaneously with its communication.

[S.C. 1988, c. 65, s. 62(2).]

(1.2) [Repealed by S.C. 1997, c. 24, s. 3(4).]

(1.3) [Repealed by S.C. 1997, c. 24, s. 3(4).]

(1.4) [Repealed by S.C. 1997, c. 24, s. 3(4).]

(1.41) [Repealed by S.C. 1997, c. 24, s. 3(4).]

(1.5) [Repealed by S.C. 1997, c. 24, s. 3(4).]

(2) [Repealed by S.C. 1997, c. 24, s. 3(4).]

(3) [Repealed by S.C. 1997, c. 24, s. 3(4).]

(4) [Repealed by S.C. 1997, c. 24, s. 3(4).]

4. [Repealed by S.C. 1997, c. 24, s. 4.]

WORKS IN WHICH COPYRIGHT MAY SUBSIST

5. Conditions for subsistence of copyright — (1) Subject to this Act, copyright shall subsist in Canada, for the term hereinafter mentioned, in every original literary, dramatic, musical and artistic work if any one of the following conditions is met:

(*a*) in the case of any work, whether published or unpublished, including a cinematographic work, the author was, at the date of the making of the work, a citizen or subject of, or a person ordinarily resident in, a treaty country;

(*b*) in the case of a cinematographic work, whether published or unpublished, the maker, at the date of the making of the cinematographic work,

(i) if a corporation, had its headquarters in a treaty country, or

(ii) if a natural person, was a citizen or subject of, or a person ordinarily resident in, a treaty country; or

(*c*) in the case of a published work, including a cinematographic work,

(i) in relation to subparagraph 2.2(1)(*a*)(i), the first publication in such a quantity as to satisfy the reasonable demands of the public, having regard to the nature of the work, occurred in a treaty country, or

   (ii)   in relation to subparagraph 2.2(1)(*a*)(ii) or (iii), the first publication occurred in a treaty country.

[S.C. 1997, c. 24, s. 5(1).]

(1.01) *Protection for older works* — For the purposes of subsection (1), a country that becomes a Berne Convention country, a WCT country or a WTO Member after the date of the making or publication of a work is deemed to have been a Berne Convention country, a WCT country or a WTO Member, as the case may be, at that date, subject to subsection (1.02) and sections 33 to 33.2.

[S.C. 2001, c. 34, s. 34; S.C. 2012, c. 20, s. 5.]

(1.02) *Limitation* — Subsection (1.01) does not confer copyright protection in Canada on a work whose term of copyright protection in the country referred to in that subsection had expired before that country became a Berne Convention country, a WCT country or a WTO Member, as the case may be.

[S.C. 1994, c. 47, s. 57(1); S.C. 2012, c. 20, s. 5.]

(1.03) *Application of subsections (1.01) and (1.02)* — Subsections (1.01) and (1.02) apply, and are deemed to have applied, regardless of whether the country in question became a Berne Convention country, a WCT country or a WTO Member before or after the coming into force of those subsections.

[S.C. 1997, c. 24, s. 5(2); S.C. 2012, c. 20, s. 5.]

(1.1) *First publication* — The first publication described in subparagraph (1)(*c*)(i) or (ii) is deemed to have occurred in a treaty country notwithstanding that it in fact occurred previously elsewhere, if the interval between those two publications did not exceed thirty days.

[S.C. 1994, c. 47, s. 57(1); S.C. 1997, c. 24, s. 5(2).]

(1.2) *Idem* — Copyright shall not subsist in Canada otherwise than as provided by subsection (1), except in so far as the protection conferred by this Act is extended as hereinafter provided to foreign countries to which this Act does not extend.

[S.C. 1993, c. 44, s. 57(1).]

(2) *Minister may extend copyright to other countries* — Where the Minister certifies by notice, published in the *Canada Gazette*, that any country that is not a treaty country grants or has undertaken to grant, either by treaty, convention, agreement or law, to citizens of Canada, the benefit of copyright on substantially the same basis as to its own citizens or copyright protection substantially equal to that conferred by this Act, the country shall, for the purpose of the rights conferred by this Act, be treated as if it were a country to which this Act extends, and the Minister may give a certificate, notwithstanding that the remedies for enforcing the rights, or the restrictions on the importation of copies of works, under the law of such country, differ from those in this Act.

[S.C. 1994, c. 47, s. 57(2).]

(2.1) [Repealed by S.C. 1994, c. 47, s. 57.]

(3) [Repealed by S.C. 1997, c. 24, s. 5(3).]

(4) [Repealed by S.C. 1997, c. 24, s. 5(3).]

(5) [Repealed by S.C. 1997, c. 24, s. 5(3).]

(6) [Repealed by S.C. 1997, c. 24, s. 5(3).]

Note: See also Transitional Provisions (section 55) of S.C. 1997, c. 24.

(7) *Reciprocity protection preserved* — For greater certainty, the protection to which a work is entitled by virtue of a notice published under subsection (2), or under that subsection as it read at any time before the coming into force of this subsection, is not affected by reason only of the country in question becoming a treaty country.

[S.C. 1994, c. 47, s. 57(3).]

TERM OF COPYRIGHT

6. Term of copyright — The term for which copyright shall subsist shall, except as otherwise expressly provided by this Act, be the life of the author, the remainder of the calendar year in which the author dies, and a period of fifty years following the end of that calendar year.

[S.C. 1993, c. 44, s. 58.]

Note: See also Transitional Provisions (section 54.1) of S.C. 1997, c. 24.

6.1. Anonymous and pseudonymous works — (1) Except as provided in section 6.2 and in subsection (2), where the identity of the author of a work is unknown, copyright in the work shall subsist until the end of 75 years following the end of the calendar year in which the work is made. However, if the work is published before the copyright expires, the copyright continues until the earlier of the end of 75 years following the end of the calendar year in which the first publication occurs and 100 years following the end of the calendar year in which the work was made.

(2) *Identity of author commonly known* — Where, during any term referred to in subsection (1), the author's identity becomes commonly known, the term provided in section 6 applies.

[S.C. 1993, c. 44, s. 58; S.C. 2020, c. 1, s. 24]

6.2. Anonymous and pseudonymous works of joint authorship — (1) Except as provided in subsection (2), where the identity of all the authors of a work of joint authorship is unknown, copyright in the work shall subsist until the end of 75 years following the end of the calendar year in which the work is made. However, if the work is published before the copyright expires, the copyright continues until the earlier of the end of 75 years following the end of the calendar year in which the first publication occurs and 100 years following the end of the calendar year in which the work was made.

(2) *Identity of author commonly known* — Where, during any term referred to in subsection (1), the identity of one or more of the authors becomes commonly known, copyright shall subsist for the life of whichever of those authors dies last, the remainder of the calendar year in which that author dies and a period of 50 years following the end of that calendar year.

[S.C. 1993, c. 44, s. 58; S.C. 2020, c. 1, s. 24]

7. Term of copyright in posthumous works — (1) Subject to subsection (2), in the case of a literary, dramatic or musical work, or an engraving, in which copyright subsists at the date of the death of the author or, in the case of a work of joint authorship, at or immediately before the date of the death of the author who dies last, but which has not been published or, in the case of a lecture or a dramatic or musical work, been performed in public or communicated to the public by telecommunication, before that date, copyright shall subsist until publication, or performance in public or communication to the public by telecommunication, whichever may first happen, for the remainder of the calendar year of the publication or of the performance in public or communication to the public by telecommunication, as the case may be, and for a period of fifty years following the end of that calendar year.

(2) *Application of subsection (1)* —Subsection (1) applies only where the work in question was published or performed in public or communicated to the public by telecommunication, as the case may be, before the coming into force of this section.

(3) *Transitional provision* — Where

(*a*) a work has not, at the coming into force of this section, been published or performed in public or communicated to the public by telecommunication,

(*b*) subsection (1) would apply to that work if it had been published or performed in public or communicated to the public by telecommunication before the coming into force of this section, and

(*c*) the relevant death referred to in subsection (1) occurred during the period of fifty years immediately before the coming into force of this section,

copyright shall subsist in the work for the remainder of the calendar year in which this section comes into force and for a period of fifty years following the end of that calendar year, whether or not the work is published or performed in public or communicated to the public by telecommunication after the coming into force of this section.

(4) *Transitional provision* — Where

(*a*) a work has not, at the coming into force of this section, been published or performed in public or communicated to the public by telecommunication,

(*b*) subsection (1) would apply to that work if it had been published or performed in public or communicated to the public by telecommunication before the coming into force of this section, and

(c) the relevant death referred to in subsection (1) occurred more than fifty years before the coming into force of this section,

copyright shall subsist in the work for the remainder of the calendar year in which this section comes into force and for a period of five years following the end of that calendar year, whether or not the work is published or performed in public or communicated to the public by telecommunication after the coming into force of this section.

[S.C. 1993, c. 44, s. 58; S.C. 1997, c. 24, s. 6.]

8. [Repealed by S.C. 1993, c. 44, s. 59.]

9. Cases of joint authorship — (1) In the case of a work of joint authorship, except as provided in section 6.2, copyright shall subsist during the life of the author who dies last, for the remainder of the calendar year of that author's death, and for a period of fifty years following the end of that calendar year, and references in this Act to the period after the expiration of any specified number of years from the end of the calendar year of the death of the author shall be construed as references to the period after the expiration of the like number of years from the end of the calendar year of the death of the author who dies last.

(2) *Nationals of other countries* — Authors who are nationals of any country, other than a country that is a party to the Canada–United States–Mexico Agreement, that grants a term of protection shorter than that mentioned in subsection (1) are not entitled to claim a longer term of protection in Canada.

[S.C. 1993, c. 44, s. 60(1); S.C. 2020, c. 1, s. 25.]

10. [Repealed by S.C. 2012, c. 20, s. 6.]

11. [Repealed by S.C. 1997, c. 24, s. 8.]

Note: See also Transitional Provisions (section 55) of S.C. 1997, c. 24.

11.1. Cinematographic works — Except for cinematographic works in which the arrangement or acting form or the combination of incidents represented give the work a dramatic character, copyright in a cinematographic work or a compilation of cinematographic works shall subsist until the end of 70 years following the end of the calendar year in which the cinematographic work or the compilation is made. However, if the cinematographic work or the compilation is published before the copyright expires, the copyright continues until the earlier of the end of 75 years following the end of the calendar year in which the first publication occurs and 100 years following the end of the calendar year in which the cinematographic work or the compilation was made.

[S.C. 1993, c. 44, s. 60(1); S.C. 1997, c. 24, s. 9; S.C. 2020, c. 1, s. 26.]

12. Where copyright belongs to Her Majesty — Without prejudice to any rights or privileges of the Crown, where any work is, or has been, prepared or published by or under the direction or control of Her Majesty or any government department, the copyright in the work shall, subject to any agreement with the author, belong to

Her Majesty and in that case shall continue for the remainder of the calendar year of the first publication of the work and for a period of fifty years following the end of that calendar year.

[S.C. 1993, c. 44, s. 60(1).]

OWNERSHIP OF COPYRIGHT

13. Ownership of copyright — (1) Subject to this Act, the author of a work shall be the first owner of the copyright therein.

(2) [Repealed by S.C. 2012, c. 20, s. 7.]

(3) *Work made in the course of employment* — Where the author of a work was in the employment of some other person under a contract of service or apprenticeship and the work was made in the course of his employment by that person, the person by whom the author was employed shall, in the absence of any agreement to the contrary, be the first owner of the copyright, but where the work is an article or other contribution to a newspaper, magazine or similar periodical, there shall, in the absence of any agreement to the contrary, be deemed to be reserved to the author a right to restrain the publication of the work, otherwise than as part of a newspaper, magazine or similar periodical.

(4) *Assignments and licences* — The owner of the copyright in any work may assign the right, either wholly or partially, and either generally or subject to limitations relating to territory, medium or sector of the market or other limitations relating to the scope of the assignment, and either for the whole term of the copyright or for any other part thereof, and may grant any interest in the right by licence, but no assignment or grant is valid unless it is in writing signed by the owner of the right in respect of which the assignment or grant is made, or by the owner's duly authorized agent.

(5) *Ownership in case of partial assignment* — Where, under any partial assignment of copyright, the assignee becomes entitled to any right comprised in copyright, the assignee, with respect to the rights so assigned, and the assignor, with respect to the rights not assigned, shall be treated for the purposes of this Act as the owner of the copyright, and this Act has effect accordingly.

(6) *Assignment of right of action* — For greater certainty, it is deemed always to have been the law that a right of action for infringement of copyright may be assigned in association with the assignment of the copyright or the grant of an interest in the copyright by licence.

(7) *Exclusive licence* — For greater certainty, it is deemed always to have been the law that a grant of an exclusive licence in a copyright constitutes the grant of an interest in the copyright by licence.

[S.C. 1997, c. 24, s. 10(2).]

14. Limitation where author is first owner of copyright — (1) Where the author of a work is the first owner of the copyright therein, no assignment of the copyright and no grant of any interest therein, made by him, otherwise than by will, after June 4, 1921, is operative to vest in the assignee or grantee any rights with respect to the copyright in the work beyond the expiration of twenty-five years from the death of the author, and the reversionary interest in the copyright expectant on the termination of that period shall, on the death of the author, notwithstanding any agreement to the contrary, devolve on his legal representatives as part of the estate of the author, and any agreement entered into by the author as to the disposition of such reversionary interest is void.

(2) *Restriction* — Nothing in subsection (1) shall be construed as applying to the assignment of the copyright in a collective work or a licence to publish a work or part of a work as part of a collective work.

Note: See also Transitional Provisions (section 55(3)) of S.C. 1997, c. 24.

(3) [Repealed by S.C. 1997, c. 24, s. 11.]

(4) [Repealed by R.S.C. 1985, c. 10 (4th Supp.), s. 3.]

14.01. [Repealed by S.C. 1997, c. 24, s. 12.]

Note: Heading preceding s. 14.01 repealed by S.C. 1997, c. 24, s. 12. See also Transitional Provisions (section 56) of S.C. 1997, c. 24.

MORAL RIGHTS

14.1. Moral rights— (1) The author of a work has, subject to section 28.2, the right to the integrity of the work and, in connection with an act mentioned in section 3, the right, where reasonable in the circumstances, to be associated with the work as its author by name or under a pseudonym and the right to remain anonymous.

(2) *No assignment of moral rights* — Moral rights may not be assigned but may be waived in whole or in part.

(3) *No waiver by assignment* — An assignment of copyright in a work does not by that act alone constitute a waiver of any moral rights.

(4) *Effect of waiver* — Where a waiver of any moral right is made in favour of an owner or a licensee of copyright, it may be invoked by any person authorized by the owner or licensee to use the work, unless there is an indication to the contrary in the waiver.
[R.S.C. 1985, c. 10 (4th Supp.), s. 4.]

Note: The above section is applicable as provided by R.S.C. 1985, c. 10 (4th Supp.), ss. 23(1) and (3).

14.2. Term — (1) Moral rights in respect of a work subsist for the same term as the copyright in the work.

(2) *Succession* — The moral rights in respect of a work pass, on the death of its

author, to

(*a*)   the person to whom those rights are specifically bequeathed;

(*b*)   where there is no specific bequest of those moral rights and the author dies testate in respect of the copyright in the work, the person to whom that copyright is bequeathed; or

(*c*)   where there is no person described in paragraph (a) or (b), the person entitled to any other property in respect of which the author dies intestate.

[R.S.C. 1985, c. 10 (4th Supp.), s. 4.]

(3) *Subsequent succession* — Subsection (2) applies, with such modifications as the circumstances require, on the death of any person who holds moral rights.

[S.C. 1997, c. 24, s. 13.]

PART II
COPYRIGHT IN PERFORMERS' PERFORMANCES, SOUND RECORDINGS AND COMMUNICATION SIGNALS AND MORAL RIGHTS IN PERFORMERS' PERFORMANCES

[S.C. 2012, c. 20, s. 8.]

Note: See also Transitional Provisions (section 55) of S.C. 1997, c. 24.

PERFORMERS' RIGHTS

COPYRIGHT

15. Copyright in performer's performance — (1) Subject to subsection (2), a performer has a copyright in the performer's performance, consisting of the sole right to do the following in relation to the performer's performance or any substantial part thereof:

(*a*)   if it is not fixed,

  (i)   to communicate it to the public by telecommunication,

  (ii)   to perform it in public, where it is communicated to the public by telecommunication otherwise than by communication signal, and

  (iii)   to fix it in any material form,

(*b*)   if it is fixed,

  (i)   to reproduce any fixation that was made without the performer's authorization,

  (ii)   where the performer authorized a fixation, to reproduce any reproduction of that fixation, if the reproduction being reproduced was made for a purpose other than that for which the performer's authorization was given, and

        (iii) where a fixation was permitted under Part III or VIII, to reproduce any reproduction of that fixation, if the reproduction being reproduced was made for a purpose other than one permitted under Part III or VIII, and

(*c*) to rent out a sound recording of it,

and to authorize any such acts.

(1.1) *Copyright in performer's performance* — Subject to subsections (2.1) and (2.2), a performer's copyright in the performer's performance consists of the sole right to do the following acts in relation to the performer's performance or any substantial part of it and to authorize any of those acts:

(*a*) if it is not fixed,

        (i) to communicate it to the public by telecommunication,

        (ii) to perform it in public, if it is communicated to the public by telecommunication otherwise than by communication signal, and

        (iii) to fix it in any material form;

(*b*) if it is fixed in a sound recording, to reproduce that fixation;

(*c*) to rent out a sound recording of it;

(*d*) to make a sound recording of it available to the public by telecommunication in a way that allows a member of the public to have access to the sound recording from a place and at a time individually chosen by that member of the public and to communicate the sound recording to the public by telecommunication in that way; and

(*e*) if it is fixed in a sound recording that is in the form of a tangible object, to sell or otherwise transfer ownership of the tangible object, as long as that ownership has never previously been transferred in or outside Canada with the authorization of the owner of the copyright in the performer's performance.

(2) *Conditions* — Subsection (1) applies only if the performer's performance

(*a*) takes place in Canada or in a Rome Convention country;

(*b*) is fixed in

        (i) a sound recording whose maker, at the time of the first fixation,

                (A) if a natural person, was a Canadian citizen or permanent resident within the meaning of subsection 2(1) of the *Immigration and Refugee Protection Act,** or a citizen or permanent resident of a Rome Convention country, or

                (B) if a corporation, had its headquarters in Canada or in a Rome

Convention country, or

 (ii) a sound recording whose first publication in such a quantity as to satisfy the reasonable demands of the public occurred in Canada or in a Rome Convention country; or

(c) is transmitted at the time of the performer's performance by a communication signal broadcast from Canada or a Rome Convention country by a broadcaster that has its headquarters in the country of broadcast.

(2.1) *Conditions for copyright* — Subsection (1.1) applies if

(a) the performer's performance takes place in Canada;

(b) the performer's performance is fixed in

 (i) a sound recording whose maker, at the time of its first fixation,

  (A) was a Canadian citizen or permanent resident as defined in subsection 2(1) of the *Immigration and Refugee Protection Act*,* in the case of a natural person, or

  (B) had its headquarters in Canada, in the case of a corporation, or

 (ii) a sound recording whose first publication in a quantity sufficient to satisfy the reasonable demands of the public occurred in Canada; or

(c) the performer's performance is transmitted at the time of its performance by a communication signal broadcast from Canada by a broadcaster that has its headquarters in Canada.

(2.2) *Conditions for copyright* — Subsection (1.1) also applies if

(a) the performer's performance takes place in a WPPT country;

(b) the performer's performance is fixed in

 (i) a sound recording whose maker, at the time of its first fixation,

  (A) was a citizen or permanent resident of a WPPT country, in the case of a natural person, or

  (B) had its headquarters in a WPPT country, in the case of a corporation, or

 (ii) a sound recording whose first publication in a quantity sufficient to satisfy the reasonable demands of the public occurred in a WPPT country; or

(c) the performer's performance is transmitted at the time of its performance by a communication signal broadcast from a WPPT country by a broadcaster that has its headquarters in that country.

[S.C. 2012, c. 20, s. 9(3).]

(3) *Publication* — The first publication is deemed to have occurred in a country referred to in paragraph (2)(*b*) notwithstanding that it in fact occurred previously elsewhere, if the interval between those two publications does not exceed thirty days.

[S.C. 1993, c. 44, s. 61; S.C. 1997, c. 24, s. 14; S.C. 2001, c. 27, s. 235; S.C. 2012, c. 20, s. 9(1), (2).]

(4) *Publication* — The first publication of a sound recording is deemed to have occurred in a WPPT country, despite an earlier publication elsewhere, if the interval between the publication in that WPPT country and the earlier publication does not exceed 30 days.

[S.C. 2012, c. 20, s. 9(4).]

---

* *Immigration and Refugee Protection Act*, S.C. 2001, c. 27

permanent resident means a person who has acquired permanent resident status and has not subsequently lost that status under section 46.

[S.C. 2001, c. 27, s. 2(1).]

---

16. Contractual arrangements — Nothing in section 15 prevents the performer from entering into a contract governing the use of the performer's performance for the purpose of broadcasting, fixation or retransmission.

[S.C. 1994, c. 47, s. 59; S.C. 1997, c. 24, s. 14.]

17. Cinematographic works — (1) Where the performer authorizes the embodiment of the performer's performance in a cinematographic work, the performer may no longer exercise, in relation to the performance where embodied in that cinematographic work, the copyright referred to in subsection 15(1).

(2) *Right to remuneration* — Where there is an agreement governing the embodiment referred to in subsection (1) and that agreement provides for a right to remuneration for the reproduction, performance in public or communication to the public by telecommunication of the cinematographic work, the performer may enforce that right against

(*a*)   the other party to the agreement or, if that party assigns the agreement, the assignee, and

(*b*)   any other person who

(i)   owns the copyright in the cinematographic work governing the reproduction of the cinematographic work, its performance in public or its communication to the public by telecommunication, and

    (ii)   reproduces the cinematographic work, performs it in public or communicates it to the public by telecommunication,

and persons referred to in paragraphs (*a*) and (*b*) are jointly and severally liable to the performer in respect of the remuneration relating to that copyright.

    (3) *Application of subsection (2)* — Subsection (2) applies only if the performer's performance is embodied in a prescribed cinematographic work.

    (4) *Exception* — If so requested by a country that is a party to the Canada–United States–Mexico Agreement, the Minister may, by a statement published in the *Canada Gazette*, grant the benefits conferred by this section, subject to any terms and conditions specified in the statement, to performers who are nationals of that country or another country that is a party to that Agreement or are Canadian citizens or permanent residents within the meaning of subsection 2(1) of the *Immigration and Refugee Protection Act** and whose performer's performances are embodied in works other than the prescribed cinematographic works referred to in subsection (3). [S.C. 1994, c. 47, s. 59; S.C. 1997, c. 24, s. 14; S.C. 2001, c. 27, s. 236; S.C. 2020, c. 1, s. 27.]

MORAL RIGHTS

17.1. Moral rights — (1) In the cases referred to in subsections 15(2.1) and (2.2), a performer of a live aural performance or a performance fixed in a sound recording has, subject to subsection 28.2(1), the right to the integrity of the performance, and—in connection with an act mentioned in subsection 15(1.1) or one for which the performer has a right to remuneration under section 19—the right, if it is reasonable in the circumstances, to be associated with the performance as its performer by name or under a pseudonym and the right to remain anonymous.

    (2) *No assignment of moral rights* — Moral rights may not be assigned but may be waived in whole or in part.

    (3) *No waiver by assignment* — An assignment of copyright in a performer's performance does not by itself constitute a waiver of any moral rights.

    (4) *Effect of waiver* — If a waiver of any moral right is made in favour of an owner or a licensee of a copyright, it may be invoked by any person authorized by the owner or licensee to use the performer's performance, unless there is an indication to the contrary in the waiver. [S.C. 2012, c. 20, s. 10.]

17.2. Application and term — (1) Subsection 17.1(1) applies only in respect of a performer's performance that occurs after the coming into force of that subsection. The moral rights subsist for the same term as the copyright in that performer's performance.

    (2) *Succession*— The moral rights in respect of a performer's performance pass, on the performer's death, to

(a)   the person to whom those rights are specifically bequeathed;

(b)   if there is not a specific bequest of those moral rights and the performer dies testate in respect of the copyright in the performer's performance, the person to whom that copyright is bequeathed; or

(c)   if there is not a person as described in paragraph (a) or (b), the person entitled to any other property in respect of which the performer dies intestate.

(3) *Subsequent succession* — Subsection (2) applies, with any modifications that the circumstances require, on the death of any person who holds moral rights. [S.C. 2012, c. 20, s. 10.]

---

* *Immigration and Refugee Protection Act*, S.C. 2001, c. 27

permanent resident means a person who has acquired permanent resident status and has not subsequently lost that status under section 46.
[S.C. 2001, c. 27, s. 2(1).]

RIGHTS OF SOUND RECORDING MAKERS

18. Copyright in sound recordings — (1) Subject to subsection (2), the maker of a sound recording has a copyright in the sound recording, consisting of the sole right to do the following in relation to the sound recording or any substantial part thereof:

(a)   to publish it for the first time,

(b)   to reproduce it in any material form, and

(c)   to rent it out,

and to authorize any such acts.

(1.1) *Copyright in sound recordings* — Subject to subsections (2.1) and (2.2), a sound recording maker's copyright in the sound recording also includes the sole right to do the following acts in relation to the sound recording or any substantial part of it and to authorize any of those acts:

(a)   to make it available to the public by telecommunication in a way that allows a member of the public to have access to it from a place and at a time individually chosen by that member of the public and to communicate it to the public by telecommunication in that way; and

(b)   if it is in the form of a tangible object, to sell or otherwise transfer ownership of the tangible object, as long as that ownership has never previously been transferred in or outside Canada with the authorization of the owner of the copyright in the sound recording.

(2) *Conditions for copyright*— Subsection (1) applies only if

(*a*)   at the time of the first fixation or, if that first fixation was extended over a considerable period, during any substantial part of that period, the maker of the sound recording

   (i)   was a Canadian citizen or permanent resident as defined in subsection 2(1) of the *Immigration and Refugee Protection Act,*

   (ii)   was a citizen or permanent resident of a Berne Convention country, a Rome Convention country, a WPPT country or a country that is a WTO Member, or

   (iii)   had its headquarters in one of those countries, in the case of a corporation; or

(*b*)   the first publication of the sound recording in a quantity sufficient to satisfy the reasonable demands of the public occurred in any country referred to in paragraph (*a*).

[S.C. 2012, c. 20, s. 11(2).]

(2.1) *Conditions for copyright* — Subsection (1.1) applies if

(*a*)   at the time of the first fixation or, if that first fixation was extended over a considerable period, during any substantial part of that period, the maker of the sound recording

   (i)   was a Canadian citizen or permanent resident as defined in subsection 2(1) of the *Immigration and Refugee Protection Act,** or

   (ii)   had its headquarters in Canada, in the case of a corporation; or

(*b*)   the first publication of the sound recording in a quantity sufficient to satisfy the reasonable demands of the public occurred in Canada.

(2.2) *Conditions for copyright*— Subsection (1.1) also applies if

(*a*)   at the time of the first fixation or, if that first fixation was extended over a considerable period, during any substantial part of that period, the maker of the sound recording

   (i)   was a citizen or permanent resident of a WPPT country, or

   (ii)   had its headquarters in a WPPT country, in the case of a corporation; or

(*b*)   the first publication of the sound recording in a quantity sufficient to satisfy the reasonable demands of the public occurred in a WPPT country.

[S.C. 2012, c. 20, s. 11(4).]

(3) *Publication* — The first publication is deemed to have occurred in a country referred to in paragraph (2)(*a*) notwithstanding that it in fact occurred previously

elsewhere, if the interval between those two publications does not exceed thirty days.

[S.C. 1994, c. 47, s. 59; S.C. 1997, c. 24, s. 14; S.C. 2001, c. 27, s. 237; S.C. 2012, c. 20, s. 11(1), (3).]

(4) *Publication* — The first publication of a sound recording is deemed to have occurred in a WPPT country, despite an earlier publication elsewhere, if the interval between the publication in that WPPT country and the earlier publication does not exceed 30 days.

[S.C. 2012, c. 20, s. 11(5).]

---

* *Immigration and Refugee Protection Act*, S.C. 2001, c. 27

permanent resident means a person who has acquired permanent resident status and has not subsequently lost that status under section 46.

[S.C. 2001, c. 27, s. 2(1).]

PROVISIONS APPLICABLE TO BOTH PERFORMERS AND SOUND RECORDING MAKERS

19. Right to remuneration – Canada — (1) If a sound recording has been published, the performer and maker are entitled, subject to subsection 20(1), to be paid equitable remuneration for its performance in public or its communication to the public by telecommunication, except for a communication in the circumstances referred to in paragraph 15(1.1)(*d*) or 18(1.1)(*a*) and any retransmission.

(1.1) *Right to remuneration – Rome Convention country* — If a sound recording has been published, the performer and maker are entitled, subject to subsections 20(1.1) and (2), to be paid equitable remuneration for its performance in public or its communication to the public by telecommunication, except for

(*a*)   a communication in the circumstances referred to in paragraph 15(1.1)(*d*) or 18(1.1)(*a*), if the person entitled to the equitable remuneration is entitled to the right referred to in those paragraphs for that communication; and

(*b*)   any retransmission.

(1.2) *Right to remuneration – WPPT country* — If a sound recording has been published, the performer and maker are entitled, subject to subsections 20(1.2) and (2.1), to be paid equitable remuneration for its performance in public or its communication to the public by telecommunication, except for a communication in the circumstances referred to in paragraph 15(1.1)(*d*) or 18(1.1)(*a*) and any retransmission.

(2) *Royalties* — For the purpose of providing the remuneration mentioned in this

COPYRIGHT ACT

section, a person who performs a published sound recording in public or communicates it to the public by telecommunication is liable to pay royalties

(*a*)   in the case of a sound recording of a musical work, to the collective society authorized under Part VII.1 to collect them; or

(*b*)   in the case of a sound recording of a literary work or dramatic work, to either the maker of the sound recording or the performer.

(3) *Division of royalties* — The royalties, once paid pursuant to paragraph (2)(*a*) or (*b*), shall be divided so that

(*a*)   the performer or performers receive in aggregate fifty per cent; and

(*b*)   the maker or makers receive in aggregate fifty per cent.

[S.C. 1994, c. 47, s. 59; S.C. 1997, c. 24, s. 14; S.C. 2012, c. 20, s. 12(1), (3); S.C. 2018, c. 27, s. 281.]

19.1. Deemed publication – Canada — Despite subsection 2.2(1), a sound recording that has been made available to the public by telecommunication in a way that allows a member of the public to access it from a place and at a time individually chosen by that member of the public, or that has been communicated to the public by telecommunication in that way, is deemed to have been published for the purposes of subsection 19(1).

[S.C. 2012, c. 20, s. 13.]

19.2. Deemed publication – WPPT country — Despite subsection 2.2(1), a sound recording that has been made available to the public by telecommunication in a way that allows a member of the public to access it from a place and at a time individually chosen by that member of the public, or that has been communicated to the public by telecommunication in that way, is deemed to have been published for the purposes of subsection 19(1.2).

[S.C. 2012, c. 20, s. 14.]

20. Conditions – Canada — (1) The right to remuneration conferred by subsection 19(1) applies only if

(*a*)   the maker was, at the date of the first fixation, a Canadian citizen or permanent resident within the meaning of subsection 2(1) of the *Immigration and Refugee Protection Act** or, if a corporation, had its headquarters in Canada; or

(*b*)   all the fixations done for the sound recording occurred in Canada.

(1.1) *Conditions – Rome Convention country* — The right to remuneration conferred by subsection 19(1.1) applies only if

(*a*)   the maker was, at the date of the first fixation, a citizen or permanent resident of a Rome Convention country or, if a corporation, had its headquarters in a Rome Convention country; or

(b) all the fixations done for the sound recording occurred in a Rome Convention country.

(1.2) *Conditions – WPPT country* — The right to remuneration conferred by subsection 19(1.2) applies only if

(a) the maker was, at the date of the first fixation, a citizen or permanent resident of a WPPT country or, if a corporation, had its headquarters in a WPPT country; or

(b) all the fixations done for the sound recording occurred in a WPPT country. [S.C. 2012, c. 20, s. 15(2).]

(2) *Exception – Rome Convention country* —Despite subsection (1.1), if the Minister is of the opinion that a Rome Convention country does not grant a right to remuneration, similar in scope and duration to that provided by subsection 19(1.1), for the performance in public or the communication to the public of a sound recording whose maker, at the date of its first fixation, was a Canadian citizen or permanent resident within the meaning of subsection 2(1) of the *Immigration and Refugee Protection Act** or, if a corporation, had its headquarters in Canada, the Minister may, by a statement published in the *Canada Gazette*, limit the scope and duration of the protection for sound recordings whose first fixation is done by a maker who is a citizen or permanent resident of that country or, if a corporation, has its headquarters in that country.

(2.1) *Exception – WPPT country* — Despite subsection (1.2), if the Minister is of the opinion that a WPPT country does not grant a right to remuneration, similar in scope and duration to that provided by subsection 19(1.2), for the performance in public or the communication to the public of a sound recording whose maker, at the date of its first fixation, was a Canadian citizen or permanent resident within the meaning of subsection 2(1) of the *Immigration and Refugee Protection Act* or, if a corporation, had its headquarters in Canada, the Minister may, by a statement published in the *Canada Gazette*, limit the scope and duration of the protection for sound recordings whose first fixation is done by a maker who is a citizen or permanent resident of that country or, if a corporation, has its headquarters in that country.
[S.C. 2012, c. 20, s. 15(4).]

(3) [Repealed by S.C. 2020, c. 1, s. 28.]

(4) [Repealed by S.C. 2020, c. 1, s. 28.]
[S.C. 1994, c. 47, s. 59; S.C. 1997, c. 24, s. 14; S.C. 2001, c. 27, s. 238; S.C. 2012, c. 20, s. 15(1); S.C. 2020, c. 1, s. 28.]

Note: For countries which are subject to limited application of the right to remuneration, see Statement Limiting the Right to Equitable Remuneration of

Certain Rome Convention or WPPT Countries reproduced in this publication.

---

* *Immigration and Refugee Protection Act*, **S.C. 2001, c. 27**

permanent resident **means a person who has acquired permanent resident status and has not subsequently lost that status under section 46.**
[S.C. 2001, c. 27, s. 2(1).]

RIGHTS OF BROADCASTERS

21. Copyright in communication signals — (1) Subject to subsection (2), a broadcaster has a copyright in the communication signals that it broadcasts, consisting of the sole right to do the following in relation to the communication signal or any substantial part thereof:

(*a*)   to fix it,

(*b*)   to reproduce any fixation of it that was made without the broadcaster's consent,

(*c*)   to authorize another broadcaster to retransmit it to the public simultaneously with its broadcast, and

(*d*)   in the case of a television communication signal, to perform it in a place open to the public on payment of an entrance fee,

and to authorize any act described in paragraph (*a*), (*b*) or (*d*).

(2) *Conditions for copyright* — Subsection (1) applies only if the broadcaster

(*a*)   at the time of the broadcast, had its headquarters in Canada, in a country that is a WTO Member or in a Rome Convention country; and

(*b*)   broadcasts the communication signal from that country.

(3) *Exception* — Notwithstanding subsection (2), if the Minister is of the opinion that a Rome Convention country or a country that is a WTO Member does not grant the right mentioned in paragraph (1)(*d*), the Minister may, by a statement published in the *Canada Gazette*, declare that broadcasters that have their headquarters in that country are not entitled to that right.
[S.C. 1994, c. 47, s. 59; S.C. 1997, c. 24, s. 14.]

RECIPROCITY

22. Reciprocity — (1) If the Minister is of the opinion that a country other than a Rome Convention country or a WPPT country grants or has undertaken to grant

(*a*)   to performers and to makers of sound recordings, or

(*b*) to broadcasters

that are Canadian citizens or permanent residents of Canada within the meaning of subsection 2(1) of the *Immigration and Refugee Protection Act** or, if corporations, have their headquarters in Canada, as the case may be, whether by treaty, convention, agreement or law, benefits substantially equivalent to those conferred by this Part, the Minister may, by a statement published in the *Canada Gazette*,

(*c*) grant the benefits conferred by this Part

    (i) to performers and to makers of sound recordings, or

    (ii) to broadcasters

as the case may be, that are citizens, subjects or permanent residents of or, if corporations, have their headquarters in that country, and

(*d*) declare that that country shall, as regards those benefits, be treated as if it were a country to which this Part extends.

[S.C. 2012, c. 20, s. 16(1).]

(2) *Reciprocity* — If the Minister is of the opinion that a country other than a Rome Convention country or a WPPT country neither grants nor has undertaken to grant

(*a*) to performers, and to makers of sound recordings, or

(*b*) to broadcasters

that are Canadian citizens or permanent residents of Canada within the meaning of subsection 2(1) of the *Immigration and Refugee Protection Act** or, if corporations, have their headquarters in Canada, as the case may be, whether by treaty, convention, agreement or law, benefits substantially equivalent to those conferred by this Part, the Minister may, by a statement published in the *Canada Gazette*,

(*c*) grant the benefits conferred by this Part to performers, makers of sound recordings or broadcasters that are citizens, subjects or permanent residents of or, if corporations, have their headquarters in that country, as the case may be, to the extent that that country grants that those benefits to performers, makers of sound recordings or broadcasters that are Canadian citizens or permanent residents within the meaning of subsection 2(1) of the *Immigration and Refugee Protection Act** or, if corporations, have their headquarters in Canada, and

(*d*) declare that that country shall, as regards those benefits, be treated as if it were a country to which this Part extends.

[S.C. 2012, c. 20, s. 16(2).]

(3) *Application of Act* — Any provision of this Act that the Minister specifies in a statement referred to in subsection (1) or (2)

(*a*)   applies in respect of performers, makers of sound recordings or broadcasters covered by that statement, as if they were citizens of or, if corporations, had their headquarters in Canada; and

(*b*)   applies in respect of a country covered by that statement, as if that country were Canada.

(4) *Application of Act* — Subject to any exceptions that the Minister may specify in a statement referred to in subsection (1) or (2), the other provisions of this Act also apply in the way described in subsection (3).
[S.C. 1994, c. 47, s. 59; S.C. 1997, c. 24, s. 14; S.C. 2001, c. 27, s. 239.]

---

* *Immigration and Refugee Protection Act*, S.C. 2001, c. 27

permanent resident means a person who has acquired permanent resident status and has not subsequently lost that status under section 46.
[S.C. 2001, c. 27, s. 2(1).]

TERM OF RIGHTS

23. Term of copyright – performer's performance — (1) Subject to this Act, copyright in a performer's performance subsists until the end of 50 years after the end of the calendar year in which the performance occurs. However,

(*a*)   if the performance is fixed in a sound recording before the copyright expires, the copyright continues until the end of 70 years after the end of the calendar year in which the first fixation of the performance in a sound recording occurs; and

(*b*)   if a sound recording in which the performance is fixed is published before the copyright expires, the copyright continues until the earlier of the end of 75 years after the end of the calendar year in which the first such publication occurs and the end of 100 years after the end of the calendar year in which the first fixation of the performance in a sound recording occurs.

(1.1) *Term of copyright – sound recording* — Subject to this Act, copyright in a sound recording subsists until the end of 70 years after the end of the calendar year in which the first fixation of the sound recording occurs. However, if the sound recording is published before the copyright expires, the copyright continues until the earlier of the end of 75 years after the end of the calendar year in which the first publication of the sound recording occurs and the end of 100 years after the end of the calendar year in which that first fixation occurs.

(1.2) *Term of copyright – communication signal* — Subject to this Act, copyright in a communication signal subsists until the end of 50 years after the end of the calendar year in which the communication signal is broadcast.

(2) *Term of right to remuneration* — The rights to remuneration conferred on performers and makers by section 19 have the same terms, respectively, as those provided by subsections (1) and (1.1).

(3) *Application of subsections (1) to (2)*— Subsections (1) to (2) apply whether the fixation, performance or broadcast occurred before or after the coming into force of this section.

(4) *Berne Convention countries, Rome Convention countries, WTO Members* — Where the performer's performance, sound recording or communication signal meets the requirements set out in section 15, 18 or 21, as the case may be, a country that becomes a Berne Convention country, a Rome Convention country or a WTO Member after the date of the fixation, performance or broadcast is, as of becoming a Berne Convention country, Rome Convention country or WTO Member, as the case may be, deemed to have been such at the date of the fixation, performance or broadcast.

(5) *Where term of protection expired* — Subsection (4) does not confer any protection in Canada where the term of protection in the country referred to in that subsection had expired before that country became a Berne Convention country, Rome Convention country or WTO Member, as the case may be.
[S.C. 1994, c. 47, s. 59; S.C. 1997, c. 24, s. 14; S.C. 2012, c. 20, s. 17; S.C. 2015, c. 36, s. 81; S.C. 2020, c. 1, s. 29.]

Note: S.C. 2015, c. 36, s. 82, effective June 23, 2015 (R.A.), contained the following provision:

82. *No revival of copyright* — Paragraph 23(1)(b) and subsection 23(1.1) of the *Copyright Act*, as enacted by section 81, do not have the effect of reviving the copyright, or a right to remuneration, in a sound recording or performer's performance fixed in a sound recording in which the copyright or the right to remuneration had expired on the coming into force of those provisions.

OWNERSHIP OF COPYRIGHT

24. Ownership of copyright — The first owner of the copyright

  (*a*)   in a performer's performance, is the performer;

  (*b*)   in a sound recording, is the maker; or

  (*c*)   in a communication signal, is the broadcaster that broadcasts it.
[S.C. 1994, c. 47, s. 59; S.C. 1997, c. 24, s. 14.]

25. Assignment of rights — Subsections 13(4) to (7) apply, with such modifications as the circumstances require, in respect of the rights conferred by this Part on performers, makers of sound recordings and broadcasters.
[S.C. 1994, c. 47, s. 59; S.C. 1997, c. 24, s. 14.]

PERFORMERS' RIGHTS — WTO COUNTRIES

26. Performer's performance in WTO country — (1) Where a performer's performance takes place on or after January 1, 1996 in a country that is a WTO Member, the performer has, as of the date of the performer's performance, a copyright in the performer's performance, consisting of the sole right to do the following in relation to the performer's performance or any substantial part thereof:

   (*a*) if it is not fixed, to communicate it to the public by telecommunication and to fix it in a sound recording, and

   (*b*) if it has been fixed in a sound recording without the performer's authorization, to reproduce the fixation or any substantial part thereof,

and to authorize any such acts.

(2) *Where country joins WTO after Jan. 1, 1996* — Where a performer's performance takes place on or after January 1, 1996 in a country that becomes a WTO Member after the date of the performer's performance, the performer has the copyright described in subsection (1) as of the date the country becomes a WTO Member.

(3) *Performer's performances before Jan. 1, 1996* — Where a performer's performance takes place before January 1, 1996 in a country that is a WTO Member, the performer has, as of January 1, 1996, the sole right to do and to authorize the act described in paragraph (1)(*b*).

(4) *Where country joins WTO after Jan. 1, 1996* — Where a performer's performance takes place before January 1, 1996 in a country that becomes a WTO Member on or after January 1, 1996, the performer has the right described in subsection (3) as of the date the country becomes a WTO Member.

(5) *Term of performer's rights* — The rights conferred by this section subsist for the remainder of the calendar year in which the performer's performance takes place and a period of fifty years following the end of that calendar year.

(6) *Assignment of rights* — Subsections 13(4) to (7) apply, with such modifications as the circumstances require, in respect of a performer's rights conferred by this section.

(7) *Limitation* — Notwithstanding an assignment of a performer's right conferred by this section, the performer, as well as the assignee, may

   (*a*) prevent the reproduction of

      (i) any fixation of the performer's performance, or

      (ii) any substantial part of such a fixation,

   where the fixation was made without the performer's consent or the assignee's consent; and

(b) prevent the importation of any fixation of the performer's performance, or any reproduction of such a fixation, that the importer knows or ought to have known was made without the performer's consent or the assignee's consent.

[S.C. 1994, c. 47, s. 59; S.C. 1997, c. 24, s. 14.]

PART III
INFRINGEMENT OF COPYRIGHT AND MORAL RIGHTS AND EXCEPTIONS TO INFRINGEMENT

[S.C. 1997, c. 24, s. 15.]

INFRINGEMENT OF COPYRIGHT

GENERAL

27. Infringement generally — (1) It is an infringement of copyright for any person to do, without the consent of the owner of the copyright, anything that by this Act only the owner of the copyright has the right to do.

(2) *Secondary infringement* — It is an infringement of copyright for any person to

(a)   sell or rent out,

(b)   distribute to such an extent as to affect prejudicially the owner of the copyright,

(c)   by way of trade distribute, expose or offer for sale or rental, or exhibit in public,

(d)   possess for the purpose of doing anything referred to in paragraphs (a) to (c), or

(e)   import into Canada for the purpose of doing anything referred to in paragraphs (a) to (c),

a copy of a work, sound recording or fixation of a performer's performance or of a communication signal that the person knows or should have known infringes copyright or would infringe copyright if it had been made in Canada by the person who made it.

(2.1) *Clarification* — For greater certainty, a copy made outside Canada does not infringe copyright under subsection (2) if, had it been made in Canada, it would have been made under a limitation or exception under this Act.

(2.11) *Secondary infringement – exportation* — It is an infringement of copyright for any person, for the purpose of doing anything referred to in paragraphs (2)(a) to (c), to export or attempt to export a copy—of a work, sound recording or fixation of a performer's performance or of a communication signal—that the person knows or should have known was made without the consent of the owner of the copyright in the country where the copy was made.

[S.C. 2014, c. 32, s. 3.]

(2.12) *Exception* — Subsection (2.11) does not apply with respect to a copy that was made under a limitation or exception under this Act or, if it was made outside Canada, that would have been made under such a limitation or exception had it been made in Canada.

[S.C. 2014, c. 32, s. 3.]

(2.2) *Secondary infringement related to lesson* — It is an infringement of copyright for any person to do any of the following acts with respect to anything that the person knows or should have known is a lesson, as defined in subsection 30.01(1), or a fixation of one:

(*a*)   to sell it or to rent it out;

(*b*)   to distribute it to an extent that the owner of the copyright in the work or other subject-matter that is included in the lesson is prejudicially affected;

(*c*)   by way of trade, to distribute it, expose or offer it for sale or rental or exhibit it in public;

(*d*)   to possess it for the purpose of doing anything referred to in any of paragraphs (*a*) to (*c*);

(*e*)   to communicate it by telecommunication to any person other than a person referred to in paragraph 30.01(3)(*a*); or

(*f*)   to circumvent or contravene any measure taken in conformity with paragraph 30.01(6)(*b*), (*c*) or (*d*).

(2.3) *Infringement – provision of services* — It is an infringement of copyright for a person, by means of the Internet or another digital network, to provide a service primarily for the purpose of enabling acts of copyright infringement if an actual infringement of copyright occurs by means of the Internet or another digital network as a result of the use of that service.

(2.4) *Factors* — In determining whether a person has infringed copyright under subsection (2.3), the court may consider

(*a*)   whether the person expressly or implicitly marketed or promoted the service as one that could be used to enable acts of copyright infringement;

(*b*)   whether the person had knowledge that the service was used to enable a significant number of acts of copyright infringement;

(*c*)   whether the service has significant uses other than to enable acts of copyright infringement;

(*d*)   the person's ability, as part of providing the service, to limit acts of copyright infringement, and any action taken by the person to do so;

(*e*) any benefits the person received as a result of enabling the acts of copyright infringement; and

(*f*) the economic viability of the provision of the service if it were not used to enable acts of copyright infringement.

(3) *Knowledge of importer* — In determining whether there is an infringement under subsection (2) in the case of an activity referred to in any of paragraphs (2)(*a*) to (*d*) in relation to a copy that was imported in the circumstances referred to in paragraph (2)(*e*), it is irrelevant whether the importer knew or should have known that the importation of the copy infringed copyright.

(4) *Plates* — It is an infringement of copyright for any person to make or possess a plate that has been specifically designed or adapted for the purpose of making infringing copies of a work or other subject-matter.

(5) *Public performance for profit* — It is an infringement of copyright for any person, for profit, to permit a theatre or other place of entertainment to be used for the performance in public of a work or other subject-matter without the consent of the owner of the copyright unless that person was not aware, and had no reasonable ground for suspecting, that the performance would be an infringement of copyright.

(6) [Repealed by S.C. 1997, c. 24, s. 15.]

[R.S.C. 1985, c. 1 (3rd Supp.), s. 13; R.S.C. 1985, c. 10 (4th Supp.), s. 5; S.C. 1993, c. 44, s. 64; S.C. 1997, c. 24, s. 15; S.C. 2012, c. 20, s. 18.]

PARALLEL IMPORTATION OF BOOKS

27.1. Importation of books — (1) Subject to any regulations made under subsection (6), it is an infringement of copyright in a book for any person to import the book where

(*a*) copies of the book were made with the consent of the owner of the copyright in the book in the country where the copies were made, but were imported without the consent of the owner of the copyright in the book in Canada; and

(*b*) the person knows or should have known that the book would infringe copyright if it was made in Canada by the importer.

(2) *Secondary infringement* — Subject to any regulations made under subsection (6), where the circumstances described in paragraph (1)(*a*) exist, it is an infringement of copyright in an imported book for any person who knew or should have known that the book would infringe copyright if it was made in Canada by the importer to

(*a*) sell or rent out the book;

(*b*) by way of trade, distribute, expose or offer for sale or rental, or exhibit in public, the book; or

(c)   possess the book for the purpose of any of the activities referred to in paragraph (a) or (b).

(3) *Limitation* — Subsections (1) and (2) only apply where there is an exclusive distributor of the book and the acts described in those subsections take place in the part of Canada or in respect of the particular sector of the market for which the person is the exclusive distributor.

(4) *Exclusive distributor* — An exclusive distributor is deemed, for the purposes of entitlement to any of the remedies under Part IV in relation to an infringement under this section, to derive an interest in the copyright in question by licence.

(5) *Notice* — No exclusive distributor, copyright owner or exclusive licensee is entitled to a remedy under Part IV in relation to an infringement under this section unless, before the infringement occurred, notice has been given within the prescribed time and in the prescribed manner to the person referred to in subsection (1) or (2), as the case may be, that there is an exclusive distributor of the book.

(6) *Regulations*— The Governor in Council may, by regulation, establish terms and conditions for the importation of certain categories of books, including remaindered books, books intended solely for re-export and books imported by special order
[S.C. 1997, c. 24, ss. 15 and 62(1).]

Note: See also Transitional Provisions of S.C. 1997, c. 24.

28. [Repealed by S.C. 1997, c. 24, s. 15.]

28.01. [Renumbered as section 31 by S.C. 1997, c. 24, s. 16 and repositioned accordingly.]

28.02. [Repealed by S.C. 1997, c. 24, s. 17.]

28.03. [Repealed by S.C. 1997, c. 24, s. 17.]

Note: Heading preceding ss. 28.02 and 28.03 also repealed by S.C. 1997, c. 24, s. 17.

MORAL RIGHTS INFRINGEMENT

28.1. Infringement generally — Any act or omission that is contrary to any of the moral rights of the author of a work or of the performer of a performer's performance is, in the absence of the author's or performer's consent, an infringement of those rights.
[S.C. 2012, c. 20, s. 19.]

28.2. Nature of right of integrity — (1) The author's or performer's right to the integrity of a work or performer's performance is infringed only if the work or the performance is, to the prejudice of its author's or performer's honour or reputation,

(a)   distorted, mutilated or otherwise modified; or

89

(*b*) used in association with a product, service, cause or institution.

(2) *Where prejudice deemed* — In the case of a painting, sculpture or engraving, the prejudice referred to in subsection (1) shall be deemed to have occurred as a result of any distortion, mutilation or other modification of the work.

(3) *When work not distorted, etc.*— For the purposes of this section,

(*a*) a change in the location of a work, the physical means by which a work is exposed or the physical structure containing a work, or

(*b*) steps taken in good faith to restore or preserve the work

shall not, by that act alone, constitute a distortion, mutilation or other modification of the work.

[R.S.C. 1985, c. 10 (4th Supp.), s. 6; S.C. 2012, c. 20, s. 20.]

EXCEPTIONS
[S.C. 1997, c. 24, s. 18(1).]

FAIR DEALING

29. Research, private study, etc. — Fair dealing for the purpose of research, private study, education, parody or satire does not infringe copyright.
[S.C. 2012, c. 20, s. 21.]

29.1. Criticism or review — Fair dealing for the purpose of criticism or review does not infringe copyright if the following are mentioned:

(*a*) the source; and

(*b*) if given in the source, the name of the

    (i) author, in the case of a work,

    (ii) performer, in the case of a performer's performance,

    (iii) maker, in the case of a sound recording, or

    (iv) broadcaster, in the case of a communication signal.

[S.C. 1997, c. 24, s. 18(1).]

29.2. News reporting — Fair dealing for the purpose of news reporting does not infringe copyright if the following are mentioned:

(*a*) the source; and

(*b*) if given in the source, the name of the

    (i) author, in the case of a work,

    (ii) performer, in the case of a performer's performance,

    (iii) maker, in the case of a sound recording, or

(iv) broadcaster, in the case of a communication signal.
[S.C. 1997, c. 24, s. 18(1).]

NON-COMMERCIAL USER-GENERATED CONTENT

29.21. Non-commercial user-generated content — (1) It is not an infringement of copyright for an individual to use an existing work or other subject-matter or copy of one, which has been published or otherwise made available to the public, in the creation of a new work or other subject-matter in which copyright subsists and for the individual — or, with the individual's authorization, a member of their household — to use the new work or other subject-matter or to authorize an intermediary to disseminate it, if

(*a*) the use of, or the authorization to disseminate, the new work or other subject-matter is done solely for non-commercial purposes;

(*b*) the source — and, if given in the source, the name of the author, performer, maker or broadcaster — of the existing work or other subject-matter or copy of it are mentioned, if it is reasonable in the circumstances to do so;

(*c*) the individual had reasonable grounds to believe that the existing work or other subject-matter or copy of it, as the case may be, was not infringing copyright; and

(*d*) the use of, or the authorization to disseminate, the new work or other subject-matter does not have a substantial adverse effect, financial or otherwise, on the exploitation or potential exploitation of the existing work or other subject-matter — or copy of it — or on an existing or potential market for it, including that the new work or other subject-matter is not a substitute for the existing one.

(2) *Definitions* — The following definitions apply in subsection (1).

intermediary means a person or entity who regularly provides space or means for works or other subject-matter to be enjoyed by the public.

use means to do anything that by this Act the owner of the copyright has the sole right to do, other than the right to authorize anything.
[S.C. 2012, c. 20, s. 22.]

REPRODUCTION FOR PRIVATE PURPOSES

29.22. Reproduction for private purposes — (1) It is not an infringement of copyright for an individual to reproduce a work or other subject-matter or any substantial part of a work or other subject-matter if

(*a*) the copy of the work or other subject-matter from which the reproduction is made is not an infringing copy;

(*b*) the individual legally obtained the copy of the work or other subject-matter from which the reproduction is made, other than by borrowing it or renting it, and owns or is authorized to use the medium or device on which it is reproduced;

(c) the individual, in order to make the reproduction, did not circumvent, as defined in section 41, a technological protection measure, as defined in that section, or cause one to be circumvented;

(d) the individual does not give the reproduction away; and

(e) the reproduction is used only for the individual's private purposes.

(2) *Meaning of **medium or device*** — For the purposes of paragraph (1)(*b*), a ***medium or device*** includes digital memory in which a work or subject-matter may be stored for the purpose of allowing the telecommunication of the work or other subject-matter through the Internet or other digital network.

(3) *Limitation – audio recording medium* — In the case of a work or other subject-matter that is a musical work embodied in a sound recording, a performer's performance of a musical work embodied in a sound recording or a sound recording in which a musical work or a performer's performance of a musical work is embodied, subsection (1) does not apply if the reproduction is made onto an audio recording medium as defined in section 79.

(4) *Limitation – destruction of reproductions*— Subsection (1) does not apply if the individual gives away, rents or sells the copy of the work or other subject-matter from which the reproduction is made without first destroying all reproductions of that copy that the individual has made under that subsection.
[S.C. 2012, c. 20, s. 22.]

Fixing Signals and Recording Programs for Later Listening or Viewing

29.23. Reproduction for later listening or viewing — (1) It is not an infringement of copyright for an individual to fix a communication signal, to reproduce a work or sound recording that is being broadcast or to fix or reproduce a performer's performance that is being broadcast, in order to record a program for the purpose of listening to or viewing it later, if

(a) the individual receives the program legally;

(b) the individual, in order to record the program, did not circumvent, as defined in section 41, a technological protection measure, as defined in that section, or cause one to be circumvented;

(c) the individual makes no more than one recording of the program;

(d) the individual keeps the recording no longer than is reasonably necessary in order to listen to or view the program at a more convenient time;

(e)   the individual does not give the recording away; and

(f)   the recording is used only for the individual's private purposes.

(2) *Limitation* — Subsection (1) does not apply if the individual receives the work, performer's performance or sound recording under an on-demand service.

(3) *Definitions* — The following definitions apply in this section.

broadcast means any transmission of a work or other subject-matter by telecommunication for reception by the public, but does not include a transmission that is made solely for performance in public.

on-demand service means a service that allows a person to receive works, performer's performances and sound recordings at times of their choosing.

[S.C. 2012, c. 20, s. 22.]

BACKUP COPIES

29.24. Backup copies — (1) It is not an infringement of copyright in a work or other subject-matter for a person who owns — or has a licence to use — a copy of the work or subject-matter (in this section referred to as the "source copy") to reproduce the source copy if

(a)   the person does so solely for backup purposes in case the source copy is lost, damaged or otherwise rendered unusable;

(b)   the source copy is not an infringing copy;

(c)   the person, in order to make the reproduction, did not circumvent, as defined in section 41, a technological protection measure, as defined in that section, or cause one to be circumvented; and

(d)   the person does not give any of the reproductions away.

(2) *Backup copy becomes source copy* — If the source copy is lost, damaged or otherwise rendered unusable, one of the reproductions made under subsection (1) becomes the source copy.

(3) *Destruction* — The person shall immediately destroy all reproductions made under subsection (1) after the person ceases to own, or to have a licence to use, the source copy.

[S.C. 2012, c. 20, s. 22.]

ACTS UNDERTAKEN WITHOUT MOTIVE OF GAIN

29.3. Motive of gain — (1) No action referred to in section 29.4, 29.5, 30.2 or 30.21 may be carried out with motive of gain.

(2) *Cost recovery* — An educational institution, library, archive or museum, or person acting under its authority does not have a motive of gain where it or the person acting under its authority, does anything referred to in section 29.4, 29.5,

30.2 or 30.21 and recovers no more than the costs, including overhead costs, associated with doing that act.

[S.C. 1997, c. 24, s. 18(1).]

EDUCATIONAL INSTITUTIONS

29.4. Reproduction for instruction — (1) It is not an infringement of copyright for an educational institution or a person acting under its authority for the purposes of education or training on its premises to reproduce a work, or do any other necessary act, in order to display it.

(2) *Reproduction for examinations, etc.* — It is not an infringement of copyright for an educational institution or a person acting under its authority to

(*a*) reproduce, translate or perform in public on the premises of the educational institution, or

(*b*) communicate by telecommunication to the public situated on the premises of the educational institution

a work or other subject-matter as required for a test or examination.

(3) *If work commercially available* — Except in the case of manual reproduction, the exemption from copyright infringement provided by subsections (1) and (2) does not apply if the work or other subject-matter is commercially available, within the meaning of paragraph (a) of the definition *commercially available* in section 2, in a medium that is appropriate for the purposes referred to in those subsections.

[S.C. 2012, c. 20, s. 23.]

29.5. Performances — It is not an infringement of copyright for an educational institution or a person acting under its authority to do the following acts if they are done on the premises of an educational institution for educational or training purposes and not for profit, before an audience consisting primarily of students of the educational institution, instructors acting under the authority of the educational institution or any person who is directly responsible for setting a curriculum for the educational institution:

(*a*) the live performance in public, primarily by students of the educational institution, of a work;

(*b*) the performance in public of a sound recording, or of a work or performer's performance that is embodied in a sound recording, as long as the sound recording is not an infringing copy or the person responsible for the performance has no reasonable grounds to believe that it is an infringing copy;

(*c*) the performance in public of a work or other subject-matter at the time of its communication to the public by telecommunication; and

(*d*) the performance in public of a cinematographic work, as long as the work is not an infringing copy or the person responsible for the performance has no reasonable grounds to believe that it is an infringing copy.

[S.C. 1997, c. 24, s. 18(1); S.C. 2012, c. 20, s. 24.]

29.6. News and commentary — (1) It is not an infringement of copyright for an educational institution or a person acting under its authority to

(a) make, at the time of its communication to the public by telecommunication, a single copy of a news program or a news commentary program, excluding documentaries, for the purposes of performing the copy for the students of the educational institution for educational or training purposes; and

(b) perform the copy in public before an audience consisting primarily of students of the educational institution on its premises for educational or training purposes.

(2) [Repealed by S.C. 2012, c. 20, s. 25(3).]

[S.C. 2012, c. 20, s. 25.]

29.7. Reproduction of broadcast — (1) Subject to subsection (2) and section 29.9, it is not an infringement of copyright for an educational institution or a person acting under its authority to

(a) make a single copy of a work or other subject-matter at the time that it is communicated to the public by telecommunication; and

(b) keep the copy for up to thirty days to decide whether to perform the copy for educational or training purposes.

(2) *Royalties for reproduction* — An educational institution that has not destroyed the copy by the expiration of the thirty days infringes copyright in the work or other subject-matter unless it pays any royalties, and complies with any terms and conditions, fixed under this Act for the making of the copy.

(3) *Royalties for performance* — It is not an infringement of copyright for the educational institution or a person acting under its authority to perform the copy in public for educational or training purposes on the premises of the educational institution before an audience consisting primarily of students of the educational institution if the educational institution pays the royalties and complies with any terms and conditions fixed under this Act for the performance in public.

[S.C. 1997, c. 24, s. 18(1).]

29.8. Unlawful reception — The exceptions to infringement of copyright provided for under sections 29.5 to 29.7 do not apply where the communication to the public by telecommunication was received by unlawful means.

[S.C. 1997, c. 24, s. 18(1).]

29.9. Records and marking — (1) Where an educational institution or person acting under its authority (*a*)   [Repealed by S.C. 2012, c. 20, s. 26.]

(*b*)   makes a copy of a work or other subject-matter communicated to the public by telecommunication and performs it pursuant to section 29.7,

the educational institution shall keep a record of the information prescribed by regulation in relation to the making of the copy, the destruction of it or any performance in public of it for which royalties are payable under this Act and shall, in addition, mark the copy in the manner prescribed by regulation.

(2) *Regulations* — The Board may, with the approval of the Governor in Council, make regulations

(*a*)   prescribing the information in relation to the making, destruction, performance and marking of copies that must be kept under subsection (1),

(*b*)   prescribing the manner and form in which records referred to in that subsection must be kept and copies destroyed or marked, and

(*c*)   respecting the sending of information to collective societies that carry on the business of collecting royalties referred to in subsection 29.7(2) or (3).

[S.C. 1997, c. 24, s. 18(1); S.C. 2012, c. 20, s. 26; S.C. 2018, c. 27, s. 282.]

30. Literary collections — The publication in a collection, mainly composed of non-copyright matter, intended for the use of educational institutions, and so described in the title and in any advertisements issued by the publisher, of short passages from published literary works in which copyright subsists and not themselves published for the use of educational institutions, does not infringe copyright in those published literary works if

(*a*)   not more than two passages from works by the same author are published by the same publisher within five years;

(*b*)   the source from which the passages are taken is acknowledged; and

(*c*)   the name of the author, if given in the source, is mentioned.

[S.C. 1997, c. 24, s. 18(1).]

Note: S.C. 1997, c. 24, s. 18(2) provides that section 30 of the Act, as enacted by section 18(1) of S.C. 1997, c. 24, does not apply in respect of collections referred to in section 30 that are published before the coming into force of section 30 (Sept. 1/97). Such collections continue to be governed by paragraph 27(2)(*d*) of the Act as it read before the coming into force of section 15 of S.C. 1997, c. 24 (Sept. 1/97).

30.01. Meaning of *lesson* — (1) For the purposes of this section, *lesson* means a lesson, test or examination, or part of one, in which, or during the course of which, an act is done in respect of a work or other subject-matter by an educational institution or a person acting under its authority that would otherwise be an infringement of copyright but is permitted under a limitation or exception under this Act.

(2) *Application* — This section does not apply so as to permit any act referred to in paragraph (3)(*a*), (*b*) or (*c*) with respect to a work or other subject-matter whose use in the lesson constitutes an infringement of copyright or for whose use in the lesson the consent of the copyright owner is required.

(3) *Communication by telecommunication* — Subject to subsection (6), it is not an infringement of copyright for an educational institution or a person acting under its authority

(*a*) to communicate a lesson to the public by telecommunication for educational or training purposes, if that public consists only of students who are enrolled in a course of which the lesson forms a part or of other persons acting under the authority of the educational institution;

(*b*) to make a fixation of the lesson for the purpose of the act referred to in paragraph (*a*); or

(*c*) to do any other act that is necessary for the purpose of the acts referred to in paragraphs (*a*) and (*b*).

(4) *Participation by telecommunication* — A student who is enrolled in a course of which the lesson forms a part is deemed to be a person on the premises of the educational institution when the student participates in or receives the lesson by means of communication by telecommunication under paragraph (3)(*a*).

(5) *Reproducing lessons* — It is not an infringement of copyright for a student who has received a lesson by means of communication by telecommunication under paragraph (3)(*a*) to reproduce the lesson in order to be able to listen to or view it at a more convenient time. However, the student shall destroy the reproduction within 30 days after the day on which the students who are enrolled in the course to which the lesson relates have received their final course evaluations.

(6) *Conditions* — The educational institution and any person acting under its authority, except a student, shall

(*a*) destroy any fixation of the lesson within 30 days after the day on which the students who are enrolled in the course to which the lesson relates have received their final course evaluations;

(*b*) take measures that can reasonably be expected to limit the communication by telecommunication of the lesson to the persons referred to in paragraph (3)(*a*);

(*c*) take, in relation to the communication by telecommunication of the lesson in digital form, measures that can reasonably be expected to prevent the students from fixing, reproducing or communicating the lesson other than as they may do under this section; and

(*d*) take, in relation to a communication by telecommunication in digital form, any measure prescribed by regulation.

[S.C. 2012, c. 20, s. 27.]

30.02. Exception – digital reproduction of works — (1) Subject to subsections (3) to (5), it is not an infringement of copyright for an educational institution that has a reprographic reproduction licence under which the institution is authorized to make reprographic reproductions of works in a collective society's repertoire for an educational or training purpose

(*a*)   to make a digital reproduction – of the same general nature and extent as the reprographic reproduction authorized under the licence – of a paper form of any of those works;

(*b*)   to communicate the digital reproduction by telecommunication for an educational or training purpose to persons acting under the authority of the institution; or

(*c*)   to do any other act that is necessary for the purpose of the acts referred to in paragraphs (*a*) and (*b*).

(2) *Exception* — Subject to subsections (3) to (5), it is not an infringement of copyright for a person acting under the authority of the educational institution to whom the work has been communicated under paragraph (1)(*b*) to print one copy of the work.

(3) *Conditions* — An educational institution that makes a digital reproduction of a work under paragraph (1)(*a*) shall

(*a*)   pay to the collective society, with respect to all the persons to whom the digital reproduction is communicated by the institution under paragraph (1)(*b*), the royalties that would be payable if one reprographic reproduction were distributed by the institution to each of those persons, and comply with the licence terms and conditions applicable to a reprographic reproduction to the extent that they are reasonably applicable to a digital reproduction;

(*b*)   take measures to prevent the digital reproduction from being communicated by telecommunication to any persons who are not acting under the authority of the institution;

(*c*)   take measures to prevent a person to whom the work has been communicated under paragraph (1)(*b*) from printing more than one copy, and to prevent any other reproduction or communication of the digital reproduction; and

(*d*)   take any measure prescribed by regulation.

(4) *Restriction* — An educational institution may not make a digital reproduction of a work under paragraph (1)(*a*) if

(*a*)   the institution has entered into a digital reproduction agreement respecting the work with a collective society under which the institution may make a digital reproduction of the work, may communicate the digital reproduction by telecommunication to persons acting under the authority of the institution and may permit those persons to print at least one copy of the work;

(*b*) there is a tariff approved under section 70 that is applicable to the digital reproduction of the work, to the communication of the digital reproduction by telecommunication to persons acting under the authority of the institution and to the printing by those persons of at least one copy of the work; or

(*c*) the institution has been informed by the collective society that is authorized to enter into reprographic agreements with respect to the work that the owner of the copyright in the work has informed it, under subsection (5), that the owner refuses to authorize the collective society to enter into a digital reproduction agreement with respect to the work.

(5) *Restriction* — If the owner of the copyright in a work informs the collective society that is authorized to enter into reprographic agreements with respect to the work that the owner refuses to authorize it to enter into digital reproduction agreements with respect to the work, the collective society shall inform the educational institutions with which it has entered into reprographic reproduction agreements with respect to the work that they are not permitted to make digital reproductions under subsection (1).

(6) *Deeming provision* — The owner of the copyright in a work who, in respect of the work, has authorized a collective society to enter into a reprographic reproduction agreement with an educational institution is deemed to have authorized the society to enter into a digital reproduction agreement with the institution – subject to the same restrictions as a reprographic reproduction agreement – unless the owner has refused to give this authorization under subsection (5) or has authorized another collective society to enter into a digital reproduction agreement with respect to the work.

(7) *Maximum amount that may be recovered* — In proceedings against an educational institution for making a digital reproduction of a paper form of a work, or for communicating such a reproduction by telecommunication for an educational or training purpose to persons acting under the authority of the institution, the owner of the copyright in the work may not recover an amount more than

(*a*) in the case where there is a digital reproduction licence that meets the conditions described in paragraph (4)(*a*) in respect of the work – or, if none exists in respect of the work, in respect of a work of the same category – the amount of royalties that would be payable under that licence in respect of those acts or, if there is more than one applicable licence, the greatest amount of royalties payable under any of those licences; and

(*b*) in the case where there is no licence described in paragraph (*a*) but there is a reprographic reproduction licence in respect of the work – or, if none exists in respect of the work, in respect of a work of the same category – the amount of royalties that would be payable under that licence in respect of those acts or, if there is more than one applicable licence, the greatest amount of royalties payable under any of those licences.

(8) *No damages* — The owner of the copyright in a work may not recover any damages against a person acting under the authority of the educational institution who, in respect of a digital reproduction of the work that is communicated to the person by telecommunication, prints one copy of the work if, at the time of the printing, it was reasonable for the person to believe that the communication was made in accordance with paragraph (1)(*b*).
[S.C. 2012, c. 20, s. 27; S.C. 2018, c. 27, s. 283.]

30.03. Royalties – digital reproduction agreement — (1) If an educational institution has paid royalties to a collective society for the digital reproduction of a work under paragraph 30.02(3)(*a*) and afterwards the institution enters into a digital reproduction agreement described in paragraph 30.02(4)(*a*) with any collective society,

(*a*) in the case where the institution would — under that digital reproduction agreement — pay a greater amount of royalties for the digital reproduction of that work than what was payable under paragraph 30.02(3)(*a*), the institution shall pay to the collective society to which it paid royalties under that paragraph the difference between

(i) the amount of royalties that the institution would have had to pay for the digital reproduction of that work if the agreement had been entered into on the day on which the institution first made a digital reproduction under paragraph 30.02(1)(*a*), and

(ii) the amount of royalties that the institution paid to the society under paragraph 30.02(3)(*a*) for the digital reproduction of that work from the day on which that paragraph comes into force until the day on which they enter into the digital reproduction agreement; and

(*b*) in the case where the institution would — under that digital reproduction agreement — pay a lesser amount of royalties for the digital reproduction of that work than what was payable under paragraph 30.02(3)(*a*), the collective society to which the institution paid royalties under that paragraph shall pay to the institution the difference between

(i) the amount of royalties that the institution paid to the society under paragraph 30.02(3)(*a*) for the digital reproduction of that work from the day on which that paragraph comes into force until the day on which they enter into the digital reproduction agreement, and

(ii) the amount of royalties that the institution would have had to pay for the digital reproduction of that work if the agreement had been entered into on the day on which the institution first made a digital reproduction under paragraph 30.02(1)(*a*).

(2) *Royalties tariff* — If an educational institution has paid royalties to a collective society for the digital reproduction of a work under paragraph 30.02(3)(*a*) and afterwards a tariff applies to the digital reproduction of that work under paragraph 30.02(4)(*b*),

(*a*)   in the case where the institution would — under the tariff — pay a greater amount of royalties for the digital reproduction of that work than what was payable under paragraph 30.02(3)(*a*), the institution shall pay to the collective society to which it paid royalties under that paragraph the difference between

    (i)   the amount of royalties that the institution would have had to pay for the digital reproduction of that work if the tariff had been approved on the day on which the institution first made a digital reproduction under paragraph 30.02(1)(*a*), and

    (ii)   the amount of royalties that the institution paid to the society under paragraph 30.02(3)(*a*) for the digital reproduction of that work from the day on which that paragraph comes into force until the day on which the tariff is approved; and

(*b*)   in the case where the institution would — under the tariff — pay a lesser amount of royalties for the digital reproduction of that work than what was payable under paragraph 30.02(3)(*a*), the collective society to which the institution paid royalties under that paragraph shall pay to the institution the difference between

    (i)   the amount of royalties that the institution paid to the society under paragraph 30.02(3)(*a*) for the digital reproduction of that work from the day on which that paragraph comes into force until the day on which the tariff is approved, and

    (ii)   the amount of royalties that the institution would have had to pay for the digital reproduction of that work if the tariff had been approved on the day on which the institution first made a digital reproduction under paragraph 30.02(1)(*a*).

[S.C. 2012, c. 20, s. 27; S.C. 2018, c. 27, s. 284(E).]

30.04. Work available through Internet — (1) Subject to subsections (2) to (5), it is not an infringement of copyright for an educational institution, or a person acting under the authority of one, to do any of the following acts for educational or training purposes in respect of a work or other subject-matter that is available through the Internet:

(*a*) reproduce it;

(*b*) communicate it to the public by telecommunication, if that public primarily consists of students of the educational institution or other persons acting under its authority;

(*c*) perform it in public, if that public primarily consists of students of the educational institution or other persons acting under its authority; or

(*d*) do any other act that is necessary for the purpose of the acts referred to in paragraphs (*a*) to (*c*).

(2) *Conditions* — Subsection (1) does not apply unless the educational institution or person acting under its authority, in doing any of the acts described in that subsection in respect of the work or other subject-matter, mentions the following:

(*a*) the source; and

(*b*) if given in the source, the name of

(i) the author, in the case of a work,

(ii) the performer, in the case of a performer's performance,

(iii) the maker, in the case of a sound recording, and

(iv) the broadcaster, in the case of a communication signal.

(3) *Non-application* — Subsection (1) does not apply if the work or other subject-matter — or the Internet site where it is posted – is protected by a technological protection measure that restricts access to the work or other subject-matter or to the Internet site.

(4) *Non-application* — Subsection (1) does not permit a person to do any act described in that subsection in respect of a work or other subject-matter if

(*a*) that work or other subject-matter – or the Internet site where it is posted — is protected by a technological protection measure that restricts the doing of that act; or

(*b*) a clearly visible notice – and not merely the copyright symbol — prohibiting that act is posted at the Internet site where the work or other subject-matter is posted or on the work or other subject-matter itself.

(5) *Non-application* — Subsection (1) does not apply if the educational institution or person acting under its authority knows or should have known that the work or other subject-matter was made available through the Internet without the consent of the copyright owner.

(6) *Regulations* — The Governor in Council may make regulations for the purposes of paragraph (4)(*b*) prescribing what constitutes a clearly visible notice. [S.C. 2012, c. 20, s. 27.]

Libraries, Archives and Museums

30.1. Management and maintenance of collection — (1) It is not an infringement of copyright for a library, archive or museum or a person acting under the authority of a library, archive or museum to make, for the maintenance or management of its permanent collection or the permanent collection of another library, archive or museum, a copy of a work or other subject-matter, whether published or unpublished, in its permanent collection

(*a*)   if the original is rare or unpublished and is

     (i)   deteriorating, damaged or lost, or

     (ii)   at risk of deterioration or becoming damaged or lost;

(*b*)   for the purposes of on-site consultation if the original cannot be viewed, handled or listened to because of its condition or because of the atmospheric conditions in which it must be kept;

(*c*)   in an alternative format if the library, archive or museum or a person acting under the authority of the library, archive or museum considers that the original is currently in a format that is obsolete or is becoming obsolete, or that the technology required to use the original is unavailable or is becoming unavailable;

[S.C. 2012, c. 20, s. 28.]

(*d*)   for the purposes of internal record-keeping and cataloguing;

(*e*)   for insurance purposes or police investigations; or

(*f*)   if necessary for restoration.

(2) *Limitation* — Paragraphs (1)(*a*) to (*c*) do not apply where an appropriate copy is commercially available in a medium and of a quality that is appropriate for the purposes of subsection (1).

(3) *Destruction of intermediate copies* — If a person must make an intermediate copy in order to make a copy under subsection (1), the person must destroy the intermediate copy as soon as it is no longer needed.

(4) *Regulations* — The Governor in Council may make regulations with respect to the procedure for making copies under subsection (1).

30.2. Research or private study— (1) It is not an infringement of copyright for a library, archive or museum or a person acting under its authority to do anything on behalf of any person that the person may do personally under section 29 or 29.1.

(2) *Copies of articles for research, etc.* — It is not an infringement of copyright for a library, archive or museum or a person acting under the authority of a library, archive or museum to make, by reprographic reproduction, for any person requesting to use the copy for research or private study, a copy of a work that is, or

that is contained in, an article published in

(*a*)   a scholarly, scientific or technical periodical; or

(*b*)   a newspaper or periodical, other than a scholarly, scientific or technical periodical, if the newspaper or periodical was published more than one year before the copy is made.

(3) *Restriction* — Paragraph (2)(*b*) does not apply in respect of a work of fiction or poetry or a dramatic or musical work.

(4) *Conditions* — A library, archive or museum may provide the person for whom the copy is made under subsection (2) with the copy only on the condition that

(*a*)   the person is provided with a single copy of the work; and

(*b*)   the library, archive or museum informs the person that the copy is to be used solely for research or private study and that any use of the copy for a purpose other than research or private study may require the authorization of the copyright owner of the work in question.

(5) *Patrons of other libraries, etc.* — Subject to subsection (5.02), a library, archive or museum, or a person acting under the authority of one, may do, on behalf of a patron of another library, archive or museum, anything under subsection (1) or (2) that it is authorized by this section to do on behalf of one of its own patrons.

(5.01) *Deeming* — For the purpose of subsection (5), the making of a copy of a work other than by reprographic reproduction is deemed to be a making of a copy of the work that may be done under subsection (2).

(5.02) *Limitation regarding copies in digital form* — A library, archive or museum, or a person acting under the authority of one, may, under subsection (5), provide a copy in digital form to a person who has requested it through another library, archive or museum if the providing library, archive or museum or person takes measures to prevent the person who has requested it from

(*a*)   making any reproduction of the digital copy, including any paper copies, other than printing one copy of it;

(*b*)   communicating the digital copy to any other person; and

(*c*)   using the digital copy for more than five business days from the day on which the person first uses it.

[S.C. 1997, c. 24, s. 18(1); S.C. 1999, c. 31, s. 59; S.C. 2012, c. 20, s. 29.]

(5.1) *Destruction of intermediate copies* — Where an intermediate copy is made in order to copy a work referred to in subsection (5), once the copy is given to the patron, the intermediate copy must be destroyed.

(6) *Regulations* — The Governor in Council may, for the purposes of this section, make regulations

(*a*) defining "newspaper" and "periodical";

(*b*) defining scholarly, scientific and technical periodicals;

(*c*) prescribing the information to be recorded about any action taken under subsection (1) or (5) and the manner and form in which the information is to be kept; and

(*d*) prescribing the manner and form in which the conditions set out in subsection (4) are to be met.

[S.C. 1997, c. 24, s. 18(1).]

30.21. Copying works deposited in archive — (1) Subject to subsections (3) and (3.1), it is not an infringement of copyright for an archive to make, for any person requesting to use the copy for research or private study, a copy of an unpublished work that is deposited in the archive and provide the person with it.

(2) *Notice* — When a person deposits a work in an archive, the archive must give the person notice that it may copy the work in accordance with this section.

(3) *Conditions for copying of works* — The archive may copy the work only on the condition that

(*a*) the person who deposited the work, if a copyright owner, did not, at the time the work was deposited, prohibit its copying; and

(*b*) copying has not been prohibited by any other owner of copyright in the work.

(3.1) *Condition for providing copy* — The archive may provide the person for whom a copy is made under subsection (1) with the copy only on the condition that

(*a*) the person is provided with a single copy of the work; and

(*b*) the archive informs the person that the copy is to be used solely for research or private study and that any use of the copy for a purpose other than research or private study may require the authorization of the copyright owner of the work in question.

(4) *Regulations* — The Governor in Council may prescribe by regulation the manner and form in which the conditions in subsection (3) and (3.1) may be met.

(5) to (7) [Repealed by S.C. 2004, c. 11, s. 21(3).]

[S.C. 1997, c. 24, s. 18(1); S.C. 1999, c. 31, s. 60; S.C. 2004, c. 11, s. 21; S.C. 2012, c. 20, s. 30.]

Ed. Note: S.C. 2004, c. 11, s. 21(4) provides as follows:

Application — Subsection (1) applies in respect of unpublished works deposited in an archive on or before September 1, 1999 or at any time after that date.

MACHINES INSTALLED IN EDUCATIONAL INSTITUTIONS, LIBRARIES, ARCHIVES AND MUSEUMS

30.3. No infringement by educational institution, etc. — (1) An educational institution or a library, archive or museum does not infringe copyright where

(a) a copy of a work is made using a machine for the making, by reprographic reproduction, of copies of works in printed form;

(b) the machine is installed by or with the approval of the educational institution, library, archive or museum on its premises for use by students, instructors or staff at the educational institution or by persons using the library, archive or museum; and

(c) there is affixed in the prescribed manner and location a notice warning of infringement of copyright.

(2) *Application* — Subsection (1) only applies if, in respect of a reprographic reproduction,

(a) the educational institution, library, archive or museum has entered into an agreement with a collective society that is authorized by copyright owners to grant licences on their behalf;

(b) the Board has, in accordance with subsection 71(2), fixed the royalty rates and related terms and conditions;

(c) a tariff has been approved in accordance with section 70; or

(d) a collective society has filed a proposed tariff in accordance with section 68.

(3) *Order* — Where a collective society offers to negotiate or has begun to negotiate an agreement referred to in paragraph (2)(a), the Board may, at the request of either party, order that the educational institution, library, archive or museum be treated as an institution to which subsection (1) applies, during the period specified in the order.

(4) *Agreement with copyright owner* — Where an educational institution, library, archive or museum has entered into an agreement with a copyright owner other than a collective society respecting reprographic reproduction, subsection (1) applies only in respect of the works of the copyright owner that are covered by the agreement.

(5) *Regulations* — The Governor in Council may, for the purposes of paragraph 1(c), prescribe by regulation the manner of affixing and location of notices and the dimensions, form and contents of notices.

[S.C. 1997, c. 24, s. 18(1); S.C. 2018, c. 27, s. 285.]

LIBRARIES, ARCHIVES AND MUSEUMS IN EDUCATIONAL INSTITUTIONS

30.4. Application to libraries, etc. within educational institutions — For greater certainty, the exceptions to infringement of copyright provided for under sections 29.4 to 30.3 and 45 also apply in respect of a library, archive or museum that forms part of an educational institution.
[S.C. 1997, c. 24, s. 18(1).]

LIBRARY AND ARCHIVES OF CANADA

30.5. Permitted acts — It is not an infringement of copyright for the Librarian and Archivist of Canada under the *Library and Archives of Canada Act,** to

(*a*)   make a copy of a work or other subject-matter in taking a representative sample for the purpose of preservation under subsection 8(2) of that Act;

(*b*)   effect the fixation of a copy of a publication, as defined in section 2 of that Act, that is provided by telecommunication in accordance with subsection 10(1) of that Act;

(*c*)   make a copy of a recording, as defined in subsection 11(2) of that Act, for the purposes of section 11 of that Act; or

(*d*)   at the time that a broadcasting undertaking, as defined in subsection 2(1) of the *Broadcasting Act,*** communicates a work or other subject-matter to the public by telecommunication, make a copy of the work or other subject-matter that is included in that communication.

[S.C. 1997, c. 24, s. 18(1); S.C. 2004, c. 11, s. 25.]

---

* *Library and Archives of Canada Act*, S.C. 2004, c. 11

2.

. . .

publication means any library matter that is made available in multiple copies or at multiple locations, whether without charge or otherwise, to the public generally or to qualifying members of the public by subscription or otherwise. Publications may be made available through any medium and may be in any form, including printed material, on-line items or recordings.

. . .

8. *Sampling from Internet* — **(2)** In exercising the powers referred to in paragraph (1)(*a*) and for the purpose of preservation, the Librarian and Archivist may take, at the times and in the manner that he or she considers appropriate, a representative sample of the documentary material of interest to Canada that is accessible to the public without restriction through the Internet or any similar medium.

. . . .

10. *Deposit of publications* — (1) Subject to the regulations, the publisher who makes a publication available in Canada shall, at the publisher's own expense, provide two copies of the publication to the Librarian and Archivist — who shall acknowledge their receipt — within

(a)   in any case other than one referred to in paragraph (*b*), seven days after the day it is made available; or

(b)   in the case of a publication that is in a class prescribed under paragraph (2)(*d*), seven days after receiving a written request from the Librarian and Archivist or any longer period specified in the request.

. . .

11. *Providing archival quality copy* — (1) If the Librarian and Archivist determines that a recording that was made available to the public in Canada has historical or archival value, he or she may by a written request require any other person who is legally entitled to provide such a copy to provide to the Librarian and Archivist, in accordance with the terms specified, a copy of that recording in the form and quality that the Librarian and Archivist determines is suitable for archival purposes and specifies in the request.

(2) *Definition of recording* — In this section, *recording* means anything that requires a machine in order to use its content, whether sounds, images or other information.

(3) *Payment for copy* — The Librarian and Archivist shall reimburse the person, other than Her Majesty in right of Canada or one of Her agents, who provides a copy under subsection (1) for the actual cost of making that copy.

(4) *Binding on Crown in right of a province*— This section binds Her Majesty in right of a province.

(5) *Property* — Copies provided to the Librarian and Archivist under this section belong to Her Majesty and form part of the collection of the Library and Archives of Canada.

** *Broadcasting Act*, S.C. 1991, c. 11

broadcasting undertaking includes a distribution undertaking, a programming undertaking and a network;

COMPUTER PROGRAMS

30.6. Permitted acts — It is not an infringement of copyright in a computer program for a person who owns a copy of the computer program that is authorized by the owner of the copyright, or has a licence to use a copy of the computer program, to

(a) reproduce the copy by adapting, modifying or converting it, or translating it into another computer language, if the person proves that the reproduced copy

    (i) is essential for the compatibility of the computer program with a particular computer,

    (ii) is solely for the person's own use, and

    (iii) was destroyed immediately after the person ceased to be the owner of the copy of the computer program or to have a licence to use it; or

(b) reproduce for backup purposes the copy or a reproduced copy referred to in paragraph (a) if the person proves that the reproduction for backup purposes was destroyed immediately after the person ceased to be the owner of the copy of the computer program or to have a licence to use it.

[S.C. 1997, c. 24, s. 18(1); S.C. 2012, c. 20, s. 31.]

30.61. Interoperability of computer programs — (1) It is not an infringement of copyright in a computer program for a person who owns a copy of the computer program that is authorized by the owner of the copyright, or has a licence to use a copy of the computer program, to reproduce the copy if

(a) they reproduce the copy for the sole purpose of obtaining information that would allow the person to make the program and another computer program interoperable; and

(b) they do not use or disclose that information, except as necessary to make the program and another computer program interoperable or to assess that interoperability.

(2) *No limitation* — In the case where that information is used or disclosed as necessary to make another computer program interoperable with the program, subsection (1) applies even if the other computer program incorporates the information and is then sold, rented or otherwise distributed.

[S.C. 2012, c. 20, s. 31.]

ENCRYPTION RESEARCH

30.62. Encryption research — (1) Subject to subsections (2) and (3), it is not an infringement of copyright for a person to reproduce a work or other subject-matter for the purposes of encryption research if

(*a*)   it would not be practical to carry out the research without making the copy;

(*b*)   the person has lawfully obtained the work or other subject-matter; and

(*c*)   the person has informed the owner of the copyright in the work or other subject-matter.

(2) *Limitation* — Subsection (1) does not apply if the person uses or discloses information obtained through the research to commit an act that is an offence under the *Criminal Code*.*

(3) *Limitation – computer program* — Subsection (1) applies with respect to a computer program only if, in the event that the research reveals a vulnerability or a security flaw in the program and the person intends to make the vulnerability or security flaw public, the person gives adequate notice of the vulnerability or security flaw and of their intention to the owner of copyright in the program. However, the person need not give that adequate notice if, in the circumstances, the public interest in having the vulnerability or security flaw made public without adequate notice outweighs the owner's interest in receiving that notice.

[S.C. 2012, c. 20, s. 31.]

---

*R.S.C. 1985, c. C-46

SECURITY

30.63. Security — (1) Subject to subsections (2) and (3), it is not an infringement of copyright for a person to reproduce a work or other subject-matter for the sole purpose, with the consent of the owner or administrator of a computer, computer system or computer network, of assessing the vulnerability of the computer, system or network or of correcting any security flaws.

(2) *Limitation* — Subsection (1) does not apply if the person uses or discloses information obtained through the assessment or correction to commit an act that is an offence under the *Criminal Code*.*

(3) *Limitation computer program* — Subsection (1) applies with respect to a computer program only if, in the event that the assessment or correction reveals a vulnerability or a security flaw in the program and the person intends to make the vulnerability or security flaw public, the person gives adequate notice of the vulnerability or security flaw and of their intention to the owner of copyright in the program. However, the person need not give that adequate notice if, in the circumstances, the public interest in having the vulnerability or security flaw made public without adequate notice outweighs the owner's interest in receiving that

notice.
[S.C. 2012, c. 20, s. 31.]

---

*R.S.C. 1985, c. C-46

INCIDENTAL INCLUSION

30.7. Incidental use — It is not an infringement of copyright to incidentally and not deliberately

(*a*)   include a work or other subject-matter in another work or other subject-matter; or

(*b*)   do any act in relation to a work or other subject-matter that is incidentally and not deliberately included in another work or other subject-matter.

[S.C. 1997, c. 24, s. 18(1).]

TEMPORARY REPRODUCTIONS FOR TECHNOLOGICAL PROCESSES

30.71. Temporary reproductions — It is not an infringement of copyright to make a reproduction of a work or other subject-matter if

(*a*)   the reproduction forms an essential part of a technological process;

(*b*)   the reproduction's only purpose is to facilitate a use that is not an infringement of copyright; and

(*c*)   the reproduction exists only for the duration of the technological process.

[S.C. 2012, c. 20, s. 32.]

EPHEMERAL RECORDINGS

30.8. Ephemeral recordings — (1) It is not an infringement of copyright for a programming undertaking to fix or reproduce in accordance with this section a performer's performance or work, other than a cinematographic work, that is performed live or a sound recording that is performed at the same time as the performer's performance or work, if the undertaking

(*a*)   is authorized to communicate the performer's performance, work or sound recording to the public by telecommunication;

(*b*)   makes the fixation or the reproduction itself, for its own broadcasts;

(*c*)   does not synchronize the fixation or reproduction with all or part of another recording, performer's performance or work; and

(*d*)   does not cause the fixation or reproduction to be used in an advertisement intended to sell or promote, as the case may be, a product, service, cause or

111

institution.

(2) *Record keeping* — The programming undertaking must record the dates of the making and destruction of all fixations and reproductions and any other prescribed information about the fixation or reproduction, and keep the record current.

(3) *Right of access by copyright owners* — The programming undertaking must make the record referred to in subsection (2) available to owners of copyright in the works, sound recordings or performer's performances, or their representatives, within twenty-four hours after receiving a request.

(4) *Destruction* — The programming undertaking must destroy the fixation or reproduction within thirty days after making it, unless

(*a*)   the copyright owner authorizes its retention; or

(*b*)   it is deposited in an archive, in accordance with subsection (6).

(5) *Royalties* — Where the copyright owner authorizes the fixation or reproduction to be retained after the thirty days, the programming undertaking must pay any applicable royalty.

(6) *Archive* — Where the programming undertaking considers a fixation or reproduction to be of an exceptional documentary character, the undertaking may, with the consent of an official archive, deposit it in the official archive and must notify the copyright owner, within thirty days, of the deposit of the fixation or reproduction.

(7) *Definition of **official archive*** — In subsection (6), **official archive** means the Library and Archives of Canada or any archive established under the law of a province for the preservation of the official archives of the province.

(8) *Application* — This section does not apply where a licence is available from a collective society to make the fixation or reproduction of the performer's performance, work or sound recording.

(9) *Telecommunications by networks* — A broadcasting undertaking, as defined in the *Broadcasting Act*,* may make a single reproduction of a fixation or reproduction made by a programming undertaking and communicate it to the public by telecommunication, within the period referred to in subsection (4), if the broadcasting undertaking meets the conditions set out in subsection (1) and is part of a prescribed network that includes the programming undertaking.

(10) *Limitations* — The reproduction and communication to the public by telecommunication must be made

(*a*)   in accordance with subsections (2) to (6); and

(*b*)   within thirty days after the day on which the programming undertaking made the fixation or reproduction.

(11) *Definition of **programming undertaking*** — In this section, ***programming undertaking*** means

(*a*) a programming undertaking as defined in the *Broadcasting Act*;*

(*b*) a programming undertaking described in paragraph (*a*) that originates programs within a network, as defined in the *Broadcasting Act*;* or

(*c*) a distribution undertaking as defined in the *Broadcasting Act*,* in respect of the programs that it originates.

The undertaking must hold a broadcasting licence issued by the Canadian Radio-television and Telecommunications Commission under the *Broadcasting Act*, or be exempted from this requirement by the Canadian Radio-television and Telecommunications Commission.*

[S.C. 1997, c. 24, s. 18(1); S.C. 2004, c. 11, s. 26; S.C. 2012, c. 20, s. 33.]

------

* *Broadcasting Act*, S.C. 1991, c. 11

broadcasting undertaking **includes a distribution undertaking, a programming undertaking and a network;**

distribution undertaking **means an undertaking for the reception of broadcasting and the retransmission thereof by radio waves or other means of telecommunication to more than one permanent or temporary residence or dwelling unit or to another such undertaking;**

network **includes any operation where control over all or any part of the programs or program schedules of one or more broadcasting undertakings is delegated to another undertaking or person;**

programming undertaking **means an undertaking for the transmission of programs, either directly by radio waves or other means of telecommunication or indirectly through a distribution undertaking, for reception by the public by means of broadcasting receiving apparatus;**

30.9. Ephemeral recordings – broadcasting undertaking — (1) It is not an infringement of copyright for a broadcasting undertaking to reproduce in accordance with this section a sound recording, or a performer's performance or work that is embodied in a sound recording, solely for the purpose of their broadcasting, if the undertaking

(*a*) owns the copy of the sound recording, performer's performance or work and that copy is authorized by the owner of the copyright, or has a licence to use the copy;

(*b*) is authorized to communicate the sound recording, performer's performance or work to the public by telecommunication;

113

(c) makes the reproduction itself, for its own broadcasts;

(d) does not synchronize the reproduction with all or part of another recording, performer's performance or work; and

(e) does not cause the reproduction to be used in an advertisement intended to sell or promote, as the case may be, a product, service, cause or institution.

(2) *Record keeping* — The broadcasting undertaking must record the dates of the making and destruction of all reproductions and any other prescribed information about the reproduction, and keep the record current.

(3) *Right of access by copyright owners* — The broadcasting undertaking must make the record referred to in subsection (2) available to owners of copyright in the sound recordings, performer's performances or works, or their representatives, within twenty-four hours after receiving a request.

(4) *Destruction* — The broadcasting undertaking must destroy the reproduction when it no longer possesses the sound recording, or performer's performance or work embodied in the sound recording, or its licence to use the sound recording, performer's performance or work expires, or at the latest within 30 days after making the reproduction, unless the copyright owner authorizes the reproduction to be retained.

(5) *Royalty* — If the copyright owner authorizes the reproduction to be retained, the broadcasting undertaking must pay any applicable royalty.

(6) [Repealed by S.C. 2012, c. 20, s. 34(3).]

(7) *Definition of **broadcasting undertaking*** — In this section, ***broadcasting undertaking*** means a broadcasting undertaking as defined in the *Broadcasting Act** that holds a broadcasting licence issued by the Canadian Radio-television and Telecommunications Commission under that Act.

[S.C. 1997, c. 24, s. 18(1); S.C. 2012, c. 20, s. 34.]

---

* *Broadcasting Act*, S.C. 1991, c. 11
broadcasting undertaking includes a distribution undertaking, a programming undertaking and a network;

RETRANSMISSION

31. Interpretation — (1) In this section,

new media retransmitter means a person whose retransmission is lawful under the *Broadcasting Act* only by reason of the *Exemption Order for New Media Broadcasting Undertakings* issued by the Canadian Radio-television and Telecommunications Commission as Appendix A to Public Notice CRTC 1999-197, as amended from time to time;

retransmitter means a person who performs a function comparable to that of a cable retransmission system, but does not include a new media retransmitter;

signal means a signal that carries a literary, dramatic, musical or artistic work and is transmitted for free reception by the public by a terrestrial radio or terrestrial television station.

(2) *Retransmission of local and distant signals* — It is not an infringement of copyright for a retransmitter to communicate to the public by telecommunication any literary, dramatic, musical or artistic work if

(*a*)   the communication is a retransmission of a local or distant signal;

(*b*)   the retransmission is lawful under the *Broadcasting Act*;*

(*c*)   the signal is retransmitted simultaneously and without alteration, except as otherwise required or permitted by or under the laws of Canada;

(*d*)   in the case of the retransmission of a distant signal, the retransmitter has paid any royalties, and complied with any terms and conditions, fixed under this Act; and

(*e*)   the retransmitter complies with the applicable conditions, if any, referred to in paragraph 3(*b*).

(3) *Regulations* — The Governor in Council may make regulations

(*a*)   defining "local signal" and "distant signal" for the purposes of subsection (2); and

(*b*)   prescribing conditions for the purposes of paragraph (2)(*e*), and specifying whether any such condition applies to all retransmitters or only to a class of retransmitter.

[S.C. 1988, c. 65, s. 63; S.C. 1997, c. 24, s. 16; S.C. 2002, c. 26, s. 2.]

***S.C. 1991, c. 11**

NETWORK SERVICES

31.1. Network services — (1) A person who, in providing services related to the operation of the Internet or another digital network, provides any means for the telecommunication or the reproduction of a work or other subject-matter through the Internet or that other network does not, solely by reason of providing those means, infringe copyright in that work or other subject-matter.

(2) *Incidental acts* — Subject to subsection (3), a person referred to in subsection (1) who caches the work or other subject-matter, or does any similar act in relation to it, to make the telecommunication more efficient does not, by virtue of that act alone, infringe copyright in the work or other subject-matter.

(3) *Conditions for application* — Subsection (2) does not apply unless the person, in respect of the work or other subject-matter,

(a) does not modify it, other than for technical reasons;

(b) ensures that any directions related to its caching or the doing of any similar act, as the case may be, that are specified in a manner consistent with industry practice by whoever made it available for telecommunication through the Internet or another digital network, and that lend themselves to automated reading and execution, are read and executed; and

(c) does not interfere with the use of technology that is lawful and consistent with industry practice in order to obtain data on the use of the work or other subject-matter.

(4) *Hosting* — Subject to subsection (5), a person who, for the purpose of allowing the telecommunication of a work or other subject-matter through the Internet or another digital network, provides digital memory in which another person stores the work or other subject-matter does not, by virtue of that act alone, infringe copyright in the work or other subject-matter.

(5) *Condition for application* — Subsection (4) does not apply in respect of a work or other subject-matter if the person providing the digital memory knows of a decision of a court of competent jurisdiction to the effect that the person who has stored the work or other subject-matter in the digital memory infringes copyright by making the copy of the work or other subject-matter that is stored or by the way in which he or she uses the work or other subject-matter.

(6) *Exception* — Subsections (1), (2) and (4) do not apply in relation to an act that constitutes an infringement of copyright under subsection 27(2.3).
[S.C. 2012, c. 20, s. 35.]

PERSONS WITH PERCEPTUAL DISABILITIES

32. Reproduction in alternate format — (1) It is not an infringement of copyright for a person with a perceptual disability, for a person acting at the request of such a person or for a non-profit organization acting for the benefit of such a person to

(a) reproduce a literary, musical, artistic or dramatic work, other than a cinematographic work, in a format specially designed for persons with a perceptual disability;

(a.1) fix a performer's performance of a literary, musical, artistic or dramatic work, other than a cinematographic work, in a format specially designed for persons with a perceptual disability;

(*a*.2) reproduce a sound recording, or a fixation of a performer's performance referred to in paragraph (*a*.1), in a format specially designed for persons with a perceptual disability;

(*b*) translate, adapt or reproduce in sign language a literary or dramatic work, other than a cinematographic work, in a format specially designed for persons with a perceptual disability;

(*b*.1) provide a person with a perceptual disability with, or provide such a person with access to, a work or other subject-matter to which any of paragraphs (*a*) to (*b*) applies, in a format specially designed for persons with a perceptual disability, and do any other act that is necessary for that purpose; or

(*c*) perform in public a literary or dramatic work, other than a cinematographic work, in sign language, either live or in a format specially designed for persons with a perceptual disability.

(2) *Limitation* — Subsection (1) does not apply if the work or other subject-matter is commercially available, within the meaning of paragraph (*a*) of the definition *commercially available* in section 2, in a format specially designed to meet the needs of the person with a perceptual disability referred to in that subsection.

(3) [Repealed by S.C. 2016, c. 4, s. 1.]

[S.C. 1997, c. 24, s. 19; S.C. 2012, c. 20, s. 36; S.C. 2016, c. 4, s. 1.]

32.01. Print disability – outside Canada — (1) Subject to this section, it is not an infringement of copyright for a non-profit organization acting for the benefit of persons with a print disability to do any of the following:

(*a*) for the purpose of doing any of the acts set out in paragraph (*b*),

(i) reproduce a literary, musical, artistic or dramatic work, other than a cinematographic work, in a format specially designed for persons with a print disability,

(ii) fix a performer's performance of a literary, musical, artistic or dramatic work, other than a cinematographic work, in a format specially designed for persons with a print disability, or

(iii) reproduce a sound recording, or a fixation of a performer's performance referred to in subparagraph (ii), in a format specially designed for persons with a print disability;

(*b*) provide either of the following with, or provide either of the following with access to, a work or other subject-matter to which any of subparagraphs (*a*)(i) to (iii) applies, in a format specially designed for persons with a print disability, and do any other act that is necessary for that purpose:

117

(i)   a non-profit organization, in a country other than Canada, acting for the benefit of persons with a print disability in that country, or

(ii)   a person with a print disability, in a country other than Canada, who has made a request to be provided with, or provided with access to, the work or other subject-matter through a non-profit organization acting for the benefit of persons with a print disability in that country.

(2) *Available in other country* — Paragraph (1)(*b*) does not apply if the work or other subject-matter, in the format specially designed for persons with a print disability, is available in the other country within a reasonable time and for a reasonable price and may be located in that country with reasonable effort.

(3) *Marrakesh Treaty country* — An injunction is the only remedy that the owner of the copyright in the work or other subject-matter has against a non-profit organization relying on the exception set out in paragraph (1)(*b*) if

(*a*)   the other country referred to in that paragraph is a Marrakesh Treaty country; and

(*b*)   the non-profit organization infringes copyright by reason only that the work or other subject-matter, in the format described in subsection (2), is available, and may be located, as described in that subsection.

The owner of the copyright bears the burden of demonstrating that the work or other subject-matter, in the format described in subsection (2), is available, and may be located, as described in that subsection.

(3.1) *Not Marrakesh Treaty country* — An injunction is the only remedy that the owner of the copyright in the work or other subject-matter has against a non-profit organization relying on the exception set out in paragraph (1)(*b*) if

(*a*)   the other country referred to in that paragraph is not a Marrakesh Treaty country;

(*b*)   the non-profit organization infringes copyright by reason only that the work or other subject-matter, in the format described in subsection (2), is available, and may be located, as described in that subsection; and

(*c*)   the non-profit organization demonstrates that it had reasonable grounds to believe that the work or other subject-matter, in the format described in subsection (2), was not available, and could not be located, as described in that subsection.

(4) *Royalty* — A non-profit organization relying on the exception set out in subsection (1) shall pay, in accordance with the regulations, any royalty established under the regulations to the copyright owner.

(5) *If copyright owner cannot be located* — If the organization cannot locate the

copyright owner, despite making reasonable efforts to do so, the organization shall pay, in accordance with the regulations, any royalty established under the regulations to a collective society.

(6) *Reports* — A non-profit organization relying on the exception set out in subsection (1) shall submit reports to an authority, in accordance with the regulations, on the organization's activities under this section.

(7) *Regulations* — The Governor in Council may make regulations

(*a*) requiring that, before a non-profit organization provides, or provides access to, a work or other subject-matter under paragraph (1)(*b*), the organization enter into a contract with respect to the use of the work or other subject-matter with, as the case may be, the recipient non-profit organization or the non-profit organization through which the request was made;

(*b*) respecting the form and content of such contracts;

(*c*) respecting any royalties to be paid under subsections (4) and (5);

(*d*) respecting to which collective society a royalty is payable in relation to works or other subject-matter, or classes of works or other subject-matter, for the purposes of subsection (5);

(*e*) respecting what constitutes reasonable efforts for the purposes of subsection (5); and

(*f*) respecting the reports to be made, and the authorities to which the reports are to be submitted, under subsection (6).

(8) *Definitions* — The following definitions apply in this section.

Marrakesh Treaty country means a country that is a party to the Marrakesh Treaty to Facilitate Access to Published Works for Persons Who Are Blind, Visually Impaired, or Otherwise Print Disabled, done at Marrakesh on June 27, 2013.

print disability means a disability that prevents or inhibits a person from reading a literary, musical, artistic or dramatic work in its original format and includes such a disability resulting from

(*a*) severe or total impairment of sight or the inability to focus or move one's eyes;

(*b*) the inability to hold or manipulate a book; or

(*c*) an impairment relating to comprehension.

[S.C. 2012, c. 20, s. 37; S.C. 2016, c. 4, s. 2.]

32.02. Definition of *non-profit organization* — In sections 32 and 32.01, ***non-profit organization*** includes a department, agency or other portion of any order of government, including a municipal or local government, when it is acting on a non-profit basis.

[S.C. 2016, c. 4, s. 3.]

---

* *Immigration and Refugee Protection Act*, S.C. 2001, c. 27

permanent resident means a person who has acquired permanent resident status and has not subsequently lost that status under section 46.

STATUTORY OBLIGATIONS

32.1. No infringement — (1) It is not an infringement of copyright for any person

   (*a*)   to disclose, pursuant to the *Access to Information Act*,* a record within the meaning of that Act, or to disclose, pursuant to any like Act of the legislature of a province, like material;

   (*b*)   to disclose, pursuant to the *Privacy Act*,** personal information within the meaning of that Act, or to disclose, pursuant to any like Act of the legislature of a province, like information;

   (*c*)   to make a copy of an object referred to in section 14 of the *Cultural Property Export and Import Act*,† for deposit in an institution pursuant to a direction under that section; and

   (*d*)   to make a fixation or copy of a work or other subject-matter in order to comply with the *Broadcasting Act*†† or any rule, regulation or other instrument made under it.

(2) *Limitation* — Nothing in paragraph (1)(*a*) or (*b*) authorizes a person to whom a record or information is disclosed to do anything that, by this Act, only the owner of the copyright in the record, personal information or like information, as the case may be, has a right to do.

(3) *Destruction of fixation or copy* —Unless the *Broadcasting Act* otherwise provides, a person who makes a fixation or copy under paragraph (1)(*d*) shall destroy it immediately on the expiration of the period for which it must be kept pursuant to that Act, rule, regulation or other instrument.

[S.C. 1997, c. 24, s. 19.]

---

* *Access to Information Act*, R.S.C. 1985, c. A-1

record means any documentary material, regardless of medium or form;

[S.C. 2006, c. 9, s. 141]

** *Privacy Act*, R.S.C. 1985, c. P-21

personal information means information about an identifiable individual that is recorded in any form including, without restricting the generality of the foregoing,

(a)   information relating to the race, national or ethnic origin, colour, religion, age or marital status of the individual,

(b)   information relating to the education or the medical, criminal or employment history of the individual or information relating to financial transactions in which the individual has been involved,

(c)   any identifying number, symbol or other particular assigned to the individual,

(d)   the address, fingerprints or blood type of the individual,

(e)   the personal opinions or views of the individual except where they are about another individual or about a proposal for a grant, an award or a prize to be made to another individual by a government institution or a part of a government institution specified in the regulations,

(f)   correspondence sent to a government institution by the individual that is implicitly or explicitly of a private or confidential nature, and replies to such correspondence that would reveal the contents of the original correspondence,

(g)   the views or opinions of another individual about the individual,

(h)   the views or opinions of another individual about a proposal for a grant, an award or a prize to be made to the individual by an institution or a part of an institution referred to in paragraph (e), but excluding the name of the other individual where it appears with the views or opinions of the other individual, and

(i)   the name of the individual where it appears with other personal information relating to the individual or where the disclosure of the name itself would reveal information about the individual,

but, for the purposes of sections 7, 8 and 26 and section 19 of the *Access to Information Act*, does not include

(j)   information about an individual who is or was an officer or employee of a government institution that relates to the position or functions of the individual including,

(i)   the fact that the individual is or was an officer or employee of the government institution,

(ii)   the title, business address and telephone number of the individual,

(iii)   the classification, salary range and responsibilities of the position held by the individual,

　(iv)　the name of the individual on a document prepared by the individual in the course of employment, and

　(v)　the personal opinions or views of the individual given in the course of employment,

(*j*.1)　the fact that an individual is or was a *ministerial adviser* or a member of a *ministerial staff*, as those terms are defined in subsection 2(1) of the *Conflict of Interest Act*, as well as the individual's name and title;

(*k*)　information about an individual who is or was performing services under contract for a government institution that relates to the services performed, including the terms of the contract, the name of the individual and the opinions or views of the individual given in the course of the performance of those services,

(*l*)　information relating to any discretionary benefit of a financial nature, including the granting of a licence or permit, conferred on an individual, including the name of the individual and the exact nature of the benefit, and

(*m*)　information about an individual who has been dead for more than twenty years;

[S.C. 2019, c. 18, s. 47.]

---

† *Cultural Property Export and Import Act*, R.S.C. 1985, c. C-51

14. Deposit of copy — No export permit shall, unless it is issued under section 7, be issued under this Act for an object within a class of objects prescribed under paragraph 39(*d*), where the object is included in the Control List, until a copy of that object has been deposited by the person applying for the permit in such institution as the Minister may direct.

---

††S.C. 1991, c. 11

MISCELLANEOUS

32.2. Permitted acts — (1) It is not an infringement of copyright

(*a*)　for an author of an artistic work who is not the owner of the copyright in the work to use any mould, cast, sketch, plan, model or study made by the author for the purpose of the work, if the author does not thereby repeat or imitate the main design of the work;

(*b*)　for any person to reproduce, in a painting, drawing, engraving, photograph or cinematographic work

(i) an architectural work, provided the copy is not in the nature of an architectural drawing or plan, or

(ii) a sculpture or work of artistic craftsmanship or a cast or model of a sculpture or work of artistic craftsmanship, that is permanently situated in a public place or building;

(c) for any person to make or publish, for the purposes of news reporting or news summary, a report of a lecture given in public, unless the report is prohibited by conspicuous written or printed notice affixed before and maintained during the lecture at or about the main entrance of the building in which the lecture is given, and, except while the building is being used for public worship, in a position near the lecturer;

(d) for any person to read or recite in public a reasonable extract from a published work;

(e) for any person to make or publish, for the purposes of news reporting or news summary, a report of an address of a political nature given at a public meeting; or

(f) for an individual to use for private or non-commercial purposes, or permit the use of for those purposes, a photograph or portrait that was commissioned by the individual for personal purposes and made for valuable consideration, unless the individual and the owner of the copyright in the photograph or portrait have agreed otherwise.

(2) *Further permitted acts* — It is not an infringement of copyright for a person to do any of the following acts without motive of gain at any agricultural or agricultural-industrial exhibition or fair that receives a grant from or is held by its directors under federal, provincial or municipal authority:

(a) the live performance in public of a musical work;

(b) the performance in public of a sound recording embodying a musical work or a performer's performance of a musical work; or

(c) the performance in public of a communication signal carrying

(i) the live performance in public of a musical work, or

(ii) a sound recording embodying a musical work or a performer's performance of a musical work.

(3) *Further permitted acts* — No religious organization or institution, educational institution and no charitable or fraternal organization shall be held liable to pay any compensation for doing any of the following acts in furtherance of a religious, educational or charitable object:

(*a*) the live performance in public of a musical work;

(*b*) the performance in public of a sound recording embodying a musical work or a performer's performance of a musical work; or

(*c*) the performance in public of a communication signal carrying

(i) the live performance in public of a musical work, or

(ii) a sound recording embodying a musical work or a performer's performance of a musical work.

[S.C. 1997, c. 24, s. 19; S.C. 2012, c. 20, s. 38.]

INTERPRETATION

32.3. No right to equitable remuneration — For the purposes of sections 29 to 32.2, an act that does not infringe copyright does not give rise to a right to remuneration conferred by section 19.

[S.C. 1997, c. 24, s. 19.]

COMPENSATION FOR ACTS DONE BEFORE RECOGNITION OF COPYRIGHT OF PERFORMERS AND BROADCASTERS

32.4. Certain rights and interests protected — (1) Notwithstanding section 27, where a person has, before the later of January 1, 1996 and the day on which a country becomes a WTO member, incurred an expenditure or liability in connection with, or in preparation for, the doing of an act that would have infringed copyright under section 26 commencing on the later of those days, had that country been a WTO member, any right or interest of that person that

(*a*) arises from or in connection with the doing of that act, and

(*b*) is subsisting and valuable on the later of those days

is not prejudiced or diminished by reason only that that country has become a WTO member, except as provided by an order of the Board made under subsection 78(3).

(2) *Compensation* — Notwithstanding subsection (1), a person's right or interest that is protected by that subsection terminates if and when the owner of the copyright pays that person such compensation as is agreed to between the parties or, failing agreement, as is determined by the Board in accordance with section 78.

(3) *Limitation* — Nothing in subsections (1) and (2) affects any right of a performer available in law or equity.

[S.C. 1997, c. 24, s. 19.]

32.5. Certain rights and interests protected — (1) Notwithstanding section 27, where a person has, before the later of the coming into force of Part II and the day on which a country becomes a Rome Convention country, incurred an expenditure or liability in connection with, or in preparation for, the doing of an act that would have infringed copyright under section 15 or 21 commencing on the later of those days, had Part II been in force or had that country been a Rome Convention country, any right or interest of that person that

(*a*) arises from or in connection with the doing of that act, and

(*b*) is subsisting and valuable on the later of those days

is not prejudiced or diminished by reason only that Part II has come into force or that the country has become a Rome Convention country, except as provided by an order of the Board made under subsection 78(3).

(2) *Compensation* — Notwithstanding subsection (1), a person's right or interest that is protected by that subsection terminates if and when the owner of the copyright pays that person such compensation as is agreed to between the parties or, failing agreement, as is determined by the Board in accordance with section 78.

(3) *Limitation* — Nothing in subsections (1) and (2) affects any right of a performer available in law or equity.

[S.C. 1997, c. 24, s. 19.]

32.6. Certain rights and interests protected — Despite sections 27, 28.1 and 28.2, if a person has, before the day on which subsection 15(1.1), 17.1(1) or 18(1.1) applies in respect of a particular performers' performance or sound recording, incurred an expenditure or a liability in connection with, or in preparation for, the doing of an act that would, if done after that day, have infringed rights under that subsection, any right or interest of that person that arises from, or in connection with, the doing of that act and that is subsisting and valuable on that day is not, for two years after the day on which this section comes into force, prejudiced or diminished by reason only of the subsequent application of that subsection in respect of the performers' performance or sound recording.

[S.C. 2012, c. 20, s. 39.]

COMPENSATION FOR ACTS DONE BEFORE RECOGNITION OF COPYRIGHT OR MORAL RIGHTS

33. Certain rights and interests protected — (1) Despite subsections 27(1), (2) and (4) and sections 27.1, 28.1 and 28.2, if a person has, before the later of January 1, 1996 and the day on which a country becomes a treaty country other than a WCT country, incurred an expenditure or liability in connection with, or in preparation for, the doing of an act that, if that country had been such a treaty country, would have infringed copyright in a work or moral rights in respect of a work, any right or interest of that person that arises from, or in connection with, the doing of that act and that is subsisting and valuable on the later of those days is not, except as provided by an order of the Board made under subsection 78(3), prejudiced or diminished by reason only of that country having become such a treaty country.

(2) *Compensation* — Notwithstanding subsection (1), a person's right or interest that is protected by that subsection terminates, as against the copyright owner or author, if and when that copyright owner or the author, as the case may be, pays that person such compensation as is agreed to between the parties or, failing agreement, as is determined by the Board in accordance with section 78.
[S.C. 1997, c. 24, s. 19; S.C. 2012, c. 20, s. 40.]

33.1. Certain rights and interests protected — (1) Despite subsections 27(1), (2) and (4) and sections 27.1, 28.1 and 28.2, if a person has, before the later of the day on which this section comes into force and the day on which a country that is a treaty country but not a WCT country becomes a WCT country, incurred an expenditure or liability in connection with, or in preparation for, the doing of an act that, if that country had been a WCT country, would have infringed a right under paragraph 3(1)(j), any right or interest of that person that arises from, or in connection with, the doing of that act and that is subsisting and valuable on the later of those days is not, except as provided by an order of the Board made under subsection 78(3), prejudiced or diminished by reason only of that country having become a WCT country.

(2) *Compensation* — Despite subsection (1), a person's right or interest that is protected by that subsection terminates as against the copyright owner if and when the owner pays the person any compensation that is agreed to between the parties or, failing agreement, that is determined by the Board in accordance with section 78.
[S.C. 2012, c. 20, s. 41.]

33.2. Certain rights and interests protected — (1) Despite subsections 27(1), (2) and (4) and sections 27.1, 28.1 and 28.2, if a person has, before the later of the day on which this section comes into force and the day on which a country that is not a treaty country becomes a WCT country, incurred an expenditure or a liability in connection with, or in preparation for, the doing of an act that, if that country had been a WCT country, would have infringed copyright in a work or moral rights in respect of a work, any right or interest of that person that arises from, or in connection with, the doing of that act and that is subsisting and valuable on the later of those days is not, except as provided by an order of the Board made under subsection 78(3), prejudiced or diminished by reason only of that country having become a WCT country.

(2) *Compensation* — Despite subsection (1), a person's right or interest that is protected by that subsection terminates as against the copyright owner if and when that owner pays the person any compensation that is agreed to between the parties or, failing agreement, that is determined by the Board in accordance with section 78.
[S.C. 2012, c. 20, s. 41.]

PART IV
REMEDIES

[S.C. 1997, c. 24, s. 19.]

CIVIL REMEDIES

Infringement of Copyright and Moral Rights

[S.C. 2012, c. 20, s. 42.]

34. Copyright — (1) Where copyright has been infringed, the owner of the copyright is, subject to this Act, entitled to all remedies by way of injunction, damages, accounts, delivery up and otherwise that are or may be conferred by law for the infringement of a right.

(1.01) [Repealed by S.C. 1997, c. 24, s. 20(1).]

(1.02) [Repealed by S.C. 1997, c. 24, s. 20(1).]

(1.03) [Repealed by S.C. 1997, c. 24, s. 20(1).]

(1.1) [Repealed by S.C. 1997, c. 24, s. 20(1).]

(2) *Moral rights* — In any proceedings for an infringement of a moral right of an author, the court may grant to the holder of those rights all remedies by way of injunction, damages, accounts, delivery up and otherwise that are or may be conferred by law for the infringement of a right.

(3) *Costs* — The costs of all parties in any proceedings in respect of the infringement of a right conferred by this Act shall be in the discretion of the court.

(4) *Summary proceedings* — The following proceedings may be commenced or proceeded with by way of application or action and shall, in the case of an application, be heard and determined without delay and in a summary way:

(*a*)   proceedings for infringement of copyright or moral rights;

(*b*)   proceedings taken under section 44.12, 44.2 or 44.4; and

(*c*)   proceedings taken in respect of

(i)   a tariff approved by the Board under Part VII.1 or VIII, or

(ii)   agreements referred to in subsection 67(3).

[S.C. 2014, c. 32, s. 6; S.C. 2018, c. 27, s. 286.]

(5) *Practice and procedure* — The rules of practice and procedure, in civil matters, of the court in which proceedings are commenced by way of application apply to those proceedings, but where those rules do not provide for the proceedings to be heard and determined without delay and in a summary way, the court may give such directions as it considers necessary in order to so provide.

(6) *Actions* — The court in which proceedings are instituted by way of application may, where it considers it appropriate, direct that the proceeding be proceeded with as an action.

(7) *Meaning of application* — In this section, *application* means a proceeding that is commenced other than by way of a writ or statement of claim.

[R.S.C. 1985, c. 10 (4th Supp.), s. 8; S.C. 1993, c. 15, s. 3; S.C. 1993, c. 44, ss. 65, 78(b); S.C. 1994, c. 47, s. 62; S.C. 1997, c. 24, s. 20(1); S.C. 2012, c. 20, s. 43.]

34.1. Presumptions respecting copyright and ownership — (1) In any civil proceedings taken under this Act in which the defendant puts in issue either the existence of the copyright or the title of the plaintiff to it,

(*a*) copyright shall be presumed, unless the contrary is proved, to subsist in the work, performer's performance, sound recording or communication signal, as the case may be; and

(*b*) the author, performer, maker or broadcaster, as the case may be, shall, unless the contrary is proved, be presumed to be the owner of the copyright.

(2) *Where no grant registered* — Where any matter referred to in subsection (1) is at issue and no assignment of the copyright, or licence granting an interest in the copyright, has been registered under this Act,

(*a*) if a name purporting to be that of

    (i) the author of the work,

    (ii) the performer of the performer's performance,

    (iii) the maker of the sound recording, or

    (iv) the broadcaster of the communication signal

is printed or otherwise indicated thereon in the usual manner, the person whose name is so printed or indicated shall, unless the contrary is proved, be presumed to be the author, performer, maker or broadcaster;

(*b*) if

    (i) no name is so printed or indicated, or if the name so printed or indicated is not the true name of the author, performer, maker or broadcaster or the name by which that person is commonly known, and

    (ii) a name purporting to be that of the publisher or owner of the work, performer's performance, sound recording or communication signal is printed or otherwise indicated thereon in the usual manner,

the person whose name is printed or indicated as described in subparagraph (ii) shall, unless the contrary is proved, be presumed to be the owner of the copyright in question; and (*c*) if, on a cinematographic work, a name purporting to be that of the maker of the cinematographic work appears in the usual manner, the person so named shall, unless the contrary is proved, be presumed to be the maker of the cinematographic work.

[S.C. 1997, c. 24, s. 20(1); S.C. 2012, c. 20, s. 44.]

35. Liability for infringement — (1) Where a person infringes copyright, the person is liable to pay such damages to the owner of the copyright as the owner has suffered due to the infringement and, in addition to those damages, such part of the profits that the infringer has made from the infringement and that were not taken into account in calculating the damages as the court considers just.

(2) *Proof of profits* — In proving profits,

(*a*) the plaintiff shall be required to prove only receipts or revenues derived from the infringement; and

(*b*) the defendant shall be required to prove every element of cost that the defendant claims.

[S.C. 1997, c. 24, s. 20(1).]

36. [Repealed by S.C. 2012, c. 20, s. 45.]

37. [Repealed by S.C. 2012, c. 20, s. 45.]

38. Recovery of possession of copies, plates — (1) Subject to subsection (2), the owner of the copyright in a work or other subject-matter may

(*a*) recover possession of all infringing copies of that work or other subject-matter, and of all plates used or intended to be used for the production of infringing copies, and

(*b*) take proceedings for seizure of those copies or plates before judgment if, under the law of Canada or of the province in which those proceedings are taken, a person is entitled to take such proceedings,

as if those copies or plates were the property of the copyright owner.

(2) *Powers of court* — On application by

(*a*) a person from whom the copyright owner has recovered possession of copies or plates referred to in subsection (1),

(*b*) a person against whom proceedings for seizure before judgment of copies or plates referred to in subsection (1) have been taken, or

(*c*) any other person who has an interest in those copies or plates,

a court may order that those copies or plates be destroyed, or may make any other order that it considers appropriate in the circumstances.

(3) *Notice to interested persons* — Before making an order under subsection (2),

the court shall direct that notice be given to any person who has an interest in the copies or plates in question, unless the court is of the opinion that the interests of justice do not require such notice to be given.

(4) *Circumstances court to consider* — In making an order under subsection (2), the court shall have regard to all the circumstances, including

(*a*) the proportion, importance and value of the infringing copy or plate, as compared to the substrate or carrier embodying it; and

(*b*) the extent to which the infringing copy or plate is severable from, or a distinct part of, the substrate or carrier embodying it.

(5) *Limitation* — Nothing in this Act entitles the copyright owner to damages in respect of the possession or conversion of the infringing copies or plates.
[S.C. 1997, c. 24, s. 20(1).]

Note: S.C. 1997, c. 24, s. 20(2), which was repealed before coming into force by S.C. 2008, c. 20, s. 3, provided that section 38 of the *Copyright Act*, as it read immediately before the coming into force of S.C. 1997, c. 24, s. 20(1) would continue to apply in respect of proceedings commenced but not concluded before the coming into force of S.C. 1997, c. 24, s. 20(1).

38.1. Statutory damages — (1) Subject to this section, a copyright owner may elect, at any time before final judgment is rendered, to recover, instead of damages and profits referred to in subsection 35(1), an award of statutory damages for which any one infringer is liable individually, or for which any two or more infringers are liable jointly and severally,

(*a*) in a sum of not less than $500 and not more than $20,000 that the court considers just, with respect to all infringements involved in the proceedings for each work or other subject-matter, if the infringements are for commercial purposes; and

(*b*) in a sum of not less than $100 and not more than $5,000 that the court considers just, with respect to all infringements involved in the proceedings for all works or other subject-matter, if the infringements are for non-commercial purposes.

(1.1) *Infringement of subsection 27(2.3)* — An infringement under subsection 27(2.3) may give rise to an award of statutory damages with respect to a work or other subject-matter only if the copyright in that work or other subject-matter was actually infringed as a result of the use of a service referred to in that subsection.

(1.11) *Deeming – infringement of subsection 27(2.3)* — For the purpose of subsection (1), an infringement under subsection 27(2.3) is deemed to be for a commercial purpose.

(1.12) *Infringements not involved in proceedings* — If the copyright owner has made an election under subsection (1) with respect to a defendant's infringements that are for non-commercial purposes, they are barred from recovering statutory damages under this section from that defendant with respect to any other of the defendant's infringements that were done for non-commercial purposes before the institution of the proceedings in which the election was made.

(1.2) *No other statutory damages* — If a copyright owner has made an election under subsection (1) with respect to a defendant's infringements that are for non-commercial purposes, every other copyright owner is barred from electing to recover statutory damages under this section in respect of that defendant for any of the defendant's infringements that were done for non-commercial purposes before the institution of the proceedings in which the election was made.

(2) *If defendant unaware of infringement* — If a copyright owner has made an election under subsection (1) and the defendant satisfies the court that the defendant was not aware and had no reasonable grounds to believe that the defendant had infringed copyright, the court may reduce the amount of the award under paragraph (1)(*a*) to less than $500, but not less than $200.

(3) *Special case* — In awarding statutory damages under paragraph (1)(*a*) or subsection (2), the court may award, with respect to each work or other subject-matter, a lower amount than $500 or $200, as the case may be, that the court considers just, if

(*a*) either

   (i) there is more than one work or other subject-matter in a single medium, or

   (ii) the award relates only to one or more infringements under subsection 27(2.3); and

(*b*) the awarding of even the minimum amount referred to in that paragraph or that subsection would result in a total award that, in the court's opinion, is grossly out of proportion to the infringement.

(4) *Limitation – certain acts* — A collective society or copyright owner who has authorized a collective society to act on their behalf may make an election under this section with respect to an act set out in subsection (4.1) only if applicable royalties are set out in an approved tariff or fixed under subsection 71(2) and the defendant has not paid them. If they make the election, the collective society or copyright owner may only recover, in lieu of any other remedy of a monetary nature provided by this Act, an award of statutory damages in respect of such acts in a sum of not less than three and not more than ten times the amount of the applicable royalties, as the court considers just.

(4.1) *Acts for the purposes of subsection (4)* — Subsection (4) applies with respect to the following acts:

(*a*) the performance in public of musical works or dramatico-musical works, of

131

performer's performances of such works, or of sound recordings embodying such works or performances; and

(*b*) the communication to the public by telecommunication of musical works or dramatico-musical works, other than as described in subsection 31(2), of performer's performances of such works, or of sound recordings embodying such works or performances.

(5) *Factors to consider* — In exercising its discretion under subsections (1) to (4), the court shall consider all relevant factors, including

(*a*) the good faith or bad faith of the defendant;

(*b*) the conduct of the parties before and during the proceedings;

(*c*) the need to deter other infringements of the copyright in question; and

(*d*) in the case of infringements for non-commercial purposes, the need for an award to be proportionate to the infringements, in consideration of the hardship the award may cause to the defendant, whether the infringement was for private purposes or not, and the impact of the infringements on the plaintiff.

(6) *No award* — No statutory damages may be awarded against

(*a*) an educational institution or a person acting under its authority that has committed an act referred to in section 29.6 or 29.7 and has not paid any royalties or complied with any terms and conditions fixed under this Act in relation to the commission of the act;

(*b*) an educational institution, library, archive or museum that is sued in the circumstances referred to in section 38.2;

(*c*) a person who infringes copyright under paragraph 27(2)(*e*) or section 27.1, where the copy in question was made with the consent of the copyright owner in the country where the copy was made; or

(*d*) an educational institution that is sued in the circumstances referred to in subsection 30.02(7) or a person acting under its authority who is sued in the circumstances referred to in subsection 30.02(8).

(7) *Exemplary or punitive damages not affected* — An election under subsection (1) does not affect any right that the copyright owner may have to exemplary or punitive damages.

[S.C. 1997, c. 24, s. 20(1); S.C. 2012, c. 20, s. 46; S.C. 2018, c. 27, s. 287.]

Note: S.C. 1997, c. 24, s. 20(3) provides that section 38.1 of the *Copyright Act*, as enacted by S.C. 1997, c. 24, s. 20(1) applies

(*a*) to proceedings commenced after the date of the coming into force of that subsection; and (*b*) where the infringement to which those proceedings relate occurred after that date.

38.2. Maximum amount that may be recovered — (1) An owner of copyright in a work who has not authorized a collective society to authorize its reprographic reproduction may recover, in proceedings against an educational institution, library, archive or museum that has reproduced the work, a maximum amount equal to the amount of royalties that would have been payable to the society in respect of the reprographic reproduction, if it were authorized, either

(*a*) under any agreement entered into with the collective society; or

(*b*) under a tariff approved by the Board under section 70.

(2) *Agreements with more than one collective society* — Where agreements respecting reprographic reproduction have been signed with more than one collective society or where more than one tariff applies or where both agreements and tariffs apply, the maximum amount that the copyright owner may recover is the largest amount of the royalties provided for in any of those agreements or tariffs.

(3) *Application* — Subsections (1) and (2) apply only where

(*a*) the collective society is entitled to authorize, or the tariff provides for the payment of royalties in respect of, the reprographic reproduction of that category of work; and

(*b*) copying of that general nature and extent is covered by the agreement or tariff.

[S.C. 1997, c. 24, s. 20(1); S.C. 2018, c. 27, s. 288.]

39. Injunction only remedy when defendant not aware of copyright — (1) Subject to subsection (2), in any proceedings for infringement of copyright, the plaintiff is not entitled to any remedy other than an injunction in respect of the infringement if the defendant proves that, at the date of the infringement, the defendant was not aware and had no reasonable ground for suspecting that copyright subsisted in the work or other subject-matter in question.

(2) *Exception where copyright registered* — Subsection (1) does not apply if, at the date of the infringement, the copyright was duly registered under this Act.

[S.C. 1997, c. 24, s. 20(1).]

39.1. Wide injunction — (1) When granting an injunction in respect of an infringement of copyright in a work or other subject-matter, the court may further enjoin the defendant from infringing the copyright in any other work or subject-matter if

(*a*) the plaintiff is the owner of the copyright or the person to whom an interest in the copyright has been granted by licence; and

(*b*) the plaintiff satisfies the court that the defendant will likely infringe the copyright in those other works or subject-matter unless enjoined by the court from doing so.

(2) *Application of injunction* — An injunction granted under subsection (1) may extend to works or other subject-matter

(*a*) in respect of which the plaintiff was not, at the time the proceedings were commenced, the owner of the copyright or the person to whom an interest in the copyright has been granted by licence; or

(*b*) that did not exist at the time the proceedings were commenced.
[S.C. 1997, c. 24, s. 20(1).]

Note: S.C. 1997, c. 24, s. 20(4) provides that section 39.1 of the *Copyright Act*, as enacted by S.C. 1997, c. 24, s. 20(1), applies in respect of

(*a*) proceedings commenced but not concluded before the coming into force of S.C. 1997, c. 24, s. 20(1); and

(*b*) proceedings commenced after the coming into force of S.C. 1997, c. 24, s. 20(1).

40. No injunction in case of a building — (1) Where the construction of a building or other structure that infringes or that, if completed, would infringe the copyright in some other work has been commenced, the owner of the copyright is not entitled to obtain an injunction in respect of the construction of that building or structure or to order its demolition.

(2) *Certain remedies inapplicable* — Sections 38 and 42 do not apply in any case in respect of which subsection (1) applies.
[S.C. 1997, c. 24, s. 21.]

TECHNOLOGICAL PROTECTION MEASURES AND RIGHTS MANAGEMENT INFORMATION

41. Definitions — The following definitions apply in this section and in sections 41.1 to 41.21.

circumvent means,

(*a*) in respect of a technological protection measure within the meaning of paragraph (*a*) of the definition **technological protection measure**, to descramble a scrambled work or decrypt an encrypted work or to otherwise avoid, bypass, remove, deactivate or impair the technological protection measure, unless it is done with the authority of the copyright owner; and

(*b*) in respect of a technological protection measure within the meaning of paragraph (*b*) of the definition **technological protection measure**, to avoid, bypass, remove, deactivate or impair the technological protection measure.

technological protection measure means any effective technology, device or component that, in the ordinary course of its operation,

(*a*) controls access to a work, to a performer's performance fixed in a sound recording or to a sound recording and whose use is authorized by the copyright owner; or

(*b*) restricts the doing — with respect to a work, to a performer's performance fixed in a sound recording or to a sound recording – of any act referred to in section 3, 15 or 18 and any act for which remuneration is payable under section 19.

[S.C. 2012, c. 20, s. 47.]

41.1. Prohibition — (1) No person shall

(*a*) circumvent a technological protection measure within the meaning of paragraph (*a*) of the definition ***technological protection measure*** in section 41;

(*b*) offer services to the public or provide services if

    (i) the services are offered or provided primarily for the purposes of circumventing a technological protection measure,

    (ii) the uses or purposes of those services are not commercially significant other than when they are offered or provided for the purposes of circumventing a technological protection measure, or

    (iii) the person markets those services as being for the purposes of circumventing a technological protection measure or acts in concert with another person in order to market those services as being for those purposes; or

(*c*) manufacture, import, distribute, offer for sale or rental or provide — including by selling or renting — any technology, device or component if

    (i) the technology, device or component is designed or produced primarily for the purposes of circumventing a technological protection measure,

    (ii) the uses or purposes of the technology, device or component are not commercially significant other than when it is used for the purposes of circumventing a technological protection measure, or

    (iii) the person markets the technology, device or component as being for the purposes of circumventing a technological protection measure or acts in concert with another person in order to market the technology, device or component as being for those purposes.

(2) *Circumvention of technological protection measure* — The owner of the copyright in a work, a performer's performance fixed in a sound recording or a

sound recording in respect of which paragraph (1)(*a*) has been contravened is, subject to this Act and any regulations made under section 41.21, entitled to all remedies — by way of injunction, damages, accounts, delivery up and otherwise — that are or may be conferred by law for the infringement of copyright against the person who contravened that paragraph.

(3) *No statutory damages* — The owner of the copyright in a work, a performer's performance fixed in a sound recording or a sound recording in respect of which paragraph (1)(*a*) has been contravened may not elect under section 38.1 to recover statutory damages from an individual who contravened that paragraph only for his or her own private purposes.

(4) *Services, technology, device or component* — Every owner of the copyright in a work, a performer's performance fixed in a sound recording or a sound recording in respect of which a technological protection measure has been or could be circumvented as a result of the contravention of paragraph (1)(*b*) or (*c*) is, subject to this Act and any regulations made under section 41.21, entitled to all remedies — by way of injunction, damages, accounts, delivery up and otherwise — that are or may be conferred by law for the infringement of copyright against the person who contravened paragraph (1)(*b*) or (*c*).
[S.C. 2012, c. 20, s. 47.]

41.11. Law enforcement and national security — (1) Paragraph 41.1(1)(*a*) does not apply if a technological protection measure is circumvented for the purposes of an investigation related to the enforcement of any Act of Parliament or any Act of the legislature of a province, or for the purposes of activities related to the protection of national security.

(2) *Services* — Paragraph 41.1(1)(*b*) does not apply if the services are provided by or for the persons responsible for carrying out such an investigation or such activities.

(3) *Technology, device or component* — Paragraph 41.1(1)(*c*) does not apply if the technology, device or component is manufactured, imported or provided by the persons responsible for carrying out such an investigation or such activities, or is manufactured, imported, provided or offered for sale or rental as a service provided to those persons.
[S.C. 2012, c. 20, s. 47.]

41.12. Interoperability of computer programs — (1) Paragraph 41.1(1)(*a*) does not apply to a person who owns a computer program or a copy of one, or has a licence to use the program or copy, and who circumvents a technological protection measure that protects that program or copy for the sole purpose of obtaining information that would allow the person to make the program and any other computer program interoperable.

(2) *Services* — Paragraph 41.1(1)(*b*) does not apply to a person who offers

services to the public or provides services for the purposes of circumventing a technological protection measure if the person does so for the purpose of making the computer program and any other computer program interoperable.

(3) *Technology, device or component* — Paragraph 41.1(1)(*c*) does not apply to a person who manufactures, imports or provides a technology, device or component for the purposes of circumventing a technological protection measure if the person does so for the purpose of making the computer program and any other computer program interoperable and

(*a*) uses that technology, device or component only for that purpose; or

(*b*) provides that technology, device or component to another person only for that purpose.

(4) *Sharing of information* — A person referred to in subsection (1) may communicate the information obtained under that subsection to another person for the purposes of allowing that person to make the computer program and any other computer program interoperable.

(5) *Limitation* — A person to whom the technology, device or component referred to in subsection (3) is provided or to whom the information referred to in subsection (4) is communicated may use it only for the purpose of making the computer program and any other computer program interoperable.

(6) *Non-application* — However, a person is not entitled to benefit from the exceptions under subsections (1) to (3) or (5) if, for the purposes of making the computer program and any other computer program interoperable, the person does an act that constitutes an infringement of copyright.

(7) *Non-application* — Furthermore, a person is not entitled to benefit from the exception under subsection (4) if, for the purposes of making the computer program and any other computer program interoperable, the person does an act that constitutes an infringement of copyright or an act that contravenes any Act of Parliament or any Act of the legislature of a province.
[S.C. 2012, c. 20, s. 47.]

41.13. Encryption research — (1) Paragraph 41.1(1)(*a*) does not apply to a person who, for the purposes of encryption research, circumvents a technological protection measure by means of decryption if

(*a*) it would not be practical to carry out the research without circumventing the technological protection measure;

(*b*) the person has lawfully obtained the work, the performer's performance fixed in a sound recording or the sound recording that is protected by the technological protection measure; and

(*c*) the person has informed the owner of the copyright in the work, the

137

performer's performance fixed in a sound recording or the sound recording who has applied the technological protection measure.

(2) *Non-application* — However, a person acting in the circumstances referred to in subsection (1) is not entitled to benefit from the exception under that subsection if the person does an act that constitutes an infringement of copyright or an act that contravenes any Act of Parliament or any Act of the legislature of a province.

(3) *Technology, device or component* — Paragraph 41.1(1)(*c*) does not apply to a person referred to in subsection (1) who manufactures a technology, device or component for the purposes of circumventing a technological protection measure that is subject to paragraph 41.1(1)(*a*) if the person does so for the purpose of encryption research and

(*a*) uses that technology, device or component only for that purpose; or

(*b*) provides that technology, device or component only for that purpose to another person who is collaborating with the person.

[S.C. 2012, c. 20, s. 47.]

41.14. Personal information — (1) Paragraph 41.1(1)(*a*) does not apply to a person who circumvents a technological protection measure if

(*a*) the work, performer's performance fixed in a sound recording or sound recording that is protected by the technological protection measure is not accompanied by a notice indicating that its use will permit a third party to collect and communicate personal information relating to the user or, in the case where it is accompanied by such a notice, the user is not provided with the option to prevent the collection and communication of personal information without the user's use of it being restricted; and

(*b*) the only purpose of circumventing the technological protection measure is to verify whether it permits the collection or communication of personal information and, if it does, to prevent it.

(2) *Services, technology, device or component* — Paragraphs 41.1(1)(*b*) and (*c*) do not apply to a person who offers services to the public or provides services, or manufactures, imports or provides a technology, device or component, for the purposes of circumventing a technological protection measure in accordance with subsection (1), to the extent that the services, technology, device or component do not unduly impair the technological protection measure.

[S.C. 2012, c. 20, s. 47.]

41.15. Security — (1) Paragraph 41.1(1)(*a*) does not apply to a person who circumvents a technological protection measure that is subject to that paragraph for the sole purpose of, with the consent of the owner or administrator of a computer, computer system or computer network, assessing the vulnerability of the computer, system or network or correcting any security flaws.

(2) *Services* — Paragraph 41.1(1)(*b*) does not apply if the services are provided to a person described in subsection (1).

(3) *Technology, device or component* — Paragraph 41.1(1)(*c*) does not apply if the technology, device or component is manufactured or imported by a person described in subsection (1), or is manufactured, imported, provided – including by selling or renting – offered for sale or rental or distributed as a service provided to that person.

(4) *Non-application* — A person acting in the circumstances referred to in subsection (1) is not entitled to benefit from the exception under that subsection if the person does an act that constitutes an infringement of copyright or an act that contravenes any Act of Parliament or any Act of the legislature of a province.
[S.C. 2012, c. 20, s. 47.]

41.16. Persons with perceptual disabilities — (1) Paragraph 41.1(1)(*a*) does not apply to a person with a perceptual disability, to another person acting at their request or to a non-profit organization, as defined in section 32.02, acting for their benefit, if that person or organization circumvents a technological protection measure solely for one or more of the following purposes:

(*a*) to make a work, a performer's performance fixed in a sound recording or a sound recording perceptible to the person with a perceptual disability;

(*b*) to permit a person, or a non-profit organization referred to in subsection 32(1), to benefit from the exception set out in section 32;

(*c*) to permit a non-profit organization referred to in subsection 32.01(1) to benefit from the exception set out in section 32.01.

(2) *Services, technology, device or component* — Paragraphs 41.1(1)(*b*) and (*c*) do not apply to a person who offers or provides services to persons or non-profit organizations referred to in subsection (1) or who manufactures, imports or provides a technology, device or component, for the sole purpose of enabling those persons or non-profit organizations to circumvent a technological protection measure in accordance with that subsection.
[S.C. 2012, c. 20, s. 47; S.C. 2016, c. 4, s. 4.]

41.17. Broadcasting undertakings — Paragraph 41.1(1)(*a*) does not apply to a broadcasting undertaking that circumvents a technological protection measure for the sole purpose of making an ephemeral reproduction of a work, a performer's performance fixed in a sound recording or a sound recording in accordance with section 30.9, unless the owner of the copyright in the work, the performer's performance fixed in a sound recording or the sound recording that is protected by the technological protection measure makes available the necessary means to enable the making of such a reproduction in a timely manner in light of the broadcasting undertaking's business requirements.
[S.C. 2012, c. 20, s. 47.]

41.18. Radio apparatus — (1) Paragraph 41.1(1)(*a*) does not apply to a person who circumvents a technological protection measure on a radio apparatus for the sole purpose of gaining access to a telecommunications service by means of the radio apparatus.

(2) *Services or technology, device or component* — Paragraphs 41.1(1)(*b*) and (*c*) do not apply to a person who offers the services to the public or provides the services, or manufactures, imports or provides the technology, device or component, for the sole purpose of facilitating access to a telecommunications service by means of a radio apparatus.

(3) *Definitions* — The following definitions apply in this section.

radio apparatus has the same meaning as in section 2 of the *Radiocommunication Act*.*

telecommunications service has the same meaning as in subsection 2(1) of the *Telecommunications Act*.**

[S.C. 2012, c. 20, s. 47.]

---

* *Radiocommunication Act*, R.S.C. 1985, c. R-2

radio apparatus means a device or combination of devices intended for, or capable of being used for, radiocommunication;

** *Telecommunications Act*, S.C. 1993, c. 38

telecommunications service means a service provided by means of telecommunications facilities and includes the provision in whole or in part of telecommunications facilities and any related equipment, whether by sale, lease or otherwise;

41.19. Reduction of damages — A court may reduce or remit the amount of damages it awards in the circumstances described in subsection 41.1(1) if the defendant satisfies the court that the defendant was not aware, and had no reasonable grounds to believe, that the defendant's acts constituted a contravention of that subsection.

[S.C. 2012, c. 20, s. 47.]

41.20. Injunction only remedy — If a court finds that a defendant that is a library, archive or museum or an educational institution has contravened subsection 41.1(1) and the defendant satisfies the court that it was not aware, and had no reasonable grounds to believe, that its actions constituted a contravention of that subsection, the plaintiff is not entitled to any remedy other than an injunction.

[S.C. 2012, c. 20, s. 47.]

41.21. Regulations — (1) The Governor in Council may make regulations excluding from the application of section 41.1 any technological protection measure that protects a work, a performer's performance fixed in a sound recording or a sound recording, or classes of them, or any class of such technological protection measures, if the Governor in Council considers that the application of that section to the technological protection measure or class of technological protection measures would unduly restrict competition in the aftermarket sector in which the technological protection measure is used.

(2) *Regulations* — The Governor in Council may make regulations

(a) prescribing additional circumstances in which paragraph 41.1(1)(*a*) does not apply, having regard to the following factors:

(i) whether not being permitted to circumvent a technological protection measure that is subject to that paragraph could adversely affect the use a person may make of a work, a performer's performance fixed in a sound recording or a sound recording when that use is authorized,

(ii) whether the work, the performer's performance fixed in a sound recording or the sound recording is commercially available,

(iii) whether not being permitted to circumvent a technological protection measure that is subject to that paragraph could adversely affect criticism, review, news reporting, commentary, parody, satire, teaching, scholarship or research that could be made or done in respect of the work, the performer's performance fixed in a sound recording or the sound recording,

(iv) whether being permitted to circumvent a technological protection measure that is subject to that paragraph could adversely affect the market for the work, the performer's performance fixed in a sound recording or the sound recording or its market value,

(v) whether the work, the performer's performance fixed in a sound recording or the sound recording is commercially available in a medium and in a quality that is appropriate for non-profit archival, preservation or educational uses, and

(vi) any other relevant factor; and

(b) requiring the owner of the copyright in a work, a performer's performance fixed in a sound recording or a sound recording that is protected by a technological protection measure to provide access to the work, performer's performance fixed in a sound recording or sound recording to persons who are entitled to the benefit of any of the limitations on the application of paragraph 41.1(1)(*a*) prescribed under paragraph (*a*). The regulations may prescribe the manner in which, and the time within which, access is to be provided, as well as any conditions that the owner of the copyright is to comply with.

[S.C. 2012, c. 20, s. 47.]

41.22. Prohibition – rights management information — (1) No person shall knowingly remove or alter any rights management information in electronic form without the consent of the owner of the copyright in the work, the performer's performance or the sound recording, if the person knows or should have known that the removal or alteration will facilitate or conceal any infringement of the owner's copyright or adversely affect the owner's right to remuneration under section 19.

(2) *Removal or alteration of rights management information* — The owner of the copyright in a work, a performer's performance fixed in a sound recording or a sound recording is, subject to this Act, entitled to all remedies – by way of injunction, damages, accounts, delivery up and otherwise – that are or may be conferred by law for the infringement of copyright against a person who contravenes subsection (1).

(3) *Subsequent acts* — The copyright owner referred to in subsection (2) has the same remedies against a person who, without the owner's consent, knowingly does any of the following acts with respect to any material form of the work, the performer's performance fixed in a sound recording or the sound recording and knows or should have known that the rights management information has been removed or altered in a way that would give rise to a remedy under that subsection:

(a)   sells it or rents it out;

(b)   distributes it to an extent that the copyright owner is prejudicially affected;

(c)   by way of trade, distributes it, exposes or offers it for sale or rental or exhibits it in public;

(d)   imports it into Canada for the purpose of doing anything referred to in any of paragraphs (a) to (c); or

(e)   communicates it to the public by telecommunication.

(4) *Definition of* **rights management information** — In this section, *rights management information* means information that

(a)   is attached to or embodied in a copy of a work, a performer's performance fixed in a sound recording or a sound recording, or appears in connection with its communication to the public by telecommunication; and

(b)   identifies or permits the identification of the work or its author, the performance or its performer, the sound recording or its maker or the holder of any rights in the work, the performance or the sound recording, or concerns the terms or conditions of the work's, performance's or sound recording's use.

[S.C. 2012, c. 20, s. 47.]

GENERAL PROVISIONS

41.23. Protection of separate rights — (1) Subject to this section, the owner of any copyright, or any person or persons deriving any right, title or interest by assignment or grant in writing from the owner, may individually for himself or herself, as a party to the proceedings in his or her own name, protect and enforce any right that he or she holds, and, to the extent of that right, title and interest, is entitled to the remedies provided by this Act.

(2) *Copyright owner to be made party* — If proceedings under subsection (1) are taken by a person other than the copyright owner, the copyright owner shall be made a party to those proceedings, except

(*a*) in the case of proceedings taken under section 44.12, 44.2 or 44.4;

(*b*) in the case of interlocutory proceedings, unless the court is of the opinion that the interests of justice require the copyright owner to be a party; and

(*c*) in any other case in which the court is of the opinion that the interests of justice do not require the copyright owner to be a party.

[S.C. 2014, c. 32, s. 6.]

(3) *Owner's liability for costs* — A copyright owner who is made a party to proceedings under subsection (2) is not liable for any costs unless the copyright owner takes part in the proceedings.

(4) *Apportionment of damages, profits* — If a copyright owner is made a party to proceedings under subsection (2), the court, in awarding damages or profits, shall, subject to any agreement between the person who took the proceedings and the copyright owner, apportion the damages or profits referred to in subsection 35(1) between them as the court considers appropriate.

[S.C. 2012, c. 20, s. 47.]

41.24. Concurrent jurisdiction of Federal Court — The Federal Court has concurrent jurisdiction with provincial courts to hear and determine all proceedings, other than the prosecution of offences under sections 42 and 43, for the enforcement of a provision of this Act or of the civil remedies provided by this Act.

[S.C. 2012, c. 20, s. 47.]

PROVISIONS RESPECTING PROVIDERS OF NETWORK SERVICES OR INFORMATION LOCATION TOOLS

41.25. Notice of claimed infringement — (1) An owner of the copyright in a work or other subject-matter may send a notice of claimed infringement to a person who provides

(*a*) the means, in the course of providing services related to the operation of the

Internet or another digital network, of telecommunication through which the electronic location that is the subject of the claim of infringement is connected to the Internet or another digital network;

(b) for the purpose set out in subsection 31.1(4), the digital memory that is used for the electronic location to which the claim of infringement relates; or

(c) an information location tool as defined in subsection 41.27(5).

(2) *Form and content of notice* — A notice of claimed infringement shall be in writing in the form, if any, prescribed by regulation and shall

(a) state the claimant's name and address and any other particulars prescribed by regulation that enable communication with the claimant;

(b) identify the work or other subject-matter to which the claimed infringement relates;

(c) state the claimant's interest or right with respect to the copyright in the work or other subject-matter;

(d) specify the location data for the electronic location to which the claimed infringement relates;

(e) specify the infringement that is claimed;

(f) specify the date and time of the commission of the claimed infringement; and

(g) contain any other information that may be prescribed by regulation.

(3) *Prohibited content* — A notice of claimed infringement shall not contain

(a) an offer to settle the claimed infringement;

(b) a request or demand, made in relation to the claimed infringement, for payment or for personal information;

(c) a reference, including by way of hyperlink, to such an offer, request or demand; and

(d) any other information that may be prescribed by regulation.

[S.C. 2012, c. 20, s. 47; S.C. 2018, c. 27, s. 243.]

41.26. Obligations related to notice — (1) A person described in paragraph 41.25(1)(a) or (b) who receives a notice of claimed infringement that complies with subsections 41.25(2) and (3) shall, on being paid any fee that the person has lawfully charged for doing so,

(a) as soon as feasible forward the notice electronically to the person to whom the electronic location identified by the location data specified in the notice belongs and inform the claimant of its forwarding or, if applicable, of the reason why it was not possible to forward it; and

(*b*) retain records that will allow the identity of the person to whom the electronic location belongs to be determined, and do so for six months beginning on the day on which the notice of claimed infringement is received or, if the claimant commences proceedings relating to the claimed infringement and so notifies the person before the end of those six months, for one year after the day on which the person receives the notice of claimed infringement.

(2) *Fees related to notices* — The Minister may, by regulation, fix the maximum fee that a person may charge for performing his or her obligations under subsection (1). If no maximum is fixed by regulation, the person may not charge any amount under that subsection.

(3) *Damages related to notices* — A claimant's only remedy against a person who fails to perform his or her obligations under subsection (1) is statutory damages in an amount that the court considers just, but not less than $5,000 and not more than $10,000.

(4) *Regulations – change of amounts* — The Governor in Council may, by regulation, increase or decrease the minimum or maximum amount of statutory damages set out in subsection (3).

[S.C. 2012, c. 20, s. 47; S.C. 2018, c. 27, s. 244.]

41.27. Injunctive relief only – providers of information location tools — (1) In any proceedings for infringement of copyright, the owner of the copyright in a work or other subject-matter is not entitled to any remedy other than an injunction against a provider of an information location tool that is found to have infringed copyright by making a reproduction of the work or other subject-matter or by communicating that reproduction to the public by telecommunication.

(2) *Conditions for application* — Subsection (1) applies only if the provider, in respect of the work or other subject-matter,

(*a*) makes and caches, or does any act similar to caching, the reproduction in an automated manner for the purpose of providing the information location tool;

(*b*) communicates that reproduction to the public by telecommunication for the purpose of providing the information that has been located by the information location tool;

(*c*) does not modify the reproduction, other than for technical reasons;

(*d*) complies with any conditions relating to the making or caching, or doing of any act similar to caching, of reproductions of the work or other subject-matter, or to the communication of the reproductions to the public by telecommunication, that were specified in a manner consistent with industry practice by whoever made the work or other subject-matter available through the Internet or another digital network and that lend themselves to automated reading and execution; and

(e) does not interfere with the use of technology that is lawful and consistent with industry practice in order to obtain data on the use of the work or other subject-matter.

(3) *Limitation* — If the provider receives a notice of claimed infringement, relating to a work or other subject-matter, that complies with subsections 41.25(2) and (3) after the work or other subject-matter has been removed from the electronic location set out in the notice, then subsection (1) applies, with respect to reproductions made from that electronic location, only to infringements that occurred before the day that is 30 days – or the period that may be prescribed by regulation – after the day on which the provider receives the notice.

(4) *Exception* — Subsection (1) does not apply to the provision of the information location tool if the provision of that tool constitutes an infringement of copyright under subsection 27(2.3).

(4.1) *Factors – scope of injunction* — If it grants an injunction as set out in subsection (1), the court shall, among any other relevant factors, consider the following in establishing the terms of the injunction:

(a) the harm likely to be suffered by the copyright owner if steps are not taken to prevent or restrain the infringement; and

(b) the burden imposed on the provider and on the operation of the information location tool, including

    (i) the aggregate effect of the injunction and any injunctions from other proceedings,

    (ii) whether implementing the injunction would be technically feasible and effective in addressing the infringement,

    (iii) whether implementing the injunction would interfere with the use of the information location tool for non-infringing acts, and

    (iv) the availability of less burdensome and comparably effective means of preventing or restraining the infringement.

(4.2) *Limitation* — A court is not permitted to grant an injunction under section 39.1 against a provider who is the subject of an injunction set out in subsection (1).

(5) *Meaning of **information location tool*** — In this section, **information location tool** means any tool that makes it possible to locate information that is available through the Internet or another digital network.
[S.C. 2012, c. 20, s. 47; S.C. 2018, c. 27, s. 245.]

CRIMINAL REMEDIES

[S.C. 1997, c. 24, s. 23.]

42. Offences — (1) Every person commits an offence who knowingly

(*a*) makes for sale or rental an infringing copy of a work or other subject-matter in which copyright subsists,

(*b*) sells or rents out, or by way of trade exposes or offers for sale or rental, an infringing copy of a work or other subject-matter in which copyright subsists,

(*c*) distributes infringing copies of a work or other subject-matter in which copyright subsists, either for the purpose of trade or to such an extent as to affect prejudicially the owner of the copyright,

(*d*) by way of trade exhibits in public an infringing copy of a work or other subject-matter in which copyright subsists,

(*e*) possesses, for sale, rental, distribution for the purpose of trade or exhibition in public by way of trade, an infringing copy of a work or other subject-matter in which copyright subsists;

(*f*) imports, for sale or rental, into Canada any infringing copy of a work or other subject-matter in which copyright subsists; or

(*g*) exports or attempts to export, for sale or rental, an infringing copy of a work or other subject-matter in which copyright subsists.

(2) *Possession and performance offences* — Every person commits an offence who knowingly

(*a*) makes or possesses any plate that is specifically designed or adapted for the purpose of making infringing copies of any work or other subject-matter in which copyright subsists, or

(*b*) for private profit causes to be performed in public, without the consent of the owner of the copyright, any work or other subject-matter in which copyright subsists

(*c*) [Repealed by S.C. 2014, c. 32, s. 4.]

(*d*) [Repealed by S.C. 2014, c. 32, s. 4.]

(2.1) *Punishment* — Every person who commits an offence under subsection (1) or (2) is liable

(*a*) on conviction on indictment, to a fine of not more than $1,000,000 or to imprisonment for a term of not more than five years or to both; or

(*b*) on summary conviction, to a fine of not more than $25,000 or to imprisonment for a term of not more than six months or to both.

(3) *Power of court to deal with copies or plates* — The court before which any proceedings under this section are taken may, on conviction, order that all copies of the work or other subject-matter that appear to it to be infringing copies, or all plates in the possession of the offender predominantly used for making infringing copies, be destroyed or delivered up to the owner of the copyright or otherwise dealt with as the court may think fit.

(3.01) *Notice* — Before making an order under subsection (3), the court shall require that notice be given to the owner of the copies or plates and to any other person who, in the court's opinion, appears to have a right or interest in them, unless the court is of the opinion that the interests of justice do not require that the notice be given.

(3.1) *Circumvention of technological protection measure* — Every person, except a person who is acting on behalf of a library, archive or museum or an educational institution, is guilty of an offence who knowingly and for commercial purposes contravenes section 41.1 and is liable

(*a*)   on conviction on indictment, to a fine not exceeding $1,000,000 or to imprisonment for a term not exceeding five years or to both; or

(*b*)   on summary conviction, to a fine not exceeding $25,000 or to imprisonment for a term not exceeding six months or to both.

(3.2) *Offence – infringement related to rights management information* — Every person, except a person who is acting on behalf of a library, archive or museum or an educational institution, commits an offence who knowingly and for commercial purposes

(*a*)   removes or alters any rights management information in electronic form without the consent of the owner of the copyright in the work, the performer's performance fixed in a sound recording or the sound recording, if the person knows that the removal or alteration will facilitate or conceal any infringement of the owner's copyright or adversely affect the owner's right to remuneration under section 19; or

(*b*)   does any of the acts referred to in paragraphs 41.22(3)(a) to (e) with respect to any material form of the work, the performer's performance fixed in a sound recording or the sound recording without the consent of the owner of the copyright and knows that

     (i)   the rights management information in electronic form has been removed or altered without the consent of the owner of the copyright, and

     (ii)   the removal or alteration will facilitate or conceal any infringement of the owner's copyright or adversely affect the owner's right to remuneration under section 19.

(3.3) *Punishment* — Every person who commits an offence under subsection (3.2) is liable

(*a*) on conviction on indictment to a fine of not more than $1,000,000 or to imprisonment for a term of not more than five years or to both; or

(*b*) on summary conviction to a fine of not more than $25,000 or to imprisonment for a term of not more than six months or to both.

(3.4) *Definition of rights management information* — In subsection (3.2), **rights management information** has the same meaning as in subsection 41.22(4).

(4) *Limitation period* — Proceedings by summary conviction in respect of an offence under this section may be instituted at any time within, but not later than, two years after the time when the offence was committed.

(5) *Parallel importation* — For the purposes of this section, a copy of a work or other subject-matter is not infringing if the copy was made with the consent of the owner of the copyright in the country where the copy was made.

[R.S.C. 1985, c. 10 (4th Supp.), s. 10; S.C. 1997, c. 24, s. 24; S.C. 2012, c. 20, s. 48; S.C. 2014, c. 32, s. 4; S.C. 2020, c. 1, s. 30.]

43. Infringement in case of dramatic, operatic or musical work — (1) Any person who, without the written consent of the owner of the copyright or of the legal representative of the owner, knowingly performs or causes to be performed in public and for private profit the whole or any part, constituting an infringement, of any dramatic or operatic work or musical composition in which copyright subsists in Canada is guilty of an offence and liable on summary conviction to a fine not exceeding two hundred and fifty dollars and, in the case of a second or subsequent offence, either to that fine or to imprisonment for a term not exceeding two months or to both.

(2) *Change or suppression of title or author's name* — Any person who makes or causes to be made any change in or suppression of the title, or the name of the author, of any dramatic or operatic work or musical composition in which copyright subsists in Canada, or who makes or causes to be made any change in the work or composition itself without the written consent of the author or of his legal representative, in order that the work or composition may be performed in whole or in part in public for private profit, is guilty of an offence and liable on summary conviction to a fine not exceeding five hundred dollars and, in the case of a second or subsequent offence, either to that fine or to imprisonment for a term not exceeding four months or to both.

LIMITATION OR PRESCRIPTION PERIOD

43.1. Limitation or prescription period for civil remedies — (1) Subject to subsection (2), a court may award a remedy for any act or omission that has been done contrary to this Act only if

(a) the proceedings for the act or omission giving rise to a remedy are commenced within three years after it occurred, in the case where the plaintiff knew, or could reasonably have been expected to know, of the act or omission at the time it occurred; or

(b) the proceedings for the act or omission giving rise to a remedy are commenced within three years after the time when the plaintiff first knew of it, or could reasonably have been expected to know of it, in the case where the plaintiff did not know, and could not reasonably have been expected to know, of the act or omission at the time it occurred.

(2) *Restriction* — The court shall apply the limitation or prescription period set out in paragraph (1)(*a*) or (*b*) only in respect of a party who pleads a limitation period.

[S.C. 2012, c. 20, s. 49.]

Note: See also Transitional Provisions (section 62) of S.C. 2012, c. 20.

IMPORTATION AND EXPORTATION

[S.C. 1994, c. 47, s. 65; S.C. 1997, c. 24, s. 26; S.C. 2014, c. 32, s. 5.]

INTERPRETATION

44. Definitions — The following definitions apply in sections 44.02 to 44.4.

court means the Federal Court or the superior court of a province.

customs officer has the meaning assigned by the definition *officer* in subsection 2(1) of the *Customs Act.**

duties has the same meaning as in subsection 2(1) of the *Customs Act.**

Minister means the Minister of Public Safety and Emergency Preparedness.

release has the same meaning as in subsection 2(1) of the *Customs Act.**

working day means a day other than a Saturday or a holiday.

[R.S.C. 1985, c. 41 (3rd Supp.), s. 116; S.C. 1997, c. 36, s. 205; S.C. 1999, c. 17, s. 119; S.C. 2005, c. 38, s. 139(b); S.C. 2014, c. 32, s. 5.]

---

* *Customs Act*, **R.S.C. 1985, c. 1 (2nd Supp.)**

duties **means any duties or taxes levied or imposed on imported goods under the** *Customs Tariff*, **the** *Excise Act, 2001*, **the** *Excise Tax Act*, **the** *Special Import Measures Act* **or any other Act of Parliament, but, for the purposes of subsection 3(1), paragraphs 59(3)(b) and 65(1)(b), sections 69 and 73 and subsections 74(1), 75(2) and 76(1), does not include taxes imposed under Part IX of the** *Excise Tax Act*;

. . .

officer **means a person employed in the administration or enforcement of this**

Act, the *Customs Tariff* or the *Special Import Measures Act* and includes any member of the Royal Canadian Mounted Police;

. . .

release means

(a) in respect of goods, to authorize the removal of the goods from a customs office, sufferance warehouse, bonded warehouse or duty free shop for use in Canada, and

(b) in respect of goods to which paragraph 32(2)(b) applies, to receive the goods at the place of business of the importer, owner or consignee;

[S.C. 1995, c. 41, s. 1; S.C. 1997, c. 36, s. 147; S.C. 2002, c. 22, s. 328; S.C. 2001, c. 25, s. 1.]

PROHIBITION AND DETENTION BY CUSTOMS OFFICER

PROHIBITION

44.01. Prohibition on importation or exportation — (1) Copies of a work or other subject-matter in which copyright subsists shall not be imported or exported if

(a) they were made without the consent of the owner of the copyright in the country where they were made; and

(b) they infringe copyright or, if they were not made in Canada, they would infringe copyright had they been made in Canada by the person who made them.

(2) *Exception* — Subsection (1) does not apply to copies that are imported or exported by an individual in their possession or baggage if the circumstances, including the number of copies, indicate that the copies are intended only for their personal use.

[S.C. 2014, c. 32, s. 5; S.C. 2020, c. 1, s. 31.]

REQUEST FOR ASSISTANCE

44.02. Request for assistance — (1) The owner of copyright in a work or other subject-matter may file with the Minister, in the form and manner specified by the Minister, a request for assistance in pursuing remedies under this Act with respect to copies imported or exported in contravention of section 44.01.

(2) *Information in request* — The request for assistance shall include the copyright owner's name and address in Canada and any other information that is required by the Minister, including information about the work or other subject-matter in question.

(3) *Validity period* — A request for assistance is valid for a period of two years beginning on the day on which it is accepted by the Minister. The Minister may, at the request of the copyright owner, extend the period for two years, and may do so more than once.

(4) *Security* — The Minister may, as a condition of accepting a request for assistance or of extending a request's period of validity, require that the copyright owner furnish security, in an amount and form fixed by the Minister, for the payment of an amount for which the copyright owner becomes liable under section 44.07.

(5) *Update* — The copyright owner shall inform the Minister in writing, as soon as practicable, of any changes to

(*a*)   the subsistence of the copyright that is the subject of the request for assistance; or

(*b*)   the ownership of that copyright.

[S.C. 2014, c. 32, s. 5.]

MEASURES RELATING TO DETAINED COPIES

44.03. Provision of information by customs officer — A customs officer who is detaining copies of a work or other subject-matter under section 101 of the *Customs Act** may, in the officer's discretion, to obtain information about whether the importation or exportation of the copies is prohibited under section 44.01, provide the owner of copyright in that work or subject-matter with a sample of the copies and with any information about the copies that the customs officer reasonably believes does not directly or indirectly identify any person.

[S.C. 2014, c. 32, s. 5.]

** *Customs Act*, R.S.C. 1985, c. 1 (2nd Supp.)**

101. *Detention of controlled goods* — Goods that have been imported or are about to be exported may be detained by an officer until he is satisfied that the goods have been dealt with in accordance with this Act, and any other Act of Parliament that prohibits, controls or regulates the importation or exportation of goods, and any regulations made thereunder.

44.04. Provision of information to pursue remedy — (1) A customs officer who is detaining copies of a work or other subject-matter under section 101 of the *Customs Act** and who has reasonable grounds to suspect that the importation or exportation of the copies is prohibited under section 44.01 may, in the officer's discretion, if the Minister has accepted a request for assistance with respect to the work or subject-matter filed by the owner of copyright in it, provide that owner with a sample of the copies and with information about the copies that could assist them in pursuing a remedy under this Act, such as

(*a*)   a description of the copies and of their characteristics;

(*b*)   the name and address of their owner, importer, exporter and consignee and of the person who made them and of any other person involved in their movement;

(*c*)   their quantity;

(*d*)   the countries in which they were made and through which they passed in transit; and

(*e*)   the day on which they were imported, if applicable.

(2) *Detention* — Subject to subsection (3), the customs officer shall not detain, for the purpose of enforcing section 44.01, the copies for more than 10 working days — or, if the copies are perishable, for more than five days — after the day on which the customs officer first sends or makes available a sample or information to the copyright owner under subsection (1). At the request of the copyright owner made while the copies are detained for the purpose of enforcing section 44.01, the customs officer may, having regard to the circumstances, detain non-perishable copies for one additional period of not more than 10 working days.

(3) *Notice of proceedings* — If, before the copies are no longer detained for the purpose of enforcing section 44.01, the owner of copyright has provided the Minister, in the manner specified by the Minister, with a copy of a document filed with a court commencing proceedings to obtain a remedy under this Act with respect to the detained copies, the customs officer shall continue to detain them until the Minister is informed in writing that

(*a*)   the proceedings are finally disposed of, settled or abandoned;

(*b*)   a court directs that the copies are no longer to be detained for the purpose of the proceedings; or

(*c*)   the copyright owner consents to the copies no longer being so detained.

(4) *Continued detention* — The occurrence of any of the events referred to in paragraphs (3)(*a*) to (*c*) does not preclude a customs officer from continuing to detain the copies under the *Customs Act** for a purpose other than the proceedings. [S.C. 2014, c. 32, s. 5; S.C. 2020, c. 1, s. 32.]

---

* *Customs Act*, **R.S.C. 1985, c. 1 (2nd Supp.)**

101. *Detention of controlled goods* — Goods that have been imported or are about to be exported may be detained by an officer until he is satisfied that the goods have been dealt with in accordance with this Act, and any other Act of Parliament that prohibits, controls or regulates the importation or

exportation of goods, and any regulations made thereunder.

44.05. Restriction on information use — section 44.03 — (1) A person who receives a sample or information that is provided under section 44.03 shall not use the information, or information that is derived from the sample, for any purpose other than to give information to the customs officer about whether the importation or exportation of the copies is prohibited under section 44.01.

(2) *Restriction on information use – subsection 44.04(1)* — A person who receives a sample or information that is provided under subsection 44.04(1) shall not use the information, or information that is derived from the sample, for any purpose other than to pursue remedies under this Act.

(3) *For greater certainty* — For greater certainty, subsection (2) does not prevent the confidential communication of information about the copies for the purpose of reaching an out-of-court settlement.
[S.C. 2014, c. 32, s. 5.]

44.06. Inspection — After a sample or information has been provided under subsection 44.04(1), a customs officer may, in the officer's discretion, give the owner, importer, exporter and consignee of the detained copies and the owner of copyright an opportunity to inspect the copies.
[S.C. 2014, c. 32, s. 5.]

44.07. Liability for charges — (1) The owner of copyright who has received a sample or information under subsection 44.04(1) is liable to Her Majesty in right of Canada for the storage and handling charges for the detained copies—and, if applicable, for the charges for destroying them—for the period beginning on the day after the day on which a customs officer first sends or makes available a sample or information to that owner under that subsection and ending on the first day on which one of the following occurs:

(a)   the copies are no longer detained for the purpose of enforcing section 44.01 or, if subsection 44.04(3) applies, for the purpose of the proceedings referred to in that subsection;

(b)   the Minister receives written notification in which the owner states that the importation or exportation of the copies does not, with respect to the owner's copyright, contravene section 44.01;

(c)   the Minister receives written notification in which the owner states that they will not, while the copies are detained for the purpose of enforcing section 44.01, commence proceedings to obtain a remedy under this Act with respect to them.

(2) *Exception – paragraph (1)(a)* —Despite paragraph (1)(a), if the copies are forfeited under subsection 39(1) of the *Customs Act** and the Minister did not,

before the end of the detention of the copies for the purpose of enforcing section 44.01, receive a copy of a document filed with a court commencing proceedings to obtain a remedy under this Act with respect to the detained copies or the written notification referred to in paragraph (1)(*b*) or (*c*), the period ends on the day on which the copies are forfeited.

(3) *Exception – paragraph (1)(c)* — Despite paragraph (1)(*c*), if the copies are forfeited under subsection 39(1) of the *Customs Act** after the Minister has received the written notification referred to in that paragraph, the period ends on the day on which the copies are forfeited.

(4) *Joint and several or solidary liability* — The owner and the importer or exporter of copies that are forfeited in the circumstances set out in subsection (2) or (3) are jointly and severally, or solidarily, liable to the owner of copyright for all the charges under subsection (1) paid by the copyright owner with respect to the period

(*a*)   in the circumstances referred to in subsection (2), beginning on the day on which the copies are no longer detained for the purpose of enforcing section 44.01 and ending on the day on which the copies are forfeited; and

(*b*)   in the circumstances referred to in subsection (3), beginning on the day on which the Minister receives the written notification referred to in paragraph (1)(*c*) and ending on the day on which the copies are forfeited.

(5) *Exception* — Subsections (1) to (3) do not apply if

(*a*)   the detention of the copies for the purpose of enforcing section 44.01 ends before the expiry of 10 working days — or, if the copies are perishable, before the expiry of five days — after the day on which the customs officer first sends or makes available a sample or information to the copyright owner under subsection 44.04(1); and

(*b*)   the Minister has not, by the end of the detention, received a copy of a document filed with a court commencing proceedings to obtain a remedy under this Act with respect to the detained copies or the written notification referred to in paragraph (1)(*b*) or (*c*).

[S.C. 2014, c. 32, s. 5.]

---

* *Customs Act*, **R.S.C. 1985, c. 1 (2nd Supp.)**

39. *Unclaimed goods forfeit* — **(1) Goods that have not been removed from a place of safe-keeping referred to in section 37 within such period of time after they were deposited therein as may be prescribed are, at the termination of that period of time, forfeit.**

No Liability

44.08. No liability — Neither Her Majesty nor a customs officer is liable for any loss or damage suffered in relation to the enforcement or application of sections 44.01 to 44.04 and 44.06 because of

    (*a*)   the detention of copies of a work or other subject-matter, except if the detention contravenes subsection 44.04(2);

    (*b*)   the failure to detain copies; or

    (*c*)   the release or cessation of detention of any copies, except if the release or cessation contravenes subsection 44.04(3).

[S.C. 2014, c. 32, s. 5.]

Powers of Court Relating to Detained Copies

44.09. Application to court — (1) In the course of proceedings referred to in subsection 44.04(3), the court may, on the application of the Minister or a party to the proceedings,

    (*a*)   impose conditions on the storage or detention of the copies that are the subject of the proceedings; or

    (*b*)   direct that the copies are no longer to be detained for the purpose of the proceedings, on any conditions that the court may impose, if their owner, importer, exporter or consignee furnishes security in an amount fixed by the court.

(2) *Minister's consent* — If a party applies to have the detained copies stored in a place other than a bonded warehouse or a sufferance warehouse, as those terms are defined in subsection 2(1) of the *Customs Act,** the Minister must consent to the storage of the copies in that place before a condition to that effect is imposed under subsection (1).

(3) *Customs Act* — The court may impose a condition described in subsection (2) despite section 31 of the *Customs Act.**

(4) *Continued detention* — A direction under paragraph (1)(*b*) that the copies are no longer to be detained for the purpose of the proceedings does not preclude a customs officer from continuing to detain the copies under the *Customs Act** for another purpose.

(5) *Security* — In the course of proceedings referred to in subsection 44.04(3), the court may, on the application of the Minister or a party to the proceedings, require the owner of copyright to furnish security, in an amount fixed by the court,

    (*a*)   to cover duties, storage and handling charges, and any other amount that may become chargeable against the copies; and

    (*b*)   to answer any damages that may, because of the detention of the copies, be

sustained by the owner, importer, exporter or consignee of the copies.
[S.C. 2014, c. 32, s. 5.]

* *Customs Act*, **R.S.C. 1985, c. 1 (2nd Supp.)**

2. *Definitions* **— (1) In this Act,**

bonded warehouse means a place licensed as a bonded warehouse by the
Minister under subsection 91(1) of the *Customs Tariff*;

sufferance warehouse means a place licensed as a sufferance warehouse by the
Minister under section 24;
[S.C. 1997, c. 36, s. 147.]

. . .

31. *Release* **— Subject to section 19, no goods shall be removed from a
customs office, sufferance warehouse, bonded warehouse or duty free shop
by any person other than an officer in the performance of his or her duties
under this or any other Act of Parliament unless the goods have been
released by an officer or by any prescribed means.**
[S.C. 2001, c. 25, s. 20.]

44.1. Damages against copyright owner — (1) The court may award damages
against the owner of copyright who commenced proceedings referred to in
subsection 44.04(3) to the owner, importer, exporter or consignee of the copies who
is a party to the proceedings for losses, costs or prejudice suffered as a result of the
detention of the copies if the proceedings are dismissed or discontinued.

(2) *Damages awarded to copyright owner* — Any damages under subsection
34(1) awarded to the owner of copyright in proceedings referred to in subsection
44.04(3) are to include the charges incurred by the copyright owner as a result of
storing, handling or, if applicable, destroying the detained copies.
[S.C. 1993, c. 44, s. 66; S.C. 1997, c. 24, s. 27; S.C. 2005, c. 38, ss. 142(*d*), 145(2)(*j*); S.C.
2014, c. 32, s. 5.]

PROHIBITION RESULTING FROM NOTICE

44.11. Importation of certain copyright works prohibited — Copies made
outside Canada of any work in which copyright subsists that if made in Canada
would infringe copyright and as to which the owner of the copyright gives notice in
writing to the Canada Border Services Agency that the owner desires that the copies
not be imported into Canada, shall not be so imported and are deemed to be included
in tariff item No. 9897.00.00 in the List of Tariff Provisions set out in the schedule
to the *Customs Tariff*,* with section 136 of that Act applying accordingly.

[S.C. 2014, c. 32, s. 5.]

---

* *Customs Tariff*, S.C. 1997, c. 36

136. *Prohibited imports* — (1) The importation of goods of tariff item No. 9897.00.00, 9898.00.00 or 9899.00.00 is prohibited.

(2) *Subsection 10(1) does not apply* — Subsection 10(1) does not apply in respect of goods referred to in subsection (1).

COURT-ORDERED DETENTION

44.12. Power of court — (1) A court may make an order described in subsection (3) if the court is satisfied that

(*a*) copies of the work are about to be imported into Canada, or have been imported into Canada but have not been released;

(*b*) the copies were either

(i) made without the consent of the person who is owner of the copyright in the country where they were made, or

(ii) made elsewhere than in a country to which this Act extends; and

(*c*) the copies would infringe copyright if they were made in Canada by the importer and the importer knows or should have known this.

(2) *Who may apply* — A court may make an order described in subsection (3) on application by the owner of the copyright in a work in Canada.

(3) *Order of court* — In an order made under subsection (1), the court may

(*a*) direct the Minister

(i) to take reasonable measures, on the basis of information reasonably required by the Minister and provided by the applicant, to detain the copies of the work, and

(ii) to notify the applicant and the importer, immediately after detaining the copies of the work, of the detention and the reasons for the detention; and

(*b*) provide for any other matters that the court considers appropriate.

(4) *How application made* — An application for an order under subsection (1) may be made in an action or otherwise, and either on notice or *ex parte*, except that it must always be made on notice to the Minister.

(5) *Security* — Before making an order under subsection (1), the court may

require the applicant to furnish security, in an amount fixed by the court,

(*a*) to cover duties, storage and handling charges and any other amount that may become chargeable against the copies of the work; and

(*b*) to answer any damages that may by reason of the order be incurred by the owner, importer or consignee of the work.

(6) *Application for directions* — The Minister may apply to the court for directions in implementing an order made under subsection (1).

(7) *Minister may allow inspection* — The Minister may give the applicant or the importer an opportunity to inspect the detained copies of the work for the purpose of substantiating or refuting, as the case may be, the applicant's claim.

(8) *If applicant fails to commence action* — Unless an order made under subsection (1) provides otherwise, the Minister shall, subject to the *Customs Act** and to any other Act of Parliament that prohibits, controls or regulates the importation or exportation of goods, release the copies of the work without further notice to the applicant if, within 10 working days after the applicant has been notified under subparagraph (3)(*a*)(ii), the applicant has not notified the Minister that they have commenced a proceeding for a final determination by the court of the issues referred to in paragraphs (1)(*b*) and (*c*).

(9) *If court finds in plaintiff's favour* — If, in a proceeding commenced under this section, the court is satisfied that the circumstances referred to in paragraphs (1)(*b*) and (*c*) existed, the court may make any order that it considers appropriate in the circumstances, including an order that the copies of the work be destroyed, or that they be delivered up to the plaintiff as the plaintiff's property absolutely.

(10) *Other remedies not affected* — For greater certainty, nothing in this section affects any remedy available under any other provision of this Act or any other Act of Parliament.
[S.C. 2014, c. 32, s. 5.]

---

* *Customs Act*, **R.S.C. 1985, c. 1 (2nd Supp.)**

44.2. Importation of books — (1) A court may, subject to this section, make an order described in section 44.12(3) in relation to a book where the court is satisfied that

(*a*) copies of the book are about to be imported into Canada, or have been imported into Canada but have not yet been released;

(*b*) copies of the book were made with the consent of the owner of the copyright in the book in the country where the copies were made, but were imported without the consent of the owner in Canada of the copyright in the book; and

(c) the copies would infringe copyright if they were made in Canada by the importer and the importer knows or should have known this.

[S.C. 2014, c. 32, s. 6.]

(2) *Who may apply* — A court may make an order described in section 44.12(3) in relation to a book on application by

(a) the owner of the copyright in the book in Canada;

(b) the exclusive licensee of the copyright in the book in Canada; or

(c) the exclusive distributor of the book.

[S.C. 2014, c. 32, s. 6.]

(3) *Limitation* — Subsections (1) and (2) only apply where there is an exclusive distributor of the book and the acts described in those subsections take place in the part of Canada or in respect of the particular sector of the market for which the person is the exclusive distributor.

(4) *Application of certain provisions* — Subsections 44.12(3) to (10) apply, with such modifications as the circumstances require, in respect of an order made under subsection (1).

[S.C. 1994, c. 47, s. 66; S.C. 1997, c. 24, s. 28; S.C. 2014, c. 32, s. 6.]

44.3. Limitation — No exclusive licensee of the copyright in a book in Canada, and no exclusive distributor of a book, may obtain an order under section 44.2 against another exclusive licensee of the copyright in that book in Canada or against another exclusive distributor of that book.

[S.C. 1997, c. 24, s. 28.]

44.4. Importation of other subject-matter — Section 44.12 applies, with such modifications as the circumstances require, in respect of a sound recording, performer's performance or communication signal, where a fixation or a reproduction of a fixation of it

(a) is about to be imported into Canada, or has been imported into Canada but has not yet been released;

(b) either

(i)   was made without the consent of the person who then owned the copyright in the sound recording, performer's performance or communication signal, as the case may be, in the country where the fixation or reproduction was made, or

(ii) was made elsewhere than in a country to which Part II extends; and

(c) would infringe the right of the owner of copyright in the sound recording, performer's performance or communication signal if it was made in Canada

160

by the importer and the importer knows or should have known this.
[S.C. 1997, c. 24, s. 28; S.C. 2014, c. 32, s. 6.]

45. Exceptions — (1) Notwithstanding anything in this Act, it is lawful for a person

(*a*) to import for their own use not more than two copies of a work or other subject-matter made with the consent of the owner of the copyright in the country where it was made;

(*b*) to import for use by a department of the Government of Canada or a province copies of a work or other subject-matter made with the consent of the owner of the copyright in the country where it was made;

(*c*) at any time before copies of a work or other subject-matter are made in Canada, to import any copies, except copies of a book, made with the consent of the owner of the copyright in the country where the copies were made, that are required for the use of a library, archive, museum or educational institution;

(*d*) to import, for the use of a library, archive, museum or educational institution, not more than one copy of a book that is made with the consent of the owner of the copyright in the country where the book was made; and

(*e*) to import copies, made with the consent of the owner of the copyright in the country where they were made, of any used books, except textbooks of a scientific, technical or scholarly nature for use within an educational institution in a course of instruction.

(2) *Satisfactory evidence —* An officer of customs may, in the officer's discretion, require a person seeking to import a copy of a work or other subject-matter under this section to produce satisfactory evidence of the facts necessary to establish the person's right to import the copy.
[S.C. 1994, c. 47, s. 67(4); S.C. 1997, c. 24, ss. 28 and 62(1).]

Note: S.C. 1997, c. 24, s. 62(3) provides that notwithstanding the coming into force provisions of S.C. 1997, c. 24, s. 62 paragraph (1)(*d*), paragraph 45(1)(*e*) of the Act, as enacted by section 28 of S.C. 1997, c. 24, shall be read as follows for the period beginning on June 30, 1996 and ending on the day that is sixty days after the day on which S.C. 1997, c. 24 is assented to (Royal Assent—April 25, 1997):

(*e*) to import copies, made with the consent of the owner of the copyright in the country where they were made, of any used books.

PART V
ADMINISTRATION

[S.C. 1997, c. 24, s. 29.]

COPYRIGHT OFFICE

46. Copyright Office — The Copyright Office shall be attached to the Patent Office.

47. Powers of Commissioner and Registrar — The Commissioner of Patents shall exercise the powers conferred and perform the duties imposed on him by this Act under the direction of the Minister, and, in the absence of the Commissioner of Patents or if the Commissioner is unable to act, the Registrar of Copyrights or other officer temporarily appointed by the Minister may, as Acting Commissioner, exercise those powers and perform those duties under the direction of the Minister.

48. Registrar — There shall be a Registrar of Copyrights.

49. Register of Copyrights, certificates and certified copies — The Commissioner of Patents, the Registrar of Copyrights or an officer, clerk or employee of the Copyright Office may sign certificates and certified copies of the Register of Copyrights.

[S.C. 1992, c. 1, s. 47; S.C. 1993, c. 15, s. 4.]

50. Other duties of Registrar — The Registrar of Copyrights shall perform such other duties in connection with the administration of this Act as may be assigned to him by the Commissioner of Patents.

51. [Repealed by S.C. 1992, c. 1, s. 48.]

52. Control of business and officials — The Commissioner of Patents shall, subject to the Minister, oversee and direct the officers, clerks and employees of the Copyright Office, have general control of the business thereof and perform such other duties as are assigned to him by the Governor in Council.

53. Register to be evidence — (1) The Register of Copyrights is evidence of the particulars entered in it, and a copy of an entry in the Register is evidence of the particulars of the entry if it is certified by the Commissioner of Patents, the Registrar of Copyrights or an officer, clerk or employee of the Copyright Office as a true copy.

[S.C. 1992, c. 1, s. 49; S.C. 1993, c. 15, s. 5(1).]

(2) *Owner of copyright* — A certificate of registration of copyright is evidence that the copyright subsists and that the person registered is the owner of the copyright.

[S.C. 1997, c. 24, s. 30.]

(2.1) *Assignee* — A certificate of registration of an assignment of copyright is evidence that the right recorded on the certificate has been assigned and that the assignee registered is the owner of that right.

[S.C. 1997, c. 24, s. 30.]

(2.2) *Licensee* — A certificate of registration of a licence granting an interest in a copyright is evidence that the interest recorded on the certificate has been granted and that the licensee registered is the holder of that interest.

[S.C. 1997, c. 24, s. 30.]

(3) *Admissibility* — A certified copy or certificate appearing to have been issued under this section is admissible in all courts without proof of the signature or official

character of the person appearing to have signed it.
[S.C. 1993, c. 15, s. 5(2).]

REGISTRATION

54. Register of Copyrights — (1) The Minister shall cause to be kept at the Copyright Office a register to be called the Register of Copyrights in which may be entered

(a) the names or titles of works and of other subject-matter in which copyright subsists;

(b) the names and addresses of authors, performers, makers of sound recordings, broadcasters, owners of copyright, assignees of copyright, and persons to whom an interest in copyright has been granted by licence; and

(c) such other particulars as may be prescribed by regulation.
[S.C. 1997, c. 24, s. 31(1).]

(2) [Repealed by S.C. 1997, c. 24, s. 31(1).]

(3) *Single entry sufficient*—In the case of an encyclopaedia, newspaper, review, magazine or other periodical work, or work published in a series of books or parts, it is not necessary to make a separate entry for each number or part, but a single entry for the whole work is sufficient.

(4) *Indices —* There shall also be kept at the Copyright Office such indices of the Register established under this section as may be prescribed by regulation.
[S.C. 1997, c. 24, s. 31(2).]

(5) *Inspection and extracts —* The Register and indices established under this section shall at all reasonable times be open to inspection, and any person is entitled to make copies of or take extracts from the Register.
[S.C. 1992, c. 1, s. 50(2); S.C. 1997, c. 24, s. 31(2).]

(6) *Former registration effective —* Any registration made under the *Copyright Act*, chapter 70 of the Revised Statutes of Canada, 1906, has the same force and effect as if made under this Act.

(7) *Subsisting copyright —* Any work in which copyright, operative in Canada, subsisted immediately before January 1, 1924 is registrable under this Act.

55. Copyright in works — (1) Application for the registration of a copyright in a work may be made by or on behalf of the author of the work, the owner of the copyright in the work, an assignee of the copyright, or a person to whom an interest in the copyright has been granted by licence.

(2) *Application for registration —* An application under subsection (1) must be filed with the Copyright Office, be accompanied by the fee prescribed by or determined under the regulations, and contain the following information:

163

(a)   the name and address of the owner of the copyright in the work;

(b)   a declaration that the applicant is the author of the work, the owner of the copyright in the work, an assignee of the copyright, or a person to whom an interest in the copyright has been granted by licence;

(c)   the category of the work;

(d)   the title of the work;

(e)   the name of the author and, if the author is dead, the date of the author's death, if known;

(f)   in the case of a published work, the date and place of the first publication; and

(g)   any additional information prescribed by regulation.
[S.C. 1997, c. 24, s. 32.]

56. Copyright in subject-matter other than works — (1) Application for the registration of a copyright in subject-matter other than a work may be made by or on behalf of the owner of the copyright in the subject-matter, an assignee of the copyright, or a person to whom an interest in the copyright has been granted by licence.

(2) *Application for registration* — An application under subsection (1) must be filed with the Copyright Office, be accompanied by the fee prescribed by or determined under the regulations, and contain the following information:

(a)   the name and address of the owner of the copyright in the subject-matter;

(b)   a declaration that the applicant is the owner of the copyright in the subject-matter, an assignee of the copyright, or a person to whom an interest in the copyright has been granted by licence;

(c)   whether the subject-matter is a performer's performance, a sound recording or a communication signal;

(d)   the title, if any, of the subject-matter;

(e)   the date of

  (i)   in the case of a performer's performance, its first fixation in a sound recording or, if it is not fixed in a sound recording, its first performance,

  (ii)   in the case of a sound recording, the first fixation, or

  (iii)   in the case of a communication signal, its broadcast; and

(f)   any additional information prescribed by regulation.
[S.C. 1993, c. 15, s. 6; S.C. 1997, c. 24, s. 32.]

56.1. Recovery of damages — Where a person purports to have the authority to apply for the registration of a copyright under section 55 or 56 on behalf of another person, any damage caused by a fraudulent or erroneous assumption of such authority is recoverable in any court of competent jurisdiction.
[S.C. 1997, c. 24, s. 32.]

57. Registration of assignment or licence — (1) The Registrar of Copyrights shall register an assignment of copyright, or a licence granting an interest in a copyright, on being furnished with

(*a*)   the original instrument or a certified copy of it, or other evidence satisfactory to the Registrar of the assignment or licence; and

(*b*)   the fee prescribed by or determined under the regulations.
[S.C. 1997, c. 24, s. 33(1).]

(2) [Repealed by S.C. 1992, c. 1, s. 51(1).]

(3) *When assignment or licence is void* — Any assignment of copyright, or any licence granting an interest in a copyright, shall be adjudged void against any subsequent assignee or licensee for valuable consideration without actual notice, unless the prior assignment or licence is registered in the manner prescribed by this Act before the registering of the instrument under which the subsequent assignee or licensee claims.
[S.C. 1997, c. 24, s. 33(2).]

(4) *Rectification of Register by the Court* — The Federal Court may, on application of the Registrar of Copyrights or of any interested person, order the rectification of Register of Copyrights by

(*a*)   the making of any entry wrongly omitted to be made in the Register,

(*b*)   the expunging of any entry wrongly made in or remaining on the Register, or

(*c*)   the correction of any error or defect in the Register,

and any rectification of the Register under this subsection shall be retroactive from such date as the Court may order.
[S.C. 1992, c. 1, s. 51; S.C. 1993, c. 15, s. 7.]

58. Execution of instruments — (1) Any assignment of a copyright, or any licence granting an interest in a copyright, may be executed, subscribed or acknowledged at any place in a treaty country, a Rome Convention country or a WPPT country by the assignor, licensor or secured or hypothecary debtor, before any notary public, commissioner or other official, or the judge of any court, who is authorized by law to administer oaths or certify documents in that place and who also subscribes their signature and affixes to, or impresses on, the assignment or licence their official seal or the seal of the court of which they are a judge.

165

[S.C. 2012, c. 20, s. 50.]

(2) *Execution of instruments* — Any assignment of copyright, or any licence granting an interest in a copyright, may be executed, subscribed or acknowledged by the assignor, licensor or mortgagor, in any other foreign country before any notary public, commissioner or other official or the judge of any court of the foreign country, who is authorized to administer oaths or perform notarial acts in that foreign country and whose authority shall be proved by the certificate of a diplomatic or consular officer of Canada performing their functions in that foreign country.

[S.C. 1997, c. 24, s. 34(1).]

(3) *Seals to be evidence* — The official seal or seal of the court or the certificate of a diplomatic or consular officer is evidence of the execution of the instrument, and the instrument with the seal or certificate affixed or attached thereto is admissible as evidence in any action or proceeding brought under this Act without further proof.

(4) *Other testimony* — The provisions of subsections (1) and (2) shall be deemed to be permissive only, and the execution of any assignment of copyright, or any licence granting an interest in a copyright, may in any case be proved in accordance with the applicable rules of evidence.

[S.C. 1997, c. 24, s. 34(2).]

FEES

59. Fees regulations — The Governor in Council may make regulations

(a) prescribing fees, or the manner of determining fees, to be paid for anything required or authorized to be done in the administration of this Act; and

(b) prescribing the time and manner in which the fees must be paid.

[S.C. 1993, c. 15, s. 8.]

PART VI
MISCELLANEOUS PROVISIONS

[S.C. 1997, c. 24, s. 35.]

SUBSTITUTED RIGHT

[S.C. 1993, c. 15, s. 9.]

60. Subsistence of substituted right — (1) Where any person is immediately before January 1, 1924 entitled to any right in any work that is set out in column I of Schedule I, or to any interest in such a right, he is, as from that date, entitled to the substituted right set out in column II of that Schedule, or to the same interest in the substituted right, and to no other right or interest, and the substituted right shall subsist for the term for which it would have subsisted if this Act had been in force at the date when the work was made, and the work had been one entitled to copyright thereunder.

(2) *Where author has assigned the right* — Where the author of any work in which any right that is set out in column I of Schedule I subsists on January 1, 1924 has, before that date, assigned the right or granted any interest therein for the whole term of the right, then at the date when, but for the passing of this Act, the right would have expired, the substituted right conferred by this section shall, in the absence of express agreement, pass to the author of the work, and any interest therein created before January 1, 1924 and then subsisting shall determine, but the person who immediately before the date at which the right would have expired was the owner of the right or interest is entitled at his option either

(*a*) on giving such notice as is hereinafter mentioned, to an assignment of the right or the grant of a similar interest therein for the remainder of the term of the right for such consideration as, failing agreement, may be determined by arbitration, or

(*b*) without any assignment or grant, to continue to reproduce or perform the work in like manner as therefore subject to the payment, if demanded by the author within three years after the date at which the right would have expired, of such royalties to the author as, failing agreement, may be determined by arbitration, or, where the work is incorporated in a collective work and the owner of the right or interest is the proprietor of that collective work, without any payment,

and the notice referred to in paragraph (*a*) must be given not more than one year or less than six months before the date at which the right would have so expired, and must be sent by registered post to the author, or, if he cannot with reasonable diligence be found, advertised in the Canada Gazette.

(3) *Definition of author* — For the purposes of this section, ***author*** includes the legal representatives of a deceased author.

(4) *Works made before this Act in force* — Subject to this Act, copyright shall not subsist in any work made before January 1, 1924 otherwise than under and in accordance with the provisions of this section.

CLERICAL ERRORS

[S.C. 1997, c. 24, s. 36.]

61. Clerical errors do not invalidate — Clerical errors in any instrument of record in the Copyright Office do not invalidate the instrument, but they may be corrected under the authority of the Registrar of Copyrights.

[S.C. 1992, c. 1, s. 52; S.C. 1993, c. 15, s. 10.]

REGULATIONS

[S.C. 1997, c. 24, s. 37(1).]

62. Regulations — (1) The Governor in Council may make regulations

  (*a*)   for the purposes of paragraph 30.01(6)(*d*), respecting measures, which may vary according to circumstances specified in the regulations;

  (*b*)   for the purposes of paragraph 30.02(3)(*d*), respecting measures, which may vary according to circumstances specified in the regulations;

  (*c*)   prescribing the form of a notice of claimed infringement referred to in section 41.25 and prescribing the information that must be and that is not permitted to be contained in it;

  (*d*)   prescribing anything that by this Act is to be prescribed by regulation; and

  (*e*)   generally for carrying out the purposes and provisions of this Act.

(2) *Rights saved* — The Governor in Council may make orders for altering, revoking or varying any order in council made under this Act, but any order made under this section does not affect prejudicially any rights or interests acquired or accrued at the date when the order comes into operation, and shall provide for the protection of those rights and interests.

[S.C. 2012, c. 20, s. 51; S.C. 2018, c. 27, s. 246.]

INDUSTRIAL DESIGNS AND TOPOGRAPHIES

[S.C. 1997, c. 24, s. 38.]

63. [Repealed by S.C. 1997, c. 24, s. 38.]

64. Interpretation — (1) In this section and section 64.1,

article means any thing that is made by hand, tool or machine;

design means features of shape, configuration, pattern or ornament and any combination of those features that, in a finished article, appeal to and are judged solely by the eye;

useful article means an article that has a utilitarian function and includes a model of any such article;

utilitarian function, in respect of an article, means a function other than merely serving as a substrate or carrier for artistic or literary matter.

Note: Section 26 of R.S.C. 1985, c. 10 (4th Supp.), states, "subsection 64(1) and section 64.1 of the *Copyright Act*, as enacted by section 11, apply in respect of any alleged infringement of copyright occurring prior to, on or after the day on which section 11 comes into force."

(2) *Non-infringement re certain designs* — Where copyright subsists in a design applied to a useful article or in an artistic work from which the design is derived and, by or under the authority of any person who owns the copyright in Canada or who owns the copyright elsewhere,

(a) the article is reproduced in a quantity of more than fifty, or

(b) where the article is a plate, engraving or cast, the article is used for producing more than fifty useful articles,

it shall not thereafter be an infringement of the copyright or the moral rights for anyone

(c) to reproduce the design of the article or a design not differing substantially from the design of the article by

(i) making the article, or

(ii) making a drawing or other reproduction in any material form of the article, or

(d) to do with an article, drawing or reproduction that is made as described in paragraph (c) anything that the owner of the copyright has the sole right to do with the design or artistic work in which the copyright subsists.

(3) *Exception* — Subsection (2) does not apply in respect of the copyright or the moral rights in an artistic work in so far as the work is used as or for

(a) a graphic or photographic representation that is applied to the face of an article;

(b) a trademark or a representation thereof or a label;

(c) material that has a woven or knitted pattern or that is suitable for piece goods or surface coverings or for making wearing apparel;

(d) an architectural work of art that is a building or a model of a building;
[S.C. 1993, c. 44, s. 68; S.C. 2014, c. 20, s. 366(E).]

(e) a representation of a real or fictitious being, event or place that is applied to an article as a feature of shape, configuration, pattern or ornament;

(f) articles that are sold as a set, unless more than fifty sets are made; or

(g) such other work or article as may be prescribed by regulation.
[S.C. 1997, c. 24, s. 39.]

(4) *Idem* — Subsections (2) and (3) apply only in respect of designs created after the coming into force of this subsection, and section 64 of this Act and the *Industrial Design Act,** as they read immediately before the coming into force of this subsection, as well as the rules made under them, continue to apply in respect of designs created before that coming into force.
[R.S.C. 1985, c. 10 (4th Supp.), s. 11.]

*R.S.C. 1985, c. I-9

Note: The reference to section 64 pertains to section 46 of R.S.C. 1970, c. C-30.*

* Copyright Act, R.S.C. 1970, c. C-30

46. *Application of Act to designs* — **(1) This Act does not apply to designs capable of being registered under the** *Industrial Design Act***, except designs that, though capable of being so registered, are not used or intended to be used as models or patterns to be multiplied by any industrial process.**

(2) *Rules for determining use of design* — **General rules, under the** *Industrial Design Act***, may be made for determining the conditions under which a design shall be deemed to be used for such purposes as aforesaid.**

64.1. Non-infringement re useful article features — (1) The following acts do not constitute an infringement of the copyright or moral rights in a work:

(*a*) applying to a useful article features that are dictated solely by a utilitarian function of the article;

(*b*) by reference solely to a useful article, making a drawing or other reproduction in any material form of any features of the article that are dictated solely by a utilitarian function of the article;

(*c*) doing with a useful article having only features described in paragraph (*a*) or doing with a drawing or reproduction that is made as described in paragraph (*b*) anything that the owner of the copyright has the sole right to do with the work; and

(*d*) using any method or principle of manufacture or construction.

(2) *Exception* — Nothing in subsection (1) affects

(*a*) the copyright, or

(*b*) the moral rights, if any,

in any sound recording, cinematograph film or other contrivance by means of which a work may be mechanically reproduced or performed.

[R.S.C. 1985, c. 10 (4th Supp.), s. 11; S.C. 1997, c. 24, s. 40.]

Note: Section 26 of R.S.C. 1985, c. 10 (4th Supp.), states, "subsection 64(1) and section 64.1 of the *Copyright Act*, as enacted by section 11, apply in respect of any alleged infringement of copyright occurring prior to, on or after the day on which section 11 comes into force."

64.2. Application of act to topographies — (1) This Act does not apply, and shall be deemed never to have applied, to any topography or to any design, however expressed, that is intended to generate all or part of a topography.

170

COPYRIGHT ACT

(2) *Computer programs* — For greater certainty, the incorporation of a computer program into an integrated circuit product or the incorporation of a work into such a computer program may constitute and infringement of the copyright or moral rights in a work.

(3) *Definitions* — In this section, *topography* and *integrated circuit product* have the same meaning as in the *Integrated Circuit Topography Act.**
[S.C. 1990, c. 37, s. 33.]

---

* *Integrated Circuit Topography Act*, S.C. 1990, c. 37

integrated circuit product **means a product in a final or intermediate form, that is intended to perform an electronic function and in which the elements, at least one of which is an active element, and some or all of the interconnections, are integrally formed in or on, or both in and on, a piece of material;**

topography **means the design, however expressed, of the disposition of**

(*a*) **the interconnections, if any, and the elements for the making of an integrated circuit product, or**

(*b*) **the elements, if any, and the interconnections for the making of a customization layer or layers to be added to an integrated circuit product in an intermediate form.**

---

65. [Repealed by S.C. 1993, c. 44, s. 69.]

PART VII
COPYRIGHT BOARD

[S.C. 1997, c. 24, s. 41; S.C. 2018, c. 27, s. 289.]

66. Establishment — (1) There is established a Board to be known as the Copyright Board, consisting of not more than five members, including a Chair and a Vice-chair, to be appointed by the Governor in Council.

(2) *Service* — The members of the Board shall be appointed to serve either full-time or part-time.

(3) *Chair* — The Chair must be a judge, either sitting or retired, of a superior court.

(4) *Tenure* — Each member of the Board shall hold office during good behaviour for a term not exceeding five years, but may be removed at any time by the Governor in Council for cause.

(5) *Re-appointment* — A member of the Board is eligible to be re-appointed once only.

(6) *Prohibition* — A member of the Board shall not be employed in the public service within the meaning of the *Federal Public Sector Labour Relations Act* during the member's term of office.

(7) *Members deemed public service employees* — A full-time member of the Board, other than the Chair, is deemed to be employed in

(a)   the public service for the purposes of the *Public Service Superannuation Act;* * and

(b)   the federal public administration for the purposes of any regulations made pursuant to section 9 of the *Aeronautics Act.* **

[R.S.C. 1985, c. 10 (4th Supp.), s. 12; S.C. 2003, c. 22, s. 154; S.C. 2003, c. 22, ss. 154, 224 (z.20) and 225(s); S.C. 2017, c. 9, s. 55; S.C. 2018, c. 27, s. 290.]

---

*R.S.C. 1985, c. P-36

** *Aeronautics Act,* **R.S.C. 1985, c. A-2**

9. *Regulations establishing compensation payable for death or injury* — (1) The Governor in Council may make regulations establishing the compensation to be paid and the persons to whom and the manner in which such compensation shall be payable for the death or injury of any person employed in the federal public administration or employed under the direction of any department in the federal public administration that results directly from a flight undertaken by that person in the course of duty in the federal public administration.

(2) *Idem* — Regulations made under subsection (1) shall not extend to the payment of compensation for any death or injury in respect of which provision for the payment of other compensation or a gratuity or pension is made by any other Act, unless the claimant elects to accept the compensation instead of the other compensation, gratuity or pension under that other Act.

[R.S.C. 1985, c. 33 (1st Supp.), s. 1; S.C. 2003, c. 22, s. 89.]

66.1. Duties of Chair —   (1) The Chair shall direct the work of the Board and apportion its work among its members.

(2) *Absence or incapacity of Chair* — If the Chair is absent or incapacitated or if the office of Chair is vacant, the Vice-chair has all the powers and functions of the Chair during the absence, incapacity or vacancy.

(3) *Duties of Vice-chair* — The Vice-chair is the chief executive officer of the

Board and has supervision over and direction of the Board and its staff.
[R.S.C. 1985, c. 10 (4th Supp.), s. 12; S.C. 2018, c. 27, s. 291(E).]

66.2. Remuneration and expenses — The members of the Board shall be paid such remuneration as may be fixed by the Governor in Council and are entitled to be paid reasonable travel and living expenses incurred by them in the course of their duties under this Act while absent from their ordinary place of residence.
[R.S.C. 1985, c. 10 (4th Supp.), s. 12.]

66.3. Conflict of interest prohibited — (1) A member of the Board shall not, directly or indirectly, engage in any activity, have any interest in a business or accept or engage in any office or employment that is inconsistent with the member's duties.

(2) *Termination of conflict of interest* — Where a member of the Board becomes aware that he is in a conflict of interest contrary to subsection (1), the member shall, within one hundred and twenty days, terminate the conflict or resign.
[R.S.C. 1985, c. 10 (4th Supp.), s. 12.]

66.4. Staff — (1) Such officers and employees as are necessary for the proper conduct of the work of the Board shall be appointed in accordance with the *Public Service Employment Act.* *

(2) *Idem* — The officers and employees referred to in subsection (1) shall be deemed to be employed in the public service for the purposes of the *Public Service Superannuation Act.* **

(3) *Technical assistance* — The Board may engage on a temporary basis the services of persons having technical or specialized knowledge to advise and assist in the performance of its duties and the Board may, in accordance with Treasury Board directives, fix and pay the remuneration and expenses of those persons.
[R.S.C. 1985, c. 10 (4th Supp.), s. 12; S.C. 2003, c. 22, s. 225(5).]

---

*S.C. 2003, c. 22, ss. 12, 13

**R.S.C. 1985, c. P-36

66.5. Concluding matters after membership expires — (1) A member of the Board whose term expires may conclude the matters that the member has begun to consider.

(2) *Decisions* — Matters before the Board shall be decided by a majority of the members of the Board and the presiding member shall have a second vote in the case of a tie.
[R.S.C. 1985, c. 10 (4th Supp.), s. 12.]

66.501. Fair and equitable — The Board shall fix royalty and levy rates and any related terms and conditions under this Act that are fair and equitable, in consideration of

(*a*) what would have been agreed upon between a willing buyer and a willing seller acting in a competitive market with all relevant information, at arm's length and free of external constraints;

(*b*) the public interest

(*c*) any regulation made under subsection 66.91(1); and

(*d*) any other criterion that the Board considers appropriate.
[S.C. 2018, c. 27, s. 292.]

66.502. Informal and expeditious — All matters before the Board shall be dealt with as informally and expeditiously as the circumstances and considerations of fairness permit but, in any case, within any period or no later than any day provided for under this Act.
[S.C. 2018, c. 27, s. 292.]

66.503. For greater certainty — For greater certainty, any person or entity may authorize any other person or entity to act on their behalf in any matter before the Board.
[S.C. 2018, c. 27, s. 292.]

66.504. Case manager — (1) The Chair may assign a member, officer or employee of the Board or a person engaged under subsection 66.4(3) to act as a case manager of a matter before the Board.

(2) *Powers* — The case manager may give any directions or make any orders with respect to the case management of the matter, but is not permitted to make a direction or order that is inconsistent with

(*a*) this Act;

(*b*) regulations made under subsection 66.6(1), unless authorized to do so under regulations made under paragraph 66.6(1.1)(*b*); or

(*c*) regulations made under paragraph 66.91(2)(*a*) to (*c*), unless authorized to do so under regulations made under paragraph 66.91(2)(*d*).

(3) *Deemed direction or order of Board* — A direction given, or an order made, by a case manager is deemed to be a direction or order of the Board, including for the purposes of paragraph 28(1)(*j*) of the *Federal Courts Act*.

(4) *Delegation* — The Chair may delegate his or her power under subsection (1) to the Vice-chair.
[S.C. 2018, c. 27, s. 292.]

66.51. Interim decisions — The Board may, on application, make an interim decision.

[R.S.C. 1985, c. 10 (4th Supp.), s. 12.]

66.52. Variation of decisions — A decision of the Board respecting royalties or their related terms and conditions that is made under subsection 70(1), 71(2), 76.1(1) or 83(8) may, on application, be varied by the Board if, in its opinion, there has been a material change in circumstances since the decision was made.
[R.S.C. 1985, c. 10 (4th Supp.), s. 12; S.C. 1988, c. 65, s. 64; S.C. 1997, c. 24, s. 42; S.C. 2018, c. 27, s. 293.]

66.6. Regulations — (1) The Board may, with the approval of the Governor in Council, make regulations governing

(a) the practice and procedure in respect of the Board's hearings, including the number of members of the Board that constitutes a quorum;

(b) the time and manner in which applications and notices must be made or given;

(c) the establishment of forms for the making or giving of applications and notices; and

(d) the carrying out of the work of the Board, the management of its internal affairs and the duties of its officers and employees.

(1.1) *Case management* — The Board may, with the approval of the Governor in Council, make regulations governing the case management of matters before the Board, including regulations

(a) governing the directions a case manager may give and the orders they may make; and

(b) authorizing a case manager to give a direction or make an order that adapts, restricts or excludes the application of any provision of regulations made under subsection (1) to a matter or any step in a matter.

(2) *Publication of proposed regulations* — A copy of each regulation that the Board proposes to make under subsection (1) or (1.1) shall be published in the *Canada Gazette* at least 60 days before the regulation's proposed effective date, and a reasonable opportunity shall be given to interested persons to make representations with respect to the regulation.

(3) *Exception* — No proposed regulation that has been published pursuant to subsection (2) need again be published under that subsection, whether or not it has been altered as a result of representations made with respect thereto.
[R.S.C. 1985, c. 10 (4th Supp.), s. 12; S.C. 2018, c. 27, s. 294.]

66.7. General powers, etc. — (1) The Board has, with respect to the attendance, swearing and examination of witnesses, the production and inspection of documents, the enforcement of its decisions and other matters necessary or proper for the due exercise of its jurisdiction, all such powers, rights and privileges as are vested in a superior court of record.

(2) *Enforcement of decisions* — Any decision of the Board may, for the purposes of its enforcement, be made an order of the Federal Court or of any superior court and is enforceable in the same manner as an order thereof.

(3) *Procedure* — To make a decision of the Board an order of a court, the usual practice and procedure of the court in such matters may be followed or a certified copy of the decision may be filed with the registrar of the court and thereupon the decision becomes an order of the court.

(4) *Effect of variation of decision* — Where a decision of the Board that has been made an order of a court is varied by a subsequent decision of the Board, the order of the court shall be deemed to have been varied accordingly and the subsequent decision may, in the same manner, be made an order of the court.

[R.S.C. 1985, c. 10 (4th Supp.), s. 12.]

66.71. Distribution, publication of notices — Independently of any other provision of this Act relating to the distribution or publication of information or documents by the Board, the Board may at any time cause to be distributed or published, in any manner and on any terms and conditions that it sees fit, any notice that it sees fit to be distributed or published.

[S.C. 1997, c. 24, s. 43.]

66.8. Studies — The Board shall conduct such studies with respect to the exercise of its powers as are requested by the Minister.

[R.S.C. 1985, c. 10 (4th Supp.), s. 12.]

66.9. Report — (1) The Board shall, not later than August 31 in each year, submit to the Governor in Council through the Minister an annual report on the Board's activities for the preceding year describing briefly the applications made to the Board, the Board's decisions and any other matter that the Board considers relevant.

(2) *Tabling* — The Minister shall cause a copy of each annual report to be laid before each House of Parliament on any of the first fifteen days on which that House is sitting after the Minister receives the report.

[R.S.C. 1985, c. 10 (4th Supp.), s. 12.]

66.91. Regulations — (1) The Governor in Council may make regulations issuing policy directions to the Board and establishing general criteria to be applied by the Board or to which the Board must have regard

(*a*) in establishing fair and equitable royalties to be paid pursuant to this Act; and

(*b*) in rendering its decisions in any matter within its jurisdiction.

(2) *Regulations regarding time* — The Governor in Council may make regulations

(*a*) establishing the day by which, or the period within which, a matter before the Board — and any procedural step in the matter, whether set out in a provision of this Act or not — must be completed;

(*b*) establishing the minimum length of the effective period for the purposes of subsections 68.1(2) and 83(4);

(*c*) establishing a day for the purposes of paragraph 73.4(*b*); and

(*d*) authorizing the Board or a case manager to give a direction or make an order that adapts, restricts or excludes the application of any provision of regulations made under any of paragraphs (*a*) to (*c*) to a matter or any step in a matter.

(3) *Inconsistency or conflict* — Regulations made under subsection (2) prevail over regulations made under subsection 66.6(1) or (1.1) to the extent of an inconsistency or conflict between them.

[S.C. 1997, c. 24, s. 44; S.C. 2018, c. 27, s. 295.]

PART VII.1
COLLECTIVE ADMINISTRATION OF COPYRIGHT
COLLECTIVE SOCIETIES

[S.C. 1997, c. 24, s. 45; S.C. 2018, c. 27, s. 296.]

67. Filing of proposed tariffs — (1) A collective society may file a proposed tariff with the Board for the purpose of establishing royalties with respect to rights the collective society administers under section 3, 15, 18, 19 or 21.

(2) *Mandatory filing for certain royalties* — However, a collective society shall file a proposed tariff with the Board for the purpose of establishing royalties referred to in subsection 29.7(2) or (3) or paragraph 31(2)(*d*).

(3) *Entering into agreements* — A collective society may enter into agreements for the purpose of establishing royalties with respect to rights the collective society administers under section 3, 15, 18, 19 or 21, other than royalties referred to in subsection 29.7(2) or (3) or paragraph 31(2)(*d*).

[R.S.C. 1985, c. 10 (1st Supp.), s. 1; R.S.C. 1985, c. 10 (4th Supp.), s. 12; S.C. 1993, c. 23, s. 3; S.C. 1997, c. 24, s. 45; S.C. 2018, c. 27, s. 296.]

67.1. Designation of collective society – paragraph 19(2)(*a*) — On application by a collective society, the Board may designate the collective society as the sole collective society authorized to collect all royalties referred to in paragraph 19(2)(*a*) with respect to a sound recording of a musical work.

[R.S.C. 1985, c. 10 (4th Supp.), s. 12; S.C. 1997, c. 24, s. 45; S.C. 2001, c. 34, s. 35(E); S.C. 2012, c. 20, s. 52; S.C. 2018, c. 27, s. 296.]

67.2. Requests regarding repertoire — A collective society shall answer, within a reasonable time, all reasonable requests from any person for information about its repertoire of works, performer's performances, sound recordings or communication signals.

[R.S.C. 1985, c. 10 (4th Supp.), s. 12; S.C. 1993, c. 23, s. 4; S.C. 1993, c. 44, ss. 71, 79; S.C. 1997, c. 24, s. 45; S.C. 2018, c. 27, s. 296.]

67.3. [Repealed by S.C. 1997, c. 24, s. 45.]

TARIFFS
PROPOSED TARIFFS

68. Filing — A proposed tariff must be filed no later than October 15 of the second calendar year before the calendar year in which the proposed tariff is to take effect or, if a day is established under regulations made under subsection 66.91(2), no later than that day.

[R.S.C. 1985, c. 10 (4th Supp.), s. 13; S.C. 1993, c. 23, s. 5; S.C. 1997, c. 24, s. 45; S.C. 2012, c. 20, s. 58; S.C. 2018, c. 27, s. 296.]

68.1 Form and content — (1) A proposed tariff must be filed in both official languages and include

(*a*) the acts to which the tariff is to apply;

(*b*) the proposed royalty rates and any related terms and conditions; and

(*c*) the effective period of the proposed tariff.

(2) *Minimum effective period* — A proposed tariff's effective period must be at least three calendar years or, if a minimum period is established under regulations made under subsection 66.91(2), at least that minimum period.

[S.C. 1997, c. 24, s. 45; S.C. 2018, c. 27, s. 296.]

68.2. Publication and notification — The Board, in the manner that it sees fit,

(*a*) shall publish the proposed tariff as well as a notice that any objection to the proposed tariff must be filed within the period set out in subsection 68.3(2); and

(*b*) may distribute a notice — or cause it to be distributed or published, on any terms and conditions that the Board sees fit — of the publication of the tariff and of the notice referred to in paragraph (*a*) to any person affected by the proposed tariff.

[S.C. 1997, c. 24, s. 45; S.C. 2012, c. 20, s. 54; S.C. 2018, c. 27, s. 296.]

68.3. Filing of objection — (1) An objection to a proposed tariff may be filed with the Board by

(*a*) an educational institution, if the proposed tariff is filed for the purpose of collecting royalties referred to in subsection 29.7(2) or (3);

(*b*) a *retransmitter*, as defined in subsection 31(1), if the proposed tariff is filed for the purpose of collecting royalties referred to in paragraph 31(2)(*d*); or

(*c*)   any user, in any other case.

(2) *Time for filing objection* — An objection shall be filed no later than the 30th day after the day on which the Board published the proposed tariff under paragraph 68.2(*a*) or, if a day is established under the regulations made under subsection 66.91(2), no later than that day.

(3) *Copy to collective society* — The Board shall provide a copy of the filed objection to the collective society.
[S.C. 2018, c. 27, s. 296.]

68.4. Reply to objection— (1) The collective society may file a reply to an objection with the Board.

(2) *Copy to be provided* — The Board shall provide a copy of the filed reply to the person or entity that filed the objection.
[S.C. 2018, c. 27, s. 296.]

WITHDRAWAL OR AMENDMENT OF PROPOSED TARIFF
[S.C. 1997, c. 24, s. 45; S.C. 2018, c. 27, s. 296.]

69. Request to withdraw or amend — A collective society may, before a proposed tariff filed by it has been approved by the Board, make an application to the Board requesting that

(*a*)   the proposed tariff be withdrawn; or

(*b*)   a reference to an act set out in the proposed tariff be excluded from the approved tariff for all of the proposed effective period or, despite subsection 68.1(2), for a portion of that period.
[R.S.C. 1985, c. 10 (4th Supp.), s. 14; S.C. 1993, c. 44, s. 73; S.C. 1997, c. 24, s. 52(F); S.C. 2018, c. 27, s. 296.]

69.1. Approval by Board — (1) The Board shall approve an application made under section 69 if it is satisfied that

(*a*)   the collective society has provided sufficient public notice of its intention to make the application;

(*b*)   every person who, in respect of the proposed effective period, has paid royalties that would not be payable if the application were approved has

   (i)   consented to the application,

   (ii)   received a refund of the royalties, or

   (iii)   entered into an agreement under subsection 67(3) that covers the act, repertoire or proposed effective period that is the subject of the application; and

179

(c)   in the case of an application made under paragraph 69(*b*) with respect to a portion of the proposed effective period, the application is not made for the purpose of improperly circumventing the required minimum effective period.

(2) *For greater certainty* — For greater certainty, the approval of an application made under section 69 does not preclude the collective society from filing, in accordance with this Act, a proposed tariff that deals in whole or in part with the act, repertoire or proposed effective period that was the subject of the application.

[S.C. 2018, c. 27, s. 296.]

APPROVAL OF TARIFFS

70. Approval — (1) The Board shall — within the period, if any, that is established under regulations made under subsection 66.91(2) — approve the proposed tariff after making any alterations to the royalty rates and the related terms and conditions, or fixing any new related terms and conditions, that the Board considers appropriate.

(2) *Factors – performances of musical works and sound recordings* — In approving a proposed tariff for the performance in public or the communication to the public by telecommunication of performer's performances of musical works, or of sound recordings embodying such performer's performances, the Board shall ensure that

(a)   the tariff applies in respect of performer's performances and sound recordings only in the situations referred to in section 20;

(b)   the tariff does not, because of linguistic and content requirements of Canada's broadcasting policy set out in section 3 of the *Broadcasting Act*, place some users that are subject to that Act at a greater financial disadvantage than others; and

(c)   the payment of royalties by users under section 19 will be made in a single payment.

(3) *Small cable transmission system* — The Board shall fix a preferential royalty rate for small cable transmission systems in approving a tariff for

(a)   the performance in public of musical works or dramatico-musical works, of performer's performances of such works, or of sound recordings embodying such works; or

(b)   the communication to the public by telecommunication of musical works or dramatico-musical works, other than as described in subsection 31(2), of performer's performances of such works, or of sound recordings embodying such works.

(4) *Small retransmission systems* — The Board shall fix a preferential royalty rate for small retransmission systems in approving a tariff for royalties referred to in

paragraph 31(2)(*d*).

(5) *For greater certainty* — For greater certainty, the Board may determine, in respect of any tariff that it approves, the portion of the royalties that is to be paid to each collective society.

(6) *No discrimination* — For greater certainty, the Board must not discriminate between owners of copyright on the ground of their nationality or residence in approving a tariff for royalties referred to in subsection 29.7(2) or (3) or paragraph 31(2)(*d*).

(7) *Regulations* — The Governor in Council may make regulations defining "small cable transmission system" and "small retransmission system" for the purposes of this section.

[R.S.C. 1985, c. 10 (4th Supp.), s. 15; S.C. 2018, c. 27, s. 296; S.C. 2020, c. 1, s. 33.]

70.1. Publication of approved tariff — The Board shall publish the approved tariff in the *Canada Gazette* and provide a copy of it, together with the reasons for the Board's decision, to

    (*a*)   the collective society that filed the proposed tariff;

    (*b*)   every collective society that is authorized to collect royalties under the tariff;

    (*c*)   every person or entity that filed an objection under section 68.3; and

    (*d*)   any other person or entity that, in the Board's opinion, ought to receive the copy and reasons.

[R.S.C. 1985, c. 10 (4th Supp.), s. 16; S.C. 1997, c. 24, s. 46; S.C. 2018, c. 27, s. 296.]

70.11. [Repealed by S.C. 2018, c. 27, s. 296.]

70.12. [Repealed by S.C. 2018, c. 27, s. 296.]

70.13. [Repealed by S.C. 2018, c. 27, s. 296.]

70.14. [Repealed by S.C. 2018, c. 27, s. 296.]

70.15. [Repealed by S.C. 2018, c. 27, s. 296.]

70.16. [Repealed by S.C. 2018, c. 27, s. 296.].

70.17. [Repealed by S.C. 2018, c. 27, s. 296.]

70.18. [Repealed by S.C. 2018, c. 27, s. 296.]

70.19. [Repealed by S.C. 2018, c. 27, s. 296.]

70.191. [Repealed by S.C. 2018, c. 27, s. 296.]

70.2. [Repealed by S.C. 2018, c. 27, s. 296.]

70.3. [Repealed by S.C. 2018, c. 27, s. 296.]

70.4. [Repealed by S.C. 2018, c. 27, s. 296.]

70.5. [Repealed by S.C. 2018, c. 27, s. 296.]

70.6. [Repealed by S.C. 2018, c. 27, s. 296.]

70.61. [Repealed by S.C. 1997, c. 24, s. 50.]

70.62. [Repealed by S.C. 1997, c. 24, s. 50.]

70.63. [Repealed by S.C. 1997, c. 24, s. 50.]

70.64. [Repealed by S.C. 1997, c. 24, s. 50.]

70.65. [Repealed by S.C. 1997, c. 24, s. 50.]

70.66. [Repealed by S.C. 1997, c. 24, s. 50.]

70.67. [Repealed by S.C. 1997, c. 24, s. 50.]

70.7. [Repealed by S.C. 1997, c. 24, s. 50.]

70.8. [Repealed by S.C. 1997, c. 24, s. 50.]

FIXING OF ROYALTY RATES IN INDIVIDUAL CASES

71. Application to fix — (1) If a collective society and a user are unable to agree on royalties to be paid with respect to rights under section 3, 15, 18, 19 or 21, other than royalties referred to in subsection 29.7(2) or (3) or paragraph 31(2)(*d*), or are unable to agree on any related terms and conditions, the collective society or user may, after giving notice to the other party, apply to the Board to fix the royalty rates or any related terms and conditions, or both.

(2) *Fixing royalties, etc.* — The Board may, for a period that the Board may specify, fix the royalty rates or their related terms and conditions, or both, as the case may be.

(3) *Application of subsections 70(2) and (3)* — Subsections 70(2) and (3) apply, with any necessary modifications, to the fixing of royalty rates or terms and conditions, or both, by the Board under subsection (2).

(4) *For greater certainty* — For greater certainty, the Board may deny an application made under subsection (1) or any part of one.

(5) *Copy of decision and reasons* — The Board shall send a copy of the decision and the reasons for it to the collective society and the user.

(6) *Definition of user* — In this section, *user* means

(*a*)   a user who is not otherwise authorized to do an act referred to in section 3, 15, 18 or 21 in respect of the works, performer's performances, sound recordings or communication signals included in a collective society's repertoire; or (*b*) a user who is required to pay, in respect of sound recordings included in a collective society's repertoire, a royalty referred to in section 19 that has not otherwise been fixed or agreed on.

[S.C. 1997, c. 24, s. 50; S.C. 2012, c. 20, s. 55; S.C. 2018, c. 27, s. 296.]

71.1. Agreement — The Board shall not proceed with an application under section 71 in respect of any matter in issue on which an agreement has been reached, if a notice is filed with the Board that such an agreement has been reached.

[S.C. 2018, c. 27, s. 296.]

SPECIAL RULES RELATED TO ROYALTY RATES

72. Special royalty rates — (1) Subsections (2) and (3) apply despite the tariffs approved by the Board under section 70, or despite the royalty rates fixed under subsection 71(2), for the performance in public or the communication to the public by telecommunication of performer's performances of musical works or of sound recordings embodying such performer's performances.

(2) *Wireless transmission systems* — For wireless transmission systems, other than community systems and public transmission systems, broadcasters shall pay

(*a*) $100 on the first $1.25 million of annual advertising revenues in respect of each year; and

(*b*) 100% of the royalties set out in the approved tariff or fixed under subsection 71(2) for that year on any portion of annual advertising revenues exceeding $1.25 million.

(3) *Community systems* — For community systems, broadcasters shall pay royalties of $100 in respect of each year.

(4) *Effect of paying royalties* — The payment of the royalties set out in subsection (2) or (3) fully discharges all liabilities of the system in question in respect of the approved tariffs or the royalties fixed under subsection 71(2).

(5) *Definition of advertising revenues* — The Board may, by regulation, define "advertising revenues" for the purposes of subsection (2).

(6) *Regulations* — The Governor in Council may make regulations defining "community system", "public transmission system" and "wireless transmission system" for the purposes of this section.

[S.C. 1997, c. 24, s. 50; S.C. 1999, c. 31, s. 61; S.C. 2002, c. 26, s. 3; S.C. 2018, c. 27, s. 296.]

72.1. Radio performances in places other than theatres — (1) In respect of public performances by means of any radio receiving set in any place other than a theatre that is ordinarily and regularly used for entertainments to which an admission charge is made, no royalties shall be collectable from the owner or user of the radio receiving set, but the Board shall, in so far as possible, provide for the collection in advance from radio broadcasting stations of royalties appropriate to the conditions produced by the provisions of this subsection and shall fix the amount of the same.

(2) *Expenses to be taken into account* — In fixing royalties under subsection (1), the Board shall take into account all expenses of collection and other outlays, if any, saved or savable by, for or on behalf of the owner of the copyright or performing right concerned or their agents, in consequence of that subsection.
[S.C. 2018, c. 27, s. 296.]

EFFECTS RELATED TO TARIFFS AND FIXING OF ROYALTY RATES
PERMITTED ACTS AND ENFORCEMENT

73. Effect of fixing royalties — Without prejudice to any other remedies available to it, the collective society concerned may collect the royalties specified in an approved tariff or fixed by the Board under subsection 71(2) for the applicable period and, in default of their payment, recover them in a court of competent jurisdiction.
[S.C. 1997, c. 24, s. 50; S.C. 1999, c. 31, s. 62; S.C. 2002, c. 26, s. 4; S.C. 2018, c. 27, s. 296.]

73.1. Order – compliance with terms and conditions — Without prejudice to any other remedies available to it, the collective society concerned may apply to a court of competent jurisdiction for an order directing a person to comply with any terms and conditions that are set out in an approved tariff or that are fixed by the Board under subsection 71(2).
[S.C. 2018, c. 27, s. 296.]

73.2. Continuation of rights — If a proposed tariff's effective period begins before the proposed tariff is approved, and immediately after the expiry of the previous tariff, then, from the start of the effective period of the proposed tariff until the earlier of its approval and the end of its effective period,

(*a*)   any person authorized under the previous tariff to do an act that is referred to in section 3, 15, 18 or 21 and that is covered by the proposed tariff may do so; and

(*b*)   the collective society may collect the royalties in accordance with the previous tariff.
[S.C. 2018, c. 27, s. 296.]

73.3. Proceedings barred – tariff — No proceedings may be brought against a person for the infringement of a right with respect to an act referred to in section 3, 15, 18 or 21 if

(*a*)   the person has paid or offered to pay the royalties set out in an approved tariff that apply with respect to that act;

(*b*)   in the case where section 73.2 applies with respect to that act, the person has paid or offered to pay the royalties referred to in paragraph 73.2(*b*); or (*c*) in the case where no tariff has been approved with respect to that act and section 73.2 does not apply with respect to it, the person has offered to pay the royalties that are included in a proposed tariff and that will apply to that act once the tariff is approved.

[S.C. 2018, c. 27, s. 296.]

73.4. Approval of request made under section 69 — If the Board approves an application made under section 69, no proceedings may be brought against a person for the infringement of a right with respect to an act referred to in section 3, 15, 18 or 21 if

(*a*) the proposed tariff, if approved, will not apply to the act as a result of the Board's approval of the application; and

(*b*) the act occurs during the effective period set out in the proposed tariff and before the first anniversary of the day on which the collective society made its application under section 69 or, if a day has been established by regulations made under subsection 66.91(2), before that day.

[S.C. 2018, c. 27, s. 296.]

73.5. Effect of fixing of royalties — (1) If any royalties or related terms and conditions are fixed under subsection 71(2) in respect of a person, the person may, during the applicable period and on paying or offering to pay the applicable royalties, do the act referred to in section 3, 15, 18 or 21 with respect to which the royalties or related terms and conditions are fixed, subject to those related terms and conditions and to the terms and conditions established by the collective society and the person.

(2) *Authority during application* — If an application is made under subsection 71(1), a person in respect of whom royalties or terms and conditions may be fixed may, until the Board's final decision on the application, do an act referred to in section 3, 15, 18 or 21 to which the application applies if the person has offered to pay the applicable royalties in accordance with any applicable related terms and conditions.

[S.C. 2018, c. 27, s. 296.]

EFFECTS OF AGREEMENT

74. No application — An approved tariff and any royalty rates and related terms and conditions fixed by the Board under subsection 71(2), as well as sections 73.2 to 73.5, do not apply to a person in respect of the matters covered by an agreement referred to in subsection 67(3) that applies to the person.

[S.C. 1997, c. 24, s. 50; S.C. 2018, c. 27, s. 296.]

CLAIM BY COPYRIGHT OWNER — PARTICULAR ROYALTIES

75. Claims by non-members — (1) An owner of copyright who does not authorize a collective society to collect, for that person's benefit, royalties referred to in paragraph 31(2)(d) is, if the work is communicated to the public by telecommunication during a period when an approved tariff that is applicable to that kind of work is effective, entitled to be paid those royalties by the collective society that is designated by the Board, of its own motion or on application, subject to the same conditions as those to which a person who has so authorized that collective society is subject.

(2) *Payment to non-members* — An owner of copyright who does not authorize a collective society to collect, for that person's benefit, royalties referred to in subsection 29.7(2) or (3) is, if such royalties are payable during a period when an approved tariff that is applicable to that kind of work or other subject matter is effective, entitled to be paid those royalties by the collective society that is designated by the Board, of its own motion or on application, subject to the same conditions as those to which a person who has so authorized that collective society is subject.

(3) *Exclusion of other remedies* — The entitlement referred to in subsections (1) and (2) is the only remedy of the owner of the copyright for the payment of royalties for the communication, making of the copy or sound recording or performance in public, as the case may be.

(4) *Measures* — The Board may, for the purposes of this section,

(*a*) require a collective society to file with the Board information relating to payments of royalties collected by it to the persons who have authorized it to collect those royalties; and

(*b*) by regulation, establish periods of not less than 12 months within which the entitlements referred to in subsections (1) and (2) must be exercised, beginning on

(i) the making of the copy, in the case of royalties referred to in subsection 29.7(2),

(ii) the performance in public, in the case of royalties referred to in subsection 29.7(3), or

(iii) the communication to the public by telecommunication, in the case of royalties referred to in paragraph 31(2)(*d*).

[S.C. 1997, c. 24, s. 50; S.C. 2018, c. 27, s. 296.]

EXAMINATION OF AGREEMENTS

76. Definition of *Commissioner* — (1) For the purposes of this section and section 76.1, *Commissioner* means the Commissioner of Competition appointed under the *Competition Act*.

(2) *Filing agreement with the Board* — If a collective society enters into an agreement under subsection 67(3) with a user, either party may file a copy of the

agreement with the Board within 15 days after it is entered into.

(3) *Non-application of section 45 of Competition Act —* Section 45 of the *Competition Act* does not apply in respect of any royalties or related terms and conditions arising under an agreement filed in accordance with subsection (2).

(4) *Access by Commissioner —* The Commissioner may have access to the copy of an agreement filed in accordance with subsection (2).

(5) *Request for examination —* If the Commissioner considers that an agreement filed in accordance with subsection (2) is contrary to the public interest, he or she may, after advising the parties, request that the Board examine it.

[S.C. 1997, c. 27, s. 50; S.C. 2012, c. 20, s. 56; S.C. 2018, c. 27, s. 296.]

76.1. Examination and fixing of royalty — (1) The Board shall consider a request by the Commissioner to examine an agreement and may, after giving the Commissioner and the parties to the agreement an opportunity to present their arguments, alter the royalties and any related terms and conditions arising under the agreement or fix new related terms and conditions.

(2) *Copy of decision and reasons —* The Board shall send a copy of the decision and the reasons for it to the parties and to the Commissioner.

[S.C. 2018, c. 27, s. 296.]

PART VII.2
CERTAIN APPLICATIONS TO BOARD

[S.C. 2018, c. 27, s. 296.]

OWNERS WHO CANNOT BE LOCATED

77. Circumstances in which licence may be issued by Board — (1) Where, on application to the Board by a person who wishes to obtain a licence to use

(*a*)   a published work,

(*b*)   a fixation of a performer's performance,

(*c*)   a published sound recording, or

(*d*)   a fixation of a communication signal

in which copyright subsists, the Board is satisfied that the applicant has made reasonable efforts to locate the owner of the copyright and that the owner cannot be located, the Board may issue to the applicant a licence to do an act mentioned in section 3, 15, 18 or 21, as the case may be.

(2) *Conditions of licence —* A licence issued under subsection (1) is non-exclusive and is subject to such terms and conditions as the Board may establish.

(3) *Payment to owner —* The owner of a copyright may, not later than five years after the expiration of a licence issued pursuant to subsection (1) in respect of the

copyright, collect the royalties fixed in the licence or, in default of their payment, commence an action to recover them in a court of competent jurisdiction.

(4) *Regulations* — The Copyright Board may make regulations governing the issuance of licences under subsection (1).

[S.C. 1997, c. 24, s. 50.]

COMPENSATION FOR ACTS DONE BEFORE RECOGNITION OF COPYRIGHT OR MORAL RIGHTS

78. Board may determine compensation — (1) Subject to subsection (2), for the purposes of subsections 32.4(2), 32.5(2), 33(2), 33.1(2) and 33.2(2) the Board may, on application by any of the parties referred to in one of those provisions, determine the amount of the compensation referred to in that provision that the Board considers reasonable, having regard to all the circumstances, including any judgment of a court in an action between the parties for the enforcement of a right mentioned in subsection 32.4(3) or 32.5(3).

(2) *Limitation* — The Board shall not

(*a*) proceed with an application under subsection (1) where a notice is filed with the Board that an agreement regarding the matters in issue has been reached; or

(*b*) where a court action between the parties for enforcement of a right referred to in subsection 32.4(3) or 32.5(3), as the case may be, has been commenced, continue with an application under subsection (1) until the court action is finally concluded.

(3) *Interim orders* — Where the Board proceeds with an application under subsection (1), it may, for the purpose of avoiding serious prejudice to any party, make an interim order requiring a party to refrain from doing any act described in the order until the determination of compensation is made under subsection (1).

[S.C. 1997, c. 24, s. 50; S.C. 2012, c. 20, s. 57.]

PART VIII
PRIVATE COPYING

[S.C. 1997, c. 24, s. 50.]

INTERPRETATION

79. Definitions — In this Part,

audio recording medium means a recording medium, regardless of its material form, onto which a sound recording may be reproduced and that is of a kind ordinarily used by individual consumers for that purpose, excluding any prescribed kind of recording medium;

blank audio recording medium means

188

(*a*) an audio recording medium onto which no sounds have ever been fixed, and

(*b*) any other prescribed audio recording medium;

collecting body means the collective society, or other society, association or corporation, that is designated as the collecting body under subsection 83(8);

eligible author means an author of a musical work, whether created before or after the coming into force of this Part, that is embodied in a sound recording, whether made before or after the coming into force of this Part, if copyright subsists in Canada in that musical work;

eligible maker means a maker of a sound recording that embodies a musical work, whether the first fixation of the sound recording occurred before or after the coming into force of this Part, if

(*a*) both the following two conditions are met:

  (i) the maker, at the date of that first fixation, if a corporation, had its headquarters in Canada or, if a natural person, was a Canadian citizen or permanent resident of Canada within the meaning of the subsection 2(1) of the *Immigration and Refugee Protection Act*,* and

  (ii) copyright subsists in Canada in the sound recording, or

(*b*) the maker, at the date of that first fixation, if a corporation, had its headquarters in a country referred to in a statement published under section 85 or, if a natural person, was a citizen, subject or permanent resident of such a country;

eligible performer means the performer of a performer's performance of a musical work, whether it took place before or after the coming into force of this Part, if the performer's performance is embodied in a sound recording and

(*a*) both the following two conditions are met:

  (i) the performer was, at the date of the first fixation of the sound recording, a Canadian citizen or permanent resident within the meaning of subsection 2(1) of the *Immigration and Refugee Protection Act*,* and

  (ii) copyright subsists in Canada in the performer's performance, or

(*b*) the performer was, at the date of the first fixation of the sound recording, a citizen, subject or permanent resident of a country referred to in a statement published under section 85;

prescribed means prescribed by regulations made under this Part.

[S.C. 1997, c. 24, s. 50; S.C. 2001, c. 27, s. 240.]

---

* *Immigration and Refugee Protection Act*, S.C. 2001, c. 27

permanent resident means a person who has acquired permanent resident status and has not subsequently lost that status under section 46.

[S.C. 2001, c. 27, s. 2(1).]

COPYING FOR PRIVATE USE

80. Where no infringement of copyright — (1) Subject to subsection (2), the act of reproducing all or any substantial part of

(a) a musical work embodied in a sound recording,

(b) a performer's performance of a musical work embodied in a sound recording, or

(c) a sound recording in which a musical work, or a performer's performance of a musical work, is embodied

onto an audio recording medium for the private use of the person who makes the copy does not constitute an infringement of the copyright in the musical work, the performer's performance or the sound recording.

(2) *Limitation* — Subsection (1) does not apply if the act described in that subsection is done for the purpose of doing any of the following in relation to any of the things referred to in paragraphs (1)(a) to (c):

(a) selling or renting out, or by way of trade exposing or offering for sale or rental;

(b) distributing, whether or not for the purpose of trade;

(c) communicating to the public by telecommunication; or

(d) performing, or causing to be performed, in public.

[S.C. 1997, c. 24, s. 50.]

RIGHT OF REMUNERATION

81. Right of remuneration — (1) Subject to and in accordance with this Part, eligible authors, eligible performers and eligible makers have a right to receive remuneration from manufacturers and importers of blank audio recording media in respect of the reproduction for private use of

(a) a musical work embodied in a sound recording;

(b) a performer's performance of a musical work embodied in a sound recording; or

(c) a sound recording in which a musical work, or a performer's performance of a musical work, is embodied.

(2) *Assignment of rights* — Subsections 13(4) to (7) apply, with such modifica-

tions as the circumstances require, in respect of the rights conferred by subsection (1) on eligible authors, performers and makers.

[S.C. 1997, c. 24, s. 50.]

LEVY ON BLANK AUDIO RECORDING MEDIA

82. Liability to pay levy — (1) Every person who, for the purpose of trade, manufactures a blank audio recording medium in Canada or imports a blank audio recording medium into Canada

- (*a*) is liable, subject to subsection (2) and section 86, to pay a levy to the collecting body on selling or otherwise disposing of those blank audio recording media in Canada; and

- (*b*) shall, in accordance with subsection 83(8), keep statements of account of the activities referred to in paragraph (*a*), as well as of exports of those blank audio recording media, and shall furnish those statements to the collecting body.

(2) *No levy for exports* — No levy is payable where it is a term of the sale or other disposition of the blank audio recording medium that the medium is to be exported from Canada, and it is exported from Canada.

[S.C. 1997, c. 24, s. 50.]

83. Filing of proposed tariffs — (1) Subject to subsection (14), each collective society may file with the Board a proposed tariff for the benefit of those eligible authors, eligible performers and eligible makers who, by assignment, grant of licence, appointment of the society as their agent or otherwise, authorize it to act on their behalf for that purpose, but no person other than a collective society may file any such tariff.

(2) *Filing of proposed tariff* — A proposed tariff must be filed no later than October 15 of the second calendar year before the calendar year in which the proposed tariff is to take effect or, if a day is established under regulations made under subsection 66.91(2), no later than that day.

(3) *Form and content* — A proposed tariff must be filed in both official languages and include

- (*a*) the proposed levy rates and any related terms and conditions; and

- (*b*) the effective period of the proposed tariff. It may also include a suggestion as to whom the Board should designate under paragraph (8)(*b*).

(4) *Minimum effective period* — A proposed tariff's effective period must be at least three calendar years or, if a minimum period is established under regulations made under subsection 66.91(2), at least that minimum period.

(5) *Publication* — The Board, in the manner that it sees fit, shall publish the proposed tariff and a notice that any person or entity who files an objection must do

so no later than the 30th day after the day on which the Board made the proposed tariff public or, if a day is established under regulations made under subsection 66.91(2), no later than that day.

(6) *Copy of objection* — The Board shall provide a copy of the filed objection to each collective society concerned.

(7) *Reply* — Each collective society concerned may file a reply to an objection with the Board.

(7.1) *Copy to objecto r*— The Board shall provide a copy of the filed reply to the person or entity that filed the objection.

(8) *Approval* — The Board shall, within the period that is established under regulations made under subsection 66.91(2),

(*a*)　approve a proposed tariff, after making any alterations to the levy rates and the related terms and conditions, or fixing any new related terms and conditions, that the Board considers appropriate; and

(*b*)　subject to subsection (8.2), designate as the collecting body the collective society or other society, association or corporation that, in the Board's opinion, will best fulfil the objects of sections 82, 84 and 86.

(8.1) *Terms and conditions* — The related terms and conditions may include terms and conditions such as the form, content and frequency of the statements of account referred to in subsection 82(1), measures for the protection of confidential information contained in those statements, and the times at which the levies are payable.

(8.2) *Designation* — The Board is not obligated to designate a collecting body under paragraph (8)(*b*) if it has previously done so, and a designation under that paragraph remains in effect until the Board, under a proposed tariff or on a separate application, makes another designation.

(9) *Publication of approved tariffs* — The Board shall publish the approved tariff in the *Canada Gazette* and provide a copy of it, together with the reasons for the Board's decision, to

(*a*)　the collecting body;

(*b*)　each collective society that filed a proposed tariff;

(*c*)　every person or entity that filed an objection under subsection (5); and

(*d*)　any other person or entity that, in the Board's opinion, ought to receive the copy and reasons.

(10) *Continuation of rights* — If a proposed tariff's effective period begins before the proposed tariff is approved and that effective period begins immediately after the expiry of the previous tariff, then — from the start of the effective period of the

proposed tariff until the earlier of its approval and the end of its effective period — the collecting body may collect the levies in accordance with the previous tariff.

(11) *Authors, etc., not represented by collective society* — An eligible author, eligible performer or eligible maker who does not authorize a collective society to file a proposed tariff under subsection (1) is entitled, in relation to

(*a*)　a musical work,

(*b*)　a performer's performance of a musical work, or

(*c*)　a sound recording in which a musical work, or a performer's performance of a musical work, is embodied,

as the case may be, to be paid by the collective society that is designated by the Board, of the Board's own motion or on application, the remuneration referred to in section 81 if such remuneration is payable during a period when an approved tariff that is applicable to that kind of work, performer's performance or sound recording is effective, subject to the same conditions as those to which a person who has so authorized that collective society is subject.

(12) *Exclusion of other remedies* — The entitlement referred to in subsection (11) is the only remedy of the eligible author, eligible performer or eligible maker referred to in that subsection in respect of the reproducing of sound recordings for private use.

(13) *Powers of Board* — The Board may, for the purposes of subsections (11) and (12),

(*a*)　require a collective society to file with the Board information relating to payments of moneys received by the society pursuant to section 84 to the persons who have authorized it to file a tariff under subsection (1); and

(*b*)　by regulation, establish the periods, which shall not be less than twelve months, beginning when the applicable approved tariff ceases to be effective, within which the entitlement referred to in subsection (11) must be exercised.

(14) *Single proposed tariff* — Where all the collective societies that intend to file a proposed tariff authorize a particular person or body to file a single proposed tariff on their behalf, that person or body may do so, and in that case this section applies, with such modifications as the circumstances require, in respect of that proposed tariff.

[S.C. 1997, c. 24, s. 50; S.C. 2018, c. 27, s. 297.]

DISTRIBUTION OF LEVIES PAID

84. Distribution by collecting body — As soon as practicable after receiving the levies paid to it, the collecting body shall distribute the levies to the collective societies representing eligible authors, eligible performers and eligible makers, in the proportions fixed by the Board.

[S.C. 1997, c. 24, s. 50.]

85. Reciprocity — (1) Where the Minister is of the opinion that another country grants or has undertaken to grant to performers and makers of sound recordings that are Canadian citizens or permanent residents of Canada within the meaning of subsection 2(1) of the *Immigration and Refugee Protection Act** or, if corporations, have their headquarters in Canada, as the case may be, whether by treaty, convention, agreement or law, benefits substantially equivalent to those conferred by this Part, the Minister may, by a statement published in the *Canada Gazette*,

(a)   grant the benefits conferred by this Part to performers or makers of sound recordings that are citizens, subjects or permanent residents of or, if corporations, have their headquarters in that country; and

(b)   declare that that country shall, as regards those benefits, be treated as if it were a country to which this Part extends.

(2) *Reciprocity* — Where the Minister is of the opinion that another country neither grants nor has undertaken to grant to performers or makers of sound recordings that are Canadian citizens or permanent residents of Canada within the meaning of subsection 2(1) of the *Immigration and Refugee Protection Act** or, if corporations, have their headquarters in Canada, as the case may be, whether by treaty, convention, agreement or law, benefits substantially equivalent to those conferred by this Part, the Minister may, by a statement published in the *Canada Gazette*,

(a)   grant the benefits conferred by this Part to performers or makers of sound recordings that are citizens, subjects or permanent residents of or, if corporations, have their headquarters in that country, as the case may be, to the extent that that country grants those benefits to performers or makers of sound recordings that are Canadian citizens or permanent residents within the meaning of subsection 2(1) of the *Immigration and Refugee Protection Act** or, if corporations, have their headquarters in Canada; and

(b)   declare that that country shall, as regards those benefits, be treated as if it were a country to which this Part extends.

(3) *Application of Act* — Any provision of this Act that the Minister specifies in a statement referred to in subsection (1) or (2)

(a)   applies in respect of performers or makers of sound recordings covered by that statement, as if they were citizens of or, if corporations, had their headquarters in Canada; and

(b)   applies in respect of a country covered by that statement, as if that country were Canada.

(4) *Application of Act* — Subject to any exceptions that the Minister may specify in a statement referred to in subsection (1) or (2), the other provisions of this Act also apply in the way described in subsection (3).

[S.C. 1997, c. 24, s. 50; S.C. 2001, c. 27, s. 241.]

---

* *Immigration and Refugee Protection Act*, S.C. 2001, c. 27

permanent resident means a person who has acquired permanent resident status and has not subsequently lost that status under section 46.

[S.C. 2001, c. 27, s. 2(1).]

EXEMPTION FROM LEVY

86. Where no levy payable — (1) No levy is payable under this Part where the manufacturer or importer of a blank audio recording medium sells or otherwise disposes of it to a society, association or corporation that represents persons with a perceptual disability.

(2) *Refunds* — Where a society, association or corporation referred to in subsection (1)

(*a*) purchases a blank audio recording medium in Canada from a person other than the manufacturer or importer, and

(*b*) provides the collecting body with proof of that purchase, on or before June 30 in the calendar year following the calendar year in which the purchase was made,

the collecting body is liable to pay forthwith to the society, association or corporation an amount equal to the amount of the levy paid in respect of the blank audio recording medium purchased.

(3) *If registration system exists* — If regulations made under paragraph 87(*a*) provide for the registration of societies, associations or corporations that represent persons with a perceptual disability, subsections (1) and (2) shall be read as referring to societies, associations or corporations that are so registered.

[S.C. 1997, c. 24, s. 50.]

REGULATIONS

87. Regulations— The Governor in Council may make regulations

(*a*) respecting the exemptions and refunds provided for in section 86, including, without limiting the generality of the foregoing,

    (i) regulations respecting procedures governing those exemptions and refunds,

      (ii)   regulations respecting applications for those exemptions and refunds, and

      (iii)   regulations for the registration of societies, associations or corporations that represent persons with a perceptual disability;

  (*b*)   prescribing anything that by this Part is to be prescribed; and

  (*c*)   generally for carrying out the purposes and provisions of this Part.
[S.C. 1997, c. 24, s. 50.]

CIVIL REMEDIES

88. Right of recovery— (1) Without prejudice to any other remedies available to it, the collecting body may, for the period specified in an approved tariff, collect the levies due to it under the tariff and, in default of their payment, recover them in a court of competent jurisdiction.

(2) *Failure to pay royalties* — The court may order a person who fails to pay any levy due under this Part to pay an amount not exceeding five times the amount of the levy to the collecting body. The collecting body must distribute the payment in the manner set out in section 84.

(3) *Order directing compliance* — Where any obligation imposed by this Part is not complied with, the collecting body may, in addition to any other remedy available, apply to a court of competent jurisdiction for an order directing compliance with that obligation.

(4) *Factors to consider* — Before making an order under subsection (2), the court must take into account

  (*a*)   whether the person who failed to pay the levy acted in good faith or bad faith;

  (*b*)   the conduct of the parties before and during the proceedings; and

  (*c*)   the need to deter persons from failing to pay levies.
[S.C. 1997, c. 24, s. 50.]

PART IX
GENERAL PROVISIONS
[S.C. 1997, c. 24, s. 50.]

89. No copyright, etc., except by statute — No person is entitled to copyright otherwise than under and in accordance with this Act or any other Act of Parliament, but nothing in this section shall be construed as abrogating any right or jurisdiction in respect of a breach of trust or confidence.
[S.C. 1997, c. 24, s. 50.]

90. Interpretation — No provision of this Act relating to

(a)   copyright in performer's performances, sound recordings or communication signals, or

(b)   the right of performers or makers to remuneration shall be construed as prejudicing any rights conferred by Part I or, in and of itself, as prejudicing the amount of royalties that the Board may fix in respect of those rights.

[S.C. 1997, c. 24, s. 50.]

91. Adherence to Berne and Rome Conventions — The Governor in Council shall take such measures as are necessary to secure the adherence of Canada to

(a)   the Convention for the Protection of Literary and Artistic Works concluded at Berne on September 9, 1886, as revised by the Paris Act of 1971; and

(b)   the International Convention for the Protection of Performers, Producers of Phonograms and Broadcasting Organizations, done at Rome on October 26, 1961.

[S.C. 1997, c. 24, s. 50.]

92. Review of Act — Five years after the day on which this section comes into force and at the end of each subsequent period of five years, a committee of the Senate, of the House of Commons or of both Houses of Parliament is to be designated or established for the purpose of reviewing this Act.

[S.C. 1997, c. 24, s. 50; S.C. 2012, c. 20, s. 58.]

TRANSITIONAL PROVISIONS

TRANSITIONAL PROVISIONS OF R.S.C. 1985, c. 10 (4TH SUPP.)

23. Application re moral rights — (1) The rights referred to in section 14.1 of the *Copyright Act*, as enacted by section 4, subsist in respect of a work even if the work was created before the coming into force of section 4.

(2) *Restriction* — A remedy referred to in subsection 34(1.1) of the *Copyright Act*, as enacted by section 8, may only be obtained where the infringement of the moral rights of the author occurs after the coming into force of section 8.

(3) *Idem* — Notwithstanding subsection (1) and the repeal by section 3 of subsection 14(4) of the *Copyright Act*, the rights referred to in section 14.1 of that Act, as enacted by section 4, are not enforceable against

(a)   a person who, on the coming into force of this section, is the owner of the copyright in, or holds a licence in relation to, a work, or

(b)   a person authorized by a person described in paragraph (a) to do an act mentioned in section 3 of that Act,

in respect of any thing done during the period for which the person described in paragraph (a) is the owner or while the licence is in force, and the rights referred to in subsection 14(4) of that Act continue to be enforceable against a person described in paragraph (*a*) or (*b*) during that period as if subsection 14(4) were not repealed.

24. Application re computer programs — Subsection 1(2), the definition *computer program* in subsection 1(3) and section 5 apply in respect of a computer program that was made prior to the day on which those provisions come into force but where, by virtue only of subsections 1(2) and (3) and this section, copyright subsists in a computer program that was made prior to May 27, 1987, nothing done in respect of the computer program before May 27, 1987 shall be construed to constitute an infringement of the copyright.

25. Making of records, perforated rolls, etc. — It shall be deemed not to be an infringement of copyright in any musical, literary or dramatic work for any person to make within Canada during the six months following the coming into force of section 7 records, perforated rolls or other contrivances by means of which sounds may be reproduced and by means of which the work may be mechanically performed, if the person proves

(*a*)   that before the coming into force of section 7, the person made such contrivances in respect of that work in accordance with section 29 or 30 of the *Copyright Act* and any regulation made under section 33 of that Act, as they read immediately before the coming into force of section 7; and

(*b*)   that the making would, had it occurred before the coming into force of section 7, have been deemed not to have been an infringement of copyright by section 29 or 30 of the *Copyright Act*, as it read immediately before the coming into force of section 7.

26. Infringements before coming into force — Subsection 64(1) and section 64.1 of the *Copyright Act*, as enacted by section 11, apply in respect of any alleged infringement of copyright occurring prior to, on or after the day on which section 11 comes into force.

TRANSITIONAL PROVISIONS OF S.C. 1993, c. 44

60.

. . .

(2) *Application of amendments to s. 10* — Subject to subsection 75(2) of this Act, section 10 of the *Copyright Act*, as enacted by subsection (1) of this section, applies to all photographs, whether made before or after the coming into force of this section.

(3) *Application of amendments to s. 11* — Except as provided by section 75 of this Act,

(*a*)   section 11 of the *Copyright Act*, as enacted by subsection (1) of this section, applies only in respect of contrivances made after the coming into force of this section; and (b)　section 11 of the *Copyright Act*, as it read immediately before the coming into force of this section, continues to apply in respect of contrivances made before the coming into force of this section.

. . .

75. Application of certain amendments — (1) Subject to subsection (2), amendments to the *Copyright Act* made by this Act relating to the term of copyright apply in respect of all works, whether made before or after the coming into force of this section.

(2) *Idem* — Where the term of the copyright in a work expires before the coming into force of this section, nothing in this Act shall be construed as extending or reviving that term.

76. Cinematographs — (1) Except as provided by subsection (2) of this section, the *Copyright Act*, as amended by this Act, applies in respect of all cinematographs, whether made before or after the coming into force of this section, subject to subsection 75(2) of this Act.

(2) *Idem* — Section 10 of the *Copyright Act*, as that section read immediately before the coming into force of this section and in so far as it governs who is the author of a photograph, continues to apply in respect of all cinematographs made before the coming into force of this section that were, before the coming into force of this section, protected as photographs.

77. Application of section 5 — Nothing in section 5 of the *Copyright Act*, as amended by this Act, confers copyright on works made before the coming into force of this section that did not qualify for copyright under section 5 of the *Copyright Act* as it read immediately before the coming into force of this section.

TRANSITIONAL PROVISIONS OF S.C. 1997, c. 24

18. (2) Section 30 of the Act, as enacted by subsection (1) of this section, does not apply in respect of collections referred to in section 30 that are published before the coming into force of section 30. Such collections continue to be governed by paragraph 27(2)(*d*) of the Act as it read before the coming into force of section 15 of this Act.

. . .

20.

(4) Section 39.1 of the *Copyright Act*, as enacted by subsection (1) of this section, applies in respect of

(a)　proceedings commenced but not concluded before the coming into force of subsection (1) of this section; and

(b)　proceedings commenced after the coming into force of subsection (1) of this section.

. . .

54. For greater certainty, all notices published under subsection 5(2) of the *Copyright Act* before the coming into force of this section are deemed to have been validly made and to have had force and effect in accordance with their terms.

54.1. Section 6 of the *Copyright Act* applies to a photograph in which copyright subsists on the date of the coming into force of this section, if the author is

(a) a natural person who is the author of the photograph referred to in subsection 10(2) of the *Copyright Act*, as enacted by section 7 of this Act; or

(b) the natural person referred to in subsection 10(1.1) of the *Copyright Act*, as enacted by section 7 of this Act.

55. (1) Part II of the *Copyright Act*, as enacted by section 14 of this Act, shall be construed as a replacement for subsections 5(3) to (6) and section 11 of the *Copyright Act* as those provisions read immediately before the coming into force of subsection 5(3) and section 8, respectively, of this Act.

(2) The rights conferred by Part II of the *Copyright Act*, as enacted by section 14 of this Act, shall not be construed as diminishing the rights conferred by subsections 5(3) to (6) and section 11 of the *Copyright Act* as those provisions read immediately before the coming into force of subsection 5(3) and section 8, respectively, of this Act, in relation to records, perforated rolls and other contrivances by means of which sounds may be mechanically reproduced that were made before the coming into force of subsection 5(3) and section 8, respectively, of this Act.

(3) Where an assignment of copyright or a grant of any interest therein

(a) was made before the coming into force of Part II of the *Copyright Act*, as enacted by section 14 of this Act, and

(b) was made by the maker of a sound recording who was a natural person,

subsections 14(1) and (2) of the *Copyright Act* continue to apply in respect of that assignment or grant, with such modifications as the circumstances require, as if the sound recording was the work referred to in those subsections and the maker of the sound recording was its author.

56. Nothing in this Act shall be construed as diminishing the right conferred by section 14.01 of the *Copyright Act* as that section read immediately before the coming into force of section 12 of this Act.

57. For greater certainty, the amendments to the *Copyright Act* that eliminate references to "British subject" and "Her Majesty's Realms and Territories" do not affect any copyright or moral rights that subsisted in Canada immediately before the coming into force of those amendments.

58. Nothing in this Act shall be construed as reviving a copyright that expired before the coming into force of this section.

58.1. No agreement concluded before April 25, 1996 that assigns a right or grants an interest by licence in a right that would be a copyright or a right to remuneration under this Act shall be construed as assigning or granting any rights conferred for the first time by this Act, unless the agreement specifically provides for the assignment or grant.

. . .

62. Coming into force — (1) The following provisions come into force or are deemed to have come into force on June 30, 1996:

(a) the definitions *exclusive distributor, educational institution* and *library, archive or museum* in section 2 of the *Copyright Act*, as enacted by subsection 1(5) of this Act;

(b) section 2.6 of the *Copyright Act*, as enacted by section 2 of this Act;

(c) section 27.1 of the *Copyright Act*, as enacted by section 15 of this Act; and

(d) section 45 of the *Copyright Act*, as enacted by section 28 of this Act.

(2) Notwithstanding subsection (1), the definition *exclusive distributor* referred to in paragraph (1)(a) shall be read as follows during the period beginning on June 30, 1996 and ending on the day that is sixty days after the day on which this Act is assented to:

exclusive distributor means, in relation to a book, a person who has, before or after the coming into force of this definition, been appointed in writing, by the owner or exclusive licensee of the copyright in the book in Canada, as

(a) the only distributor of the book in Canada or any part of Canada, or

(b) the only distributor of the book in Canada or any part of Canada in respect of a particular sector of the market.

(3) Notwithstanding paragraph (1)(d), paragraph 45(1)(e) of the *Copyright Act*, as enacted by section 28 of this Act, shall be read as follows for the period beginning on June 30, 1996 and ending on the day that is sixty days after the day on which this Act is assented to:

(e) to import copies, made with the consent of the owner of the copyright in the country where they were made, of any used books.

63. (1) No exclusive distributor, within the meaning assigned to that expression by subsection 62(2) of this Act, copyright owner or exclusive licensee is entitled to a remedy referred to in the *Copyright Act* in relation to an infringement referred to in subsection 27.1(1) or (2) of that Act, as enacted by section 15 of this Act, during the period beginning on June 30, 1996 and ending on the day on which this Act is assented to, unless

(a) before the infringement occurred, notice in writing has been given to the person referred to in subsection 27.1(1) or (2) of that Act, as enacted by section 15 of this Act, as the case may be, that

    (i)   there is an exclusive distributor of the book in Canada, and

    (ii)   section 27.1 of that Act came into force or was deemed to have come into force on June 30, 1996; and

  (b)   in the case of an infringement referred to in section 27.1 of that Act, as enacted by section 15 of this Act, the remedy is only in relation to a book that was imported during that period and forms part of the inventory of the person referred to in section 27.1 of that Act on the day on which this Act is assented to.

(2) No exclusive distributor, copyright owner or exclusive licensee is entitled to a remedy referred to in subsection (1) against an educational institution, library, archive or museum.

(3) For greater certainty, the expiration of the period referred to in subsection 62(2) of this Act does not affect the right of an exclusive distributor to continue, after the expiration of that period, legal proceedings validly commenced during that period.

TRANSITIONAL PROVISIONS OF S.C. 2004, C. 11

21. (4) Application — Application 21 (4) Subsection (1) applies in respect of unpublished works deposited in an archive on or before September 1, 1999 or at any time after that date.

TRANSITIONAL PROVISIONS OF S.C. 2012, C. 20

59. No revival of copyright in photograph — (1) The repeal of section 10 of the *Copyright Act* by section 6 does not have the effect of reviving copyright in any photograph in which, on the coming into force of that section 6, copyright had expired.

(2) *Cases where corporations were deemed to be authors —* In any case in which, immediately before the coming into force of section 6, a corporation is deemed, by virtue of subsection 10(2) of the *Copyright Act* as it read before the coming into force of that section 6, to be the author of a photograph in which copyright subsists at that time, the copyright in that photograph continues to subsist for the term determined in accordance with sections 6, 6.1, 6.2, 9, 11.1 or 12 of the *Copyright Act* as if its author were the individual who would have been considered the author of the photograph apart from that subsection 10(2).

(3) *Cases where individuals were deemed to be authors —* In any case in which an individual is deemed to be the author of a photograph, by virtue of subsection 10(2) of the *Copyright Act* as it read before the coming into force of section 6, the individual continues, after the coming into force of that section 6, to be the author of that photograph for the purposes of the *Copyright Act.*

60. Engraving, photograph or portrait — Subsection 13(2) of the *Copyright Act*, as it read immediately before the coming into force of section 7, continues to apply with respect to any engraving, photograph or portrait the plate or original of which was commissioned before the coming into force of that section 7.

61. No revival of copyright — Subsections 23(1) to (2) of the *Copyright Act*, as enacted by section 17, do not have the effect of reviving the copyright, or a right to remuneration, in any performer's performance or sound recording in which the copyright or the right to remuneration had expired on the coming into force of those subsections.

62. Limitation or prescription period — (1) Subsection 43.1(1) of the *Copyright Act*, as enacted by section 49, applies only to proceedings with respect to an act or omission that occurred after the coming into force of that section.

(2) *Former limitation or prescription period continued* — Subsection 41(1) of the *Copyright Act*, as it read immediately before the coming into force of section 47, applies to proceedings with respect to an infringement that occurred before the coming into force of that section.

TRANSITIONAL PROVISIONS OF S.C. 2015, C. 36

82. No revival of copyright — Paragraph 23(1)(*b*) and subsection 23(1.1) of the *Copyright Act*, as enacted by section 81, do not have the effect of reviving the copyright, or a right to remuneration, in a sound recording or performer's performance fixed in a sound recording in which the copyright or the right to remuneration had expired on the coming into force of those provisions.

TRANSITIONAL PROVISIONS OF S.C. 2018, C. 27

299. Paragraphs 66.501(*a*) and (*b*) — The Copyright Board is not required to consider the criteria set out in paragraphs 66.501(*a*) and (*b*) of the *Copyright Act*, as enacted by section 292 of this Act, in a matter in which it fixes royalty rates, levies or any related terms and conditions if the matter is commenced before the day on which this section comes into force.

300. Subsections 68.1(2) and 83(4) — Neither subsection 68.1(2) nor subsection 83(4) of the *Copyright Act*, as enacted by sections 296 and 297 of this Act, respectively, applies with respect to a proposed tariff filed before the day on which this section comes into force.

301. Subsection 67.1(4) — Subsection 67.1(4) of the *Copyright Act*, as it read immediately before the day on which this section comes into force, continues to apply with respect to

(*a*) an infringement referred to in that subsection that occurred before that day; and

(*b*) the recovery of royalties to be paid under section 19 of that Act in relation to an act that occurred before that day.

TRANSITIONAL PROVISION OF S.C. 2020, C. 1

34. No revival of copyright — Sections 6.1, 6.2 and 11.1, paragraphs 23(1)(*a*) and (*b*) and subsection 23(1.1) of the *Copyright Act*, as enacted by sections 24, 26 and 29, respectively, do not have the effect of reviving the copyright or a right to remuneration in any work, performer's performance fixed in a sound recording or sound recording in which the copyright or the right to remuneration had expired on the coming into force of those provisions of that Act.

SCHEDULE I

(Section 60)

EXISTING RIGHTS

Column I Existing Right	Column II Substituted Right
Works other than Dramatic and Musical Works Copyright	Copyright as defined by this Act.[1]
Musical and Dramatic Works Both copyright and performing right	Copyright as defined by this Act.
Copyright, but not performing right	Copyright as defined by this Act, except the sole right to perform the work or any substantial part thereof in public.
Performing right, but not copyright	The sole right to perform the work in public, but none of the other rights comprised in copyright as defined by this Act.

For the purposes of this Schedule the following expressions, where used in column I thereof, have the following meanings:

Copyright in the case of a work that according to the law in force immediately before January 1, 1924 has not been published before that date and statutory copyright wherein depends on publication,
includes the right at common law, if any, to restrain publication or other dealing with the work;

Performing right, in the case of a work that has not been performed in public before January 1, 1924, includes the right at common law, if any, to restrain the

---

[1] In the case of an essay, article or portion forming part of and first published in a review, magazine or other periodical or work of a like nature, the right shall be subject to any right of publishing the essay, article or portion in a separate form to which the author is entitled on January 1, 1924 or would if this Act had not been passed have become entitled under section 18 of *An Act to amend the Law of Copyright*, being chapter 45 of the Statutes of the United Kingdom, 1842.

performance thereof in public.
[1976-77, c. 28, s. 10.]

Schedule II [Repealed by S.C. 1993, c. 44, s. 74.]

Schedule III [Repealed by S.C. 1993, c. 44, s. 74.]

UNIVERSAL COPYRIGHT CONVENTION

(For the list of contracting countries to the Universal Copyright Convention, see http://www.unesco.org/eri/la/convention.asp?KO=15381&language=E&order=alpha)

UNIVERSAL COPYRIGHT CONVENTION 1952 (REVISED IN 1971)

The Contracting States,

Moved by the desire to assure in all countries copyright protection of literary, scientific and artistic works,

Convinced that a system of copyright protection appropriate to all nations of the world and expressed in a universal convention, additional to, and without impairing international systems already in force, will ensure respect for the rights of the individual and encourage the development of literature, the sciences and the arts,

Persuaded that such a universal copyright system will facilitate a wider dissemination of works of the human mind and increase international understanding,

Have agreed as follows:

Article I

Each Contracting State undertakes to provide for the adequate and affective protection of the rights of authors and other copyright proprietors in literary, scientific and artistic works, including writings, musical, dramatic and cinematographic works, and paintings, engravings and sculpture.

Article II

1. Published works of nationals of any Contracting State and works first published in that State shall enjoy in each other Contracting State the same protection as that other State accords to works of its nationals first published in its own territory.

2. Unpublished works of nationals of each Contracting State shall enjoy in each other Contracting State the same protection as that other State accords to unpublished works of its own nationals.

3. For the purpose of this Convention any Contracting State may, by domestic legislation, assimilate to its own nationals any person domiciled in that State.

Article III

1. Any Contracting State which, under its domestic law, requires as a condition of copyright, compliance with formalities such as deposit, registration, notice, notarial certificates, payment of fees or manufacture or publication in that Contracting State, shall regard these requirements as satisfied with respect to all works protected in accordance with this Convention and first published outside its territory and the author of which is not one of its nationals, if from the time of the first publication all the copies of the work published with the authority of the author or other copyright proprietor bear the symbol © accompanied by the name of the copyright proprietor and the year of first publication placed in such manner and location as to give reasonable notice of claim of copyright.

2. The provisions of paragraph 1 of this article shall not preclude any Contracting State from requiring formalities or other conditions for the acquisition and enjoyment of copyright in respect of works first published in its territory or works of its nationals wherever published.

3. The provisions of paragraph 1 of this article shall not preclude any Contracting State from providing that a person seeking judicial relief must, in bringing the action, comply with procedural requirements, such as that the complainant must appear through domestic counsel or that the complainant must deposit with the court or an administrative office, or both, a copy of the work involved in the litigation; provided that failure to comply with such requirements shall not affect the validity of the copyright, nor shall any such requirement be imposed upon a national of another Contracting State if such requirement is not imposed on nationals of the State in which protection is claimed.

4. In each Contracting State there shall be legal means of protecting without formalities the unpublished works of nationals of other Contracting States.

5. If a Contracting State grants protection for more than one term of copyright and the first term is for a period longer than one of the minimum periods prescribed in article IV, such State shall not be required to comply with the provisions of paragraph 1 of this article III in respect of the second or any subsequent term of copyright.

Article IV

1. The duration of protection of a work shall be governed, in accordance with the provisions of article II and this article, by the law of the Contracting State in which protection is claimed.

2. The term of protection for works protected under this Convention shall not be less than the life of the author and 25 years after his death.

However, any Contracting State which, on the effective date of this Convention in that State, has limited this term for certain classes of works to a period computed from the first publication of the work, shall be entitled to maintain these exceptions and to extend them to other classes of works. For all these classes the term of protection shall not be less than 25 years from the date of first publication.

Any Contracting State which, upon the effective date of this Convention in that State, does not compute the term of protection upon the basis of the life of the author, shall be entitled to compute the term of protection from the date of the first publication of the work or from its registration prior to publication, as the case may be, provided the term of protection shall not be less than 25 years from the date of first publication or from its registration prior to publication, as the case may be.

If the legislation of a Contracting State grants two or more successive terms of protection, the duration of the first term shall not be less than one of the minimum periods specified above.

3. The provisions of paragraph 2 of this article shall not apply to photographic works or to works of applied art; provided, however, that the term of protection in those Contracting States which protect photographic works, or works of applied art in so far as they are protected as artistic works, shall not be less than ten years for each of said classes of works.

4. No Contracting State shall be obliged to grant protection to a work for a period longer than that fixed for the class of works to which the work in question belongs, in the case of unpublished works by the law of the Contracting State of which the author is a national, and in the case of published works by the law of the Contracting State in which the work has been first published.

For the purposes of the application of the preceding provision, if the law of any Contracting State grants two or more successive terms of protection, the period of protection of that State shall be considered to be the aggregate of those terms. However, if a specified work is not protected by such State during the second or any subsequent term for any reason, the other Contracting States shall not be obliged to protect it during the second or any subsequent term.

5. For the purposes of the application of paragraph 4 of this article, the work of a national of a Contracting State, first published in a non-Contracting State, shall be treated as though first published in the Contracting State of which the author is a national.

6. For the purposes of the application of paragraph 4 of this article, in case of simultaneous publication in two or more Contracting States, the work shall be treated as though first published in the State which affords the shortest term; any work published in two or more Contracting States within thirty days of its first publication shall be considered as having been published simultaneously in said Contracting States.

Article V

1. Copyright shall include the exclusive right of the author to make, publish, and authorize the making and publication of translations of works protected under this Convention.

2. However, any Contracting State may, by its domestic legislation, restrict the right of translation of writings, but only subject to the following provisions:

If, after the expiration of a period of seven years from the date of the first publication of a writing, a translation of such writing has not been published in the national language or languages, as the case may be, of the Contracting State, by the owner of the right of translation or with his authorization, any national of such Contracting State may obtain a non-exclusive license from the competent authority thereof to translate the work and publish the work so translated in any of the national languages in which it has not been published; provided that such national, in accordance with the procedure of the State concerned, establishes either that he has requested, and been denied, authorization by the proprietor of the right to make and publish the translation, or that, after due diligence on his part, he was unable to find the owner of the right. A license may also be granted on the same conditions if all previous editions of a translation in such language are out of print.

If the owner of the right of translation cannot be found, then the applicant for a license shall send copies of his application to the publisher whose name appears on the work and, if the nationality of the owner of the right of translation is known, to the diplomatic or consular representative of the State of which such owner is a national, or to the organization which may have been designated by the government of that State. The license shall not be granted before the expiration of a period of two months from the date of the dispatch of the copies of the application.

Due provision shall be made by domestic legislation to assure to the owner of the right of translation a compensation which is just and conforms to international standards, to assure payment and transmittal of such compensation, and to assure a correct translation of the work.

The original title and the name of the author of the work shall be printed on all copies of the published translation. The license shall be valid only for publication of the translation in the territory of the Contracting State where it has been applied for. Copies so published may be imported and sold in another Contracting State if one of the national languages of such other State is the same language as that into which the work has been so translated and if the domestic law in such other State makes provision for such licenses and does not prohibit such importation and sale. Where the foregoing conditions do not exist, the importation and sale of such copies in a Contracting State shall be governed by its domestic law and its agreements. The license shall not be transferred by the license[e].

The license shall not be granted when the author has withdrawn from circulation all copies of the work.

Article VI

"Publication", as used in this Convention, means the reproduction in tangible form and the general distribution to the public of copies of a work from which it can be read or otherwise visually perceived.

Article VII

This Convention shall not apply to works or rights in works which, at the effective date of the Convention in a Contracting State where protection is claimed, are permanently in the public domain in the said Contracting State.

Article VIII

1. This Convention, which shall bear the date of September 6, 1952, shall be deposited with the Director-General of the United Nations Educational, Scientific and Cultural Organization and shall remain open for signature by all States for a period of 120 days after that date. It shall be subject to ratification or acceptance by the signatory States.

2. Any State which has not signed this Convention may accede thereto.

3. Ratification, acceptance or accession shall be effected by the deposit of an instrument to that effect with the Director-General of the United Nations Educational, Scientific and Cultural Organization.

Article IX

1. This Convention shall come into force three months after the deposit of twelve instruments of ratification, acceptance or accession, among which there shall be those of four States which are not members of the International Union for the Protection of Literary and Artistic Works.

2. Subsequently, this Convention shall come into force in respect of each State three months after that State has deposited its instrument of ratification, acceptance or accession.

Article X

1. Each State party to this Convention undertakes to adopt, in accordance with its Constitution, such measures as are necessary to ensure the application of this Convention.

2. It is understood, however, that at the time an instrument of ratification, acceptance or accession is deposited on behalf of any State, such State must be in a position under its domestic law to give effect to the terms of this Convention.

Article XI

1. An Intergovernmental Committee is hereby established with the following duties:

  (*a*) to study the problems concerning the application and operation of this Convention;

  (*b*) to make preparation for periodic revisions of this Convention;

  (*c*) to study any other problems concerning the international protection of copyright, in co-operation with the various interested international organizations, such as the United Nations Educational, Scientific and Cultural Organization, the International Union for the Protection of Literary and Artistic Works and the Organization of American States;

(*d*) to inform the Contracting States as to its activities.

2. The Committee shall consist of the representatives of twelve Contracting States to be selected with due consideration to fair geographical representation and in conformity with the Resolution relating to this article, annexed to this Convention.

The Director-General of the United Nations Educational, Scientific and Cultural Organization, the Director of the Bureau of the International Union for the Protection of Literary and Artistic Works and the Secretary-General of the Organization of American States, or their representatives, may attend meetings of the Committee in an advisory capacity.

Article XII

The Intergovernmental Committee shall convene a conference for revision of this Convention whenever it deems necessary, or at the request of at least ten Contracting States, or of a majority of the Contracting States if there are less than twenty Contracting States.

Article XIII

Any Contracting State may, at the time of deposit of its instrument of ratification, acceptance or accession, or at any time thereafter, declare by notification addressed to the Director-General of the United Nations Educational, Scientific and Cultural Organization that this Convention shall apply to all or any of the countries or territories for the international relations of which it is responsible and this Convention shall thereupon apply to the countries or territories named in such notification after the expiration of the term of three months provided for in article IX. In the absence of such notification, this Convention shall not apply to any such country or territory.

Article XIV

1. Any Contracting State may denounce this Convention in its own name or on behalf of all or any of the countries or territories as to which a notification has been given under article XIII. The denunciation shall be made by notification addressed to the Director-General of the United Nations Educational, Scientific and Cultural Organization.

2. Such denunciation shall operate only in respect of the State or of the country or territory on whose behalf it was made and shall not take effect until twelve months after the date of receipt of the notification.

Article XV

A dispute between two or more Contracting States concerning the interpretation or application of this Convention, not settled by negotiation, shall, unless the States concerned agree on some other method of settlement, be brought before the International Court of Justice for determination by it.

Article XVI

1. This Convention shall be established in English, French and Spanish. The three texts shall be signed and shall be equally authoritative.

2. Official texts of this Convention shall be established in German, Italian and Portuguese.

Any Contracting State or group of Contracting States shall be entitled to have established by the Director-General of the United Nations Educational, Scientific and Cultural Organization other texts in the language of its choice by arrangement with the Director-General.

All such texts shall be annexed to the signed texts of this Convention.

Article XVII

1. This Convention shall not in any way affect the provisions of the Berne Convention for the Protection of Literary and Artistic Works or membership in the Union created by that Convention.

2. In application of the foregoing paragraph, a Declaration has been annexed to the present article. This Declaration is an integral part of this Convention for the States bound by the Berne Convention on January 1, 1951, or which have or may become bound to it at a later date. The signature of this Convention by such States shall also constitute signature of the said Declaration, and ratification, acceptance or accession by such States shall include the Declaration as well as the Convention.

Article XVIII

This Convention shall not abrogate multilateral or bilateral copyright conventions or arrangements that are or may be in effect exclusively between two or more American Republics. In the event of any difference either between the provisions of such existing conventions or arrangements and the provisions of this Convention, or between the provisions of this Convention and those of any new convention or arrangement which may be formulated between two or more American Republics after this Convention comes into force, the convention or arrangement most recently formulated shall prevail between the parties thereto. Rights in works acquired in any Contracting State under existing conventions or arrangements before the date this Convention comes into force in such State shall not be affected.

Article XIX

This Convention shall not abrogate multilateral or bilateral conventions or

213

arrangements in effect between two or more Contracting States. In the event of any difference between the provisions of such existing conventions or arrangements and the provisions of this Convention, the provisions of this Convention shall prevail. Rights in works acquired in any Contracting State under existing conventions or arrangements before the date on which this Convention comes into force in such State shall not be affected. Nothing in this article shall affect the provisions of articles XVII and XVIII of this Convention.

Article XX

Reservations to this Convention shall not be permitted.

Article XXI

The Director-General of the United Nations Educational, Scientific and Cultural Organization shall send duly certified copies of this Convention to the States interested, to the Swiss Federal Council and to the Secretary-General of the United Nations for registration by him.

He shall also inform all interested States of the ratifications, acceptances and accessions which have been deposited, the date on which this Convention comes into force, the notifications under article XIII of this Convention, and denunciations under article XIV.

APPENDIX DECLARATION

RELATING TO ARTICLE XVII

The States which are members of the International Union for the Protection of Literary and Artistic Works, and which are signatories to the Universal Copyright Convention,

Desiring to reinforce their mutual relations on the bias of the said Union and to avoid any conflict which might result from the co-existence of the Convention of Berne and the Universal Convention,

Have, by common agreement, accepted the terms of the following declaration:

(a) Works which, according to the Berne Convention, have as their country of origin a country which has withdrawn from the International Union created by the said Convention, after January 1, 1951, shall not be protected by the Universal Copyright Convention in the countries of the Berne Union;

(b) The Universal Copyright Convention shall not be applicable to the relationships among countries of the Berne Union insofar as it relates to the protection of works having as their country of origin, within the meaning of the Berne Convention, a country of the International Union created by the said Convention.

RESOLUTION CONCERNING ARTICLE XI

THE INTERGOVERNMENTAL COPYRIGHT CONFERENCE

Having considered the problems relating to the Intergovernmental Committee provided for in Article XI of the Universal Copyright Convention.

RESOLVES

1. The first members of the Committee shall be representatives of the following twelve States, each of those States designating one representative and an alternate: Argentina, Brazil, France, India, Italy, Japan, Mexico, Spain, Switzerland, United Kingdom, and United States of America.

2. The Committee shall be constituted as soon as the Convention comes into force in accordance with article XI of this Convention.

3. The Committee shall elect its Chairman and one Vice-Chairman. It shall establish its rules of procedure having regard to the following principles:

(*a*) the normal duration of the term of office of the representatives shall be six years; with one third retiring every two years;

(*b*) before the expiration of the term of office of any members, the Committee shall decide which States shall cease to be represented on it and which States shall be called upon to designate representatives; the representatives of those States which have not ratified, accepted or acceded shall be the first to retire;

(*c*) the different parts of the world shall be fairly represented;

AND EXPRESSES THE WISH

that the United Nations Educational, Scientific, and Cultural Organization provide its Secretariat.

In faith whereof the undersigned, having deposited their respective full powers, have signed this Convention.

Done at Geneva, this sixth day of September, 1952 in a single copy.

PROTOCOL 1 ANNEXED TO THE UNIVERSAL COPYRIGHT CONVENTION CONCERNING THE APPLICATION OF THAT CONVENTION TO THE WORKS OF STATELESS PERSONS AND REFUGEES

The States parties hereto, being also parties to the Universal Copyright Convention (hereinafter referred to as the "Convention") have accepted the following provisions:

1. Stateless persons and refugees who have their habitual residence in a State party to this Protocol shall, for the purposes of the Convention, be assimilated to the nationals of that State.

2.

(*a*) This Protocol shall be signed and shall be subject to ratification or acceptance, or may be acceded to, as if the provisions of article VIII of the Convention applied hereto.

(*b*) This Protocol shall enter into force in respect of each State, on the date of deposit of the instrument of ratification, acceptance or accession of the State concerned or on the date of entry into force of the Convention with respect to such State, whichever is the later.

In faith whereof the undersigned, being duly authorized thereto, have signed this Protocol.

Done at Geneva this sixth day of September, 1952, in the English, French and Spanish languages, the three texts being equally authoritative, in a single copy which shall be deposited with the Director-General of Unesco. The Director-General shall send certified copies to the signatory States, to the Swiss Federal Council and to the Secretary-General of the United Nations for registration.

PROTOCOL 2 ANNEXED TO THE UNIVERSAL COPYRIGHT CONVENTION, CONCERNING THE APPLICATION OF THAT CONVENTION TO THE WORKS OF CERTAIN INTERNATIONAL ORGANIZATIONS

The State parties hereto, being also parties to the Universal Copyright Convention (hereinafter referred to as the "Convention"),

Have accepted the following provisions:

1.

(*a*) The protection provided for in article II (1) of the Convention shall apply to works published for the first time by the United Nations, by the United Nations, by the Specialized Agencies in relationship therewith, or by the Organization of American States;

(*b*) Similarly, article II (2) of the Convention shall apply to the said organization or agencies.

2.

(*a*) This Protocol shall be signed and shall be subject to ratification or acceptance, or may be acceded to, as if the provisions of article VIII of the Convention applied hereto.

(*b*) This Protocol shall enter into force for each State on the date of deposit of the instrument of ratification, acceptance or accession of the State concerned or on the date of entry into force of the Convention with respect to such State, whichever is the later.

In faith whereof the undersigned, being duly authorized thereto, have signed this Protocol.

Done at Geneva, this sixth day of September, 1952, in the English, French and Spanish languages, the three texts being equally authoritative, in a single copy which shall be deposited with the Director-General of the Unesco.

The Director-General shall send certificated copies to the signatory States, to the Swiss Federal Council, and to the Secretary-General of the United Nations for registration.

PROTOCOL 3 ANNEXED TO THE UNIVERSAL COPYRIGHT CONVENTION CONCERNING THE EFFECTIVE DATE OF INSTRUMENTS OF RATIFICATION OR ACCEPTANCE OF OR ACCESSION TO THAT CONVENTION

States parties hereto,

Recognizing that the application of the Universal Copyright Convention (hereinafter referred to as the "Convention") to States participating in all the international copyright systems already in force will contribute greatly to the value of the Convention;

Have agreed as follows:

1. Any State party hereto may, on depositing its instrument of ratification or acceptance of or accession to the Convention, notify the Director-General of the United Nations Educational, Scientific and Cultural Organization (hereinafter referred to as "Director-General") that that instrument shall not take effect for the purposes of Article IX of the Convention until any other State named in such notification shall have deposited its instrument.

2. The notification referred to in paragraph 1 above shall accompany the instrument to which it relates.

3. The Director-General shall inform all States signatory or which have then acceded to the Convention of any notifications received in accordance with this protocol.

4. This Protocol shall bear the same date and shall remain open for signature for the same period as the Convention.

5. It shall be subject to ratification or acceptance by the signatory States. Any State which has not signed this Protocol may accede thereto.

6. (*a*) Ratification or acceptance or accession shall be effected by the deposit of an instrument to that effect with the Director-General.

(*b*) This Protocol shall enter into force on the date of deposit of not less than four instruments of ratification or acceptance or accession. The Director-General shall inform all interested States of this date. Instruments deposited after such date shall take effect on the date of their deposit.

In faith whereof the undersigned, being duly authorized thereto, have signed this Protocol.

Done at Geneva, the sixth day of September 1952, in the English, French and Spanish languages, the three texts being equally authoritative, in a single copy which shall be annexed to the original copy of the Convention. The Director-General shall send certified copies to the signatory States to the Swiss Federal council, and to the Secretary-General of United Nations for registration.

BERNE CONVENTION FOR THE PROTECTION OF LITERARY AND ARTISTIC WORKS

(PARIS TEXT 1971, AS AMENDED ON SEPTEMBER 28, 1979)

**(For the list of contracting parties to the Berne Convention, see
http://www.wipo.int/treaties/en/ActResults.jsp?act_id=26)**

The countries of the Union, being equally animated by the desire to protect, in as
effective and uniform a manner as possible, the rights of authors in their literary and
artistic works, Recognizing the importance of the work of the Revision Conference
held at Stockholm in 1967, Have resolved to revise the Act adopted by the
Stockholm Conference, while maintaining without change Articles 1 to 20 and 22 to
26 of that Act.

Consequently, the undersigned Plenipotentiaries, having presented their full
powers, recognized as in good and due form, have agreed as follows:

Article 1

The countries to which this Convention applies constitute a Union for the
protection of the rights of authors in their literary and artistic works.

Article 2

(1) The expression "literary and artistic works" shall include every production in
the literary, scientific and artistic domain, whatever may be the mode or form of its
expression, such as books, pamphlets and other writings; lectures, addresses,
sermons and other works of the same nature; dramatic or dramatico-musical works;
choreographic works and entertainments in dumb show; musical compositions with
or without words; cinematographic works to which are assimilated works expressed
by a process analogous to cinematography; works of drawing, painting, architecture,
sculpture, engraving and lithography; photographic works to which are assimilated
works expressed by a process analogous to photography; works of applied art;
illustrations, maps, plans, sketches and three-dimensional works relative to geography, topography, architecture or science.

(2) It shall, however, be a matter for legislation in the countries of the Union to
prescribe that works in general or any specified categories of works shall not be
protected unless they have been fixed in some material form.

(3) Translations, adaptations, arrangements of music and other alterations of a
literary or artistic work shall be protected as original works without prejudice to the
copyright in the original work.

(4) It shall be a matter for legislation in the countries of the Union to determine the protection to be granted to official texts of a legislative, administrative and legal nature, and to official translations of such texts.

(5) Collections of literary or artistic works such as encyclopedias and anthologies which, by reason of the selection and arrangement of their contents, constitute intellectual creations shall be protected as such, without prejudice to the copyright in each of the works forming part of such collections.

(6) The works mentioned in this article shall enjoy protection in all countries of the Union. This protection shall operate for the benefit of the author and his successors in title.

(7) Subject to the provisions of Article 7(4) of this Convention, it shall be a matter for legislation in the countries of the Union to determine the extent of the application of their laws to works of applied art and industrial designs and models, as well as the conditions under which such works, designs and models shall be protected. Works protected in the country of origin solely as designs and models shall be entitled in another country of the Union only to such special protection as is granted in that country to designs and models; however, if no such special protection is granted in that country, such works shall be protected as artistic works.

(8) The protection of this Convention shall not apply to news of the day or to miscellaneous facts having the character of mere items of press information.

Article 2bis

(1) It shall be a matter for legislation in the countries of the Union to exclude, wholly or in part, from the protection provided by the preceding Article political speeches and speeches delivered in the course of legal proceedings.

(2) It shall also be a matter for legislation in the countries of the Union to determine the conditions under which lectures, addresses and other works of the same nature which are delivered in public may be reproduced by the press, broadcast, communicated to the public by wire and made the subject of public communication as envisaged in Article 11bis (1) of this Convention, when such use is justified by the informatory purpose.

(3) Nevertheless, the author shall enjoy the exclusive right of making a collection of his works mentioned in the preceding paragraphs.

Article 3

(1) The protection of this Convention shall apply to:

(a)   authors who are nationals of one of the countries of the Union, for their works, whether published or not;

(b)   authors who are not nationals of one of the countries of the Union, for their works first published in one of those countries, or simultaneously in a country outside the Union and in a country of the Union.

(2) Authors who are not nationals of one of the countries of the Union but who have their habitual residence in one of them shall, for the purposes of this Convention, be assimilated to nationals of that country.

(3) The expression "published works" means works published with the consent of their authors, whatever may be the means of manufacture of the copies, provided that the availability of such copies has been such as to satisfy the reasonable requirements of the public, having regard to the nature of the work. The performance of a dramatic, dramatico-musical, cinematographic or musical work, the public recitation of a literary work, the communication by wire or the broadcasting of literary or artistic works, the exhibition of a work of art and the construction of a work of architecture shall not constitute publication.

(4) A work shall be considered as having been published simultaneously in several countries if it has been published in two or more countries within thirty days of its first publication.

Article 4

The protection of this Convention shall apply, even if the conditions of Article 3 are not fulfilled, to:

(*a*) authors of cinematographic works the maker of which has his headquarters or habitual residence in one of the countries of the Union;

(*b*) authors of works of architecture, erected in a country of the Union or of other artistic works incorporated in a building or other structure located in a country of the Union.

Article 5

(1) Authors shall enjoy, in respect of works for which they are protected under this Convention, in countries of the Union other than the country of origin, the rights which their respective laws do now or may hereafter grant to their nationals, as well as the rights specially granted by this Convention.

(2) The enjoyment and the exercise of these rights shall not be subject to any formality; such enjoyment and such exercise shall be independent of the existence of protection in the country of origin of the work. Consequently, apart from the provisions of this Convention, the extent of protection, as well as the means of redress afforded to the author to protect his rights, shall be governed exclusively by the laws of the country where protection is claimed.

(3) Protection in the country of origin is governed by domestic law. However, when the author is not a national of the country of origin of the work for which he is protected under this Convention, he shall enjoy in that country the same rights as national authors.

221

(4) The country of origin shall be considered to be

(*a*) in the case of works first published in a country of the Union, that country; in the case of works published simultaneously in several countries of the Union which grant different terms of protection, the country whose legislation grants the shortest term of protection;

(*b*) in the case of works published simultaneously in a country outside the Union and in a country of the Union, the latter country;

(*c*) in the case of unpublished works or of works first published in a country outside the Union, without simultaneous publication in a country of the Union, the country of the Union of which the author is a national, provided that:

    (i) when these are cinematographic works the maker of which has his headquarters or his habitual residence in a country of the Union, the country of origin shall be that country, and

    (ii) when these are works of architecture erected in a country of the Union or other artistic works incorporated in a building or other structure located in a country of the Union, the country of origin shall be that country.

Article 6

(1) Where any country outside the Union fails to protect in an adequate manner the works of authors who are nationals of one of the countries of the Union, the latter country may restrict the protection given to the works of authors who are, at the date of the first publication thereof, nationals of the other country and are not habitually resident in one of the countries of the Union. If the country of first publication avails itself of this right, the other countries of the Union shall not be required to grant to works thus subjected to special treatment a wider protection than that granted to them in the country of first publication.

(2) No restrictions introduced by virtue of the preceding paragraph shall affect the rights which an author may have acquired in respect of a work published in a country of the Union before such restrictions were put into force.

(3) The countries of the Union which restrict the grant of copyright in accordance with this Article shall give notice thereof to the Director General of the World Intellectual Property Organization (hereinafter designated as "the Director General") by a written declaration specifying the countries in regard to which protection is restricted, and the restrictions to which rights of authors who are nationals of those countries are subjected. The Director General shall immediately communicate this declaration to all the countries of the Union.

Article 6bis

(1) Independently of the author's economic rights, and even after the transfer of the said rights, the author shall have the right to claim authorship of the work and to object to any distortion, mutilation or other modification of, or other derogatory action in relation to, the said work, which would be prejudicial to his honor or reputation.

(2) The rights granted to the author in accordance with the preceding paragraph shall, after his death, be maintained, at least until the expiry of the economic rights, and shall be exercisable by the persons or institutions authorized by the legislation of the country where protection is claimed. However, those countries whose legislation, at the moment of their ratification of or accession to this Act, does not provide for the protection after the death of the author of all the rights set out in the preceding paragraph may provide that some of these rights may, after his death, cease to be maintained.

(3) The means of redress for safeguarding the rights granted by this Article shall be governed by the legislation of the country where protection is claimed.

Article 7

(1) The term of protection granted by this Convention shall be the life of the author and fifty years after his death.

(2) However, in the case of cinematographic works, the countries of the Union may provide that the term of protection shall expire fifty years after the work has been made available to the public with the consent of the author, or, failing such an event within fifty years from the making of such a work, fifty years after the making.

(3) In the case of anonymous or pseudonymous works, the term of protection granted by this Convention shall expire fifty years after the work has been lawfully made available to the public. However, when the pseudonym adopted by the author leaves no doubt as to his identity, the term of protection shall be that provided in paragraph (1). If the author of an anonymous or pseudonymous work discloses his identity during the above-mentioned period, the term of protection applicable shall be that provided in paragraph (1). The countries of the Union shall not be required to protect anonymous or pseudonymous works in respect of which it is reasonable to presume that their author has been dead for fifty years.

(4) It shall be a matter for legislation in the countries of the Union to determine the term of protection of photographic works and that of works of applied art in so far as they are protected as artistic works; however, this term shall last at least until the end of a period of twenty-five years from the making of such a work.

(5) The term of protection subsequent to the death of the author and the terms provided by paragraphs (2), (3) and (4), shall run from the date of death or of the event referred to in those paragraphs, but such terms shall always be deemed to

begin on the 1st of January of the year following the death or such event.

(6) The countries of the Union may grant a term of protection in excess of those provided by the preceding paragraphs.

(7) Those countries of the Union bound by the Rome Act of this Convention, which grant, in their national legislation in force at the time of signature of the present Act, shorter terms of protection than those provided for in the preceding paragraphs, shall have the right to maintain such terms when ratifying or acceding to the present Act.

(8) In any case, the term shall be governed by the legislation of the country where protection is claimed; however, unless the legislation of that country otherwise provides, the term shall not exceed the term fixed in the country of origin of the work.

Article 7bis

The provisions of the preceding Article shall also apply in the case of a work of joint authorship, provided that the terms measured from the death of the author shall be calculated from the death of the last surviving author.

Article 8

Authors of literary and artistic works protected by this Convention shall enjoy the exclusive right of making and of authorizing the translation of their works throughout the term of protection of their rights in the original works.

Article 9

(1) Authors of literary and artistic works protected by this Convention shall have the exclusive right of authorizing the reproduction of these works, in any manner or form.

(2) It shall be a matter for legislation in the countries of the Union to permit the reproduction of such works in certain special cases, provided that such reproduction does not conflict with a normal exploitation of the work and does not unreasonably prejudice the legitimate interests of the author.

(3) Any sound or visual recording shall be considered as a reproduction for the purposes of this Convention.

Article 10

(1) It shall be permissible to make quotations from a work which has already been lawfully made available to the public, provided that their making is compatible with fair practice, and their extent does not exceed that justified by the purpose, including quotations from newspaper articles and periodicals in the form of press summaries.

(2) It shall be a matter for legislation in the countries of the Union, and for special agreements existing or to be concluded between them, to permit the utilization, to

the extent justified by the purpose, of literary or artistic works by way of illustration in publications, broadcasts or sound or visual recordings for teaching, provided such utilization is compatible with fair practice.

(3) Where use is made of works in accordance with the preceding paragraphs of this Article, mention shall be made of the source, and of the name of the author, if it appears thereon.

Article 10bis

(1) It shall be a matter for legislation in the countries of the Union to permit the reproduction by the press, the broadcasting or the communication to the public by wire, of articles published in newspapers or periodicals on current economic, political or religious topics, and of broadcast works of the same character, in cases in which the reproduction, broadcasting or such communication thereof is not expressly reserved. Nevertheless, the source must always be clearly indicated; the legal consequences of a breach of this obligation shall be determined by the legislation of the country where protection is claimed.

(2) It shall also be a matter for legislation in the countries of the Union to determine the conditions under which, for the purpose of reporting current events by means of photography, cinematography, broadcasting or communication to the public by wire, literary or artistic works seen or heard in the course of the event may, to the extent justified by the informatory purpose, be reproduced and made available to the public.

Article 11

(1) Authors of dramatic, dramatico-musical and musical works shall enjoy the exclusive right of authorizing:

(i)   the public performance of their works, including such public performance by any means or process;

(ii)   any communication to the public of the performance of their works.

(2) Authors of dramatic or dramatico-musical works shall enjoy, during the full term of their rights in the original works, the same rights with respect to translations thereof.

Article 11bis

(1) Authors of literary and artistic works shall enjoy the exclusive right of authorizing:

(i)   the broadcasting of their works or the communication thereof to the public by any other means of wireless diffusion of signs, sounds or images;

(ii)   any communication to the public by wire or by rebroadcasting of the broadcast of the work, when this communication is made by an organization

225

other than the original one;

(iii)   the public communication by loudspeaker or any other analogous instrument transmitting, by signs, sounds or images, the broadcast of the work.

(2) It shall be a matter for legislation in the countries of the Union to determine the conditions under which the rights mentioned in the preceding paragraph may be exercised, but these conditions shall apply only in the countries where they have been prescribed. They shall not in any circumstances be prejudicial to the moral rights of the author, nor to his right to obtain equitable remuneration which, in the absence of agreement, shall be fixed by competent authority.

(3) In the absence of any contrary stipulation, permission granted in accordance with paragraph (1) of this Article shall not imply permission to record, by means of instruments recording sounds or images, the work broadcast. It shall, however, be a matter for legislation in the countries of the Union to determine the regulations for ephemeral recordings made by a broadcasting organization by means of its own facilities and used for its own broadcasts. The preservation of these recordings in official archives may, on the ground of their exceptional documentary character, be authorized by such legislation.

Article 11ter

(1) Authors of literary works shall enjoy the exclusive right of authorizing:

(i)   the public recitation of their works, including such public recitation by any means or process;

(ii)   any communication to the public of the recitation of their works.

(2) Authors of literary works shall enjoy, during the full term of their rights in the original works, the same rights with respect to translations thereof.

Authors of literary or artistic works shall enjoy the exclusive right of authorizing adaptations, arrangements and other alterations of their works.

Article 13

(1) Each country of the Union may impose for itself reservations and conditions on the exclusive right granted to the author of a musical work and to the author of any words, the recording of which together with the musical work has already been authorized by the latter, to authorize the sound recording of that musical work, together with such words, if any; but all such reservations and conditions shall apply only in the countries which have imposed them and shall not, in any circumstances, be prejudicial to the rights of these authors to obtain equitable remuneration which, in the absence of agreement, shall be fixed by competent authority.

(2) Recordings of musical works made in a country of the Union in accordance with Article 13 (3) of the Convention signed at Rome on June 2, 1928, and at Brussels on June 26, 1948, may be reproduced in that country without the

permission of the author of the musical work until a date two years after that country becomes bound by this Act.

(3) Recordings made in accordance with paragraphs (1) and (2) of this Article and imported without permission from the parties concerned into a country where they are treated as infringing recordings shall be liable to seizure.

Article 14

(1) Authors of literary or artistic works shall have the exclusive right of authorizing:

(i) the cinematographic adaptation and reproduction of these works, and the distribution of the works thus adapted or reproduced;

(ii) the public performance and communication to the public by wire of the works thus adapted or reproduced.

(2) The adaptation into any other artistic form of a cinematographic production derived from literary or artistic works shall, without prejudice to the authorization of the author of the cinematographic production, remain subject to the authorization of the authors of the original works.

(3) The provisions of Article 13 (1) shall not apply.

Article 14bis

(1) Without prejudice to the copyright in any work which may have been adapted or reproduced, a cinematographic work shall be protected as an original work. The owner of copyright in a cinematographic work shall enjoy the same rights as the author of an original work, including the rights referred to in the preceding Article.

(2)

(a) Ownership of copyright in a cinematographic work shall be a matter for legislation in the country where protection is claimed.

(b) However, in the countries of the Union which, by legislation include among the owners of copyright in a cinematographic work authors who have brought contributions to the making of the work, such authors, if they have undertaken to bring such contributions, may not, in the absence of any contrary or special stipulation, object to the reproduction, distribution, public performance, communication to the public by wire, broadcasting or any other communication to the public, or to the subtitling or dubbing of texts, of the work.

(c) The question whether or not the form of the undertaking referred to above should, for the application of the preceding subparagraph (b), be in a written agreement or a written act of the same effect shall be a matter for the legislation of the country where the maker of the cinematographic work has his headquarters or habitual residence. However, it shall be a matter for the legislation of the country of the Union where protection is claimed to provide that the said undertaking shall be in a written agreement or a written act of the same effect. The countries whose legislation so provides shall notify the Director General by means of a written declaration, which will be immediately communicated by him to all the other countries of the Union.

(d) By "contrary or special stipulation" is meant any restrictive condition which is relevant to the aforesaid undertaking.

(3) Unless the national legislation provides to the contrary, the provisions of paragraph (2) (b) above shall not be applicable to authors of scenarios, dialogues and musical works created for the making of the cinematographic work, nor to the principal director thereof. However, those countries of the Union whose legislation does not contain rules providing for the application of the said paragraph (2) (b) to such director shall notify the Director General by means of a written declaration, which will be immediately communicated by him to all the other countries of the Union.

Article 14ter

(1) The author, or after his death the persons or institutions authorized by national legislation, shall, with respect to original works of art and original manuscripts of writers and composers, enjoy the inalienable right to an interest in any sale of the work subsequent to the first transfer by the author of the work.

(2) The protection provided by the preceding paragraph may be claimed in a country of the Union only if legislation in the country to which the author belongs so permits, and to the extent permitted by the country where this protection is claimed.

(3) The procedure for collection and the amounts shall be matters for determination by national legislation.

Article 15

(1) In order that the author of a literary or artistic work protected by this Convention shall, in the absence of proof to the contrary, be regarded as such, and consequently be entitled to institute infringement proceedings in the countries of the Union, it shall be sufficient for his name to appear on the work in the usual manner. This paragraph shall be applicable even if this name is a pseudonym, where the pseudonym adopted by the author leaves no doubt as to his identity.

(2) The person or body corporate whose name appears on a cinematographic work in the usual manner shall, in the absence of proof to the contrary, be presumed to be the maker of the said work.

(3) In the case of anonymous and pseudonymous works, other than those referred to in paragraph (1) above, the publisher whose name appears on the work shall, in

the absence of proof to the contrary, be deemed to represent the author, and in this capacity be shall be entitled to protect and enforce the author's rights. The provisions of this paragraph shall cease to apply when the author reveals his identity and establishes his claim to authorship of the work.

(4)

(*a*) In the case of unpublished works where the identity of the author is unknown, but where there is every ground to presume that he is a national of a country of the Union, it shall be a matter for legislation in that country to designate the competent authority who shall represent the author and shall be entitled to protect and enforce his rights in the countries of the Union.

(*b*) Countries of the Union which make such designation under the terms of this provision shall notify the Director General by means of a written declaration giving full information concerning the authority thus designated. The Director General shall at once communicate this declaration to all other countries of the Union.

Article 16

(1) Infringing copies of a work shall be liable to seizure in any country of the Union where the work enjoys legal protection.

(2) The provisions of the preceding paragraph shall also apply to reproductions coming from a country where the work is not protected, or has ceased to be protected.

(3) The seizure shall take place in accordance with the legislation of each country.

Article 17

The provisions of this Convention cannot in any way affect the right of the Government of each country of the Union to permit, to control, or to prohibit by legislation or regulation, the circulation, presentation, or exhibition of any work or production in regard to which the competent authority may find it necessary to exercise that right.

Article 18

(1) This Convention shall apply to all works which, at the moment of its coming into force, have not yet fallen into the public domain in the country of origin through the expiry of the term of protection.

(2) If, however, through the expiry of the term of protection which was previously granted, a work has fallen into the public domain of the country where protection is claimed, that work shall not be protected anew.

(3) The application of this principle shall be subject to any provisions contained in special conventions to that effect existing or to be concluded between countries of the Union. In the absence of such provisions, the respective countries shall

determine, each in so far as it is concerned, the conditions of application of this principle.

(4) The preceding provisions shall also apply in the case of new accessions to the Union and to cases in which protection is extended by the application of Article 7 or by the abandonment of reservations.

Article 19

The provisions of this Convention shall not preclude the making of a claim to the benefit of any greater protection which may be granted by legislation in a country of the Union.

Article 20

The Governments of the countries of the Union reserve the right to enter into special agreements among themselves, in so far as such agreements grant to authors more extensive rights than those granted by the Convention, or contain other provisions not contrary to this Convention. The provisions of existing agreements which satisfy these conditions shall remain applicable.

Article 21

(1) Special provisions regarding developing countries are included in the Appendix.

(2) Subject to the provisions of Article 28(1)(b), the Appendix forms an integral part of this Act.

Article 22

(1)

(*a*)   The Union shall have an Assembly consisting of those countries of the Union which are bound by Articles 22 to 26.

(*b*)   The Government of each country shall be represented by one delegate, who may be assisted by alternate delegates, advisors, and experts.

(*c*)   The expenses of each delegation shall be borne by the Government which has appointed it.

(2)

(*a*) The Assembly shall:

(i) deal with all matters concerning the maintenance and development of the Union and the implementation of this Convention;

(ii) give directions concerning the preparation for conferences of revision to the International Bureau of Intellectual Property (hereinafter designated as "the International Bureau") referred to in the Convention establishing the World Intellectual Property Organization (hereinafter designated as "the Organization"), due account being taken of any comments made by those countries of the Union which are not bound by Articles 22 to 26;

(iii) review and approve the reports and activities of the Director General of the Organization concerning the Union, and give him all necessary instructions concerning matters within the competence of the Union;

(iv) elect the members of the Executive Committee of the Assembly;

(v) review and approve the reports and activities of its Executive Committee, and give instructions to such Committee;

(vi) determine the program and adopt the triennial budget of the Union, and approve its final accounts;

(vii) adopt the financial regulations of the Union;

(viii) establish such committees of experts and working groups as may be necessary for the work of the Union;

(ix) determine which countries not members of the Union and which intergovernmental and international non-governmental organizations shall be admitted to its meetings as observers;

(x) adopt amendments to Articles 22 to 26;

(xi) take any other appropriate action designed to further the objectives of the Union;

(xii) exercise such other functions as are appropriate under this Convention;

(xiii) subject to its acceptance, exercise such rights as are given to it in the Convention establishing the Organization.

(*b*) With respect to matters which are of interest also to other Unions administered by the Organization, the Assembly shall make its decisions after having heard the advice of the Coordination Committee of the

231

Organization.

(3)

(*a*) Each country member of the Assembly shall have one vote.

(*b*) One half of the countries members of the Assembly shall constitute a quorum.

(*c*) Notwithstanding the provisions of subparagraph (b), if, in any session, the number of countries represented is less than one half but equal to or more than one third of the countries members of the Assembly, the Assembly may make decisions but, with the exception of decisions concerning its own procedure, all such decisions shall take effect only if the following conditions are fulfilled. The International Bureau shall communicate the said decisions to the countries members of the Assembly which were not represented and shall invite them to express in writing their vote or abstention within a period of three months from the date of the communication. If, at the expiration of this period, the number of countries having thus expressed their vote or abstention attains the number of countries which was lacking for attaining the quorum in the session itself, such decisions shall take effect provided that at the same time the required majority still obtains.

(*d*) Subject to the provisions of Article 26(2), the decisions of the Assembly shall require two thirds of the votes cast.

(*e*) Abstentions shall not be considered as votes.

(*f*) A delegate may represent, and vote in the name of, one country only.

(*g*) Countries of the Union not members of the Assembly shall be admitted to its meetings as observers.

(4)

(*a*) The Assembly shall meet once in every third calendar year in ordinary session upon convocation by the Director General and, in the absence of exceptional circumstances, during the same period and at the same place as the General Assembly of the Organization.

(*b*) The Assembly shall meet in extraordinary session upon convocation by the Director General, at the request of the Executive Committee or at the request of one fourth of the countries members of the Assembly.

(5) The Assembly shall adopt its own rules of procedure.

Article 23

(1) The Assembly shall have an Executive Committee.

(2)

(a) The Executive Committee shall consist of countries elected by the Assembly from among countries members of the Assembly. Furthermore, the country on whose territory the Organization has its headquarters shall, subject to the provisions of Article 25 (7) (b), have an ex officio seat on the Committee.

(b) The Government of each country member of the Executive Committee shall be represented by one delegate, who may be assisted by alternate delegates, advisors, and experts.

(c) The expenses of each delegation shall be borne by the Government which has appointed it.

(3) The number of countries members of the Executive Committee shall correspond to one fourth of the number of countries members of the Assembly. In establishing the number of seats to be filled, remainders after division by four shall be disregarded.

(4) In electing the members of the Executive Committee, the Assembly shall have due regard to an equitable geographical distribution and to the need for countries party to the Special Agreements which might be established in relation with the Union to be among the countries constituting the Executive Committee.

(5)

(a) Each member of the Executive Committee shall serve from the close of the session of the Assembly which elected it to the close of the next ordinary session of the Assembly.

(b) Members of the Executive Committee may be re-elected, but not more than two-thirds of them.

(c) The Assembly shall establish the details of the rules governing the election and possible re-election of the members of the Executive Committee.

(6)

(a) The Executive Committee shall:

    (i) prepare the draft agenda of the Assembly;

    (ii) submit proposals to the Assembly respecting the draft program and triennial budget of the Union, prepared by the Director General;

    (iii) approve, within the limits of the program and the triennial budget, the specific yearly budgets and programs prepared by the Director General;

233

(iv) submit, with appropriate comments, to the Assembly the periodical reports of the Director General and the yearly audit reports on the accounts;

(v) in accordance with the decisions of the Assembly and having regard to circumstances arising between two ordinary sessions of the Assembly, take all necessary measures to ensure the execution of the program of the Union by the Director General;

(vi) perform such other functions as are allocated to it under this Convention.

(b) With respect to matters which are of interest also to other Unions administered by the Organization, the Executive Committee shall make its decisions after having heard the advice of the Coordination Committee of the Organization.

(7)

(a) The Executive Committee shall meet once a year in ordinary session upon convocation by the Director General, preferably during the same period and at the same place as the Coordination Committee of the Organization.

(b) The Executive Committee shall meet in extraordinary session upon convocation by the Director General, either on his own initiative, or at the request of its Chairman or one fourth of its members.

(8)

(a) Each country member of the Executive Committee shall have one vote.

(b) One half of the members of the Executive Committee shall constitute a quorum.

(c) Decisions shall be made by a simple majority of the votes cast.

(d) Abstentions shall not be considered as votes.

(e) A delegate may represent, and vote in the name of, one country only.

(9) Countries of the Union not members of the Executive Committee shall be admitted to its meetings as observers.

(10) The Executive Committee shall adopt its own rules of procedure.

Article 24

(1)

(a) The administrative tasks with respect to the Union shall be performed by the International Bureau, which is a continuation of the Bureau of the Union united with the Bureau of the Union established by the International Convention for the Protection of Industrial Property.

(b) In particular, the International Bureau shall provide the secretariat of the various organs of the Union.

(c) The Director General of the Organization shall be the chief executive of the Union and shall represent the Union.

(2) The International Bureau shall assemble and publish information concerning the protection of copyright. Each country of the Union shall promptly communicate to the International Bureau all new laws and official texts concerning the protection of copyright.

(3) The International Bureau shall publish a monthly periodical.

(4) The International Bureau shall, on request, furnish information to any country of the Union on matters concerning the protection of copyright.

(5) The International Bureau shall conduct studies, and shall provide services, designed to facilitate the protection of copyright.

(6) The Director General and any staff member designated by him shall participate, without the right to vote, in all meetings of the Assembly, the Executive Committee, and any other committee of experts or working group. The Director General, or a staff member designated by him, shall be ex officio secretary of these bodies.

(7)

(a) The International Bureau shall, in accordance with the directions of the Assembly and in cooperation with the Executive Committee, make the preparations for the conferences of revision of the provisions of the Convention other than Articles 22 to 26.

(b) The International Bureau may consult with intergovernmental and international non-governmental organizations concerning preparations for conferences of revision.

(c) The Director General and persons designated by him shall take part, without the right to vote, in the discussions at these conferences.

(8) The International Bureau shall carry out any other tasks assigned to it.

Article 25

(1)

(*a*) The Union shall have a budget.

(*b*) The budget of the Union shall include the income and expenses proper to the Union, its contribution to the budget of expenses common to the Unions, and, where applicable, the sum made available to the budget of the Conference of the Organization.

(*c*) Expenses not attributable exclusively to the Union but also to one or more other Unions administered by the Organization shall be considered as expenses common to the Unions. The share of the Union in such common expenses shall be in proportion to the interest the Union has in them.

(2) The budget of the Union shall be established with due regard to the requirements of coordination with the budgets of the other Unions administered by the Organization.

(3) The budget of the Union shall be financed from the following sources:

(i)   contributions of the countries of the Union;

(ii) fees and charges due for services performed by the International Bureau in relation to the Union;

(iii) sale of, or royalties on, the publications of the International Bureau concerning the Union;

(iv) gifts, bequests, and subventions;

(v)   rents, interests, and other miscellaneous income.

(4)

(*a*) For the purpose of establishing its contribution towards the budget, each country of the Union shall belong to a class, and shall pay its annual contributions on the basis of a number of units fixed as follows:

Class I	25
Class II	20
Class III	15
Class IV	10
Class V	5
Class VI	3
Class VII	1

(*b*) Unless it has already done so, each country shall indicate, concurrently with depositing its instrument of ratification or accession, the class to which it wishes to belong. Any country may change class. If it chooses a lower class, the country must announce it to the Assembly at one of its ordinary sessions. Any such change shall take effect at the beginning of the calendar year following the session.

(c) The annual contribution of each country shall be an amount in the same proportion to the total sum to be contributed to the annual budget of the Union by all countries as the number of its units is to the total of the units of all contributing countries.

(d) Contributions shall become due on the first of January of each year.

(e) A country which is in arrears in the payment of its contributions shall have no vote in any of the organs of the Union of which it is a member if the amount of its arrears equals or exceeds the amount of the contributions due from it for the preceding two full years. However, any organ of the Union may allow such a country to continue to exercise its vote in that organ if, and as long as, it is satisfied that the delay in payment is due to exceptional and unavoidable circumstances.

(f) If the budget is not adopted before the beginning of a new financial period, it shall be at the same level as the budget of the previous year, in accordance with the financial regulations.

(5) The amount of the fees and charges due for services rendered by the International Bureau in relation to the Union shall be established, and shall be reported to the Assembly and the Executive Committee, by the Director General.

(6)

(a) The Union shall have a working capital fund which shall be constituted by a single payment made by each country of the Union. If the fund becomes insufficient, an increase shall be decided by the Assembly.

(b) The amount of the initial payment of each country to the said fund or of its participation in the increase thereof shall be a proportion of the contribution of that country for the year in which the fund is established or the increase decided.

(c) The proportion and the terms of payment shall be fixed by the Assembly on the proposal of the Director General and after it has heard the advice of the Coordination Committee of the Organization.

(7)

(a) In the headquarters agreement concluded with the country on the territory of which the Organization has its headquarters, it shall be provided that, whenever the working capital fund is insufficient, such country shall grant advances. The amount of these advances and the conditions on which they are granted shall be the subject of separate agreements, in each case, between such country and the Organization. As long as it remains under the obligation to grant advances, such country shall have an ex officio seat on the Executive Committee.

(b) The country referred to in subparagraph (a) and the Organization shall each have the right to denounce the obligation to grant advances, by written notification. Denunciation shall take effect three years after the end of the year in which it has been notified.

(8) The auditing of the accounts shall be effected by one or more of the countries of the Union or by external auditors, as provided in the financial regulations. They shall be designated, with their agreement, by the Assembly.

Article 26

(1) Proposals for the amendment of Articles 22, 23, 24, 25, and the present Article, may be initiated by any country member of the Assembly, by the Executive Committee, or by the Director General. Such proposals shall be communicated by the Director General to the member countries of the Assembly at least six months in advance of their consideration by the Assembly.

(2) Amendments to the Articles referred to in paragraph (1) shall be adopted by the Assembly. Adoption shall require three-fourths of the votes cast, provided that any amendment of Article 22, and of the present paragraph, shall require four fifths of the votes cast.

(3) Any amendment to the Articles referred to in paragraph (1) shall enter into force one month after written notifications of acceptance, effected in accordance with their respective constitutional processes, have been received by the Director General from three fourths of the countries members of the Assembly at the time it adopted the amendment. Any amendment to the said Articles thus accepted shall bind all the countries which are members of the Assembly at the time the amendment enters into force, or which become members thereof at a subsequent date, provided that any amendment increasing the financial obligations of countries of the Union shall bind only those countries which have notified their acceptance of such amendment.

Article 27

(1) This Convention shall be submitted to revision with a view to the introduction of amendments designed to improve the system of the Union.

(2) For this purpose, conferences shall be held successively in one of the countries of the Union among the delegates of the said countries.

(3) Subject to the provisions of Article 26 which apply to the amendment of Articles 22 to 26, any revision of this Act, including the Appendix, shall require the unanimity of the votes cast.

Article 28

(1)

(*a*)   Any country of the Union which has signed this Act may ratify it, and, if it has not signed it, may accede to it. Instruments of ratification or accession shall be deposited with the Director General.

(*b*)   Any country of the Union may declare in its instrument of ratification or accession that its ratification or accession shall not apply to Articles 1 to 21 and the Appendix, provided that, if such country has previously made a declaration under Article VI(1) of the Appendix, then it may declare in the said instrument only that its ratification or accession shall not apply to Articles 1 to 20.

(*c*)   Any country of the Union which, in accordance with sub-paragraph (b), has excluded provisions therein referred to from the effects of its ratification or accession may at any later time declare that it extends the effects of its ratification or accession to those provisions. Such declaration shall be deposited with the Director General.

(2)

(*a*)   Articles 1 to 21 and the Appendix shall enter into force three months after both of the following two conditions are fulfilled:

    (i)   at least five countries of the Union have ratified or acceded to this Act without making a declaration under paragraph (1)(b),

    (ii)   France, Spain, the United Kingdom of Great Britain and Northern Ireland, and the United States of America, have become bound by the Universal Copyright Convention as revised at Paris on July 24, 1971.

(*b*)   The entry into force referred to in sub-paragraph (a) shall apply to those countries of the Union which, at least three months before the said entry into force, have deposited instruments of ratification or accession not containing a declaration under paragraph (1)(b).

(*c*)   With respect to any country of the Union not covered by sub-paragraph (b) and which ratifies or accedes to this Act without making a declaration under paragraph (1)(b), Articles 1 to 21 and the Appendix shall enter into force three months after the date on which the Director General has notified the deposit of the relevant instrument of ratification or accession, unless a subsequent date has been indicated in the instrument deposited. In the latter case, Articles 1 to 21 and the Appendix shall enter into force with respect to that country on the date thus indicated.

(*d*)   The provisions of sub-paragraphs (a) to (c) do not affect the application of

Article VI of the Appendix.

(3) With respect to any country of the Union which ratifies or accedes to this Act with or without a declaration made under paragraph (1)(b), Articles 22 to 38 shall enter into force three months after the date on which the Director General has notified the deposit of the relevant instrument of ratification or accession, unless a subsequent date has been indicated in the instrument deposited. In the latter case, Articles 22 to 38 shall enter into force with respect to that country on the date thus indicated.

Article 29

(1) Any country outside the Union may accede to this Act and thereby become party to this Convention and a member of the Union. Instruments of accession shall be deposited with the Director General.

(2)

(*a*) Subject to sub-paragraph (b), this Convention shall enter into force with respect to any country outside the Union three months after the date on which the Director General has notified the deposit of its instrument of accession, unless a subsequent date has been indicated in the instrument deposited. In the latter case, this Convention shall enter into force with respect to that country on the date thus indicated.

(*b*) If the entry into force according to sub-paragraph (a) precedes the entry into force of Articles 1 to 21 and the Appendix according to Article 28(2)(a), the said country shall, in the meantime, be bound, instead of by Articles 1 to 21 and the Appendix, by Articles 1 to 20 of the Brussels Act of this Convention.

Article 29bis

Ratification of or accession to this Act by any country not bound by Articles 22 to 38 of the Stockholm Act of this Convention shall, for the sole purposes of Article 14(2) of the Convention establishing the Organization, amount to ratification of or accession to the said Stockholm Act with the limitation set forth in Article 28(1)(b)(i) thereof.

Article 30

(1) Subject to the exceptions permitted by paragraph (2) of this article, by Article 28(1)(b), by Article 33(2), and by the Appendix, ratification or accession shall automatically entail acceptance of all the provisions and admission to all the advantages of this Convention.

(2)

(*a*) Any country of the Union ratifying or acceding to this Act may, subject to Article V(2) of the Appendix, retain the benefit of the reservations it has previously formulated on condition that it makes a declaration to that effect at the time of the deposit of its instrument of ratification or accession.

(*b*) Any country outside the Union may declare, in acceding to this Convention and subject to Article V(2) of the Appendix, that it intends to substitute, temporarily at least, for Article 8 of this Act concerning the right of translation, the provisions of Article 5 of the Union Convention of 1886, as completed at Paris in 1896, on the clear understanding that the said provisions are applicable only to translations into a language in general use in the said country. Subject to Article I(6)(b) of the Appendix, any country has the right to apply, in relation to the right of translation of works whose country of origin is a country availing itself of such a reservation, a protection which is equivalent to the protection granted by the latter country.

(*c*) Any country may withdraw such reservations at any time by notification addressed to the Director General.

Article 31

(1) Any country may declare in its instrument of ratification or accession, or may inform the Director General by written notification at any time thereafter, that this Convention shall be applicable to all or part of those territories, designated in the declaration or notification, for the external relations of which it is responsible.

(2) Any country which has made such a declaration or given such a notification may, at any time, notify the Director General that this Convention shall cease to be applicable to all or part of such territories.

(3)

(*a*) Any declaration made under paragraph (1) shall take effect on the same date as the ratification or accession in which it was included, and any notification given under that paragraph shall take effect three months after its notification by the Director General.

(*b*) Any notification given under paragraph (2) shall take effect twelve months after its receipt by the Director General.

(4) This article shall in no way be understood as implying the recognition or tacit acceptance by a country of the Union of the factual situation concerning a territory to which this Convention is made applicable by another country of the Union by virtue of a declaration under paragraph (1).

Article 32

(1) This Act shall, as regards relations between the countries of the Union, and to

241

the extent that it applies, replace the Berne Convention of September 9, 1886, and the subsequent Acts of revision. The Acts previously in force shall continue to be applicable, in their entirety or to the extent that this Act does not replace them by virtue of the preceding sentence, in relations with countries of the Union which do not ratify or accede to this Act.

(2) Countries outside the Union which become party to this Act shall, subject to paragraph (3), apply it with respect to any country of the Union not bound by this Act or which, although bound by this Act, has made a declaration pursuant to Article 28(1)(b). Such countries recognize that the said country of the Union, in its relations with them:

(i) may apply the provisions of the most recent Act by which it is bound, and

(ii) subject to Article I(6) of the Appendix, has the right to adapt the protection to the level provided for by this Act.

(3) Any country which has availed itself of any of the faculties provided for in the Appendix may apply the provisions of the Appendix relating to the faculty or faculties of which it has availed itself in its relations with any other country of the Union which is not bound by this Act, provided that the latter country has accepted the application of the said provisions.

Article 33

(1) Any dispute between two or more countries of the Union concerning the interpretation or application of this Convention, not settled by negotiation, may, by any one of the countries concerned, be brought before the International Court of Justice by application in conformity with the Statute of the Court, unless the countries concerned agree on some other method of settlement. The country bringing the dispute before the Court shall inform the International Bureau; the International Bureau shall bring the matter to the attention of the other countries of the Union.

(2) Each country may, at the time it signs this Act or deposits its instrument of ratification or accession, declare that it does not consider itself bound by the provisions of paragraph (1). With regard to any dispute between such country and any other country of the Union, the provisions of paragraph (1) shall not apply.

(3) Any country having made a declaration in accordance with the provisions of paragraph (2) may, at any time, withdraw its declaration by notification addressed to the Director General.

Article 34

(1) Subject to Article 29*bis*, no country may ratify or accede to earlier Acts of this Convention once Articles 1 to 21 and the Appendix have entered into force.

(2) Once Articles 1 to 21 and the Appendix have entered into force, no country may make a declaration under Article 5 of the Protocol Regarding Developing Countries attached to the Stockholm Act.

Article 35

(1) This Convention shall remain in force without limitation as to time.

(2) Any country may denounce this Act by notification addressed to the Director General. Such denunciation shall constitute also denunciation of all earlier Acts and shall affect only the country making it, the Convention remaining in full force and effect as regards the other countries of the Union.

(3) Denunciation shall take effect one year after the day on which the Director General has received the notification.

(4) The right of denunciation provided by this article shall not be exercised by any country before the expiration of five years from the date upon which it becomes a member of the Union.

Article 36

(1) Any country party to this Convention undertakes to adopt, in accordance with its constitution, the measures necessary to ensure the application of this Convention.

(2) It is understood that, at the time a country becomes bound by this Convention, it will be in a position under its domestic law to give effect to the provisions of this Convention.

Article 37

(1)

(*a*) This Act shall be signed in a single copy in the French and English languages and, subject to paragraph (2), shall be deposited with the Director General.

(*b*) Official texts shall be established by the Director General, after consultation with the interested Governments, in the Arabic, German, Italian, Portuguese and Spanish languages, and such other languages as the Assembly may designate.

(*c*) In case of differences of opinion on the interpretation of the various texts, the French text shall prevail.

(2) This Act shall remain open for signature until January 31, 1972. Until that date, the copy referred to in paragraph (1)(a) shall be deposited with the Government of the French Republic.

(3) The Director General shall certify and transmit two copies of the signed text of this Act to the Governments of all countries of the Union and, on request, to the Government of any other country.

(4) The Director General shall register this Act with the Secretariat of the United Nations.

(5) The Director General shall notify the Governments of all countries of the Union of signatures, deposits of instruments of ratification or accession and any declarations included in such instruments or made pursuant to Articles 2 8(1)(c), 30(2)(a) and (b), and 33(2), entry into force of any provisions of this Act, notifications of denunciation, and notifications pursuant to Articles 30(2)(c), 31(1) and (2), 33(3), and 38(1), as well as the Appendix.

Article 38

(1) Countries of the Union which have not ratified or acceded to this Act and which are not bound by Articles 22 to 26 of the Stockholm Act of this Convention may, until April 26, 1975, exercise, if they so desire, the rights provided under the said articles as if they were bound by them. Any country desiring to exercise such rights shall give written notification to this effect to the Director General; this notification shall be effective on the date of its receipt. Such countries shall be deemed to be members of the Assembly until the said date.

(2) As long as all the countries of the Union have not become Members of the Organization, the International Bureau of the Organization shall also function as the Bureau of the Union, and the Director General as the Director of the said Bureau.

(3) Once all the countries of the Union have become Members of the Organization, the rights, obligations, and property, of the Bureau of the Union shall devolve on the International Bureau of the Organization.

APPENDIX

Article I

(1) Any country regarded as a developing country in conformity with the established practice of the General Assembly of the United Nations which ratifies or accedes to this Act, of which this Appendix forms an integral part, and which, having regard to its economic situation and its social or cultural needs, does not consider itself immediately in a position to make provision for the protection of all the rights as provided for in this Act, may, by a notification deposited with the Director General at the time of depositing its instrument of ratification or accession or, subject to Article V(1)(c), at any time thereafter, declare that it will avail itself of the faculty provided for in Article II, or of the faculty provided for in Article III, or of both of those faculties. It may, instead of availing itself of the faculty provided for in Article II, make a declaration according to Article V(1)(a).

(2)

(a) Any declaration under paragraph (1) notified before the expiration of the period of ten years from the entry into force of Articles 1 to 21 and this Appendix according to Article 28(2) shall be effective until the expiration of the said period. Any such declaration may be renewed in whole or in part for periods of ten years each by a notification deposited with the Director General not more than 15 months and not less than three months before the expiration of the ten-year period then running.

(b) Any declaration under paragraph (1) notified after the expiration of the period of ten years from the entry into force of Articles 1 to 21 and this Appendix according to Article 28(2) shall be effective until the expiration of the ten-year period then running. Any such declaration may be renewed as provided for in the second sentence of sub-paragraph (a).

(3) Any country of the Union which has ceased to be regarded as a developing country as referred to in paragraph (1) shall no longer be entitled to renew its declaration as provided in paragraph (2), and, whether or not it formally withdraws its declaration, such country shall be precluded from availing itself of the faculties referred to in paragraph (1) from the expiration of the ten-year period then running or from the expiration of a period of three years after it has ceased to be regarded as a developing country, whichever period expires later.

(4) Where, at the time when the declaration made under paragraph (1) or (2) ceases to be effective, there are copies in stock which were made under a license granted by virtue of this Appendix, such copies may continue to be distributed until their stock is exhausted.

(5) Any country which is bound by the provisions of this Act and which has deposited a declaration or a notification in accordance with Article 31(1) with respect to the application of this Act to a particular territory, the situation of which can be regarded as analogous to that of the countries referred to in paragraph (1), may, in respect of such territory, make the declaration referred to in paragraph (1) and the notification of renewal referred to in paragraph (2). As long as such declaration or notification remains in effect, the provisions of this Appendix shall be applicable to the territory in respect of which it was made.

(6)

(a) The fact that a country avails itself of any of the faculties referred to in paragraph (1) does not permit another country to give less protection to works of which the country of origin is the former country than it is obliged to grant under Articles 1 to 20.

(b) The right to apply reciprocal treatment provided for in Article 30(2)(b), second sentence, shall not, until the date on which the period applicable under Article I(3) expires, be exercised in respect of works the country of

245

origin of which is a country which has made a declaration according to Article V(1)(a).

Article II

(1) Any country which has declared that it will avail itself of the faculty provided for in this Article shall be entitled, so far as works published in printed or analogous forms of reproduction are concerned, to substitute for the exclusive right of translation provided for in Article 8 a system of non-exclusive and non-transferable licenses, granted by the competent authority under the following conditions and subject to Article IV.

(2)

(*a*) Subject to paragraph (3), if, after the expiration of a period of three years, or of any longer period determined by the national legislation of the said country, commencing on the date of the first publication of the work, a translation of such work has not been published in a language in general use in that country by the owner of the right of translation, or with his authorization, any national of such country may obtain a license to make a translation of the work in the said language and publish the translation in printed or analogous forms of reproduction.

(*b*) A license under the conditions provided for in this Article may also be granted if all the editions of the translation published in the language concerned are out of print.

(3)

(*a*) In the case of translations into a language which is not in general use in one or more developed countries which are members of the Union, a period of one year shall be substituted for the period of three years referred to in paragraph (2)(a).

(*b*) Any country referred to in paragraph (1) may, with the unanimous agreement of the developed countries which are members of the Union and in which the same language is in general use, substitute, in the case of translations into that language, for the period of three years referred to in paragraph (2)(a) a shorter period as determined by such agreement but not less than one year. However, the provisions of the foregoing sentence shall not apply where the language in question is English, French or Spanish. The Director General shall be notified of any such agreement by the Governments which have concluded it.

(4)

(a) No license obtainable after three years shall be granted under this Article until a further period of six months has elapsed, and no license obtainable after one year shall be granted under this Article until a further period of nine months has elapsed

(i) from the date on which the applicant complies with the requirements mentioned in Article IV(1), or

(ii) where the identity or the address of the owner of the right of translation is unknown, from the date on which the applicant sends, as provided for in Article IV(2), copies of his application submitted to the authority competent to grant the license.

(b) If, during the said period of six or nine months, a translation in the language in respect of which the application was made is published by the owner of the right of translation or with his authorization, no license under this Article shall be granted.

(5) Any license under this Article shall be granted only for the purpose of teaching, scholarship or research.

(6) If a translation of a work is published by the owner of the right of translation or with his authorization at a price reasonably related to that normally charged in the country for comparable works, any license granted under this Article shall terminate if such translation is in the same language and with substantially the same content as the translation published under the licence. Any copies already made before the license terminated may continue to be distributed until their stock is exhausted.

(7) For works which are composed mainly of illustrations, a license to make and publish a translation of the text and to reproduce and publish the illustrations may be granted only if the conditions of Article III are also fulfilled.

(8) No licence shall be granted under this Article when the author has withdrawn from circulation all copies of his work.

(9)

(a) A license to make a translation of a work which has been published in printed or analogous forms of reproduction may also be granted to any broadcasting organization having its headquarters in a country referred to in paragraph (1), upon an application made to the competent authority of that country by the said organization, provided that all of the following conditions are met:

(i) the translation is made from a copy made and acquired in accordance with the laws of the said country;

(ii) the translation is only for use in broadcasts intended exclusively for

247

teaching or for the dissemination of the results of specialized technical or scientific research to experts in a particular profession;

(iii) the translation is used exclusively for the purposes referred to in condition (ii) through broadcasts made lawfully and intended for recipients on the territory of the said country, including broadcasts made through the medium of sound or visual recordings lawfully and exclusively made for the purpose of such broadcasts;

(iv) all uses made of the translation are without any commercial purpose.

(b) Sound or visual recordings of a translation which was made by a broadcasting organization under a license granted by virtue of this paragraph may, for the purposes and subject to the conditions referred to in subparagraph (a) and with the agreement of that organization, also be used by any other broadcasting organization having its headquarters in the country whose competent authority granted the license in question.

(c) Provided that all of the criteria and conditions set out in subparagraph (a) are met, a license may also be granted to a broadcasting organization to translate any text incorporated in an audio-visual fixation where such fixation was itself prepared and published for the sole purpose of being used in connection with systematic instructional activities.

(d) Subject to subparagraphs (a) to (c), the provisions of the preceding paragraphs shall apply to the grant and exercise of any license granted under this paragraph.

Article III

(1) Any country which has declared that it will avail itself of the faculty provided for in this Article shall be entitled to substitute for the exclusive right of reproduction provided for in Article 9 a system of non-exclusive and non-transferable licenses, granted by the competent authority under the following conditions and subject to Article IV.

(2)

(a) If, in relation to a work to which this article applies by virtue of paragraph (7), after the expiration of

(i) the relevant period specified in paragraph (3), commencing on the date of first publication of a particular edition of the work, or

(ii) any longer period determined by national legislation of the country referred to in paragraph (1), commencing on the same date, copies of such edition have not been distributed in that country to the general public or in connection with systematic instructional activities, by the owner of the right of reproduction or with his authorization, at a price reasonably related to that normally charged in the country for comparable works, any national of such country may obtain a license to reproduce and publish such edition at that or a lower price for use in connection with systematic instructional activities.

(b) A license to reproduce and publish an edition which has been distributed as described in sub-paragraph (a) may also be granted under the conditions provided for in this article if, after the expiration of the applicable period, no authorized copies of that edition have been on sale for a period of six months in the country concerned to the general public or in connection with systematic instructional activities at a price reasonably related to that normally charged in the country for comparable works.

(3) The period referred to in paragraph (2)(a)(i) shall be five years, except that

(i)   for works of the natural and physical sciences, including mathematics, and of technology, the period shall be three years;

(ii) for works of fiction, poetry, drama and music, and for art books, the period shall be seven years.

(4)

(a) No license obtainable after three years shall be granted under this article until a period of six months has elapsed

(i)   from the date on which the applicant complies with the requirements mentioned in Article IV(1), or

(ii) where the identity or the address of the owner of the right of reproduction is unknown, from the date on which the applicant sends, as provided for in Article IV(2), copies of his application submitted to the authority competent to grant the license.

(b) Where licenses are obtainable after other periods and Article IV(2) is applicable, no license shall be granted until a period of three months has elapsed from the date of the dispatch of the copies of the application.

(c) If, during the period of six or three months referred to in subparagraphs (a) and (b), a distribution as described in paragraph (2)(a) has taken place, no license shall be granted under this article.

(d) No license shall be granted if the author has withdrawn from circulation all copies of the edition for the reproduction and publication of which the license has been applied for.

(5) A license to reproduce and publish a translation of a work shall not be granted under this article in the following cases:

(i)   where the translation was not published by the owner of the right of translation or with his authorization, or

(ii)   where the translation is not in a language in general use in the country in which the license is applied for.

(6) If copies of an edition of a work are distributed in the country referred to in paragraph (1) to the general public or in connection with systematic instructional activities, by the owner of the right of reproduction or with his authorization, at a price reasonably related to that normally charged in the country for comparable works, any license granted under this article shall terminate if such edition is in the same language and with substantially the same content as the edition which was published under the said license. Any copies already made before the license terminates may continue to be distributed until their stock is exhausted.

(7)

(*a*)   Subject to sub-paragraph (b), the works to which this article applies shall be limited to works published in printed or analogous forms of reproduction.

(*b*)   This article shall also apply to the reproduction in audio-visual form of lawfully made audio-visual fixations including any protected works incorporated therein and to the translation of any incorporated text into a language in general use in the country in which the license is applied for, always provided that the audio-visual fixations in question were prepared and published for the sole purpose of being used in connection with systematic instructional activities.

Article IV

(1) A license under Article II or Article III may be granted only if the applicant, in accordance with the procedure of the country concerned, establishes either that he has requested, and has been denied, authorization by the owner of the right to make and publish the translation or to reproduce and publish the edition, as the case may be, or that, after due diligence on his part, he was unable to find the owner of the right. At the same time as making the request, the applicant shall inform any national or international information center referred to in paragraph (2).

(2) If the owner of the right cannot be found, the applicant for a license shall send, by registered airmail, copies of his application, submitted to the authority competent to grant the license, to the publisher whose name appears on the work and to any national or international information center which may have been designated, in a notification to that effect deposited with the Director General, by the Government of the country in which the publisher is believed to have his principal place of business.

(3) The name of the author shall be indicated on all copies of the translation or reproduction published under a license granted under Article II or Article III. The title of the work shall appear on all such copies. In the case of a translation, the original title of the work shall appear in any case on all the said copies.

(4)

(*a*) No license granted under Article II or Article III shall extend to the export of copies, and any such license shall be valid only for publication of the translation or of the reproduction, as the case may be, in the territory of the country in which it has been applied for.

(*b*) For the purposes of sub-paragraph (a), the notion of export shall include the sending of copies from any territory to the country which, in respect of that territory, has made a declaration under Article I(5).

(*c*) Where a governmental or other public entity of a country which has granted a license to make a translation under Article II into a language other than English, French or Spanish sends copies of a translation published under such license to another country, such sending of copies shall not, for the purposes of sub-paragraph (a), be considered to constitute export if all of the following conditions are met:

  (i) the recipients are individuals who are nationals of the country whose competent authority has granted the license, or organizations grouping such individuals;

  (ii) the copies are to be used only for the purpose of teaching, scholarship or research;

  (iii) the sending of the copies and their subsequent distribution to recipients is without any commercial purpose; and

  (iv) the country to which the copies have been sent has agreed with the country whose competent authority has granted the license to allow the receipt, or distribution, or both, and the Director General has been notified of the agreement by the Government of the country in which the license has been granted.

(5) All copies published under a license granted by virtue of Article II or Article III shall bear a notice in the appropriate language stating that the copies are available for distribution only in the country or territory to which the said license applies.

(6)

(*a*) Due provision shall be made at the national level to ensure

  (i) that the license provides, in favor of the owner of the right of translation or of reproduction, as the case may be, for just compensation that is consistent with standards of royalties normally operating on licenses freely negotiated between persons in the two countries concerned, and

  (ii) payment and transmittal of the compensation: should national currency regulations intervene, the competent authority shall make all efforts, by the use of international machinery, to ensure transmittal in internationally convertible currency or its equivalent.

(b) Due provision shall be made by national legislation to ensure a correct translation of the work, or an accurate reproduction of the particular edition, as the case may be.

Article V

(1)

(a) Any country entitled to make a declaration that it will avail itself of the faculty provided for in Article II may, instead, at the time of ratifying or acceding to this Act:

   (i)   if it is a country to which Article 30(2)(a) applies, make a declaration under that provision as far as the right of translation is concerned;

   (ii) if it is a country to which Article 30(2)(a) does not apply, and even if it is not a country outside the Union, make a declaration as provided for in Article 30(2)(b), first sentence.

(b) In the case of a country which ceases to be regarded as a developing country as referred to in Article I(1), a declaration made according to this paragraph shall be effective until the date on which the period applicable under Article I(3) expires.

(c) Any country which has made a declaration according to this paragraph may not subsequently avail itself of the faculty provided for in Article II even if it withdraws the said declaration.

(2) Subject to paragraph (3), any country which has availed itself of the faculty provided for in Article II may not subsequently make a declaration according to paragraph (1).

(3) Any country which has ceased to be regarded as a developing country as referred to in Article I(1) may, not later than two years prior to the expiration of the period applicable under Article I(3), make a declaration to the effect provided for in Article 30(2)(b), first sentence, notwithstanding the fact that it is not a country outside the Union. Such declaration shall take effect at the date on which the period applicable under Article I(3) expires.

Article VI

(1) Any country of the Union may declare, as from the date of this Act, and at any time before becoming bound by Articles 1 to 21 and this Appendix:

   (i)   if it is a country which, were it bound by Articles 1 to 21 and this Appendix, would be entitled to avail itself of the faculties referred to in Article I(1), that it will apply the provisions of Article II or of Article III or of both to works

252

whose country of origin is a country which, pursuant to (ii) below, admits the application of those articles to such works, or which is bound by Articles 1 to 21 and this Appendix; such declaration may, instead of referring to Article II, refer to Article V;

(ii) that it admits the application of this Appendix to works of which it is the country of origin by countries which have made a declaration under (i) above or a notification under Article I.

(2) Any declaration made under paragraph (1) shall be in writing and shall be deposited with the Director General. The declaration shall become effective from the date of its deposit.

IN WITNESS WHEREOF, the undersigned, being duly authorized thereto, have signed this Act.

DONE at Paris on July 24, 1971.

AGREEMENT ON TRADE-RELATED ASPECTS OF INTELLECTUAL PROPERTY RIGHTS

**(For the list of contracting countries to the Agreement, see
https://www.wto.org/english/thewto_e/whatis_e/tif_e/org6_e.htm)**

The TRIPS Agreement is Annex 1C of the Marrakesh Agreement Establishing the World Trade Organization, signed in Marrakesh, Morocco on 15 April 1994.

PREAMBLE

Members,

Desiring to reduce distortions and impediments to international trade, and taking into account the need to promote effective and adequate protection of intellectual property rights, and to ensure that measures and procedures to enforce intellectual property rights do not themselves become barriers to legitimate trade;

Recognizing, to this end, the need for new rules and disciplines concerning:

(*a*) the applicability of the basic principles of GATT 1994 and of relevant international intellectual property agreements or conventions;

(*b*) the provision of adequate standards and principles concerning the availability, scope and use of trade-related intellectual property rights;

(*c*) the provision of effective and appropriate means for the enforcement of trade-related intellectual property rights, taking into account differences in national legal systems;

(*d*) the provision of effective and expeditious procedures for the multilateral prevention and settlement of disputes between governments; and

(*e*) transitional arrangements aiming at the fullest participation in the results of the negotiations;

Recognizing the need for a multilateral framework of principles, rules and disciplines dealing with international trade in counterfeit goods;

Recognizing that intellectual property rights are private rights;

Recognizing the underlying public policy objectives of national systems for the protection of intellectual property, including developmental and technological objectives;

Recognizing also the special needs of the least-developed country Members in respect of maximum flexibility in the domestic implementation of laws and regulations in order to enable them to create a sound and viable technological base;

Emphasizing the importance of reducing tensions by reaching strengthened commitments to resolve disputes on trade-related intellectual property issues through multilateral procedures;

Desiring to establish a mutually supportive relationship between the WTO and the World Intellectual Property Organization (referred to in this Agreement as "WIPO") as well as other relevant international organizations;

Hereby agree as follows:

PART I
GENERAL PROVISIONS AND BASIC PRINCIPLES

Article 1
NATURE AND SCOPE OF OBLIGATIONS

1. Members shall give effect to the provisions of this Agreement. Members may, but shall not be obliged to, implement in their law more extensive protection than is required by this Agreement, provided that such protection does not contravene the provisions of this Agreement. Members shall be free to determine the appropriate method of implementing the provisions of this Agreement within their own legal system and practice.

2. For the purposes of this Agreement, the term "intellectual property" refers to all categories of intellectual property that are the subject of Sections 1 through 7 of Part II.

3. Members shall accord the treatment provided for in this Agreement to the nationals of other Members. In respect of the relevant intellectual property right, the nationals of other Members shall be understood as those natural or legal persons that would meet the criteria for eligibility for protection provided for in the Paris Convention (1967), the Berne Convention (1971), the Rome Convention and the Treaty on Intellectual Property in Respect of Integrated Circuits, were all Members of the WTO members of those conventions. Any Member availing itself of the possibilities provided in paragraph 3 of Article 5 or paragraph 2 of Article 6 of the Rome Convention shall make a notification as foreseen in those provisions to the Council for Trade-Related Aspects of Intellectual Property Rights (the "Council for TRIPS").

Article 2
INTELLECTUAL PROPERTY CONVENTIONS

1. In respect of Parts II, III and IV of this Agreement, Members shall comply with Articles 1 through 12, and Article 19, of the Paris Convention (1967).

2. Nothing in Parts I to IV of this Agreement shall derogate from existing obligations that Members may have to each other under the Paris Convention, the Berne Convention, the Rome Convention and the Treaty on Intellectual Property in Respect of Integrated Circuits.

Article 3
NATIONAL TREATMENT

1. Each Member shall accord to the nationals of other Members treatment no less favourable than that it accords to its own nationals with regard to the protection of intellectual property, subject to the exceptions already provided in, respectively, the Paris Convention (1967), the Berne Convention (1971), the Rome Convention or the Treaty on Intellectual Property in Respect of Integrated Circuits. In respect of performers, producers of phonograms and broadcasting organizations, this obligation only applies in respect of the rights provided under this Agreement. Any Member availing itself of the possibilities provided in Article 6 of the Berne Convention (1971) or paragraph 1(b) of Article 16 of the Rome Convention shall make a notification as foreseen in those provisions to the Council for TRIPS.

2. Members may avail themselves of the exceptions permitted under paragraph 1 in relation to judicial and administrative procedures, including the designation of an address for service or the appointment of an agent within the jurisdiction of a Member, only where such exceptions are necessary to secure compliance with laws and regulations which are not inconsistent with the provisions of this Agreement and where such practices are not applied in a manner which would constitute a disguised restriction on trade.

Article 4
MOST-FAVOURED-NATION TREATMENT

With regard to the protection of intellectual property, any advantage, favour, privilege or immunity granted by a Member to the nationals of any other country shall be accorded immediately and unconditionally to the nationals of all other Members. Exempted from this obligation are any advantage, favour, privilege or immunity accorded by a Member:

(a) deriving from international agreements on judicial assistance or law enforcement of a general nature and not particularly confined to the protection of intellectual property;

(b) granted in accordance with the provisions of the Berne Convention (1971) or the Rome Convention authorizing that the treatment accorded be a function not of national treatment but of the treatment accorded in another country;

(c) in respect of the rights of performers, producers of phonograms and broadcasting organizations not provided under this Agreement;

(d) deriving from international agreements related to the protection of intellectual property which entered into force prior to the entry into force of the WTO Agreement, provided that such agreements are notified to the Council for TRIPS and do not constitute an arbitrary or unjustifiable discrimination against nationals of other Members.

257

Article 5
MULTILATERAL AGREEMENTS ON ACQUISITION OR MAINTENANCE OF PROTECTION

The obligations under Articles 3 and 4 do not apply to procedures provided in multilateral agreements concluded under the auspices of WIPO relating to the acquisition or maintenance of intellectual property rights.

Article 6
EXHAUSTION

For the purposes of dispute settlement under this Agreement, subject to the provisions of Articles 3 and 4 nothing in this Agreement shall be used to address the issue of the exhaustion of intellectual property rights.

Article 7
OBJECTIVES

The protection and enforcement of intellectual property rights should contribute to the promotion of technological innovation and to the transfer and dissemination of technology, to the mutual advantage of producers and users of technological knowledge and in a manner conducive to social and economic welfare, and to a balance of rights and obligations.

Article 8
PRINCIPLES

1. Members may, in formulating or amending their laws and regulations, adopt measures necessary to protect public health and nutrition, and to promote the public interest in sectors of vital importance to their socio-economic and technological development, provided that such measures are consistent with the provisions of this Agreement.

2. Appropriate measures, provided that they are consistent with the provisions of this Agreement, may be needed to prevent the abuse of intellectual property rights by right holders or the resort to practices which unreasonably restrain trade or adversely affect the international transfer of technology.

PART II
STANDARDS CONCERNING THE AVAILABILITY, SCOPE AND USE OF INTELLECTUAL PROPERTY RIGHTS

SECTION 1:
COPYRIGHT AND RELATED RIGHTS

Article 9
RELATION TO THE BERNE CONVENTION

1. Members shall comply with Articles 1 through 21 of the Berne Convention

(1971) and the Appendix thereto. However, Members shall not have rights or obligations under this Agreement in respect of the rights conferred under Article 6*bis* of that Convention or of the rights derived therefrom.

2. Copyright protection shall extend to expressions and not to ideas, procedures, methods of operation or mathematical concepts as such.

Article 10
COMPUTER PROGRAMS AND COMPILATIONS OF DATA

1. Computer programs, whether in source or object code, shall be protected as literary works under the Berne Convention (1971).

2. Compilations of data or other material, whether in machine readable or other form, which by reason of the selection or arrangement of their contents constitute intellectual creations shall be protected as such. Such protection, which shall not extend to the data or material itself, shall be without prejudice to any copyright subsisting in the data or material itself.

Article 11
RENTAL RIGHTS

In respect of at least computer programs and cinematographic works, a Member shall provide authors and their successors in title the right to authorize or to prohibit the commercial rental to the public of originals or copies of their copyright works. A Member shall be excepted from this obligation in respect of cinematographic works unless such rental has led to widespread copying of such works which is materially impairing the exclusive right of reproduction conferred in that Member on authors and their successors in title. In respect of computer programs, this obligation does not apply to rentals where the program itself is not the essential object of the rental.

Article 12
TERM OF PROTECTION

Whenever the term of protection of a work, other than a photographic work or a work of applied art, is calculated on a basis other than the life of a natural person, such term shall be no less than 50 years from the end of the calendar year of authorized publication, or, failing such authorized publication within 50 years from the making of the work, 50 years from the end of the calendar year of making.

Article 13
LIMITATIONS AND EXCEPTIONS

Members shall confine limitations or exceptions to exclusive rights to certain special cases which do not conflict with a normal exploitation of the work and do not unreasonably prejudice the legitimate interests of the right holder.

Article 14
PROTECTION OF PERFORMERS, PRODUCERS OF PHONOGRAMS (SOUND RECORDINGS) AND BROADCASTING ORGANIZATIONS

1. In respect of a fixation of their performance on a phonogram, performers shall have the possibility of preventing the following acts when undertaken

without their authorization: the fixation of their unfixed performance and the reproduction of such fixation. Performers shall also have the possibility of preventing the following acts when undertaken without their authorization: the broadcasting by wireless means and the communication to the public of their live performance.

2. Producers of phonograms shall enjoy the right to authorize or prohibit the direct or indirect reproduction of their phonograms.

3. Broadcasting organizations shall have the right to prohibit the following acts when undertaken without their authorization: the fixation, the reproduction of fixations, and the rebroadcasting by wireless means of broadcasts, as well as the communication to the public of television broadcasts of the same. Where Members do not grant such rights to broadcasting organizations, they shall provide owners of copyright in the subject matter of broadcasts with the possibility of preventing the above acts, subject to the provisions of the Berne Convention (1971).

4. The provisions of Article 11 in respect of computer programs shall apply *mutatis mutandis* to producers of phonograms and any other right holders in phonograms as determined in a Member's law. If on 15 April 1994 a Member has in force a system of equitable remuneration of right holders in respect of the rental of phonograms, it may maintain such system provided that the commercial rental of phonograms is not giving rise to the material impairment of the exclusive rights of reproduction of right holders.

5. The term of the protection available under this Agreement to performers and producers of phonograms shall last at least until the end of a period of 50 years computed from the end of the calendar year in which the fixation was made or the performance took place. The term of protection granted pursuant to paragraph 3 shall last for at least 20 years from the end of the calendar year in which the broadcast took place.

6. Any Member may, in relation to the rights conferred under paragraphs 1, 2 and 3, provide for conditions, limitations, exceptions and reservations to the extent permitted by the Rome Convention. However, the provisions of Article 18 of the Berne Convention (1971) shall also apply, *mutatis mutandis*, to the rights of performers and producers of phonograms in phonograms.

SECTION 2:
TRADEMARKS

Article 15
PROTECTABLE SUBJECT MATTER

1. Any sign, or any combination of signs, capable of distinguishing the goods or services of one undertaking from those of other undertakings, shall be capable of constituting a trademark. Such signs, in particular words including personal names, letters, numerals, figurative elements and combinations of colours as well as any combination of such signs, shall be eligible for registration as trademarks. Where signs are not inherently capable of distinguishing the relevant goods or services, Members may make registrability depend on distinctiveness acquired through use. Members may require, as a condition of registration, that signs be visually perceptible.

2. Paragraph 1 shall not be understood to prevent a Member from denying registration of a trademark on other grounds, provided that they do not derogate from the provisions of the Paris Convention (1967).

3. Members may make registrability depend on use. However, actual use of a trademark shall not be a condition for filing an application for registration. An application shall not be refused solely on the ground that intended use has not taken place before the expiry of a period of three years from the date of application.

4. The nature of the goods or services to which a trademark is to be applied shall in no case form an obstacle to registration of the trademark.

5. Members shall publish each trademark either before it is registered or promptly after it is registered and shall afford a reasonable opportunity for petitions to cancel the registration. In addition, Members may afford an opportunity for the registration of a trademark to be opposed.

Article 16
RIGHTS CONFERRED

1. The owner of a registered trademark shall have the exclusive right to prevent all third parties not having the owner's consent from using in the course of trade identical or similar signs for goods or services which are identical or similar to those in respect of which the trademark is registered where such use would result in a likelihood of confusion. In case of the use of an identical sign for identical goods or services, a likelihood of confusion shall be presumed. The rights described above shall not prejudice any existing prior rights, nor shall they affect the possibility of Members making rights available on the basis of use.

2. Article 6*bis* of the Paris Convention (1967) shall apply, *mutatis mutandis*, to services. In determining whether a trademark is well-known, Members shall take account of the knowledge of the trademark in the relevant sector of the public,

261

including knowledge in the Member concerned which has been obtained as a result of the promotion of the trademark.

3. Article 6*bis* of the Paris Convention (1967) shall apply, *mutatis mutandis*, to goods or services which are not similar to those in respect of which a trademark is registered, provided that use of that trademark in relation to those goods or services would indicate a connection between those goods or services and the owner of the registered trademark and provided that the interests of the owner of the registered trademark are likely to be damaged by such use.

Article 17
EXCEPTIONS

Members may provide limited exceptions to the rights conferred by a trademark, such as fair use of descriptive terms, provided that such exceptions take account of the legitimate interests of the owner of the trademark and of third parties.

Article 18
TERM OF PROTECTION

Initial registration, and each renewal of registration, of a trademark shall be for a term of no less than seven years. The registration of a trademark shall be renewable indefinitely.

Article 19
REQUIREMENT OF USE

1. If use is required to maintain a registration, the registration may be cancelled only after an uninterrupted period of at least three years of non-use, unless valid reasons based on the existence of obstacles to such use are shown by the trademark owner. Circumstances arising independently of the will of the owner of the trademark which constitute an obstacle to the use of the trademark, such as import restrictions on or other government requirements for goods or services protected by the trademark, shall be recognized as valid reasons for non-use.

2. When subject to the control of its owner, use of a trademark by another person shall be recognized as use of the trademark for the purpose of maintaining the registration.

Article 20
OTHER REQUIREMENTS

The use of a trademark in the course of trade shall not be unjustifiably encumbered by special requirements, such as use with another trademark, use in a special form or use in a manner detrimental to its capability to distinguish the goods or services of one undertaking from those of other undertakings. This will not preclude a requirement prescribing the use of the trademark identifying the undertaking producing the goods or services along with, but without linking it to, the trademark distinguishing the specific goods or services in question of that undertaking.

Article 21
Licensing and Assignment

Members may determine conditions on the licensing and assignment of trademarks, it being understood that the compulsory licensing of trademarks shall not be permitted and that the owner of a registered trademark shall have the right to assign the trademark with or without the transfer of the business to which the trademark belongs.

SECTION 3:
GEOGRAPHICAL INDICATIONS

Article 22
Protection of Geographical Indications

1. Geographical indications are, for the purposes of this Agreement, indications which identify a good as originating in the territory of a Member, or a region or locality in that territory, where a given quality, reputation or other characteristic of the good is essentially attributable to its geographical origin.

2. In respect of geographical indications, Members shall provide the legal means for interested parties to prevent:

(a) the use of any means in the designation or presentation of a good that indicates or suggests that the good in question originates in a geographical area other than the true place of origin in a manner which misleads the public as to the geographical origin of the good;

(b) any use which constitutes an act of unfair competition within the meaning of Article 10*bis* of the Paris Convention (1967).

3. A Member shall, *ex officio* if its legislation so permits or at the request of an interested party, refuse or invalidate the registration of a trademark which contains or consists of a geographical indication with respect to goods not originating in the territory indicated, if use of the indication in the trademark for such goods in that Member is of such a nature as to mislead the public as to the true place of origin.

4. The protection under paragraphs 1, 2 and 3 shall be applicable against a geographical indication which, although literally true as to the territory, region or locality in which the goods originate, falsely represents to the public that the goods originate in another territory.

Article 23
Additional Protection for Geographical Indications for Wines and Spirits

1. Each Member shall provide the legal means for interested parties to prevent use of a geographical indication identifying wines for wines not originating in the place indicated by the geographical indication in question or identifying spirits for spirits

not originating in the place indicated by the geographical indication in question, even where the true origin of the goods is indicated or the geographical indication is used in translation or accompanied by expressions such as "kind", "type", "style", "imitation" or the like.

2. The registration of a trademark for wines which contains or consists of a geographical indication identifying wines or for spirits which contains or consists of a geographical indication identifying spirits shall be refused or invalidated, *ex officio* if a Member's legislation so permits or at the request of an interested party, with respect to such wines or spirits not having this origin.

3. In the case of homonymous geographical indications for wines, protection shall be accorded to each indication, subject to the provisions of paragraph 4 of Article 22. Each Member shall determine the practical conditions under which the homonymous indications in question will be differentiated from each other, taking into account the need to ensure equitable treatment of the producers concerned and that consumers are not misled.

4. In order to facilitate the protection of geographical indications for wines, negotiations shall be undertaken in the Council for TRIPS concerning the establishment of a multilateral system of notification and registration of geographical indications for wines eligible for protection in those Members participating in the system.

Article 24
INTERNATIONAL NEGOTIATIONS; EXCEPTIONS

1. Members agree to enter into negotiations aimed at increasing the protection of individual geographical indications under Article 23. The provisions of paragraphs 4 through 8 below shall not be used by a Member to refuse to conduct negotiations or to conclude bilateral or multilateral agreements. In the context of such negotiations, Members shall be willing to consider the continued applicability of these provisions to individual geographical indications whose use was the subject of such negotiations.

2. The Council for TRIPS shall keep under review the application of the provisions of this Section; the first such review shall take place within two years of the entry into force of the WTO Agreement. Any matter affecting the compliance with the obligations under these provisions may be drawn to the attention of the Council, which, at the request of a Member, shall consult with any Member or Members in respect of such matter in respect of which it has not been possible to find a satisfactory solution through bilateral or plurilateral consultations between the Members concerned. The Council shall take such action as may be agreed to facilitate the operation and further the objectives of this Section.

3. In implementing this Section, a Member shall not diminish the protection of geographical indications that existed in that Member immediately prior to the date

of entry into force of the WTO Agreement.

4. Nothing in this Section shall require a Member to prevent continued and similar use of a particular geographical indication of another Member identifying wines or spirits in connection with goods or services by any of its nationals or domiciliaries who have used that geographical indication in a continuous manner with regard to the same or related goods or services in the territory of that Member either (*a*) for at least 10 years preceding 15 April 1994 or (*b*) in good faith preceding that date.

5. Where a trademark has been applied for or registered in good faith, or where rights to a trademark have been acquired through use in good faith either:

(*a*)   before the date of application of these provisions in that Member as defined in Part VI; or

(*b*)   before the geographical indication is protected in its country of origin;

measures adopted to implement this Section shall not prejudice eligibility for or the validity of the registration of a trademark, or the right to use a trademark, on the basis that such a trademark is identical with, or similar to, a geographical indication.

6. Nothing in this Section shall require a Member to apply its provisions in respect of a geographical indication of any other Member with respect to goods or services for which the relevant indication is identical with the term customary in common language as the common name for such goods or services in the territory of that Member. Nothing in this Section shall require a Member to apply its provisions in respect of a geographical indication of any other Member with respect to products of the vine for which the relevant indication is identical with the customary name of a grape variety existing in the territory of that Member as of the date of entry into force of the WTO Agreement.

7. A Member may provide that any request made under this Section in connection with the use or registration of a trademark must be presented within five years after the adverse use of the protected indication has become generally known in that Member or after the date of registration of the trademark in that Member provided that the trademark has been published by that date, if such date is earlier than the date on which the adverse use became generally known in that Member, provided that the geographical indication is not used or registered in bad faith.

8. The provisions of this Section shall in no way prejudice the right of any person to use, in the course of trade, that person's name or the name of that person's predecessor in business, except where such name is used in such a manner as to mislead the public.

9. There shall be no obligation under this Agreement to protect geographical indications which are not or cease to be protected in their country of origin, or which have fallen into disuse in that country.

SECTION 4:
INDUSTRIAL DESIGNS

Article 25
REQUIREMENTS FOR PROTECTION

1. Members shall provide for the protection of independently created industrial designs that are new or original. Members may provide that designs are not new or original if they do not significantly differ from known designs or combinations of known design features. Members may provide that such protection shall not extend to designs dictated essentially by technical or functional considerations.

2. Each Member shall ensure that requirements for securing protection for textile designs, in particular in regard to any cost, examination or publication, do not unreasonably impair the opportunity to seek and obtain such protection. Members shall be free to meet this obligation through industrial design law or through copyright law.

Article 26
PROTECTION

1. The owner of a protected industrial design shall have the right to prevent third parties not having the owner's consent from making, selling or importing articles bearing or embodying a design which is a copy, or substantially a copy, of the protected design, when such acts are undertaken for commercial purposes.

2. Members may provide limited exceptions to the protection of industrial designs, provided that such exceptions do not unreasonably conflict with the

normal exploitation of protected industrial designs and do not unreasonably prejudice the legitimate interests of the owner of the protected design, taking account of the legitimate interests of third parties.

3. The duration of protection available shall amount to at least 10 years.

SECTION 5:
PATENTS

Article 27
PATENTABLE SUBJECT MATTER

1. Subject to the provisions of paragraphs 2 and 3, patents shall be available for any inventions, whether products or processes, in all fields of technology, provided that they are new, involve an inventive step and are capable of industrial application. Subject to paragraph 4 of Article 65, paragraph 8 of Article 70 and paragraph 3 of this Article, patents shall be available and patent rights enjoyable without discrimination as to the place of invention, the field of technology and whether products are imported or locally produced.

2. Members may exclude from patentability inventions, the prevention within their territory of the commercial exploitation of which is necessary to protect *ordre public* or morality, including to protect human, animal or plant life or health or to avoid serious prejudice to the environment, provided that such exclusion is not made merely because the exploitation is prohibited by their law.

3. Members may also exclude from patentability:

(*a*) diagnostic, therapeutic and surgical methods for the treatment of humans or animals;

(*b*) plants and animals other than micro-organisms, and essentially biological processes for the production of plants or animals other than non-biological and microbiological processes. However, Members shall provide for the protection of plant varieties either by patents or by an effective *sui generis* system or by any combination thereof. The provisions of this subparagraph shall be reviewed four years after the date of entry into force of the WTO Agreement.

Article 28
RIGHTS CONFERRED

1. A patent shall confer on its owner the following exclusive rights:

(*a*) where the subject matter of a patent is a product, to prevent third parties not having the owner's consent from the acts of: making, using, offering for sale, selling, or importing for these purposes that product;

(*b*) where the subject matter of a patent is a process, to prevent third parties not having the owner's consent from the act of using the process, and from the acts of: using, offering for sale, selling, or importing for these purposes at least the product obtained directly by that process.

2. Patent owners shall also have the right to assign, or transfer by succession, the patent and to conclude licensing contracts.

Article 29
CONDITIONS ON PATENT APPLICANTS

1. Members shall require that an applicant for a patent shall disclose the invention in a manner sufficiently clear and complete for the invention to be carried out by a person skilled in the art and may require the applicant to indicate the best mode for carrying out the invention known to the inventor at the filing date or, where priority is claimed, at the priority date of the application.

2. Members may require an applicant for a patent to provide information concerning the applicant's corresponding foreign applications and grants.

Article 30
EXCEPTIONS TO RIGHTS CONFERRED

Members may provide limited exceptions to the exclusive rights conferred by a patent, provided that such exceptions do not unreasonably conflict with a normal exploitation of the patent and do not unreasonably prejudice the legitimate interests of the patent owner, taking account of the legitimate interests of third parties.

Article 31
OTHER USE WITHOUT AUTHORIZATION OF THE RIGHT HOLDER

Where the law of a Member allows for other use of the subject matter of a patent without the authorization of the right holder, including use by the government or third parties authorized by the government, the following provisions shall be respected:

(a) authorization of such use shall be considered on its individual merits;

(b) such use may only be permitted if, prior to such use, the proposed user has made efforts to obtain authorization from the right holder on reasonable commercial terms and conditions and that such efforts have not been successful within a reasonable period of time. This requirement may be waived by a Member in the case of a national emergency or other circumstances of extreme urgency or in cases of public non-commercial use. In situations of national emergency or other circumstances of extreme

urgency, the right holder shall, nevertheless, be notified as soon as reasonably practicable. In the case of public non-commercial use, where the government or contractor, without making a patent search, knows or has demonstrable grounds to know that a valid patent is or will be used by or for the government, the right holder shall be informed promptly;

(c) the scope and duration of such use shall be limited to the purpose for which it was authorized, and in the case of semi-conductor technology shall only be for public non-commercial use or to remedy a practice determined after judicial or administrative process to be anti-competitive;

(d) such use shall be non-exclusive;

(e) such use shall be non-assignable, except with that part of the enterprise or goodwill which enjoys such use;

(f) any such use shall be authorized predominantly for the supply of the domestic market of the Member authorizing such use;

(g) authorization for such use shall be liable, subject to adequate protection of the legitimate interests of the persons so authorized, to be terminated if and when the circumstances which led to it cease to exist and are unlikely to recur. The competent authority shall have the authority to review, upon motivated request, the continued existence of these circumstances;

(*h*)   the right holder shall be paid adequate remuneration in the circumstances of each case, taking into account the economic value of the authorization;

(*i*)   the legal validity of any decision relating to the authorization of such use shall be subject to judicial review or other independent review by a distinct higher authority in that Member;

(*j*)   any decision relating to the remuneration provided in respect of such use shall be subject to judicial review or other independent review by a distinct higher authority in that Member;

(*k*)   Members are not obliged to apply the conditions set forth in subparagraphs (b) and (f) where such use is permitted to remedy a practice determined after judicial or administrative process to be anti-competitive. The need to correct anti-competitive practices may be taken into account in determining the amount of remuneration in such cases. Competent authorities shall have the authority to refuse termination of authorization if and when the conditions which led to such authorization are likely to recur;

(*l*)   where such use is authorized to permit the exploitation of a patent ("the second patent") which cannot be exploited without infringing another patent ("the first patent"), the following additional conditions shall apply:

    (i)   the invention claimed in the second patent shall involve an important technical advance of considerable economic significance in relation to the invention claimed in the first patent;

    (ii)   the owner of the first patent shall be entitled to a cross-licence on reasonable terms to use the invention claimed in the second patent; and

    (iii)   the use authorized in respect of the first patent shall be non-assignable except with the assignment of the second patent.

Article 32
REVOCATION/FORFEITURE

An opportunity for judicial review of any decision to revoke or forfeit a patent shall be available.

Article 33
TERM OF PROTECTION

The term of protection available shall not end before the expiration of a period of twenty years counted from the filing date

Article 34
PROCESS PATENTS: BURDEN OF PROOF

1. For the purposes of civil proceedings in respect of the infringement of the rights of the owner referred to in paragraph 1(b) of Article 28, if the subject matter of a patent is a process for obtaining a product, the judicial authorities shall have the authority to order the defendant to prove that the process to obtain an identical product is different from the patented process. Therefore, Members shall provide, in at least one of the following circumstances, that any identical product when produced without the consent of the patent owner shall, in the absence of proof to the contrary, be deemed to have been obtained by the patented process:

(*a*) if the product obtained by the patented process is new;

(*b*) if there is a substantial likelihood that the identical product was made by the process and the owner of the patent has been unable through reasonable efforts to determine the process actually used.

2. Any Member shall be free to provide that the burden of proof indicated in paragraph 1 shall be on the alleged infringer only if the condition referred to in subparagraph (a) is fulfilled or only if the condition referred to in subparagraph (b) is fulfilled.

3. In the adduction of proof to the contrary, the legitimate interests of defendants in protecting their manufacturing and business secrets shall be taken into account.

SECTION 6:
LAYOUT-DESIGNS (TOPOGRAPHIES) OF INTEGRATED CIRCUITS

Article 35
RELATION TO THE IPIC TREATY

Members agree to provide protection to the layout-designs (topographies) of integrated circuits (referred to in this Agreement as "layout-designs") in accordance with Articles 2 through 7 (other than paragraph 3 of Article 6), Article 12 and paragraph 3 of Article 16 of the Treaty on Intellectual Property in Respect of Integrated Circuits and, in addition, to comply with the following provisions.

Article 36
SCOPE OF THE PROTECTION

Subject to the provisions of paragraph 1 of Article 37, Members shall consider unlawful the following acts if performed without the authorization of the right holder: importing, selling, or otherwise distributing for commercial purposes a protected layout-design, an integrated circuit in which a protected layout-design is incorporated, or an article incorporating such an integrated circuit only in so far as it continues to contain an unlawfully reproduced layout-design.

Article 37
ACTS NOT REQUIRING THE AUTHORIZATION OF THE RIGHT HOLDER

1. Notwithstanding Article 36, no Member shall consider unlawful the performance of any of the acts referred to in that Article in respect of an integrated circuit incorporating an unlawfully reproduced layout-design or any article incorporating such an integrated circuit where the person performing or ordering such acts did not know and had no reasonable ground to know, when acquiring the integrated circuit or article incorporating such an integrated circuit, that it incorporated an unlawfully reproduced layout-design. Members shall provide that, after the time that such person has received sufficient notice that the layout-design was unlawfully reproduced, that person may perform any of the acts with respect to the stock on hand or ordered before such time, but shall be liable to pay to the right holder a sum equivalent to a reasonable royalty such as would be payable under a freely negotiated licence in respect of such a layout-design.

2. The conditions set out in subparagraphs (a) through (k) of Article 31 shall apply *mutatis mutandis* in the event of any non-voluntary licensing of a layout-design or of its use by or for the government without the authorization of the right holder.

Article 38
TERM OF PROTECTION

1. In Members requiring registration as a condition of protection, the term of protection of layout-designs shall not end before the expiration of a period of 10 years counted from the date of filing an application for registration or from the first commercial exploitation wherever in the world it occurs.

2. In Members not requiring registration as a condition for protection, layout-designs shall be protected for a term of no less than 10 years from the date of the first commercial exploitation wherever in the world it occurs.

3. Notwithstanding paragraphs 1 and 2, a Member may provide that protection shall lapse 15 years after the creation of the layout-design.

SECTION 7:
PROTECTION OF UNDISCLOSED INFORMATION

Article 39

1. In the course of ensuring effective protection against unfair competition as provided in Article 10*bis* of the Paris Convention (1967), Members shall protect undisclosed information in accordance with paragraph 2 and data submitted to governments or governmental agencies in accordance with paragraph 3.

2. Natural and legal persons shall have the possibility of preventing information lawfully within their control from being disclosed to, acquired by, or used by others without their consent in a manner contrary to honest commercial practices so long

as such information:

(a) is secret in the sense that it is not, as a body or in the precise configuration and assembly of its components, generally known among or readily accessible to persons within the circles that normally deal with the kind of information in question;

(b) has commercial value because it is secret; and

(c) has been subject to reasonable steps under the circumstances, by the person lawfully in control of the information, to keep it secret.

3. Members, when requiring, as a condition of approving the marketing of pharmaceutical or of agricultural chemical products which utilize new chemical entities, the submission of undisclosed test or other data, the origination of which involves a considerable effort, shall protect such data against unfair commercial use. In addition, Members shall protect such data against disclosure, except where necessary to protect the public, or unless steps are taken to ensure that the data are protected against unfair commercial use.

SECTION 8:
CONTROL OF ANTI-COMPETITIVE PRACTICES IN CONTRACTUAL LICENCES

Article 40

1. Members agree that some licensing practices or conditions pertaining to intellectual property rights which restrain competition may have adverse effects on trade and may impede the transfer and dissemination of technology.

2. Nothing in this Agreement shall prevent Members from specifying in their legislation licensing practices or conditions that may in particular cases constitute an abuse of intellectual property rights having an adverse effect on competition in the relevant market. As provided above, a Member may adopt, consistently with the other provisions of this Agreement, appropriate measures to prevent or control such practices, which may include for example exclusive grantback conditions, conditions preventing challenges to validity and coercive package licensing, in the light of the relevant laws and regulations of that Member.

3. Each Member shall enter, upon request, into consultations with any other Member which has cause to believe that an intellectual property right owner that is a national or domiciliary of the Member to which the request for consultations has been addressed is undertaking practices in violation of the requesting Member's laws and regulations on the subject matter of this Section, and which wishes to secure compliance with such legislation, without prejudice to any action under the law and to the full freedom of an ultimate decision of either Member. The Member addressed shall accord full and sympathetic consideration to, and shall afford adequate opportunity for, consultations with the requesting Member, and shall

cooperate through supply of publicly available non-confidential information of relevance to the matter in question and of other information available to the Member, subject to domestic law and to the conclusion of mutually satisfactory agreements concerning the safeguarding of its confidentiality by the requesting Member.

4. A Member whose nationals or domiciliaries are subject to proceedings in another Member concerning alleged violation of that other Member's laws and regulations on the subject matter of this Section shall, upon request, be granted an opportunity for consultations by the other Member under the same conditions as those foreseen in paragraph 3.

PART III
ENFORCEMENT OF INTELLECTUAL PROPERTY RIGHTS

SECTION 1:
GENERAL OBLIGATIONS

Article 41

1. Members shall ensure that enforcement procedures as specified in this Part are available under their law so as to permit effective action against any act of infringement of intellectual property rights covered by this Agreement, including expeditious remedies to prevent infringements and remedies which constitute a deterrent to further infringements. These procedures shall be applied in such a manner as to avoid the creation of barriers to legitimate trade and to provide for safeguards against their abuse.

2. Procedures concerning the enforcement of intellectual property rights shall be fair and equitable. They shall not be unnecessarily complicated or costly, or entail unreasonable time-limits or unwarranted delays.

3. Decisions on the merits of a case shall preferably be in writing and reasoned. They shall be made available at least to the parties to the proceeding without undue delay. Decisions on the merits of a case shall be based only on evidence in respect of which parties were offered the opportunity to be heard.

4. Parties to a proceeding shall have an opportunity for review by a judicial authority of final administrative decisions and, subject to jurisdictional provisions in a Member's law concerning the importance of a case, of at least the legal aspects of initial judicial decisions on the merits of a case. However, there shall be no obligation to provide an opportunity for review of acquittals in criminal cases.

5. It is understood that this Part does not create any obligation to put in place a judicial system for the enforcement of intellectual property rights distinct from that for the enforcement of law in general, nor does it affect the capacity of Members to enforce their law in general. Nothing in this Part creates any obligation with respect to the distribution of resources as between enforcement of intellectual property

rights and the enforcement of law in general.

SECTION 2:
CIVIL AND ADMINISTRATIVE PROCEDURES AND REMEDIES

Article 42
FAIR AND EQUITABLE PROCEDURES

Members shall make available to right holders civil judicial procedures concerning the enforcement of any intellectual property right covered by this Agreement. Defendants shall have the right to written notice which is timely and contains sufficient detail, including the basis of the claims. Parties shall be allowed to be represented by independent legal counsel, and procedures shall not impose overly burdensome requirements concerning mandatory personal appearances. All parties to such procedures shall be duly entitled to substantiate their claims and to present all relevant evidence. The procedure shall provide a means to identify and protect confidential information, unless this would be contrary to existing constitutional requirements.

Article 43
EVIDENCE

1. The judicial authorities shall have the authority, where a party has presented reasonably available evidence sufficient to support its claims and has specified evidence relevant to substantiation of its claims which lies in the control of the opposing party, to order that this evidence be produced by the opposing party, subject in appropriate cases to conditions which ensure the protection of confidential information.

2. In cases in which a party to a proceeding voluntarily and without good reason refuses access to, or otherwise does not provide necessary information within a reasonable period, or significantly impedes a procedure relating to an enforcement action, a Member may accord judicial authorities the authority to make preliminary and final determinations, affirmative or negative, on the basis of the information presented to them, including the complaint or the allegation presented by the party adversely affected by the denial of access to information, subject to providing the parties an opportunity to be heard on the allegations or evidence.

Article 44
INJUNCTIONS

1. The judicial authorities shall have the authority to order a party to desist from an infringement, *inter alia* to prevent the entry into the channels of commerce in their jurisdiction of imported goods that involve the infringement of an intellectual property right, immediately after customs clearance of such goods. Members are not obliged to accord such authority in respect of protected subject matter acquired or ordered by a person prior

to knowing or having reasonable grounds to know that dealing in such subject matter would entail the infringement of an intellectual property right.

2. Notwithstanding the other provisions of this Part and provided that the provisions of Part II specifically addressing use by governments, or by third parties authorized by a government, without the authorization of the right holder are complied with, Members may limit the remedies available against such use to payment of remuneration in accordance with subparagraph (h) of Article 31. In other cases, the remedies under this Part shall apply or, where these remedies are inconsistent with a Member's law, declaratory judgments and adequate compensation shall be available.

Article 45
DAMAGES

1. The judicial authorities shall have the authority to order the infringer to pay the right holder damages adequate to compensate for the injury the right holder has suffered because of an infringement of that person's intellectual property right by an infringer who knowingly, or with reasonable grounds to know, engaged in infringing activity.

2. The judicial authorities shall also have the authority to order the infringer to pay the right holder expenses, which may include appropriate attorney's fees. In appropriate cases, Members may authorize the judicial authorities to order recovery of profits and/or payment of pre-established damages even where the infringer did not knowingly, or with reasonable grounds to know, engage in infringing activity.

Article 46
OTHER REMEDIES

In order to create an effective deterrent to infringement, the judicial authorities shall have the authority to order that goods that they have found to be infringing be, without compensation of any sort, disposed of outside the channels of commerce in such a manner as to avoid any harm caused to the right holder, or, unless this would be contrary to existing constitutional requirements, destroyed. The judicial authorities shall also have the authority to order that materials and implements the predominant use of which has been in the creation of the infringing goods be, without compensation of any sort, disposed of outside the channels of commerce in such a manner as to minimize the risks of further infringements. In considering such requests, the need for proportionality between the seriousness of the infringement and the remedies ordered as well as the interests of third parties shall be taken into account. In regard to counterfeit trademark goods, the simple removal of the trademark unlawfully affixed shall not be sufficient, other than in exceptional cases, to permit release of the goods into the channels of commerce.

Article 47
RIGHT OF INFORMATION

Members may provide that the judicial authorities shall have the authority, unless this would be out of proportion to the seriousness of the infringement, to order the infringer to inform the right holder of the identity of third persons involved in the production and distribution of the infringing goods or services and of their channels of distribution.

Article 48
INDEMNIFICATION OF THE DEFENDANT

1. The judicial authorities shall have the authority to order a party at whose request measures were taken and who has abused enforcement procedures to provide to a party wrongfully enjoined or restrained adequate compensation for the injury suffered because of such abuse. The judicial authorities shall also have the authority to order the applicant to pay the defendant expenses, which may include appropriate attorney's fees.

2. In respect of the administration of any law pertaining to the protection or enforcement of intellectual property rights, Members shall only exempt both public authorities and officials from liability to appropriate remedial measures where actions are taken or intended in good faith in the course of the administration of that law.

Article 49
ADMINISTRATIVE PROCEDURES

To the extent that any civil remedy can be ordered as a result of administrative procedures on the merits of a case, such procedures shall conform to principles equivalent in substance to those set forth in this Section.

SECTION 3:
PROVISIONAL MEASURES

Article 50

1. The judicial authorities shall have the authority to order prompt and effective provisional measures:

   (a) to prevent an infringement of any intellectual property right from occurring, and in particular to prevent the entry into the channels of commerce in their jurisdiction of goods, including imported goods immediately after customs clearance;

   (b) to preserve relevant evidence in regard to the alleged infringement.

2. The judicial authorities shall have the authority to adopt provisional measures *inaudita altera parte* where appropriate, in particular where any delay is likely to cause irreparable harm to the right holder, or where there is a demonstrable risk of

evidence being destroyed.

3. The judicial authorities shall have the authority to require the applicant to provide any reasonably available evidence in order to satisfy themselves with a sufficient degree of certainty that the applicant is the right holder and that the applicant's right is being infringed or that such infringement is imminent, and to order the applicant to provide a security or equivalent assurance sufficient to protect the defendant and to prevent abuse.

4. Where provisional measures have been adopted *inaudita altera parte*, the parties affected shall be given notice, without delay after the execution of the measures at the latest. A review, including a right to be heard, shall take place upon request of the defendant with a view to deciding, within a reasonable period after the notification of the measures, whether these measures shall be modified, revoked or confirmed.

5. The applicant may be required to supply other information necessary for the identification of the goods concerned by the authority that will execute the provisional measures.

6. Without prejudice to paragraph 4, provisional measures taken on the basis of paragraphs 1 and 2 shall, upon request by the defendant, be revoked or otherwise cease to have effect, if proceedings leading to a decision on the merits of the case are not initiated within a reasonable period, to be determined by the judicial authority ordering the measures where a Member's law so permits or, in the absence of such a determination, not to exceed 20 working days or 31 calendar days, whichever is the longer.

7. Where the provisional measures are revoked or where they lapse due to any act or omission by the applicant, or where it is subsequently found that there has been no infringement or threat of infringement of an intellectual property right, the judicial authorities shall have the authority to order the applicant, upon request of the defendant, to provide the defendant appropriate compensation for any injury caused by these measures.

8. To the extent that any provisional measure can be ordered as a result of administrative procedures, such procedures shall conform to principles equivalent in substance to those set forth in this Section.

SECTION 4:
SPECIAL REQUIREMENTS RELATED TO BORDER MEASURES

Article 51
SUSPENSION OF RELEASE BY CUSTOMS AUTHORITIES

Members shall, in conformity with the provisions set out below, adopt procedures to enable a right holder, who has valid grounds for suspecting that the importation of counterfeit trademark or pirated copyright goods may take place, to lodge an application in writing with competent authorities, administrative or judicial, for the suspension by the customs authorities of the release into free circulation of such goods. Members may enable such an application to be made in respect of goods which involve other infringements of intellectual property rights, provided that the requirements of this Section are met. Members may also provide for corresponding procedures concerning the suspension by the customs authorities of the release of infringing goods destined for exportation from their territories.

Article 52
APPLICATION

Any right holder initiating the procedures under Article 51 shall be required to provide adequate evidence to satisfy the competent authorities that, under the laws of the country of importation, there is *prima facie* an infringement of the right holder's intellectual property right and to supply a sufficiently detailed description of the goods to make them readily recognizable by the customs authorities. The competent authorities shall inform the applicant within a reasonable period whether they have accepted the application and, where determined by the competent authorities, the period for which the customs authorities will take action.

Article 53
SECURITY OR EQUIVALENT ASSURANCE

1. The competent authorities shall have the authority to require an applicant to provide a security or equivalent assurance sufficient to protect the defendant and the competent authorities and to prevent abuse. Such security or equivalent assurance shall not unreasonably deter recourse to these procedures.

2. Where pursuant to an application under this Section the release of goods involving industrial designs, patents, layout-designs or undisclosed information into free circulation has been suspended by customs authorities on the basis of a decision other than by a judicial or other independent authority, and the period provided for in Article 55 has expired without the granting of provisional relief by the duly empowered authority, and provided that all other conditions for importation have been complied with, the owner, importer, or consignee of such goods shall be entitled to their release on the posting of a security in an amount sufficient to protect the right holder for any infringement. Payment of such security shall not prejudice any other remedy available to the right holder, it being understood that the security shall be released if the right holder fails to pursue the right of action within a reasonable period of time.

Article 54
NOTICE OF SUSPENSION

The importer and the applicant shall be promptly notified of the suspension of the release of goods according to Article 51.

Article 55
DURATION OF SUSPENSION

If, within a period not exceeding 10 working days after the applicant has been served notice of the suspension, the customs authorities have not been informed that proceedings leading to a decision on the merits of the case have been initiated by a party other than the defendant, or that the duly empowered authority has taken provisional measures prolonging the suspension of the release of the goods, the goods shall be released, provided that all other conditions for importation or exportation have been complied with; in appropriate cases, this time-limit may be extended by another 10 working days. If proceedings leading to a decision on the merits of the case have been initiated, a review, including a right to be heard, shall take place upon request of the defendant with a view to deciding, within a reasonable period, whether these measures shall be modified, revoked or confirmed. Notwithstanding the above, where the suspension of the release of goods is carried out or continued in accordance with a provisional judicial measure, the provisions of paragraph 6 of Article 50 shall apply.

Article 56
INDEMNIFICATION OF THE IMPORTER AND OF THE OWNER OF THE GOODS

Relevant authorities shall have the authority to order the applicant to pay the importer, the consignee and the owner of the goods appropriate compensation for any injury caused to them through the wrongful detention of goods or through the detention of goods released pursuant to Article 55.

Article 57
RIGHT OF INSPECTION AND INFORMATION

Without prejudice to the protection of confidential information, Members shall provide the competent authorities the authority to give the right holder sufficient opportunity to have any goods detained by the customs authorities inspected in order to substantiate the right holder's claims. The competent authorities shall also have authority to give the importer an equivalent opportunity to have any such goods inspected. Where a positive determination has been made on the merits of a case, Members may provide the competent authorities the authority to inform the right holder of the names and addresses of the consignor, the importer and the consignee and of the quantity of the goods in question.

Article 58
EX OFFICIO ACTION

Where Members require competent authorities to act upon their own initiative and to suspend the release of goods in respect of which they have acquired *prima facie* evidence that an intellectual property right is being infringed:

(a) the competent authorities may at any time seek from the right holder any information that may assist them to exercise these powers;

(b)   the importer and the right holder shall be promptly notified of the suspension. Where the importer has lodged an appeal against the suspension with the competent authorities, the suspension shall be subject to the conditions, *mutatis mutandis*, set out at Article 55;

(c)   Members shall only exempt both public authorities and officials from liability to appropriate remedial measures where actions are taken or intended in good faith.

Article 59
REMEDIES

Without prejudice to other rights of action open to the right holder and subject to the right of the defendant to seek review by a judicial authority, competent authorities shall have the authority to order the destruction or disposal of infringing goods in accordance with the principles set out in Article 46. In regard to counterfeit trademark goods, the authorities shall not allow the re-exportation of the infringing goods in an unaltered state or subject them to a different customs procedure, other than in exceptional circumstances.

Article 60
DE MINIMIS IMPORTS

Members may exclude from the application of the above provisions small quantities of goods of a non-commercial nature contained in travellers' personal luggage or sent in small consignments.

SECTION 5:
CRIMINAL PROCEDURES

Article 61

Members shall provide for criminal procedures and penalties to be applied at least in cases of wilful trademark counterfeiting or copyright piracy on a commercial scale. Remedies available shall include imprisonment and/or monetary fines sufficient to provide a deterrent, consistently with the level of penalties applied for crimes of a corresponding gravity. In appropriate cases, remedies available shall also include the seizure, forfeiture and destruction of the infringing goods and of any materials and implements the predominant use of which has been in the commission of the offence. Members may provide for criminal procedures and penalties to be applied in other cases of infringement of intellectual property rights, in particular where they are committed wilfully and on a commercial scale.

280

PART IV
ACQUISITION AND MAINTENANCE OF INTELLECTUAL PROPERTY RIGHTS AND RELATED *INTER-PARTES* PROCEDURES

Article 62

1. Members may require, as a condition of the acquisition or maintenance of the intellectual property rights provided for under Sections 2 through 6 of Part II, compliance with reasonable procedures and formalities. Such procedures and formalities shall be consistent with the provisions of this Agreement.

2. Where the acquisition of an intellectual property right is subject to the right being granted or registered, Members shall ensure that the procedures for grant or registration, subject to compliance with the substantive conditions for acquisition of the right, permit the granting or registration of the right within a reasonable period of time so as to avoid unwarranted curtailment of the period of protection.

3. Article 4 of the Paris Convention (1967) shall apply *mutatis mutandis* to service marks.

4. Procedures concerning the acquisition or maintenance of intellectual property rights and, where a Member's law provides for such procedures, administrative revocation and *inter partes* procedures such as opposition, revocation and cancellation, shall be governed by the general principles set out in paragraphs 2 and 3 of Article 41.

5. Final administrative decisions in any of the procedures referred to under paragraph 4 shall be subject to review by a judicial or quasi-judicial authority. However, there shall be no obligation to provide an opportunity for such review of decisions in cases of unsuccessful opposition or administrative revocation, provided that the grounds for such procedures can be the subject of invalidation procedures.

PART V
DISPUTE PREVENTION AND SETTLEMENT

Article 63
TRANSPARENCY

1. Laws and regulations, and final judicial decisions and administrative rulings of general application, made effective by a Member pertaining to the subject matter of this Agreement (the availability, scope, acquisition, enforcement and prevention of the abuse of intellectual property rights) shall be published, or where such publication is not practicable made publicly available, in a national language, in such a manner as to enable governments and right holders to become acquainted with them. Agreements concerning the subject matter of this Agreement which are in force between the government or a governmental agency of a Member and the government or a governmental agency of another Member shall also be published.

2. Members shall notify the laws and regulations referred to in paragraph 1 to the Council for TRIPS in order to assist that Council in its review of the operation of this Agreement. The Council shall attempt to minimize the burden on Members in carrying out this obligation and may decide to waive the obligation to notify such laws and regulations directly to the Council if consultations with WIPO on the establishment of a common register containing these laws and regulations are successful. The Council shall also consider in this connection any action required regarding notifications pursuant to the obligations under this Agreement stemming from the provisions of Article 6*ter* of the Paris Convention (1967).

3. Each Member shall be prepared to supply, in response to a written request from another Member, information of the sort referred to in paragraph 1. A Member, having reason to believe that a specific judicial decision or administrative ruling or bilateral agreement in the area of intellectual property rights affects its rights under this Agreement, may also request in writing to be given access to or be informed in sufficient detail of such specific judicial decisions or administrative rulings or bilateral agreements.

4. Nothing in paragraphs 1, 2 and 3 shall require Members to disclose confidential information which would impede law enforcement or otherwise be contrary to the public interest or would prejudice the legitimate commercial interests of particular enterprises, public or private.

Article 64
DISPUTE SETTLEMENT

1. The provisions of Articles XXII and XXIII of GATT 1994 as elaborated and applied by the Dispute Settlement Understanding shall apply to consultations and the settlement of disputes under this Agreement except as otherwise specifically provided herein.

2. Subparagraphs 1(b) and 1(c) of Article XXIII of GATT 1994 shall not apply to the settlement of disputes under this Agreement for a period of five years from the date of entry into force of the WTO Agreement.

3. During the time period referred to in paragraph 2, the Council for TRIPS shall examine the scope and modalities for complaints of the type provided for under subparagraphs 1(b) and 1(c) of Article XXIII of GATT 1994 made pursuant to this Agreement, and submit its recommendations to the Ministerial Conference for approval. Any decision of the Ministerial Conference to approve such recommendations or to extend the period in paragraph 2 shall be made only by consensus, and approved recommendations shall be effective for all Members without further formal acceptance process.

PART VI
TRANSITIONAL ARRANGEMENTS

Article 65
TRANSITIONAL ARRANGEMENTS

1. Subject to the provisions of paragraphs 2, 3 and 4, no Member shall be obliged to apply the provisions of this Agreement before the expiry of a general period of one year following the date of entry into force of the WTO Agreement.

2. A developing country Member is entitled to delay for a further period of four years the date of application, as defined in paragraph 1, of the provisions of this Agreement other than Articles 3, 4 and 5.

3. Any other Member which is in the process of transformation from a centrally-planned into a market, free-enterprise economy and which is undertaking structural reform of its intellectual property system and facing special problems in the preparation and implementation of intellectual property laws and regulations, may also benefit from a period of delay as foreseen in paragraph 2.

4. To the extent that a developing country Member is obliged by this Agreement to extend product patent protection to areas of technology not so protectable in its territory on the general date of application of this Agreement for that Member, as defined in paragraph 2, it may delay the application of the provisions on product patents of Section 5 of Part II to such areas of technology for an additional period of five years.

5. A Member availing itself of a transitional period under paragraphs 1, 2, 3 or 4 shall ensure that any changes in its laws, regulations and practice made during that period do not result in a lesser degree of consistency with the provisions of this Agreement.

Article 66
LEAST-DEVELOPED COUNTRY MEMBERS

1. In view of the special needs and requirements of least-developed country Members, their economic, financial and administrative constraints, and their need for flexibility to create a viable technological base, such Members shall not be required to apply the provisions of this Agreement, other than Articles 3, 4 and 5, for a period of 10 years from the date of application as defined under paragraph 1 of Article 65. The Council for TRIPS shall, upon duly motivated request by a least-developed country Member, accord extensions of this period.

2. Developed country Members shall provide incentives to enterprises and institutions in their territories for the purpose of promoting and encouraging technology transfer to least-developed country Members in order to enable them to create a sound and viable technological base.

Article 67
TECHNICAL COOPERATION

In order to facilitate the implementation of this Agreement, developed country Members shall provide, on request and on mutually agreed terms and conditions, technical and financial cooperation in favour of developing and least-developed country Members. Such cooperation shall include assistance in the preparation of laws and regulations on the protection and enforcement of intellectual property rights as well as on the prevention of their abuse, and shall include support regarding the establishment or reinforcement of domestic offices and agencies relevant to these matters, including the training of personnel.

PART VII
INSTITUTIONAL ARRANGEMENTS; FINAL PROVISIONS

Article 68
COUNCIL FOR TRADE-RELATED ASPECTS OF INTELLECTUAL PROPERTY RIGHTS

The Council for TRIPS shall monitor the operation of this Agreement and, in particular, Members' compliance with their obligations hereunder, and shall afford Members the opportunity of consulting on matters relating to the trade-related aspects of intellectual property rights. It shall carry out such other responsibilities as assigned to it by the Members, and it shall, in particular, provide any assistance requested by them in the context of dispute settlement procedures. In carrying out its functions, the Council for TRIPS may consult with and seek information from any source it deems appropriate. In consultation with WIPO, the Council shall seek to establish, within one year of its first meeting, appropriate arrangements for cooperation with bodies of that Organization.

Article 69
INTERNATIONAL COOPERATION

Members agree to cooperate with each other with a view to eliminating international trade in goods infringing intellectual property rights. For this purpose, they shall establish and notify contact points in their administrations and be ready to exchange information on trade in infringing goods. They shall, in particular, promote the exchange of information and cooperation between customs authorities with regard to trade in counterfeit trademark goods and pirated copyright goods.

Article 70
PROTECTION OF EXISTING SUBJECT MATTER

1. This Agreement does not give rise to obligations in respect of acts which occurred before the date of application of the Agreement for the Member in question.

2. Except as otherwise provided for in this Agreement, this Agreement gives rise to obligations in respect of all subject matter existing at the date of application of

this Agreement for the Member in question, and which is protected in that Member on the said date, or which meets or comes subsequently to meet the criteria for protection under the terms of this Agreement. In respect of this paragraph and paragraphs 3 and 4, copyright obligations with respect to existing works shall be solely determined under Article 18 of the Berne Convention (1971), and obligations with respect to the rights of producers of phonograms and performers in existing phonograms shall be determined solely under Article 18 of the Berne Convention (1971) as made applicable under paragraph 6 of Article 14 of this Agreement.

3. There shall be no obligation to restore protection to subject matter which on the date of application of this Agreement for the Member in question has fallen into the public domain.

4. In respect of any acts in respect of specific objects embodying protected subject matter which become infringing under the terms of legislation in conformity with this Agreement, and which were commenced, or in respect of which a significant investment was made, before the date of acceptance of the WTO Agreement by that Member, any Member may provide for a limitation of the remedies available to the right holder as to the continued performance of such acts after the date of application of this Agreement for that Member. In such cases the Member shall, however, at least provide for the payment of equitable remuneration.

5. A Member is not obliged to apply the provisions of Article 11 and of paragraph 4 of Article 14 with respect to originals or copies purchased prior to the date of application of this Agreement for that Member.

6. Members shall not be required to apply Article 31, or the requirement in paragraph 1 of Article 27 that patent rights shall be enjoyable without discrimination as to the field of technology, to use without the authorization of the right holder where authorization for such use was granted by the government before the date this Agreement became known.

7. In the case of intellectual property rights for which protection is conditional upon registration, applications for protection which are pending on the date of application of this Agreement for the Member in question shall be permitted to be amended to claim any enhanced protection provided under

the provisions of this Agreement. Such amendments shall not include new matter.

8. Where a Member does not make available as of the date of entry into force of the WTO Agreement patent protection for pharmaceutical and agricultural chemical products commensurate with its obligations under Article 27, that Member shall:

(a)   notwithstanding the provisions of Part VI, provide as from the date of entry into force of the WTO Agreement a means by which applications for patents for such inventions can be filed;

(b)   apply to these applications, as of the date of application of this Agreement, the criteria for patentability as laid down in this Agreement as if those

285

criteria were being applied on the date of filing in that Member or, where priority is available and claimed, the priority date of the application; and

(c)   provide patent protection in accordance with this Agreement as from the grant of the patent and for the remainder of the patent term, counted from the filing date in accordance with Article 33 of this Agreement, for those of these applications that meet the criteria for protection referred to in subparagraph (b).

9. Where a product is the subject of a patent application in a Member in accordance with paragraph 8(a), exclusive marketing rights shall be granted, notwithstanding the provisions of Part VI, for a period of five years after obtaining marketing approval in that Member or until a product patent is granted or rejected in that Member, whichever period is shorter, provided that, subsequent to the entry into force of the WTO Agreement, a patent application has been filed and a patent granted for that product in another Member and marketing approval obtained in such other Member.

Article 71
REVIEW AND AMENDMENT

1. The Council for TRIPS shall review the implementation of this Agreement after the expiration of the transitional period referred to in paragraph 2 of Article 65. The Council shall, having regard to the experience gained in its implementation, review it two years after that date, and at identical intervals thereafter. The Council may also undertake reviews in the light of any relevant new developments which might warrant modification or amendment of this Agreement.

2. Amendments merely serving the purpose of adjusting to higher levels of protection of intellectual property rights achieved, and in force, in other multilateral agreements and accepted under those agreements by all Members of the WTO may be referred to the Ministerial Conference for action in accordance with paragraph 6 of Article X of the WTO Agreement on the basis of a consensus proposal from the Council for TRIPS.

Article 72
RESERVATIONS

Reservations may not be entered in respect of any of the provisions of this Agreement without the consent of the other Members.

Article 73
SECURITY EXCEPTIONS

Nothing in this Agreement shall be construed:

(a)   to require a Member to furnish any information the disclosure of which it considers contrary to its essential security interests; or (*b*)   to prevent a Member from taking any action which it considers necessary for the protection of its essential security interests;

    (i)   relating to fissionable materials or the materials from which they are derived;

    (ii)   relating to the traffic in arms, ammunition and implements of war and to such traffic in other goods and materials as is carried on directly or indirectly for the purpose of supplying a military establishment;

    (iii)   taken in time of war or other emergency in international relations; or

(*c*)   to prevent a Member from taking any action in pursuance of its obligations under the United Nations Charter for the maintenance of international peace and security.

WIPO COPYRIGHT TREATY

(adopted in Geneva on December 20, 1996,[1] ratified on May 13, 2014, and in force as of August 13, 2014)

(For the list of contracting parties to the Treaty, see http://www.wipo.int/treaties/en/ShowResults.jsp?lang=en&treaty_id=16)

PREAMBLE

The Contracting Parties,

Desiring to develop and maintain the protection of the rights of authors in their literary and artistic works in a manner as effective and uniform as possible,

Recognizing the need to introduce new international rules and clarify the interpretation of certain existing rules in order to provide adequate solutions to the questions raised by new economic, social, cultural and technological developments,

Recognizing the profound impact of the development and convergence of information and communication technologies on the creation and use of literary and artistic works,

Emphasizing the outstanding significance of copyright protection as an incentive for literary and artistic creation,

Recognizing the need to maintain a balance between the rights of authors and the larger public interest, particularly education, research and access to information, as reflected in the Berne Convention,

Have agreed as follows:

Article 1
RELATION TO THE BERNE CONVENTION

(1) This Treaty is a special agreement within the meaning of Article 20 of the Berne Convention for the Protection of Literary and Artistic Works, as regards Contracting Parties that are countries of the Union established by that Convention. This Treaty shall not have any connection with treaties other than the Berne Convention, nor shall it prejudice any rights and obligations under any other treaties.

(2) Nothing in this Treaty shall derogate from existing obligations that Contracting Parties have to each other under the Berne Convention for the Protection of Literary and Artistic Works.

(3) Hereinafter, "Berne Convention" shall refer to the Paris Act of July 24, 1971 of the Berne Convention for the Protection of Literary and Artistic Works.

(4) Contracting Parties shall comply with Articles 1 to 21 and the Appendix of the

Berne Convention.[2]

Article 2
SCOPE OF COPYRIGHT PROTECTION

Copyright protection extends to expressions and not to ideas, procedures, methods of operation or mathematical concepts as such.

Article 3
APPLICATION OF ARTICLES 2 TO 6 OF THE BERNE CONVENTION

Contracting Parties shall apply mutatis mutandis the provisions of Articles 2 to 6 of the Berne Convention in respect of the protection provided for in this Treaty.[3]

Article 4
COMPUTER PROGRAMS

Computer programs are protected as literary works within the meaning of Article 2 of the Berne Convention. Such protection applies to computer programs, whatever may be the mode or form of their expression.[4]

Article 5
COMPILATIONS OF DATA (DATABASES)

Compilations of data or other material, in any form, which by reason of the selection or arrangement of their contents constitute intellectual creations, are protected as such. This protection does not extend to the data or the material itself and is without prejudice to any copyright subsisting in the data or material contained in the compilation.[5]

Article 6
RIGHT OF DISTRIBUTION

(1) Authors of literary and artistic works shall enjoy the exclusive right of authorizing the making available to the public of the original and copies of their works through sale or other transfer of ownership.

(2) Nothing in this Treaty shall affect the freedom of Contracting Parties to determine the conditions, if any, under which the exhaustion of the right in paragraph (1) applies after the first sale or other transfer of ownership of the original or a copy of the work with the authorization of the author.[6]

Article 7
RIGHT OF RENTAL

(1) Authors of

(i)   computer programs;

(ii)   cinematographic works; and

(iii)   works embodied in phonograms, as determined in the national law of

Contracting Parties,

shall enjoy the exclusive right of authorizing commercial rental to the public of the originals or copies of their works.

(2) Paragraph (1) shall not apply

(i)   in the case of computer programs, where the program itself is not the essential object of the rental; and

(ii)   in the case of cinematographic works, unless such commercial rental has led to widespread copying of such works materially impairing the exclusive right of reproduction.

(3) Notwithstanding the provisions of paragraph (1), a Contracting Party that, on April 15, 1994, had and continues to have in force a system of equitable remuneration of authors for the rental of copies of their works embodied in phonograms may maintain that system provided that the commercial rental of works embodied in phonograms is not giving rise to the material impairment of the exclusive right of reproduction of authors.[7, 8]

Article 8
RIGHT OF COMMUNICATION TO THE PUBLIC

Without prejudice to the provisions of Articles 11(1)(ii), 11bis(1)(i) and (ii), 11ter(1)(ii), 14(1)(ii) and 14bis(1) of the Berne Convention, authors of literary and artistic works shall enjoy the exclusive right of authorizing any communication to the public of their works, by wire or wireless means, including the making available to the public of their works in such a way that members of the public may access these works from a place and at a time individually chosen by them.[9]

Article 9
DURATION OF THE PROTECTION OF PHOTOGRAPHIC WORKS

In respect of photographic works, the Contracting Parties shall not apply the provisions of Article 7(4) of the Berne Convention.

Article 10
LIMITATIONS AND EXCEPTIONS

(1) Contracting Parties may, in their national legislation, provide for limitations of or exceptions to the rights granted to authors of literary and artistic works under this Treaty in certain special cases that do not conflict with a normal exploitation of the work and do not unreasonably prejudice the legitimate interests of the author.

(2) Contracting Parties shall, when applying the Berne Convention, confine any limitations of or exceptions to rights provided for therein to certain special cases that do not conflict with a normal exploitation of the work and do not unreasonably prejudice the legitimate interests of the author.[10]

Article 11
OBLIGATIONS CONCERNING TECHNOLOGICAL MEASURES

Contracting Parties shall provide adequate legal protection and effective legal remedies against the circumvention of effective technological measures that are used by authors in connection with the exercise of their rights under this Treaty or the Berne Convention and that restrict acts, in respect of their works, which are not authorized by the authors concerned or permitted by law.

Article 12
OBLIGATIONS CONCERNING RIGHTS MANAGEMENT INFORMATION

(1) Contracting Parties shall provide adequate and effective legal remedies against any person knowingly performing any of the following acts knowing, or with respect to civil remedies having reasonable grounds to know, that it will induce, enable, facilitate or conceal an infringement of any right covered by this Treaty or the Berne Convention:

(i)   to remove or alter any electronic rights management information without authority;

(ii)   to distribute, import for distribution, broadcast or communicate to the public, without authority, works or copies of works knowing that electronic rights management information has been removed or altered without authority.

(2) As used in this Article, "rights management information" means information which identifies the work, the author of the work, the owner of any right in the work, or information about the terms and conditions of use of the work, and any numbers or codes that represent such information, when any of these items of information is attached to a copy of a work or appears in connection with the communication of a work to the public.[11]

Article 13
APPLICATION IN TIME

Contracting Parties shall apply the provisions of Article 18 of the Berne Convention to all protection provided for in this Treaty.

Article 14
PROVISIONS ON ENFORCEMENT OF RIGHTS

(1) Contracting Parties undertake to adopt, in accordance with their legal systems, the measures necessary to ensure the application of this Treaty.

(2) Contracting Parties shall ensure that enforcement procedures are available under their law so as to permit effective action against any act of infringement of rights covered by this Treaty, including expeditious remedies to prevent infringements and remedies which constitute a deterrent to further infringements.

Article 15
ASSEMBLY

(1)

(a) The Contracting Parties shall have an Assembly.

(b) Each Contracting Party shall be represented by one delegate who may be assisted by alternate delegates, advisors and experts.

(c) The expenses of each delegation shall be borne by the Contracting Party that has appointed the delegation. The Assembly may ask the World Intellectual Property Organization (hereinafter referred to as "WIPO") to grant financial assistance to facilitate the participation of delegations of Contracting Parties that are regarded as developing countries in conformity with the established practice of the General Assembly of the United Nations or that are countries in transition to a market economy.

(2)

(a) The Assembly shall deal with matters concerning the maintenance and development of this Treaty and the application and operation of this Treaty.

(b) The Assembly shall perform the function allocated to it under Article 17(2) in respect of the admission of certain intergovernmental organizations to become party to this Treaty.

(c) The Assembly shall decide the convocation of any diplomatic conference for the revision of this Treaty and give the necessary instructions to the Director General of WIPO for the preparation of such diplomatic conference.

(3)

(a) Each Contracting Party that is a State shall have one vote and shall vote only in its own name.

(b) Any Contracting Party that is an intergovernmental organization may participate in the vote, in place of its Member States, with a number of votes equal to the number of its Member States which are party to this Treaty. No such intergovernmental organization shall participate in the vote if any one of its Member States exercises its right to vote and vice versa.

(4) The Assembly shall meet in ordinary session once every two years upon convocation by the Director General of WIPO.

(5) The Assembly shall establish its own rules of procedure, including the convocation of extraordinary sessions, the requirements of a quorum and, subject to the provisions of this Treaty, the required majority for various kinds of decisions.

Article 16
INTERNATIONAL BUREAU

The International Bureau of WIPO shall perform the administrative tasks concerning the Treaty.

Article 17
ELIGIBILITY FOR BECOMING PARTY TO THE TREATY

(1) Any Member State of WIPO may become party to this Treaty.

(2) The Assembly may decide to admit any intergovernmental organization to become party to this Treaty which declares that it is competent in respect of, and has its own legislation binding on all its Member States on, matters covered by this Treaty and that it has been duly authorized, in accordance with its internal procedures, to become party to this Treaty.

(3) The European Community, having made the declaration referred to in the preceding paragraph in the Diplomatic Conference that has adopted this Treaty, may become party to this Treaty.

Article 18
RIGHTS AND OBLIGATIONS UNDER THE TREATY

Subject to any specific provisions to the contrary in this Treaty, each Contracting Party shall enjoy all of the rights and assume all of the obligations under this Treaty.

Article 19
SIGNATURE OF THE TREATY

This Treaty shall be open for signature until December 31, 1997, by any Member State of WIPO and by the European Community.

Article 20
ENTRY INTO FORCE OF THE TREATY

This Treaty shall enter into force three months after 30 instruments of ratification or accession by States have been deposited with the Director General of WIPO.

Article 21
EFFECTIVE DATE OF BECOMING PARTY TO THE TREATY

This Treaty shall bind:

(i)   the 30 States referred to in Article 20, from the date on which this Treaty has entered into force;

(ii) each other State from the expiration of three months from the date on which the State has deposited its instrument with the Director General of WIPO;

(iii) the European Community, from the expiration of three months after the deposit of its instrument of ratification or accession if such instrument has been deposited after the entry into force of this Treaty according to Article 20, or, three months after the entry into force of this Treaty if such instrument has been deposited before the entry into force of this Treaty;

(iv) any other intergovernmental organization that is admitted to become party to this Treaty, from the expiration of three months after the deposit of its instrument of accession.

Article 22
NO RESERVATIONS TO THE TREATY

No reservation to this Treaty shall be admitted.

Article 23
DENUNCIATION OF THE TREATY

This Treaty may be denounced by any Contracting Party by notification addressed to the Director General of WIPO. Any denunciation shall take effect one year from the date on which the Director General of WIPO received the notification.

Article 24
LANGUAGES OF THE TREATY

(1) This Treaty is signed in a single original in English, Arabic, Chinese, French, Russian and Spanish languages, the versions in all these languages being equally authentic.

(2) An official text in any language other than those referred to in paragraph (1) shall be established by the Director General of WIPO on the request of an interested party, after consultation with all the interested parties. For the purposes of this paragraph, "interested party" means any Member State of WIPO whose official language, or one of whose official languages, is involved and the European Community, and any other intergovernmental organization that may become party to this Treaty, if one of its official languages is involved.

Article 25
DEPOSITARY

The Director General of WIPO is the depositary of this Treaty.

---

[1] *Entry into force:* March 6, 2002.

Source: International Bureau of WIPO.

Note: The agreed statements of the Diplomatic Conference that adopted the Treaty (WIPO Diplomatic Conference on Certain Copyright and Neighboring Rights Questions) concerning certain provisions of the WCT are reproduced in endnotes below.

[2] **Agreed statements concerning Article 1(4):** The reproduction right, as set out in Article 9 of the Berne Convention, and the exceptions permitted thereunder, fully apply in the digital environment, in particular to the use of works in digital form. It is understood that the

storage of a protected work in digital form in an electronic medium constitutes a reproduction within the meaning of Article 9 of the Berne Convention.

[3] **Agreed statements concerning Article 3:** It is understood that in applying Article 3 of this Treaty, the expression "country of the Union" in Articles 2 to 6 of the Berne Convention will be read as if it were a reference to a Contracting Party to this Treaty, in the application of those Berne Articles in respect of protection provided for in this Treaty. It is also understood that the expression "country outside the Union" in those Articles in the Berne Convention will, in the same circumstances, be read as if it were a reference to a country that is not a Contracting Party to this Treaty, and that "this Convention" in Articles 2(8), 2*bis*(2), 3, 4 and 5 of the Berne Convention will be read as if it were a reference to the Berne Convention and this Treaty. Finally, it is understood that a reference in Articles 3 to 6 of the Berne Convention to a "national of one of the countries of the Union" will, when these Articles are applied to this Treaty, mean, in regard to an intergovernmental organization that is a Contracting Party to this Treaty, a national of one of the countries that is member of that organization.

[4] **Agreed statements concerning Article 4:** The scope of protection for computer programs under Article 4 of this Treaty, read with Article 2, is consistent with Article 2 of the Berne Convention and on a par with the relevant provisions of the TRIPS Agreement.

[5] **Agreed statements concerning Article 5:** The scope of protection for compilations of data (databases) under Article 5 of this Treaty, read with Article 2, is consistent with Article 2 of the Berne Convention and on a par with the relevant provisions of the TRIPS Agreement.

[6] **Agreed statements concerning Articles 6 and 7:** As used in these Articles, the expressions "copies" and "original and copies," being subject to the right of distribution and the right of rental under the said Articles, refer exclusively to fixed copies that can be put into circulation as tangible objects.

[7] **Agreed statements concerning Articles 6 and 7:** As used in these Articles, the expressions "copies" and "original and copies," being subject to the right of distribution and the right of rental under the said Articles, refer exclusively to fixed copies that can be put into circulation as tangible objects.

[8] **Agreed statements concerning Article 7:** It is understood that the obligation under Article 7(1) does not require a Contracting Party to provide an exclusive right of commercial rental to authors who, under that Contracting Party's law, are not granted rights in respect of phonograms. It is understood that this obligation is consistent with Article 14(4) of the TRIPS Agreement.

[9] **Agreed statements concerning Article 8:** It is understood that the mere provision of physical facilities for enabling or making a communication does not in itself amount to communication within the meaning of this Treaty or the Berne Convention. It is further understood that nothing in Article 8 precludes a Contracting Party from applying Article 11*bis*(2).

[10] **Agreed statement concerning Article 10:** It is understood that the provisions of Article 10 permit Contracting Parties to carry forward and appropriately extend into the digital environment limitations and exceptions in their national laws which have been considered acceptable under the Berne Convention. Similarly, these provisions should be understood to permit Contracting Parties to devise new exceptions and limitations that are appropriate in the digital network environment.

It is also understood that Article 10(2) neither reduces nor extends the scope of applicability of the limitations and exceptions permitted by the Berne Convention.

[11] **Agreed statements concerning Article 12:** It is understood that the reference to "infringement of any right covered by this Treaty or the Berne Convention" includes both exclusive rights and rights of remuneration.

It is further understood that Contracting Parties will not rely on this Article to devise or implement rights management systems that would have the effect of imposing formalities which are not permitted under the Berne Convention or this Treaty, prohibiting the free movement of goods or impeding the enjoyment of rights under this Treaty.

WIPO PERFORMANCES AND PHONOGRAMS TREATY (WPPT)

(adopted in Geneva on December 20, 1996, ratified on May 13, 2014, and in force as of August 13, 2014)[*]

(For the list of contracting parties to the Treaty, see http://www.wipo.int/treaties/en/ShowResults.jsp?lang=en&treaty_id=16)

PREAMBLE

The Contracting Parties,

Desiring to develop and maintain the protection of the rights of performers and producers of phonograms in a manner as effective and uniform as possible,

Recognizing the need to introduce new international rules in order to provide adequate solutions to the questions raised by economic, social, cultural and technological developments,

Recognizing the profound impact of the development and convergence of information and communication technologies on the production and use of performances and phonograms,

Recognizing the need to maintain a balance between the rights of performers and producers of phonograms and the larger public interest, particularly education, research and access to information,

Have agreed as follows:

CHAPTER I
GENERAL PROVISIONS

Article 1
RELATION TO OTHER CONVENTIONS

(1) Nothing in this Treaty shall derogate from existing obligations that Contracting Parties have to each other under the International Convention for the Protection of Performers, Producers of Phonograms and Broadcasting Organizations done in Rome, October 26, 1961 (hereinafter the "Rome Convention").

(2) Protection granted under this Treaty shall leave intact and shall in no way affect the protection of copyright in literary and artistic works. Consequently, no provision of this Treaty may be interpreted as prejudicing such protection.[1]

(3) This Treaty shall not have any connection with, nor shall it prejudice any rights and obligations under, any other treaties.

Article 2
DEFINITIONS

For the purposes of this Treaty:

(a) "performers" are actors, singers, musicians, dancers, and other persons who act, sing, deliver, declaim, play in, interpret, or otherwise perform literary or artistic works or expressions of folklore;

(b) "phonogram" means the fixation of the sounds of a performance or of other sounds, or of a representation of sounds, other than in the form of a fixation incorporated in a cinematographic or other audiovisual work;[2]

(c) "fixation" means the embodiment of sounds, or of the representations thereof, from which they can be perceived, reproduced or communicated through a device;

(d) "producer of a phonogram" means the person, or the legal entity, who or which takes the initiative and has the responsibility for the first fixation of the sounds of a performance or other sounds, or the representations of sounds;

(e) "publication" of a fixed performance or a phonogram means the offering of copies of the fixed performance or the phonogram to the public, with the consent of the rightholder, and provided that copies are offered to the public in reasonable quantity;[3]

(f) "broadcasting" means the transmission by wireless means for public reception of sounds or of images and sounds or of the representations thereof; such transmission by satellite is also "broadcasting"; transmission of encrypted signals is "broadcasting" where the means for decrypting are provided to the public by the broadcasting organization or with its consent;

(g) "communication to the public" of a performance or a phonogram means the transmission to the public by any medium, otherwise than by broadcasting, of sounds of a performance or the sounds or the representations of sounds fixed in a phonogram. For the purposes of Article 15, "communication to the public" includes making the sounds or representations of sounds fixed in a phonogram audible to the public.

Article 3
BENEFICIARIES OF PROTECTION UNDER THIS TREATY

(1) Contracting Parties shall accord the protection provided under this Treaty to the performers and producers of phonograms who are nationals of other Contracting Parties.

(2) The nationals of other Contracting Parties shall be understood to be those performers or producers of phonograms who would meet the criteria for eligibility

for protection provided under the Rome Convention, were all the Contracting Parties to this Treaty Contracting States of that Convention. In respect of these criteria of eligibility, Contracting Parties shall apply the relevant definitions in Article 2 of this Treaty.[4]

(3) Any Contracting Party availing itself of the possibilities provided in Article 5(3) of the Rome Convention or, for the purposes of Article 5 of the same Convention, Article 17 thereof shall make a notification as foreseen in those provisions to the Director General of the World Intellectual Property Organization (WIPO).[5]

Article 4
NATIONAL TREATMENT

(1) Each Contracting Party shall accord to nationals of other Contracting Parties, as defined in Article 3(2), the treatment it accords to its own nationals with regard to the exclusive rights specifically granted in this Treaty, and to the right to equitable remuneration provided for in Article 15 of this Treaty.

(2) The obligation provided for in paragraph (1) does not apply to the extent that another Contracting Party makes use of the reservations permitted by Article 15(3) of this Treaty.

CHAPTER II
RIGHTS OF PERFORMERS

Article 5
MORAL RIGHTS OF PERFORMERS

(1) Independently of a performer's economic rights, and even after the transfer of those rights, the performer shall, as regards his live aural performances or performances fixed in phonograms, have the right to claim to be identified as the performer of his performances, except where omission is dictated by the manner of the use of the performance, and to object to any distortion, mutilation or other modification of his performances that would be prejudicial to his reputation.

(2) The rights granted to a performer in accordance with paragraph (1) shall, after his death, be maintained, at least until the expiry of the economic rights, and shall be exercisable by the persons or institutions authorized by the legislation of the Contracting Party where protection is claimed. However, those Contracting Parties whose legislation, at the moment of their ratification of or accession to this Treaty, does not provide for protection after the death of the performer of all rights set out in the preceding paragraph may provide that some of these rights will, after his death, cease to be maintained.

(3) The means of redress for safeguarding the rights granted under this Article shall be governed by the legislation of the Contracting Party where protection is claimed.

Article 6
ECONOMIC RIGHTS OF PERFORMERS IN THEIR UNFIXED PERFORMANCES

Performers shall enjoy the exclusive right of authorizing, as regards their performances:

(i)   the broadcasting and communication to the public of their unfixed performances except where the performance is already a broadcast performance; and

(ii) the fixation of their unfixed performances.

Article 7
RIGHT OF REPRODUCTION

Performers shall enjoy the exclusive right of authorizing the direct or indirect reproduction of their performances fixed in phonograms, in any manner or form.[6]

Article 8
RIGHT OF DISTRIBUTION

(1) Performers shall enjoy the exclusive right of authorizing the making available to the public of the original and copies of their performances fixed in phonograms through sale or other transfer of ownership.

(2) Nothing in this Treaty shall affect the freedom of Contracting Parties to determine the conditions, if any, under which the exhaustion of the right in paragraph (1) applies after the first sale or other transfer of ownership of the original or a copy of the fixed performance with the authorization of the performer.[7]

Article 9
RIGHT OF RENTAL

(1) Performers shall enjoy the exclusive right of authorizing the commercial rental to the public of the original and copies of their performances fixed in phonograms as determined in the national law of Contracting Parties, even after distribution of them by, or pursuant to, authorization by the performer.

(2) Notwithstanding the provisions of paragraph (1), a Contracting Party that, on April 15, 1994, had and continues to have in force a system of equitable remuneration of performers for the rental of copies of their performances fixed in phonograms, may maintain that system provided that the commercial rental of phonograms is not giving rise to the material impairment of the exclusive right of reproduction of performers.[8]

Article 10
RIGHT OF MAKING AVAILABLE OF FIXED PERFORMANCES

Performers shall enjoy the exclusive right of authorizing the making available to the public of their performances fixed in phonograms, by wire or wireless means, in such a way that members of the public may access them from a place and at a time individually chosen by them.

CHAPTER III
RIGHTS OF PRODUCERS OF PHONOGRAMS

Article 11
RIGHT OF REPRODUCTION

Producers of phonograms shall enjoy the exclusive right of authorizing the direct or indirect reproduction of their phonograms, in any manner or form.[9]

Article 12
RIGHT OF DISTRIBUTION

(1) Producers of phonograms shall enjoy the exclusive right of authorizing the making available to the public of the original and copies of their phonograms through sale or other transfer of ownership.

(2) Nothing in this Treaty shall affect the freedom of Contracting Parties to determine the conditions, if any, under which the exhaustion of the right in paragraph (1) applies after the first sale or other transfer of ownership of the original or a copy of the phonogram with the authorization of the producer of the phonogram.[10]

Article 13
RIGHT OF RENTAL

(1) Producers of phonograms shall enjoy the exclusive right of authorizing the commercial rental to the public of the original and copies of their phonograms, even after distribution of them, by or pursuant to, authorization by the producer.

(2) Notwithstanding the provisions of paragraph (1), a Contracting Party that, on April 15, 1994, had and continues to have in force a system of equitable remuneration of producers of phonograms for the rental of copies of their phonograms, may maintain that system provided that the commercial rental of phonograms is not giving rise to the material impairment of the exclusive rights of reproduction of producers of phonograms.[11]

Article 14
RIGHT OF MAKING AVAILABLE OF PHONOGRAMS

Producers of phonograms shall enjoy the exclusive right of authorizing the making available to the public of their phonograms, by wire or wireless means, in such a way that members of the public may access them from a place and at a time individually chosen by them.

CHAPTER IV
COMMON PROVISIONS

Article 15
RIGHT TO REMUNERATION FOR BROADCASTING AND COMMUNICATION TO THE PUBLIC

(1) Performers and producers of phonograms shall enjoy the right to a single equitable remuneration for the direct or indirect use of phonograms published for commercial purposes for broadcasting or for any communication to the public.

(2) Contracting Parties may establish in their national legislation that the single equitable remuneration shall be claimed from the user by the performer or by the producer of a phonogram or by both. Contracting Parties may enact national legislation that, in the absence of an agreement between the performer and the producer of a phonogram, sets the terms according to which performers and producers of phonograms shall share the single equitable remuneration.

(3) Any Contracting Party may, in a notification deposited with the Director General of WIPO, declare that it will apply the provisions of paragraph (1) only in respect of certain uses, or that it will limit their application in some other way, or that it will not apply these provisions at all.

(4) For the purposes of this Article, phonograms made available to the public by wire or wireless means in such a way that members of the public may access them from a place and at a time individually chosen by them shall be considered as if they had been published for commercial purposes.[12, 13]

Article 16
LIMITATIONS AND EXCEPTIONS

(1) Contracting Parties may, in their national legislation, provide for the same kinds of limitations or exceptions with regard to the protection of performers and producers of phonograms as they provide for, in their national legislation, in connection with the protection of copyright in literary and artistic works.

(2) Contracting Parties shall confine any limitations of or exceptions to rights provided for in this Treaty to certain special cases which do not conflict with a normal exploitation of the performance or phonogram and do not unreasonably prejudice the legitimate interests of the performer or of the producer of the phonogram.[14, 15]

Article 17
TERM OF PROTECTION

(1) The term of protection to be granted to performers under this Treaty shall last, at least, until the end of a period of 50 years computed from the end of the year in which the performance was fixed in a phonogram.

(2) The term of protection to be granted to producers of phonograms under this Treaty shall last, at least, until the end of a period of 50 years computed from the end of the year in which the phonogram was published, or failing such publication within 50 years from fixation of the phonogram, 50 years from the end of the year in which the fixation was made.

Article 18
OBLIGATIONS CONCERNING TECHNOLOGICAL MEASURES

Contracting Parties shall provide adequate legal protection and effective legal remedies against the circumvention of effective technological measures that are used by performers or producers of phonograms in connection with the exercise of their rights under this Treaty and that restrict acts, in respect of their performances or phonograms, which are not authorized by the performers or the producers of phonograms concerned or permitted by law.

Article 19
OBLIGATIONS CONCERNING RIGHTS MANAGEMENT INFORMATION

(1) Contracting Parties shall provide adequate and effective legal remedies against any person knowingly performing any of the following acts knowing, or with respect to civil remedies having reasonable grounds to know, that it will induce, enable, facilitate or conceal an infringement of any right covered by this Treaty:

(i) to remove or alter any electronic rights management information without authority;

(ii) to distribute, import for distribution, broadcast, communicate or make available to the public, without authority, performances, copies of fixed performances or phonograms knowing that electronic rights management information has been removed or altered without authority.

(2) As used in this Article, "rights management information" means information which identifies the performer, the performance of the performer, the producer of the phonogram, the phonogram, the owner of any right in the performance or phonogram, or information about the terms and conditions of use of the performance or phonogram, and any numbers or codes that represent such information, when any of these items of information is attached to a copy of a fixed performance or a phonogram or appears in connection with the communication or making available of a fixed performance or a phonogram to the public.[16]

Article 20
FORMALITIES

The enjoyment and exercise of the rights provided for in this Treaty shall not be subject to any formality.

Article 21
RESERVATIONS

Subject to the provisions of Article 15(3), no reservations to this Treaty shall be permitted.

Article 22
APPLICATION IN TIME

(1) Contracting Parties shall apply the provisions of Article 18 of the Berne Convention, *mutatis mutandis*, to the rights of performers and producers of phonograms provided for in this Treaty.

(2) Notwithstanding paragraph (1), a Contracting Party may limit the application of Article 5 of this Treaty to performances which occurred after the entry into force of this Treaty for that Party.

Article 23
PROVISIONS ON ENFORCEMENT OF RIGHTS

(1) Contracting Parties undertake to adopt, in accordance with their legal systems, the measures necessary to ensure the application of this Treaty.

(2) Contracting Parties shall ensure that enforcement procedures are available under their law so as to permit effective action against any act of infringement of rights covered by this Treaty, including expeditious remedies to prevent infringements and remedies which constitute a deterrent to further infringements.

CHAPTER V
ADMINISTRATIVE AND FINAL CLAUSES

Article 24
ASSEMBLY

(1)

(*a*)   The Contracting Parties shall have an Assembly.

(*b*)   Each Contracting Party shall be represented by one delegate who may be assisted by alternate delegates, advisors and experts.

(*c*)   The expenses of each delegation shall be borne by the Contracting Party that has appointed the delegation. The Assembly may ask WIPO to grant financial assistance to facilitate the participation of delegations of Contracting Parties that are regarded as developing countries in conformity with the established practice of the General Assembly of the United Nations or that are countries in transition to a market economy.

(2)

(a) The Assembly shall deal with matters concerning the maintenance and development of this Treaty and the application and operation of this Treaty.

(b) The Assembly shall perform the function allocated to it under Article 26(2) in respect of the admission of certain intergovernmental organizations to become party to this Treaty.

(c) The Assembly shall decide the convocation of any diplomatic conference for the revision of this Treaty and give the necessary instructions to the Director General of WIPO for the preparation of such diplomatic conference.

(3)

(a) Each Contracting Party that is a State shall have one vote and shall vote only in its own name.

(b) Any Contracting Party that is an intergovernmental organization may participate in the vote, in place of its Member States, with a number of votes equal to the number of its Member States which are party to this Treaty. No such intergovernmental organization shall participate in the vote if any one of its Member States exercises its right to vote and vice versa.

(4) The Assembly shall meet in ordinary session once every two years upon convocation by the Director General of WIPO.

(5) The Assembly shall establish its own rules of procedure, including the convocation of extraordinary sessions, the requirements of a quorum and, subject to the provisions of this Treaty, the required majority for various kinds of decisions.

Article 25
INTERNATIONAL BUREAU

The International Bureau of WIPO shall perform the administrative tasks concerning the Treaty.

Article 26
ELIGIBILITY FOR BECOMING PARTY TO THE TREATY

(1) Any Member State of WIPO may become party to this Treaty.

(2) The Assembly may decide to admit any intergovernmental organization to become party to this Treaty which declares that it is competent in respect of, and has its own legislation binding on all its Member States on, matters covered by this Treaty and that it has been duly authorized, in accordance with its internal procedures, to become party to this Treaty.

(3) The European Community, having made the declaration referred to in the preceding paragraph in the Diplomatic Conference that has adopted this Treaty, may become party to this Treaty.

Article 27
RIGHTS AND OBLIGATIONS UNDER THE TREATY

Subject to any specific provisions to the contrary in this Treaty, each Contracting Party shall enjoy all of the rights and assume all of the obligations under this Treaty.

Article 28
SIGNATURE OF THE TREATY

This Treaty shall be open for signature until December 31, 1997, by any Member State of WIPO and by the European Community.

Article 29
ENTRY INTO FORCE OF THE TREATY

This Treaty shall enter into force three months after 30 instruments of ratification or accession by States have been deposited with the Director General of WIPO.

Article 30
EFFECTIVE DATE OF BECOMING PARTY TO THE TREATY

This Treaty shall bind:

(i) the 30 States referred to in Article 29, from the date on which this Treaty has entered into force;

(ii) each other State from the expiration of three months from the date on which the State has deposited its instrument with the Director General of WIPO;

(iii) the European Community, from the expiration of three months after the deposit of its instrument of ratification or accession if such instrument has been deposited after the entry into force of this Treaty according to Article 29, or, three months after the entry into force of this Treaty if such instrument has been deposited before the entry into force of this Treaty;

(iv) any other intergovernmental organization that is admitted to become party to this Treaty, from the expiration of three months after the deposit of its instrument of accession.

Article 31
DENUNCIATION OF THE TREATY

This Treaty may be denounced by any Contracting Party by notification addressed to the Director General of WIPO. Any denunciation shall take effect one year from the date on which the Director General of WIPO received the notification.

Article 32
LANGUAGES OF THE TREATY

(1) This Treaty is signed in a single original in English, Arabic, Chinese, French, Russian and Spanish languages, the versions in all these languages being equally authentic.

(2) An official text in any language other than those referred to in paragraph (1) shall be established by the Director General of WIPO on the request of an interested party, after consultation with all the interested parties. For the purposes of this paragraph, "interested party" means any Member State of WIPO whose official language, or one of whose official languages, is involved and the European Community, and any other intergovernmental organization that may become party to this Treaty, if one of its official languages is involved.

Article 33
DEPOSITARY

The Director General of WIPO is the depositary of this Treaty.

* *Entry into force:* May 20, 2002.

Source: International Bureau of WIPO.

Note: The agreed statements of the Diplomatic Conference that adopted the Treaty (WIPO Diplomatic Conference on Certain Copyright and Neighboring Rights Questions) concerning certain provisions of the WPPT, are reproduced in endnotes below.

[1] *Agreed statement concerning Article 1(2):* It is understood that Article 1(2) clarifies the relationship between rights in phonograms under this Treaty and copyright in works embodied in the phonograms. In cases where authorization is needed from both the author of a work embodied in the phonogram and a performer or producer owning rights in the phonogram, the need for the authorization of the author does not cease to exist because the authorization of the performer or producer is also required, and vice versa.

It is further understood that nothing in Article 1(2) precludes a Contracting Party from providing exclusive rights to a performer or producer of phonograms beyond those required to be provided under this Treaty.

[2] *Agreed statement concerning Article 2 (b):* It is understood that the definition of phonogram provided in Article 2(b) does not suggest that rights in the phonogram are in any way affected through their incorporation into a cinematographic or other audiovisual work.

[3] *Agreed statement concerning Articles 2 (e), 8, 9, 12, and 13:* As used in these Articles, the expressions "copies" and "original and copies," being subject to the right of distribution

and the right of rental under the said Articles, refer exclusively to fixed copies that can be put into circulation as tangible objects.

[4] *Agreed statement concerning Article 3(2):* For the application of Article 3(2), it is understood that fixation means the finalization of the master tape ("bande-mère").

[5] *Agreed statement concerning Article 3:* It is understood that the reference in Articles 5(a) and 16(a)(iv) of the Rome Convention to "national of another Contracting State" will, when applied to this Treaty, mean, in regard to an intergovernmental organization that is a Contracting Party to this Treaty, a national of one of the countries that is a member of that organization.

[6] *Agreed statement concerning Articles 7, 11 and 16:* The reproduction right, as set out in Articles 7 and 11, and the exceptions permitted thereunder through Article 16, fully apply in the digital environment, in particular to the use of performances and phonograms in digital form. It is understood that the storage of a protected performance or phonogram in digital form in an electronic medium constitutes a reproduction within the meaning of these Articles.

[7] *Agreed statement concerning Articles 2 (e), 8, 9, 12, and 13:* As used in these Articles, the expressions "copies" and "original and copies," being subject to the right of distribution and the right of rental under the said Articles, refer exclusively to fixed copies that can be put into circulation as tangible objects.

[8] *Agreed statement concerning Articles 2 (e), 8, 9, 12, and 13:* As used in these Articles, the expressions "copies" and "original and copies," being subject to the right of distribution and the right of rental under the said Articles, refer exclusively to fixed copies that can be put into circulation as tangible objects.

[9] *Agreed statement concerning Articles 7, 11 and 16:* The reproduction right, as set out in Articles 7 and 11, and the exceptions permitted thereunder through Article 16, fully apply in the digital environment, in particular to the use of performances and phonograms in digital form. It is understood that the storage of a protected performance or phonogram in digital form in an electronic medium constitutes a reproduction within the meaning of these Articles.

[10] *Agreed statement concerning Articles 2 (e), 8, 9, 12, and 13:* As used in these Articles, the expressions "copies" and "original and copies," being subject to the right of distribution and the right of rental under the said Articles, refer exclusively to fixed copies that can be put into circulation as tangible objects.

[11] *Agreed statement concerning Articles 2 (e), 8, 9, 12, and 13:* As used in these Articles, the expressions "copies" and "original and copies," being subject to the right of distribution and the right of rental under the said Articles, refer exclusively to fixed copies that can be put into circulation as tangible objects.

[12] *Agreed statement concerning Article 15:* It is understood that Article 15 does not represent a complete resolution of the level of rights of broadcasting and communication to the public that should be enjoyed by performers and phonogram producers in the digital age. Delegations were unable to achieve consensus on differing proposals for aspects of exclusivity to be provided in certain circumstances or for rights to be provided without the possibility of reservations, and have therefore left the issue to future resolution.

[13] *Agreed statement concerning Article 15:* It is understood that Article 15 does not prevent the granting of the right conferred by this Article to performers of folklore and producers of phonograms recording folklore where such phonograms have not been published for commercial gain.

[14] *Agreed statement concerning Articles 7, 11 and 16:* The reproduction right, as set out in Articles 7 and 11, and the exceptions permitted thereunder through Article 16, fully apply in the digital environment, in particular to the use of performances and phonograms in digital form. It is understood that the storage of a protected performance or phonogram in digital form in an electronic medium constitutes a reproduction within the meaning of these Articles.

[15] *Agreed statement concerning Article 16:* The agreed statement concerning Article 10 (on Limitations and Exceptions) of the WIPO Copyright Treaty is applicable *mutatis mutandis* also to Article 16 (on Limitations and Exceptions) of the WIPO Performances and Phonograms Treaty. [The text of the agreed statement concerning Article 10 of the WCT reads as follows: "It is understood that the provisions of Article 10 permit Contracting Parties to carry forward and appropriately extend into the digital environment limitations and exceptions in their national laws which have been considered acceptable under the Berne Convention. Similarly, these provisions should be understood to permit Contracting Parties to devise new exceptions and limitations that are appropriate in the digital network environment.

"It is also understood that Article 10(2) neither reduces nor extends the scope of applicability of the limitations and exceptions permitted by the Berne Convention."]

[16] *Agreed statement concerning Article 19:* The agreed statement concerning Article 12 (on Obligations concerning Rights Management Information) of the WIPO Copyright Treaty is applicable *mutatis mutandis* also to Article 19 (on Obligations concerning Rights Management Information) of the WIPO Performances and Phonograms Treaty. [The text of the agreed statement concerning Article 12 of the WCT reads as follows: "It is understood that the reference to 'infringement of any right covered by this Treaty or the Berne Convention' includes both exclusive rights and rights of remuneration.

"It is further understood that Contracting Parties will not rely on this Article to devise or implement rights management systems that would have the effect of imposing formalities which are not permitted under the Berne Convention or this Treaty, prohibiting the free movement of goods or impeding the enjoyment of rights under this Treaty."]

MARRAKESH TREATY TO FACILITATE ACCESS TO PUBLISHED WORKS FOR PERSONS WHO ARE BLIND, VISUALLY IMPAIRED, OR OTHERWISE PRINT DISABLED

(adopted by the Diplomatic Conference to Conclude a Treaty to Facilitate Access to Published Works by Visually Impaired Persons and Persons with Print Disabilities in Marrakesh, on June 27, 2013)

(For the list of contracting parties to the Treaty, see http://www.wipo.int/treaties/en/ShowResults.jsp?lang=en&treaty_id=843)

PREAMBLE

The Contracting Parties,

Recalling the principles of non-discrimination, equal opportunity, accessibility and full and effective participation and inclusion in society, proclaimed in the Universal Declaration of Human Rights and the United Nations Convention on the Rights of Persons with Disabilities,

Mindful of the challenges that are prejudicial to the complete development of persons with visual impairments or with other print disabilities, which limit their freedom of expression, including the freedom to seek, receive and impart information and ideas of all kinds on an equal basis with others, including through all forms of communication of their choice, their enjoyment of the right to education, and the opportunity to conduct research,

Emphasizing the importance of copyright protection as an incentive and reward for literary and artistic creations and of enhancing opportunities for everyone, including persons with visual impairments or with other print disabilities, to participate in the cultural life of the community, to enjoy the arts and to share scientific progress and its benefits,

Aware of the barriers of persons with visual impairments or with other print disabilities to access published works in achieving equal opportunities in society, and the need to both expand the number of works in accessible formats and to improve the circulation of such works,

Taking into account that the majority of persons with visual impairments or with other print disabilities live in developing and least-developed countries,

Recognizing that, despite the differences in national copyright laws, the positive

313

impact of new information and communication technologies on the lives of persons with visual impairments or with other print disabilities may be reinforced by an enhanced legal framework at the international level,

Recognizing that many Member States have established limitations and exceptions in their national copyright laws for persons with visual impairments or with other print disabilities, yet there is a continuing shortage of available works in accessible format copies for such persons, and that considerable resources are required for their effort of making works accessible to these persons, and that the lack of possibilities of cross-border exchange of accessible format copies has necessitated duplication of these efforts,

Recognizing both the importance of rightholders' role in making their works accessible to persons with visual impairments or with other print disabilities and the importance of appropriate limitations and exceptions to make works accessible to these persons, particularly when the market is unable to provide such access,

Recognizing the need to maintain a balance between the effective protection of the rights of authors and the larger public interest, particularly education, research and access to information, and that such a balance must facilitate effective and timely access to works for the benefit of persons with visual impairments or with other print disabilities,

Reaffirming the obligations of Contracting Parties under the existing international treaties on the protection of copyright and the importance and flexibility of the three-step test for limitations and exceptions established in Article 9(2) of the Berne Convention for the Protection of Literary and Artistic Works and other international instruments,

Recalling the importance of the Development Agenda recommendations, adopted in 2007 by the General Assembly of the World Intellectual Property Organization (WIPO), which aim to ensure that development considerations form an integral part of the Organization's work,

Recognizing the importance of the international copyright system and desiring to harmonize limitations and exceptions with a view to facilitating access to and use of works by persons with visual impairments or with other print disabilities,

Have agreed as follows:

Article 1
RELATION TO OTHER CONVENTIONS AND TREATIES

Nothing in this Treaty shall derogate from any obligations that Contracting Parties have to each other under any other treaties, nor shall it prejudice any rights that a Contracting Party has under any other treaties.

Article 2
DEFINITIONS

(a) "works" means literary and artistic works within the meaning of Article 2(1) of the Berne Convention for the Protection of Literary and Artistic Works, in the form of text, notation and/or related illustrations, whether published or otherwise made publicly available in any media;[1]

(b) "accessible format copy" means a copy of a work in an alternative manner or form which gives a beneficiary person access to the work, including to permit the person to have access as feasibly and comfortably as a person without visual impairment or other print disability. The accessible format copy is used exclusively by beneficiary persons and it must respect the integrity of the original work, taking due consideration of the changes needed to make the work accessible in the alternative format and of the accessibility needs of the beneficiary persons;

(c) "authorized entity" means an entity that is authorized or recognized by the government to provide education, instructional training, adaptive reading or information access to beneficiary persons on a non-profit basis. It also includes a government institution or non-profit organization that provides the same services to beneficiary persons as one of its primary activities or institutional obligations.[2] An authorized entity establishes and follows its own practices:

(i)   to establish that the persons it serves are beneficiary persons;

(ii) to limit to beneficiary persons and/or authorized entities its distribution and making available of accessible format copies;

(iii) to discourage the reproduction, distribution and making available of unauthorized copies; and

(iv) to maintain due care in, and records of, its handling of copies of works, while respecting the privacy of beneficiary persons in accordance with Article 8.

Article 3
BENEFICIARY PERSONS

A beneficiary person is a person who:

(a) is blind;

(b) has a visual impairment or a perceptual or reading disability which cannot be improved to give visual function substantially equivalent to that of a person who has no such impairment or disability and so is unable to read printed works to substantially the same degree as a person without an impairment or disability; or[3]

(c) is otherwise unable, through physical disability, to hold or manipulate a book or to focus or move the eyes to the extent that would be normally acceptable for reading;

regardless of any other disabilities.

Article 4
NATIONAL LAW LIMITATIONS AND EXCEPTIONS REGARDING ACCESSIBLE FORMAT COPIES

1.

(a) Contracting Parties shall provide in their national copyright laws for a limitation or exception to the right of reproduction, the right of distribution, and the right of making available to the public as provided by the WIPO Copyright Treaty (WCT), to facilitate the availability of works in accessible format copies for beneficiary persons. The limitation or exception provided in national law should permit changes needed to make the work accessible in the alternative format.

(b) Contracting Parties may also provide a limitation or exception to the right of public performance to facilitate access to works for beneficiary persons.

2. A Contracting Party may fulfill Article 4(1) for all rights identified therein by providing a limitation or exception in its national copyright law such that:

(a) Authorized entities shall be permitted, without the authorization of the copyright rightholder, to make an accessible format copy of a work, obtain from another authorized entity an accessible format copy, and supply those copies to beneficiary persons by any means, including by non-commercial lending or by electronic communication by wire or wireless means, and undertake any intermediate steps to achieve those objectives, when all of the following conditions are met:

   (i) the authorized entity wishing to undertake said activity has lawful access to that work or a copy of that work;

   (ii) the work is converted to an accessible format copy, which may include any means needed to navigate information in the accessible format, but does not introduce changes other than those needed to make the work accessible to the beneficiary person;

   (iii) such accessible format copies are supplied exclusively to be used by beneficiary persons; and

   (iv) the activity is undertaken on a non-profit basis;

and

(b) A beneficiary person, or someone acting on his or her behalf including a primary caretaker or caregiver, may make an accessible format copy of a work for the personal use of the beneficiary person or otherwise may assist the beneficiary person to make and use accessible format copies where the beneficiary person has lawful access to that work or a copy of that work.

3. A Contracting Party may fulfill Article 4(1) by providing other limitations or

exceptions in its national copyright law pursuant to Articles 10 and 11[4].

4. A Contracting Party may confine limitations or exceptions under this Article to works which, in the particular accessible format, cannot be obtained commercially under reasonable terms for beneficiary persons in that market. Any Contracting Party availing itself of this possibility shall so declare in a notification deposited with the Director General of WIPO at the time of ratification of, acceptance of or accession to this Treaty or at any time thereafter[5].

5. It shall be a matter for national law to determine whether limitations or exceptions under this Article are subject to remuneration.

Article 5
CROSS-BORDER EXCHANGE OF ACCESSIBLE FORMAT COPIES

1. Contracting Parties shall provide that if an accessible format copy is made under a limitation or exception or pursuant to operation of law, that accessible format copy may be distributed or made available by an authorized entity to a beneficiary person or an authorized entity in another Contracting Party.[6]

2. A Contracting Party may fulfill Article 5(1) by providing a limitation or exception in its national copyright law such that:

(a) authorized entities shall be permitted, without the authorization of the rightholder, to distribute or make available for the exclusive use of beneficiary persons accessible format copies to an authorized entity in another Contracting Party; and

(b) authorized entities shall be permitted, without the authorization of the rightholder and pursuant to Article 2(c), to distribute or make available accessible format copies to a beneficiary person in another Contracting Party;

provided that prior to the distribution or making available the originating authorized entity did not know or have reasonable grounds to know that the accessible format copy would be used for other than beneficiary persons.[7]

3. A Contracting Party may fulfill Article 5(1) by providing other limitations or exceptions in its national copyright law pursuant to Articles 5(4), 10 and 11.

4.

(a) When an authorized entity in a Contracting Party receives accessible format copies pursuant to Article 5(1) and that Contracting Party does not have obligations under Article 9 of the Berne Convention, it will ensure, consistent with its own legal system and practices, that the accessible format copies are only reproduced, distributed or made available for the benefit of beneficiary persons in that Contracting Party's jurisdiction.

(b) The distribution and making available of accessible format copies by an authorized entity pursuant to Article 5(1) shall be limited to that jurisdiction unless the Contracting Party is a Party to the WIPO Copyright Treaty or otherwise limits limitations and exceptions implementing this Treaty to the right of distribution and the right of making available to the public to certain special cases which do not conflict with a normal exploitation of the work and do not unreasonably prejudice the legitimate interests of the rightholder[8, 9].

(c)   Nothing in this Article affects the determination of what constitutes an act of distribution or an act of making available to the public.

5. Nothing in this Treaty shall be used to address the issue of exhaustion of rights.

Article 6
IMPORTATION OF ACCESSIBLE FORMAT COPIES

To the extent that the national law of a Contracting Party would permit a beneficiary person, someone acting on his or her behalf, or an authorized entity, to make an accessible format copy of a work, the national law of that Contracting Party shall also permit them to import an accessible format copy for the benefit of beneficiary persons, without the authorization of the rightholder.[10]

Article 7
OBLIGATIONS CONCERNING TECHNOLOGICAL MEASURES

Contracting Parties shall take appropriate measures, as necessary, to ensure that when they provide adequate legal protection and effective legal remedies against the circumvention of effective technological measures, this legal protection does not prevent beneficiary persons from enjoying the limitations and exceptions provided for in this Treaty[11].

Article 8
RESPECT FOR PRIVACY

In the implementation of the limitations and exceptions provided for in this Treaty, Contracting Parties shall endeavor to protect the privacy of beneficiary persons on an equal basis with others.

Article 9
COOPERATION TO FACILITATE CROSS-BORDER EXCHANGE

1. Contracting Parties shall endeavor to foster the cross-border exchange of accessible format copies by encouraging the voluntary sharing of information to assist authorized entities in identifying one another. The International Bureau of WIPO shall establish an information access point for this purpose.

2. Contracting Parties undertake to assist their authorized entities engaged in activities under Article 5 to make information available regarding their practices pursuant to Article 2(c), both through the sharing of information among authorized entities, and through making available information on their policies and practices,

including related to cross-border exchange of accessible format copies, to interested parties and members of the public as appropriate.

3. The International Bureau of WIPO is invited to share information, where available, about the functioning of this Treaty.

4. Contracting Parties recognize the importance of international cooperation and its promotion, in support of national efforts for realization of the purpose and objectives of this Treaty.[12]

Article 10
GENERAL PRINCIPLES ON IMPLEMENTATION

1. Contracting Parties undertake to adopt the measures necessary to ensure the application of this Treaty.

2. Nothing shall prevent Contracting Parties from determining the appropriate method of implementing the provisions of this Treaty within their own legal system and practice[13].

3. Contracting Parties may fulfill their rights and obligations under this Treaty through limitations or exceptions specifically for the benefit of beneficiary persons, other limitations or exceptions, or a combination thereof, within their national legal system and practice. These may include judicial, administrative or regulatory determinations for the benefit of beneficiary persons as to fair practices, dealings or uses to meet their needs consistent with the Contracting Parties' rights and obligations under the Berne Convention, other international treaties, and Article 11.

Article 11
GENERAL OBLIGATIONS ON LIMITATIONS AND EXCEPTIONS

In adopting measures necessary to ensure the application of this Treaty, a Contracting Party may exercise the rights and shall comply with the obligations that that Contracting Party has under the Berne Convention, the Agreement on Trade-Related Aspects of Intellectual Property Rights and the WIPO Copyright Treaty, including their interpretative agreements so that:

(a) in accordance with Article 9(2) of the Berne Convention, a Contracting Party may permit the reproduction of works in certain special cases provided that such reproduction does not conflict with a normal exploitation of the work and does not unreasonably prejudice the legitimate interests of the author;

(b) in accordance with Article 13 of the Agreement on Trade-Related Aspects of Intellectual Property Rights, a Contracting Party shall confine limitations or exceptions to exclusive rights to certain special cases which do not conflict with a normal exploitation of the work and do not unreasonably prejudice the legitimate interests of the rightholder;

(c) in accordance with Article 10(1) of the WIPO Copyright Treaty, a

Contracting Party may provide for limitations of or exceptions to the rights granted to authors under the WCT in certain special cases, that do not conflict with a normal exploitation of the work and do not unreasonably prejudice the legitimate interests of the author;

(d)   in accordance with Article 10(2) of the WIPO Copyright Treaty, a Contracting Party shall confine, when applying the Berne Convention, any limitations of or exceptions to rights to certain special cases that do not conflict with a normal exploitation of the work and do not unreasonably prejudice the legitimate interests of the author.

Article 12
OTHER LIMITATIONS AND EXCEPTIONS

1. Contracting Parties recognize that a Contracting Party may implement in its national law other copyright limitations and exceptions for the benefit of beneficiary persons than are provided by this Treaty having regard to that Contracting Party's economic situation, and its social and cultural needs, in conformity with that Contracting Party's international rights and obligations, and in the case of a least-developed country taking into account its special needs and its particular international rights and obligations and flexibilities thereof.

2. This Treaty is without prejudice to other limitations and exceptions for persons with disabilities provided by national law.

Article 13
ASSEMBLY

1.

(a)   The Contracting Parties shall have an Assembly.

(b)   Each Contracting Party shall be represented in the Assembly by one delegate who may be assisted by alternate delegates, advisors and experts.

(c)   The expenses of each delegation shall be borne by the Contracting Party that has appointed the delegation. The Assembly may ask WIPO to grant financial assistance to facilitate the participation of delegations of Contracting Parties that are regarded as developing countries in conformity with the established practice of the General Assembly of the United Nations or that are countries in transition to a market economy.

2.

(a)   The Assembly shall deal with matters concerning the maintenance and development of this Treaty and the application and operation of this Treaty.

(b)   The Assembly shall perform the function allocated to it under Article 15 in respect of the admission of certain intergovernmental organizations to become party to this Treaty.

320

(c) The Assembly shall decide the convocation of any diplomatic conference for the revision of this Treaty and give the necessary instructions to the Director General of WIPO for the preparation of such diplomatic conference.

3.

(a) Each Contracting Party that is a State shall have one vote and shall vote only in its own name.

(b) Any Contracting Party that is an intergovernmental organization may participate in the vote, in place of its Member States, with a number of votes equal to the number of its Member States which are party to this Treaty. No such intergovernmental organization shall participate in the vote if any one of its Member States exercises its right to vote and vice versa.

4. The Assembly shall meet upon convocation by the Director General and, in the absence of exceptional circumstances, during the same period and at the same place as the General Assembly of WIPO.

5. The Assembly shall endeavor to take its decisions by consensus and shall establish its own rules of procedure, including the convocation of extraordinary sessions, the requirements of a quorum and, subject to the provisions of this Treaty, the required majority for various kinds of decisions.

Article 14
INTERNATIONAL BUREAU

The International Bureau of WIPO shall perform the administrative tasks concerning this Treaty.

Article 15
ELIGIBILITY FOR BECOMING PARTY TO THE TREATY

1. Any Member State of WIPO may become party to this Treaty.

2. The Assembly may decide to admit any intergovernmental organization to become party to this Treaty which declares that it is competent in respect of, and has its own legislation binding on all its Member States on, matters covered by this Treaty and that it has been duly authorized, in accordance with its internal procedures, to become party to this Treaty.

3. The European Union, having made the declaration referred to in the preceding paragraph at the Diplomatic Conference that has adopted this Treaty, may become party to this Treaty.

Article 16
RIGHTS AND OBLIGATIONS UNDER THE TREATY

Subject to any specific provisions to the contrary in this Treaty, each Contracting Party shall enjoy all of the rights and assume all of the obligations under this Treaty.

Article 17
SIGNATURE OF THE TREATY

This Treaty shall be open for signature at the Diplomatic Conference in Marrakesh, and thereafter at the headquarters of WIPO by any eligible party for one year after its adoption.

Article 18
ENTRY INTO FORCE OF THE TREATY

This Treaty shall enter into force three months after 20 eligible parties referred to in Article 15 have deposited their instruments of ratification or accession.

Article 19
EFFECTIVE DATE OF BECOMING PARTY TO THE TREATY

This Treaty shall bind:

(a)   the 20 eligible parties referred to in Article 18, from the date on which this Treaty has entered into force;

(b)   each other eligible party referred to in Article 15, from the expiration of three months from the date on which it has deposited its instrument of ratification or accession with the Director General of WIPO.

Article 20
DENUNCIATION OF THE TREATY

This Treaty may be denounced by any Contracting Party by notification addressed to the Director General of WIPO. Any denunciation shall take effect one year from the date on which the Director General of WIPO received the notification.

Article 21
LANGUAGES OF THE TREATY

1. This Treaty is signed in a single original in English, Arabic, Chinese, French, Russian and Spanish languages, the versions in all these languages being equally authentic.

2. An official text in any language other than those referred to in Article 21(1) shall be established by the Director General of WIPO on the request of an interested party, after consultation with all the interested parties. For the purposes of this paragraph, "interested party" means any Member State of WIPO whose official language, or one of whose official languages, is involved and the European Union, and any other intergovernmental organization that may become party to this Treaty, if one of its official languages is involved.

Article 22
DEPOSITARY

The Director General of WIPO is the depositary of this Treaty.

Done in Marrakesh on the 27th day of June, 2013.

[1] **Agreed statement concerning Article 2(a):** For the purposes of this Treaty, it is understood that this definition includes such works in audio form, such as audiobooks.

[2] **Agreed statement concerning Article 2(c):** For the purposes of this Treaty, it is understood that "entities recognized by the government" may include entities receiving financial support from the government to provide education, instructional training, adaptive reading or information access to beneficiary persons on a non-profit basis.

[3] **Agreed statement concerning Article 3(b):** Nothing in this language implies that "cannot be improved" requires the use of all possible medical diagnostic procedures and treatments.

[4] **Agreed statement concerning Article 4(3):** It is understood that this paragraph neither reduces nor extends the scope of applicability of limitations and exceptions permitted under the Berne Convention, as regards the right of translation, with respect to persons with visual impairments or with other print disabilities.

[5] **Agreed statement concerning Article 4(4):** It is understood that a commercial availability requirement does not prejudge whether or not a limitation or exception under this Article is consistent with the three-step test.

[6] **Agreed statement concerning Article 5(1):** It is further understood that nothing in this Treaty reduces or extends the scope of exclusive rights under any other treaty.

[7] **Agreed statement concerning Article 5(2):** It is understood that, to distribute or make available accessible format copies directly to a beneficiary person in another Contracting Party, it may be appropriate for an authorized entity to apply further measures to confirm that the person it is serving is a beneficiary person and to follow its own practices as described in Article 2(c).

[8] **Agreed statement concerning Article 5(4)(b):** It is understood that nothing in this Treaty requires or implies that a Contracting Party adopt or apply the three-step test beyond its obligations under this instrument or under other international treaties.

[9] **Agreed statement concerning Article 5(4)(b):** It is understood that nothing in this Treaty creates any obligations for a Contracting Party to ratify or accede to the WCT or to comply with any of its provisions and nothing in this Treaty prejudices any rights, limitations and exceptions contained in the WCT.

[10] **Agreed statement concerning Article 6:** It is understood that the Contracting Parties have the same flexibilities set out in Article 4 when implementing their obligations under Article 6.

[11] **Agreed statement concerning Article 7:** It is understood that authorized entities, in various circumstances, choose to apply technological measures in the making, distribution and making available of accessible format copies and nothing herein disturbs such practices when in accordance with national law.

[12] **Agreed statement concerning Article 9:** It is understood that Article 9 does not imply mandatory registration for authorized entities nor does it constitute a precondition for authorized entities to engage in activities recognized under this Treaty; but it provides for a possibility for sharing information to facilitate the cross-border exchange of accessible format copies.

[13] **Agreed statement concerning Article 10(2):** It is understood that when a work qualifies as a work under Article 2(a), including such works in audio form, the limitations and exceptions provided for by this Treaty apply *mutatis mutandis* to related rights as necessary to make the accessible format copy, to distribute it and to make it available to beneficiary persons.

CANADA–UNITED STATES–MEXICO AGREEMENT

CHAPTER 20:
INTELLECTUAL PROPERTY RIGHTS

* * *

Section H: Copyright and Related Rights

Article 20.56: Definitions

For the purposes of Article 20.57 (Right of Reproduction) and Article 20.59 (Right of Distribution) through Article 20.68 (Collective Management), the following definitions apply with respect to performers and producers of phonograms:

broadcasting means the transmission by wireless means for public reception of sounds or of images and sounds or of the representations thereof; such transmission by satellite is also "broadcasting"; transmission of encrypted signals is "broadcasting" if the means for decrypting are provided to the public by the broadcasting organization or with its consent; "broadcasting" does not include transmission over computer networks or any transmissions where the time and place of reception may be individually chosen by members of the public;

communication to the public of a performance or a phonogram means the transmission to the public by any medium, other than by broadcasting, of sounds of a performance or the sounds or the representations of sounds fixed in a phonogram;

fixation means the embodiment of sounds, or of the representations thereof, from which they can be perceived, reproduced, or communicated through a device;

performers means actors, singers, musicians, dancers, and other persons who act, sing, deliver, declaim, play in, interpret, or otherwise perform literary or artistic works or expressions of folklore;

phonogram means the fixation of the sounds of a performance or of other sounds, or of a representation of sounds, other than in the form of a fixation incorporated in a cinematographic or other audio-visual work;

producer of a phonogram means a person that takes the initiative and has the responsibility for the first fixation of the sounds of a performance or other sounds, or the representations of sounds; and

publication of a performance or phonogram means the offering of copies of the performance or the phonogram to the public, with the consent of the right holder, and provided that copies are offered to the public in reasonable quantity.

Article 20.57: Right of Reproduction

Each Party shall provide[53] to authors, performers, and producers of phonograms[54] the exclusive right to authorize or prohibit all reproduction of their works, performances, or phonograms in any manner or form, including in electronic form.

Article 20.58: Right of Communication to the Public

Without prejudice to Article 11(1)(ii), Article 11*bis*(1)(i) and (ii), Article 11*ter*(1)(ii), Article 14(1)(ii), and Article 14*bis*(1) of the Berne Convention, each Party shall provide to authors the exclusive right to authorize or prohibit the communication to the public of their works, by wire or wireless means, including the making available to the public of their works in such a way that members of the public may access these works from a place and at a time individually chosen by them.[55]

Article 20.59: Right of Distribution

Each Party shall provide to authors, performers, and producers of phonograms the exclusive right to authorize or prohibit the making available to the public of the original and copies[56] of their works, performances, and phonograms through sale or other transfer of ownership.

Article 20.60: No Hierarchy

Each Party shall provide that, in cases in which authorization is needed from both the author of a work embodied in a phonogram and a performer or producer that owns rights in the phonogram, the need for the authorization of the:

(a) author does not cease to exist because the authorization of the performer or producer is also required; and

(b) performer or producer does not cease to exist because the authorization of the author is also required.

---

[53] For greater certainty, the Parties understand that it is a matter for each Party's law to prescribe that works, performances, or phonograms in general or any specified categories of works, performances and phonograms are not protected by copyright or related rights unless the work, performance, or phonogram has been fixed in some material form.

[54] References to "authors, performers, and producers of phonograms" refer also to any of their successors in interest.

[55] The Parties understand that the mere provision of physical facilities for enabling or making a communication does not in itself amount to communication within the meaning of this Chapter or the Berne Convention. The Parties further understand that nothing in this Article precludes a Party from applying Article 11*bis*(2) of the Berne Convention.

[56] The expressions "copies" and "original and copies", that are subject to the right of distribution in this Article, refer exclusively to fixed copies that can be put into circulation as tangible objects.

Article 20.61: Related Rights

1. Further to the protection afforded to performers and producers of phonograms as "nationals" under Article 20.8 (National Treatment), each Party shall accord the rights provided for in this Chapter to performances and phonograms first published or first fixed[57] in the territory of another Party.[58] A performance or phonogram is considered first published in the territory of a Party if it is published in the territory of that Party within 30 days of its original publication.

2. Each Party shall provide to performers the exclusive right to authorize or prohibit:

(a)   the broadcasting and communication to the public of their unfixed performances, unless the performance is already a broadcast performance; and

(b)   the fixation of their unfixed performances.

3. (a) Each Party shall provide to performers and producers of phonograms the exclusive right to authorize or prohibit the broadcasting or any communication to the public of their performances or phonograms, by wire or wireless means[59] and the making available to the public of those performances or phonograms in such a way that members of the public may access them from a place and at a time individually chosen by them.

(b)   Notwithstanding subparagraph (a) and Article 20.64 (Limitations and Exceptions), the application of the right referred to in subparagraph (a) to analog transmissions and non-interactive free over-the-air broadcasts, and exceptions or limitations to this right for those activities, is a matter of each Party's law.[60]

(c)   Each Party may adopt limitations to this right in respect of other

---

[57] For the purposes of this Article, fixation means the finalization of the master tape or its equivalent.

[58] For greater certainty, consistent with Article 20.8 (National Treatment), each Party shall accord to performances and phonograms first published or first fixed in the territory of another Party treatment no less favorable than it accords to performances or phonograms first published or first fixed in its own territory.

[59] For greater certainty, the obligation under this paragraph does not include broadcasting or communication to the public, by wire or wireless means, of the sounds or representations of sounds fixed in a phonogram that are incorporated in a cinematographic or other audio-visual work.

[60] For the purposes of this subparagraph the Parties understand that a Party may provide for the retransmission of non-interactive, free over-the-air broadcasts, provided that these retransmissions are lawfully permitted by that Party's government communications authority; any entity engaging in these retransmissions complies with the relevant rules, orders, or regulations of that authority; and these retransmissions do not include those delivered and

non-interactive transmissions in accordance with Article 20.64.1 (Limitations and Exceptions), provided that the limitations do not prejudice the right of the performer or producer of phonograms to obtain equitable remuneration.

Article 20.62: Term of Protection for Copyright and Related Rights

Each Party shall provide that in cases in which the term of protection of a work, performance, or phonogram is to be calculated:

(a) on the basis of the life of a natural person, the term shall be not less than the life of the author and 70 years after the author's death;[61] and

(b) on a basis other than the life of a natural person, the term shall be:

    (i) not less than 75 years from the end of the calendar year of the first authorized publication[62] of the work, performance, or phonogram, or

    (ii) failing such authorized publication within 25 years from the creation of the work, performance, or phonogram, not less than 70 years from the end of the calendar year of the creation of the work, performance, or phonogram.

Article 20.63: Application of Article 18 of the Berne Convention and Article 14.6 of the TRIPS Agreement

Each Party shall apply Article 18 of the Berne Convention and Article 14.6 of the TRIPS Agreement, *mutatis mutandis*, to works, performances, and phonograms, and the rights in and protections afforded to that subject matter as required by this Section.

Article 20.64: Limitations and Exceptions

1. With respect to this Section, each Party shall confine limitations or exceptions to exclusive rights to certain special cases that do not conflict with a normal exploitation of the work, performance, or phonogram, and do not unreasonably prejudice the legitimate interests of the right holder.

2. This Article does not reduce or extend the scope of applicability of the

---

accessed over the Internet. For greater certainty this footnote does not limit a Party's ability to avail itself of this subparagraph.

[61] The Parties understand that if a Party provides its nationals a term of copyright protection that exceeds life of the author plus 70 years, nothing in this Article or Article 20.8 (National Treatment) precludes that Party from applying Article 7(8) of the Berne Convention with respect to the term in excess of the term provided in this subparagraph of protection for works of another Party.

[62] For greater certainty, for the purposes of subparagraph (b), if a Party's law provides for the calculation of term from fixation rather than from the first authorized publication that Party may continue to calculate the term from fixation.

limitations and exceptions permitted by the TRIPS Agreement, the Berne Convention, the WCT, or the WPPT.

Article 20.65: Contractual Transfers

Each Party shall provide that for copyright and related rights, any person acquiring or holding an economic right[63] in a work, performance, or phonogram:

(a)   may freely and separately transfer that right by contract; and

(b)   by virtue of contract, including contracts of employment underlying the creation of works, performances, or phonograms, must be able to exercise that right in that person's own name and enjoy fully the benefits derived from that right.[64]

Article 20.66: Technological Protection Measures[65]

1. In order to provide adequate legal protection and effective legal remedies against the circumvention of effective technological measures that authors, performers, and producers of phonograms use in connection with the exercise of their rights and that restrict unauthorized acts in respect of their works, performances, and phonograms, each Party shall provide[66] that a person who:

(a)   knowingly, or having reasonable grounds to know,[67] circumvents without authority an effective technological measure that controls access to a protected work, performance, or phonogram;[68] or

---

[63] For greater certainty, this Article does not affect the exercise of moral rights.

[64] Nothing in this Article affects a Party's ability to establish: (i) which specific contracts underlying the creation of works, performances, or phonograms shall, in the absence of a written agreement, result in a transfer of economic rights by operation of law; and (ii) reasonable limits to protect the interests of the original right holders, taking into account the legitimate interests of the transferees.

[65] Nothing in this Agreement requires a Party to restrict the importation or domestic sale of a device that does not render effective a technological measure the only purpose of which is to control market segmentation for legitimate physical copies of a cinematographic film, and is not otherwise a violation of its law.

[66] A Party that, prior to the date of entry into force of this Agreement, maintains legal protections for technological protection measures consistent with Article 20.66.1 (Technological Protection Measures), may maintain its current scope of limitations, exceptions, and regulations regarding circumvention.

[67] For greater certainty, for the purposes of this subparagraph, a Party may provide that reasonable grounds to know may be demonstrated through reasonable evidence, taking into account the facts and circumstances surrounding the alleged illegal act.

[68] For greater certainty, no Party is required to impose civil or criminal liability under this subparagraph for a person that circumvents any effective technological measure that protects any of the exclusive rights of copyright or related rights in a protected work, performance, or phonogram, but does not control access to that work, performance, or phonogram.

(b) manufactures, imports, distributes, offers for sale or rental to the public, or otherwise provides devices, products, or components, or offers to the public or provides services, that:

   (i) are promoted, advertised, or otherwise marketed by that person for the purpose of circumventing any effective technological measure,

   (ii) have only a limited commercially significant purpose or use other than to circumvent any effective technological measure, or

   (iii) are primarily designed, produced, or performed for the purpose of circumventing any effective technological measure,

is liable and subject to the remedies provided for in Article 20.81.18 (Civil and Administrative Procedures and Remedies).[69]

Each Party shall provide for criminal procedures and penalties to be applied when a person, other than a non-profit library, archive,[70] educational institution, or public non-commercial broadcasting entity, is found to have engaged willfully and for the purposes of commercial advantage or financial gain in any of the foregoing activities.

Criminal procedures and penalties listed in subparagraphs (a), (c), and (f) of Article 20.84.6 (Criminal Procedures and Penalties) shall apply, as applicable to infringements *mutatis mutandis*, to the activities described in subparagraphs (a) and (b) of this paragraph.

2. In implementing paragraph 1, no Party shall be obligated to require that the design of, or the design and selection of parts and components for, a consumer electronics, telecommunications, or computing product provide for a response to any particular technological measure, so long as the product does not otherwise violate any measure implementing paragraph 1.

3. Each Party shall provide that a violation of a measure implementing this Article is a separate cause of action, independent of any infringement that might occur under the Party's law on copyright and related rights.

4. Each Party shall confine exceptions and limitations to measures implementing paragraph 1 to the following activities, which shall be applied to relevant measures in accordance with paragraph 5:[71]

---

[69] For greater certainty, no Party is required to impose liability under this Article and Article 20.67 (Rights Management Information) for actions taken by that Party or a third person acting with authorization or consent of the Party.

[70] For greater certainty, a Party may treat a non-profit museum as a non-profit archive.

[71] A Party may request consultations with the other Parties to consider how to address, under paragraph 4, activities of a similar nature that a Party identifies after the date this Agreement enters into force.

(a)　non-infringing reverse engineering activities with regard to a lawfully obtained copy of a computer program, carried out in good faith with respect to particular elements of that computer program that have not been readily available to the person engaged in those activities, for the sole purpose of achieving interoperability of an independently created computer program with other programs;

(b)　non-infringing good faith activities, carried out by an appropriately qualified researcher who has lawfully obtained a copy, unfixed performance, or display of a work, performance, or phonogram and who has made a good faith effort to obtain authorization for those activities, to the extent necessary for the sole purpose of research consisting of identifying and analyzing flaws and vulnerabilities of technologies for scrambling and descrambling of information;

(c)　the inclusion of a component or part for the sole purpose of preventing the access of minors to inappropriate online content in a technology, product, service, or device that itself is not prohibited under the measures implementing paragraph (1)(b);

(d)　non-infringing good faith activities that are authorized by the owner of a computer, computer system, or computer network for the sole purpose of testing, investigating, or correcting the security of that computer, computer system, or computer network;

(e)　non-infringing activities for the sole purpose of identifying and disabling a capability to carry out undisclosed collection or dissemination of personally identifying information reflecting the online activities of a natural person in a way that has no other effect on the ability of any person to gain access to any work;

(f)　lawfully authorized activities carried out by government employees, agents, or contractors for the purpose of law enforcement, intelligence, essential security, or similar governmental purposes;

(g)　access by a nonprofit library, archive, or educational institution to a work, performance, or phonogram not otherwise available to it, for the sole purpose of making acquisition decisions; and

(h)　in addition, a Party may provide additional exceptions or limitations for non-infringing uses of a particular class of works, performances, or phonograms, when an actual or likely adverse impact on those non-infringing uses is demonstrated by substantial evidence in a legislative, regulatory, or administrative proceeding in accordance with the Party's law.

5. The exceptions and limitations to measures implementing paragraph 1 for the activities set forth in paragraph 4 may only be applied as follows, and only to the extent that they do not impair the adequacy of legal protection or the effectiveness

of legal remedies against the circumvention of effective technological measures under the Party's legal system:

(a)   measures implementing paragraph (1)(a) may be subject to exceptions and limitations with respect to each activity set forth in paragraph (4);

(b)   measures implementing paragraph (1)(b), as they apply to effective technological measures that control access to a work, performance, or phonogram, may be subject to exceptions and limitations with respect to activities set forth in paragraphs (4)(a), (b), (c), (d), and (f); and

(c)   measures implementing paragraph (1)(b), as they apply to effective technological measures that protect any copyright or any rights related to copyright, may be subject to exceptions and limitations with respect to activities set forth in paragraphs (4)(a) and (f).

6. **Effective technological measure** means a technology, device, or component that, in the normal course of its operation, controls access to a protected work, performance, or phonogram, or protects copyright or rights related to copyright.[72]

Article 20.67: Rights Management Information[73]

1. In order to provide adequate and effective legal remedies to protect rights management information (RMI), each Party shall provide that any person that, without authority, and knowing, or having reasonable grounds to know, that it would induce, enable, facilitate, or conceal an infringement of the copyright or related right of authors, performers, or producers of phonograms, knowingly:[74]

(a)   removes or alters any RMI;

(b)   distributes or imports for distribution RMI knowing that the RMI has been altered without authority;[75] or

(c)   distributes, imports for distribution, broadcasts, communicates, or makes available to the public copies of works, performances, or phonograms, knowing that RMI has been removed or altered without authority, is liable and subject to the remedies set out in Article 20.81 (Civil and Administrative

---

[72] For greater certainty, a technological measure that can, in a usual case, be circumvented accidentally is not an "effective" technological measure.

[73] A Party may comply with the obligations in this Article by providing legal protection only to electronic rights management information.

[74] For greater certainty, a Party may extend the protection afforded by this paragraph to circumstances in which a person engages without knowledge in the acts in subparagraphs (a), (b), and (c), and to other related right holders.

[75] A Party may meet its obligation under this subparagraph if it provides effective protection for original compilations, provided that the acts described in this subparagraph are treated as infringements of copyright in those original compilations.

Procedures and Remedies).

2. Each Party shall provide for criminal procedures and penalties to be applied if a person is found to have engaged willfully and for purposes of commercial advantage or financial gain in any of the activities referred to in paragraph 1.

3. A Party may provide that the criminal procedures and penalties do not apply to a non-profit library, museum, archive, educational institution or public non-commercial broadcasting entity.[76]

4. For greater certainty, nothing prevents a Party from excluding from a measure that implements paragraphs 1 through 3 a lawfully authorized activity that is carried out for the purpose of law enforcement, essential security interests, or other related governmental purposes, such as the performance of a statutory function.

5. For greater certainty, nothing in this Article obligates a Party to require a right holder in a work, performance, or phonogram to attach RMI to copies of the work, performance, or phonogram, or to cause RMI to appear in connection with a communication of the work, performance, or phonogram to the public.

6. **RMI** means:

(a)   information that identifies a work, performance, or phonogram, the author of the work, the performer of the performance, or the producer of the phonogram; or the owner of a right in the work, performance, or phonogram;

(b)   information about the terms and conditions of the use of the work, performance, or phonogram; or

(c)   any numbers or codes that represent the information referred to in subparagraphs (a) and (b),

if any of these items is attached to a copy of the work, performance, or phonogram or appears in connection with the communication or making available of a work, performance, or phonogram to the public.

---

[76] For greater certainty, a Party may treat a broadcasting entity established without a profit-making purpose under its law as a public non-commercial broadcasting entity.

Article 20.68: Collective Management

The Parties recognize the important role of collective management societies for copyright and related rights in collecting and distributing royalties[77] based on practices that are fair, efficient, transparent, and accountable, which may include appropriate record keeping and reporting mechanisms.

---

[77] For greater certainty, royalties may include equitable remuneration.

BOOK IMPORTATION REGULATIONS

(SOR/99-324)

Note: SOR/99-324 filed July 28/99, gazetted August 18/99, in force September 1/99.

Amendments: SOR/2008-169 filed May 15/08, gazetted May 28/08, in force May 15/08.

INTERPRETATION

1. The definitions in this section apply in these Regulations.

Act means the *Copyright Act.*

bookseller means an individual, firm or corporation that is directly engaged in the sale of books in Canada for at least 30 consecutive days in a year and

> (*a*) whose floor space is open to the public and is located on premises consisting of floor space, including book shelves and customer aisles, of an area of at least 183 m² (600 sq. ft.); or

> (*b*) whose floor space is not open to the public and that derives 50% of his or her or its gross revenues from the sale of books.

Canadian edition means an edition of a book that is published under an agreement conferring a separate right of reproduction for the Canadian market, and that is made available in Canada by a publisher in Canada.

catalogue means a publication in printed, electronic or microfiche form that

> (*a*) is updated at least once a year;

> (*b*) lists all book titles currently in print that are available from at least one exclusive distributor; and

> (*c*) identifies the title, the International Standard Book Number, the exclusive distributor, the author and the list price in Canada for each book listed.

current exchange rate means the rate of exchange prevailing on the day on which a transaction takes place, as ascertained from a Canadian bank.

format in relation to a book, means

> (*a*) the type or quality of binding;

> (*b*) the typeface or size of print;

> (*c*) the type or quality of paper; or

> (*d*) the content, including whether the book is abridged or unabridged, or

335

illustrated.

holiday means a Saturday or a holiday as defined in subsection 35(1) of the *Interpretation Act.*

list price means the price for a book that is set out in a catalogue or printed on the cover or jacket of the book.

remaindered book means a book

(*a*) that is sold by the publisher for less than the cost of paper, printing and binding; or

(*b*) that is sold at a reduced price by the publisher and for which the author or copyright owner receives no royalty.

retailer means a person who sells books in the course of operating a business, but does not include an exclusive distributor or a book publisher.

special order means an order for a copy of a book that a bookseller or a retailer other than a bookseller does not have in stock and that the bookseller or retailer orders at the request of a customer.

APPLICATION

2. (1) These Regulations apply to

(*a*) English-language and French-language books that are imported into Canada and for which separate and distinct Canadian territorial rights have been created or contracted; and

(*b*) Canadian editions that are imported into Canada.

(2) For greater certainty, these Regulations apply to books referred to in subsection (1) that are added, after the coming into force of these Regulations, to an order placed before the coming into force of these Regulations.

(3) For greater certainty, these Regulations shall not be construed as authorizing anyone to do or to omit to do an act that would constitute an infringement of copyright under subsection 27(2) of the Act.

COMPUTATION OF TIME

3. (1) [Repealed, SOR/2008-169, s. 1.]

(2) If a period of less than seven days is provided for in these Regulations, a day that is a holiday shall not be included in computing the period.

(3) If a period for the doing of a thing is provided for in these Regulations and is expressed to end on a specified day, the period ends at the close of business on the specified day.

[SOR/2008-169, s. 1.]

NOTICE OF EXCLUSIVE DISTRIBUTOR

4. (1) An exclusive distributor, a copyright owner or an exclusive licensee shall give the notice referred to in subsection 27.1(5) of the Act to a person referred to in subsection 27.1(1) or (2) of the Act before the person places an order, in the following manner:

(*a*) in the case of a retailer other than a bookseller, in writing in accordance with subsection (2); and

(*b*) in the case of a bookseller, library or other institution established or conducted for profit that maintains a collection of documents, by setting out the fact that there is an exclusive distributor of the book in the latest edition of

(i) the *Canadian Telebook Agency Microfiche* and *Books in Print Plus—Canadian Edition*, published by R.R. Bowker, if the book is an English-language book, and the *Banque de titres de langue française*, if the book is a French-language book, or

(ii) a catalogue supplied by the exclusive distributor, copyright owner or exclusive licensee to the bookseller, library or other institution, at the request of, and in the form requested by, the bookseller, library or other institution.

(2) The notice referred to in paragraph (1)(*a*) shall be sent to the retailer at the retailer's last known address by courier, by mail, or by facsimile or other electronic means.

(3) Instead of the notice referred to in subsection (1), an exclusive distributor that represents all of the titles published by a particular publisher may send a notice to that effect to a person referred to in subsection 27(1) or (2) of the Act, at that person's last known address, by courier, by mail, or by facsimile or other electronic means, before the person places an order.

(4) A notice given in accordance with subsection (1) or (3) is valid and subsisting in respect of any title covered by the notice until the notice is revoked or amended by the exclusive distributor, copyright owner or exclusive licensee, as the case may be.

(5) The notice referred to in subsection (2) or (3) is deemed to have been received by the retailer, if it is

(*a*) delivered by courier, on the day of delivery;

(*b*) sent by mail, on the tenth day after the day on which the notice was mailed; or

(*c*) sent by facsimile or other electronic means, on the date and at the time indicated by the sending apparatus.

[SOR/2008-169, s. 2.]

IMPORTED BOOKS

5. (1) For the purpose of section 2.6 of the Act, where an order for imported books is placed, the following distribution criteria are established:

(*a*) an exclusive distributor shall

> (i) ship the books ordered to the intended recipient

>> (A) for books imported into Canada and in stock in Canada,

>>> (I) no later than three days after the day on which the exclusive distributor receives the order, in the case of English-language books, and

>>> (II) no later than five days after the day on which the exclusive distributor receives the order, in the case of French-language books,

>> (B) for books imported from the United States and not in stock in Canada, no later than 12 days after the day on which the exclusive distributor receives the order,

>> (C) for books imported from Europe and not in stock in Canada,

>>> (I) no later than 30 days after the day on which the exclusive distributor receives the order, in the case of English-language books, and

>>> (II) no later than 60 days after the day on which the exclusive distributor receives the order, in the case of French-language books, and

>> (D) for books imported from any other country and not in stock in Canada, no later than 50 days after the day on which the exclusive distributor receives the order,

> (ii) provide the book in the format requested by the person who placed the order, if the format exists, and

> (iii) subject to any law of any province with respect to prices concerning the distribution of books, provide the book at a price no greater than

>> (A) if the book is imported from the United States, the list price in the United States, plus the current exchange rate, plus 10% of the price after conversion, minus any applicable discounts, or

>> (B) if the book is imported from a country in Europe or any other country, the list price in the country from which the book is

imported, plus the current exchange rate, plus 15% of the price after conversion, minus any applicable discounts; and

(b) if the person who placed the order so requests, an exclusive distributor shall confirm to that person whether the order can be filled

(i) if the confirmation is made by telephone, no later than two days after the day on which the order is placed,

(ii) if the confirmation is sent by mail or facsimile, no later than five days after the day on which the order is placed, and

(iii) if the confirmation is sent by electronic means other than facsimile, no later than the day after the day on which the order is placed.

(2) In the case of books provided to libraries, the applicable discounts referred to in clause (1)(a)(iii)(A) shall be based on generally prevailing market conditions in North America.

(3) Subsections (1) and (2) apply to an exclusive distributor of a book in paperbound format only after the end of 12 months after the book first becomes available in that format in North America. If the exclusive distributor provides the book in that format before the end of that period, subsections (1) and (2) shall apply.

(4) If an exclusive distributor is unable to meet the criteria for an order set out in subsections (1) and (2), the person who placed the order may import the book through a person other than the exclusive distributor.
[SOR/2008-169, s. 3.]

CANADIAN EDITIONS

6. (1) For the purpose of section 2.6 of the Act, the following distribution criteria are established for Canadian editions:

(a) the exclusive distributor shall make sufficient copies of the Canadian edition available in Canada; and

(b) before an order is placed, the Canadian edition must be

(i) identified as a Canadian edition

(A) on the cover or jacket of the book,

(B) in the latest edition of the *Canadian Telebook Agency Microfiche* and of *Books in Print Plus—Canadian Edition*, published by R.R. Bowker, if the edition is an English-language edition, and in the latest edition of the *Banque de titres de langue française*, if the edition is a French-language edition, or

(C) in the latest edition of a catalogue supplied by the exclusive distributor, copyright owner or exclusive licensee to the bookseller, library or other institution, at the request of, and in the form requested by, the bookseller, library or other institution, and

(ii) listed

(A) in the latest edition of the *Canadian Telebook Agency Microfiche* and of *Books in Print Plus—Canadian Edition*, published by R.R. Bowker, if the edition is an English-language edition, and in the latest edition of the *Banque de titres de langue française*, if the edition is a French-language edition, or

(B) in the latest edition of a catalogue supplied by the exclusive distributor, copyright owner or exclusive licensee to the bookseller, library or other institution, at the request of, and in the form requested by, the bookseller, library or other institution.

(2) If an exclusive distributor is unable to meet the criteria for an order set out in subsection (1) the person who placed the order may import the book through a person other than the exclusive distributor.

REMAINDERED AND OTHER BOOKS

7. For the purpose of subsection 27.1(6) of the Act, a book may be imported if

(*a*) the book is marked as a remaindered book or the original foreign publisher has given notice to the exclusive distributor, if any, that the book has been remaindered, and the book is not sold in Canada before the end of 60 days after the day on which it was first offered for sale as a remaindered book by the original foreign publisher in the country from which the book is imported;

(*b*) the book is marked as a damaged book by the importer or the retailer; or

(*c*) the book is imported solely for the purpose of re-export, and the importer is able to provide evidence, on request, that an order for re-export has been made for the book before its importation.

TEXTBOOKS

8. For the purpose of subsection 27.1(6) of the Act, a textbook may be imported if

(*a*) at the time of importation, the importer provides documentation such as a certificate or an invoice establishing that the textbook is a used textbook;

(*b*) the textbook is to be offered for sale or distribution in Canada as a used textbook; and (*c*)   the textbook is of a scientific, technical or scholarly nature and is for use within an educational institution or an educational body established or conducted for profit.

SPECIAL ORDERS

9. (1) For the purpose of subsection 27.1(6) of the Act, a book that is the subject of a special order may be imported through a person other than the exclusive distributor if the exclusive distributor is unable to fill the order within the time specified by the person who placed the order.

(2) The exclusive distributor shall confirm within 24 hours after the special order is received whether or not the order can be filled within the time specified by the person who placed the order.

LEASED BOOKS

10. A library may import leased books through a person other than an exclusive distributor.

COMING INTO FORCE

11. These Regulations come into force on September 1, 1999.

CERTIFICATION OF COUNTRIES GRANTING EQUAL COPYRIGHT PROTECTION NOTICE

(C.R.C. 1978, c. 421)

SHORT TITLE

1. This Notice may be cited as the *Certification of Countries Granting Equal Copyright Protection Notice.*

CERTIFICATION

2. The Minister of Consumer and Corporate Affairs hereby certifies that the countries listed in the schedule grant or have undertaken to grant to citizens of Canada the benefit of copyright on substantially the same basis as to its own citizens or copyright protection substantially equal to that conferred by the *Copyright Act* and, for the purpose of the rights conferred by the said Act, such a country shall be treated as if it was a country to which the said Act extends.

SCHEDULE

(s. 2)

Andorra	Liberia
Argentina	Malawi
Cambodia	Malta
Chile	Mexico
Costa Rica	Nicaragua
Cuba	Nigeria
Ecuador	Paraguay
Guatemala	Peru
Haiti	Republic of Panama
Kenya	Venezuela
Laos	Zambia

CINEMATOGRAPHIC WORKS (RIGHT TO REMUNERATION) REGULATIONS

(SOR/99-194)

Note: SOR/99-194 filed April 22/99, gazetted May 12/99, in force April 22/99; S.C. 2002, c. 17, s. 15(a).

INTERPRETATION

1. The definitions in this section apply in these Regulations.

Canadian government film agency means a federal or provincial agency engaged in the development and production of cinematographic works.

Canadian program means a Canadian program as defined in subsection 2(1) of the Pay Television Regulations, 1990, in section 2 of the Specialty Services Regulations, 1990, and in section 2 of the Television Broadcasting Regulations, 1987.

PRESCRIBED CINEMATOGRAPHIC WORKS

2. The following are prescribed cinematographic works for the purposes of section 17 of the *Copyright Act*, namely, a cinematographic work in which a performer's performance has been embodied as a result of an agreement entered into by the performer on or after April 22, 1999:

(*a*)   in respect of which the Minister of Canadian Heritage has issued a Canadian film or video production certificate under the *Income Tax Act*;

(*b*)   that is recognized as a Canadian program by the Canadian Radio-television and Telecommunications Commission; or

(*c*)   that has received production funding from Telefilm Canada, or other Canadian government film agency.

[S.C. 2002, c. 17, s. 15(a).]

COMING INTO FORCE

3. These Regulations come into force on April 22, 1999.

COPYRIGHT REGULATIONS

(SOR/97-457)

Note: SOR/97-457 filed October 1/97, gazetted October 15/97, in force October 1/97.

Amendments: SOR/2003-211 filed June 5/03, gazetted June 18/03, in force June 5/03 except ss. 5-7, insofar as they enact s. 9 and items 1 and 4-8 of the Schedule, in force January 1/04; SOR/2007-93 filed May 3/07, gazetted May 16/07, in force June 2/07.

INTERPRETATION

1. The definitions in this section apply in these Regulations.

Act means the *Copyright Act*.

Commissioner means the Commissioner of Patents.

CORRESPONDENCE

2. (1) All correspondence intended for the Commissioner shall be addressed to the Copyright Office.

(2) Correspondence addressed to the Copyright Office may be physically delivered to the Office during ordinary business hours of the Office and shall be considered to be received by the Office on the day of the delivery.

(3) For the purposes of subsection (2), where correspondence addressed to the Copyright Office is physically delivered to the Office outside of its ordinary business hours, it shall be considered to have been delivered to the Office during ordinary business hours on the day when the Office is next open for business.

(4) Correspondence addressed to the Copyright Office may be physically delivered to an establishment that is designated by the Commissioner in the *Canadian Patent Office Record* as an establishment to which correspondence addressed to the Office may be delivered, during ordinary business hours of that establishment, and

(*a*) where the delivery is made to the establishment on a day that the Office is open for business, the correspondence shall be considered to be received by the Office on that day; and

(*b*) where the delivery is made to the establishment on a day that the Office is closed for business, the correspondence shall be considered to be received by the Office on the day when the Office is next open for business.

(5) For the purposes of subsection (4), where correspondence addressed to the

Copyright Office is physically delivered to an establishment outside of ordinary business hours of the establishment, it shall be considered to have been delivered to that establishment during ordinary business hours on the day when the establishment is next open for business.

(6) Correspondence addressed to the Copyright Office may be sent at any time by electronic or other means of transmission specified in the *Canadian Patent Office Record*.

(7) For the purposes of subsection (6), where, according to the local time of the place where the Copyright Office is located, the correspondence is delivered on a day when the Office is open for business, it shall be considered to be received by the Office on that day.

(8) For the purposes of subsection (6), where, according to the local time of the place where the Copyright Office is located, the correspondence is delivered on a day when the Office is closed for business, it shall be considered to be received by the Office on the day when the Office is next open for business.
[SOR/2003-211, s. 1.]

3. (1) Except as otherwise provided by the Act or these Regulations, communication in respect of a copyright shall be in writing, but the Commissioner may also accept oral communications.

(2) The Commissioner may request that an oral communication be confirmed in writing.
[SOR/2003-211, s. 2.]

4. (1) Any address required to be furnished pursuant to the Act or these Regulations shall be a complete mailing address and shall include the street name and number, where one exists, and the postal code.

(2) Where the Commissioner has not been notified of a change of address, the Commissioner is not responsible for any correspondence not received by an author, legal representative, any person purporting to be the agent of an author or their legal representative, or by an assignor, assignee, licensor or licensee.

APPLICATION FOR REGISTRATION OF COPYRIGHT

5. (1) An application for the registration of a copyright

(*a*)   in a work, shall be made in accordance with section 55 of the Act, and deal with the registration of only one work; or

(*b*)   in a performer's performance, sound recording or communication signal, shall be made in accordance with section 56 of the Act, and deal with the registration of only on performer's performance, sound recording or communication signal.

(2) An application for the registration of a copyright referred to in subsection (1)

shall be accompanied by the fee set out in column 2 of item 1 of the schedule.

REQUEST FOR REGISTRATION OF ASSIGNMENT OR LICENCE

6. (1) A request for the registration of an assignment of copyright, or a licence granting an interest in a copyright, shall

(*a*)   be in writing; and

(*b*)   contain the following information:

  (i)   the names and addresses of the assignor and assignee or the licensor and licensee,

  (ii)   a description of the interest being granted by assignment or licence, and

  (iii)   the title of the work, performer's performance, sound recording or communication signal, and, if available, the registration number of that work, performer's performance, sound recording or communication signal.

(2) A request for registration referred to in subsection (1) shall be accompanied by

(*a*)   the evidence required by paragraph 57(1)(*a*) of the Act; and

(*b*)   the fee set out in column 2 of item 2 of the schedule.
[SOR/2003-211, s. 3.]

GENERAL

7. Where the Commissioner determines that an application for registration of copyright, or a request for registration of an assignment of copyright, or a licence granting an interest in a copyright, is defective because it lacks any information or other item, the Commissioner shall notify the person applying for or requesting registration and that person shall have sixty days from the date of that notice to cure the defect. If the defect is not cured within that sixty day period, the Commissioner shall notify that person that the application or request has been rejected, in which case no further action may be taken for registration unless a fresh application or request is made and the applicable fee set out in the schedule for that fresh application or request is paid.

8. All applications for registration of copyright, requests for registration of an assignment of copyright or of a licence granting an interest in a copyright, and any correspondence to the Commissioner shall be legible and clear and, if in paper form, on white paper that measures at least 21 cm by 28 cm but not more than 22 cm by 35 cm, on one side only, with left and upper margins of at least 2.5 cm.
[SOR/2003-211, s. 4.]

9. The fee to be paid by a user of a service of the Copyright Office set out in column 1 of any of items 3 to 8 of the schedule is the fee set out in column 2 of that item. [SOR/2003-211, s. 5.]

REPEAL

10. The *Copyright Rules* (CRC, c. 422) are repealed.

COMING INTO FORCE

11. These Regulations come into force on October 1, 1997.

SCHEDULE
(SUBSECTION 5(2), PARAGRAPH 6(2)(B) AND SECTIONS 7 AND 9)

TARIFF OF FEES

Item	Column 1 Service	Column 2 Fee ($)
1.	Accepting an application for registration of a copyright	
	(*a*) pursuant to section 55 of the Act,	
	(i) where the application and fee are submitted on-line to the Copyright Office, via the Canadian Intellectual Property Office web site	50
	(ii) in any other case	65
	(*b*) pursuant to section 56 of the Act,	
	(i) where the application and fee are submitted on-line to the Copyright Office, via the Canadian Intellectual Property Office web site	50
	(ii) in any other case	65
2.	Accepting for registration an assignment or licence of a copyright pursuant to section 57 of the Act	65
3.	Processing a request for accelerated action on an application for registration of a copyright or for registration of an assignment, licence or other document	65
4.	Correcting a clerical error not committed by the Copyright Office in any instrument of record including, without further fee, issuing a corrected certificate of registration of copyright, pursuant to section 61 of the Act, or processing a request to include in the Register of Copyrights any other document affecting a copyright,	
	(*a*) where the request and fee are submitted on-line to the Copyright Office, via the Canadian Intellectual Property Office web site	50
	(*b*) in any other case	65
5.	Providing a certified copy in paper form of a document, other than a certified copy made under Rule 318 or 350 of the *Federal Courts Rules*,	
	(*a*) for each certification	35
	(*b*) plus, for each page	1
6.	Providing a certified copy in electronic form of a document, other than a certified copy made under Rule 318 or 350 of the *Federal Courts Rules*	
	(*a*) for each certification	35
	(*b*) plus, for each copyright to which the request relates	10

351

Item	Column 1 Service	Column 2 Fee ($)
7.	Providing a copy in paper form of a document, for each page,	
	(*a*) where the user of the service makes the copy using Copyright Office equipment	0.50
	(*b*) where the Copyright Office makes the copy	1
8.	Providing a copy in electronic form of a document:	
	(*a*) for each request	10
	(*b*) plus, if the copy is requested on a physical medium, for each physical medium requested in addition to the first	10
	(*c*) plus, for each copyright to which the request relates	10

[SOR/2003-211, ss. 6, 7; SOR/2007-93, s. 1.]

DEFINITION OF LOCAL SIGNAL AND DISTANT SIGNAL REGULATIONS

(SOR/89-254)

Note: SOR/89-254 filed May 9/89, gazetted May 24/89. The long title of the Regulations was repealed by SOR/2004-33, s. 1.

Amendments: SOR/2004-33 filed March 8/04, gazetted March 24/04, in force March 8/04; SOR/2014-80 filed April 4, 2014, gazetted April 23, 2014, in force April 23, 2014.

INTERPRETATION

1. In these Regulations, *area of transmission* means

(*a*)   in respect of a terrestrial television station

    (i)   for an analog signal, the area within the predicted Grade- B contour of the station, as determined in accordance with the method set out in the schedule, and the area within a radius of 32- km from that contour, and

    (ii)   for a digital signal, the area within the noise-limited bounding contour of the station, as determined in accordance with the document entitled *BPR-10 — Application Procedures and Rules for Digital Television (DTV) Undertakings*, Issue 1, published by the Department of Industry in August 2010, and the area within a radius of 32 km from that contour;

(*b*)   in respect of a terrestrial F.M. radio station, the area within the predicted 0.5 mV/m field strength contour of the station, as determined in accordance with the method set out in the schedule; and

(*c*)   in respect of a terrestrial A.M. radio station, the area within a radius of 32 km from the principal studio of the station.

[SOR/2004-33, s. 2; SOR/2014-80, s. 1.]

LOCAL SIGNAL AND DISTANT SIGNAL

2. (1) For the purposes of subsection 31(2) of the *Copyright Act*, *local signal* means ones of the following:

(*a*)   in respect of the entire service area of a retransmitter, the signal of a terrestrial radio or television station the area of transmission of which covers all of that area; and

(b) in respect of a portion of the service area of a retransmitter, the signal of a terrestrial radio or television station the area of transmission of which covers all of that portion.

(2) For the purposes of subsection 31(2) of the *Copyright Act*, **distant signal** means a signal that is not a local signal.
[SOR/2004-33, s. 2.]

3. [Repealed SOR/2004-33, s. 2.]

SCHEDULE

(*Section 1*)

METHOD FOR DETERMINING THE PREDICTED 0.5 MILLIVOLT PER METRE (MV/M) CONTOUR OF TERRESTRIAL F.M. RADIO STATIONS AND THE PREDICTED GRADE B CONTOUR OF TERRESTRIAL TELEVISION STATIONS

HEIGHT OF ANTENNA ABOVE AVERAGE TERRAIN (HAAT)

1. The height of an antenna above average terrain shall be determined on a topographical map by

(*a*) marking the transmitting site on the map, using the geographical coordinates of the site;

(*b*) drawing two concentric circles with radii of 3 km and 16 km, respectively, from the transmitting site marked under paragraph (*a*),

(*c*) starting at true north, drawing eight radials from the transmitting site at intervals of 45°;

(*d*) drawing, for each radial, a profile graph for the segment of terrain between 3 km and 16 km from the transmitting site, with the eight profile graphs plotted separately on rectangular coordinate paper, the distance in kilometers as the abscissa and the elevation in meters above mean sea level as the ordinate and reflecting the topography of the terrain;

(*e*) obtaining the average elevation of the terrain above mean sea level for each segment of terrain between 3 km and 16 km from the transmitting site by

    (i) using a plan meter,

    (ii) dividing the segment in equal sectors and averaging their respective median elevations, or

    (iii) averaging the elevations at a sufficient number of equally spaced points to provide a representation of the terrain; and

(*f*) obtaining the HAAT for each radial by subtracting the average terrain elevation calculated in accordance with paragraph (*e*) from the height above sea level of the centre of radiation of the antenna.

PREDICTED CONTOURS

2. (1) For F.M. radio stations, the predicted contour is defined by field strength of 0.5 mVm.

(2) For television stations, depending on the channel involved, the predicted

Grade B contour is defined by the following field strength:

(a)   47 dB above 1μV/m for channels 2 to 6;

(b)   56 dB above 1μV/m for channels 7 to 13;

(c)   64 dB above 1μV/m for channels 14 to 69.

(3) The HAAT determined in accordance with section 1 shall be ascertained for each radial and the effective radiated power (ERP) shall be ascertained in the plane of maximum radiation (in the case of directional antennas, the ERP value in the direction of each radial shall be used).

(4) The appropriate F(50,50) propagation curves (Tables I to III) shall be used with the HAAT and the ERP ascertained in accordance with subsection (3) to determine the distance from the transmitting site to the contour point on each radial.

(5) The contour points determined under subsection (4) shall be joined by a smooth curve to obtain the contour.

Note: The 40 dB line is the reference line for an effective radiated power (ERP) of 1 kW. [SOR/2004-33, s. 3.]

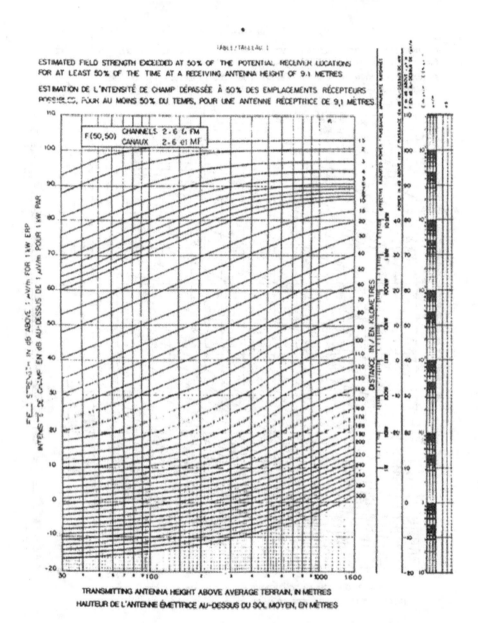

TABLE / TABLEAU 1

ESTIMATED FIELD STRENGTH EXCEEDED AT 50% OF THE POTENTIAL RECEIVER LOCATIONS FOR AT LEAST 50% OF THE TIME AT A RECEIVING ANTENNA HEIGHT OF 9.1 METRES

ESTIMATION DE L'INTENSITÉ DE CHAMP DÉPASSÉE À 50% DES EMPLACEMENTS RÉCEPTEURS POSSIBLES, POUR AU MOINS 50% DU TEMPS, POUR UNE ANTENNE RÉCEPTRICE DE 9,1 MÈTRES

TRANSMITTING ANTENNA HEIGHT ABOVE AVERAGE TERRAIN, IN METRES
HAUTEUR DE L'ANTENNE ÉMETTRICE AU-DESSUS DU SOL MOYEN, EN MÈTRES

TABLE/TABLEAU 11

ESTIMATED FIELD STRENGTH EXCEEDED AT 50% OF THE POTENTIAL RECEIVER LOCATIONS
FOR AT LEAST 50% OF THE TIME AT A RECEIVING ANTENNA HEIGHT OF 9.1 METRES.

ESTIMATION DE L'INTENSITÉ DE CHAMP DÉPASSÉE À 50% DES EMPLACEMENTS RÉCEPTEURS
POSSIBLES, POUR AU MOINS 50% DU TEMPS, POUR UNE ANTENNE RÉCEPTRICE DE 9,1 MÈTRES.

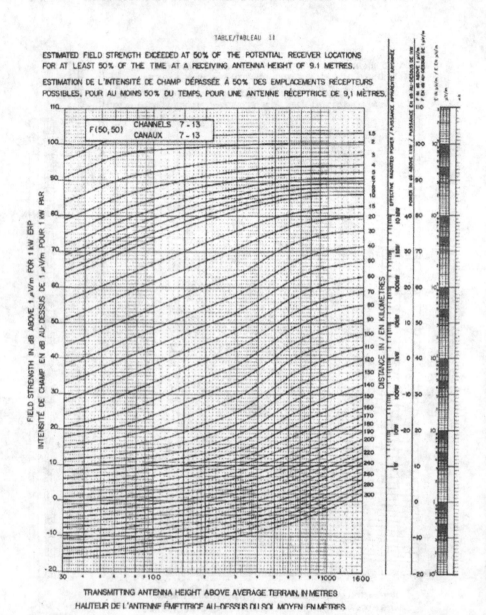

TRANSMITTING ANTENNA HEIGHT ABOVE AVERAGE TERRAIN, IN METRES
HAUTEUR DE L'ANTENNE ÉMETTRICE AU-DESSUS DU SOL MOYEN EN MÈTRES

358

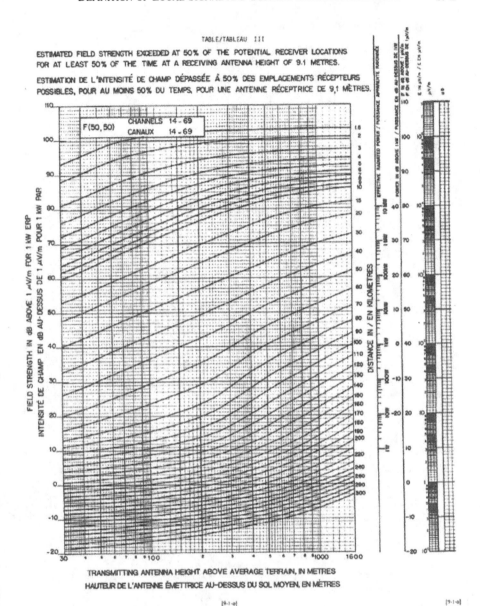

TABLE/TABLEAU III

ESTIMATED FIELD STRENGTH EXCEEDED AT 50% OF THE POTENTIAL RECEIVER LOCATIONS
FOR AT LEAST 50% OF THE TIME AT A RECEIVING ANTENNA HEIGHT OF 9.1 METRES.

ESTIMATION DE L'INTENSITÉ DE CHAMP DÉPASSÉE À 50% DES EMPLACEMENTS RÉCEPTEURS
POSSIBLES, POUR AU MOINS 50% DU TEMPS, POUR UNE ANTENNE RÉCEPTRICE DE 9,1 MÈTRES.

F(50,50)   CHANNELS 14 - 69
             CANAUX   14 - 69

TRANSMITTING ANTENNA HEIGHT ABOVE AVERAGE TERRAIN, IN METRES
HAUTEUR DE L'ANTENNE ÉMETTRICE AU-DESSUS DU SOL MOYEN, EN MÈTRES

[9-1-0]   [9-1-0]

DEFINITION OF "SMALL CABLE TRANSMISSION SYSTEM" REGULATIONS

(SOR/94-755)

Amendments: SOR/2005-148 filed May 17/05, gazetted June 1/05, in force May 17/05; SOR/2014-80, s. 2(F).

1. [Repealed by SOR/2005-148, s. 2.]*

INTERPRETATION

2. In these Regulations,

licence [Repealed by SOR/2005-148, s. 3(1).]

licensed area [Repealed by SOR/2005-148, s. 3(1).]

premises means

(*a*)   a dwelling, including a single-unit residence or a single unit within a multiple-unit residence, or

(*b*)   a room in a commercial or institutional building.

service area means an area in which premises served in accordance with the laws and regulations of Canada by a cable transmission system are located. [SOR/2005-148, s. 3.]

SMALL CABLE TRANSMISSION SYSTEM

3. (1) Subject to subsections (2) to (4) and section 4, *small cable transmission system* means a cable transmission system that transmits a signal, with or without a fee, to not more than 2,000 premises in the same service area.

(2) For the purpose of subsection (1), where a cable transmission system is included in the same unit as one or more other cable transmission systems, the number of premises to which the cable transmission system transmits a signal is deemed to be equal to the total number of premises to which all cable transmission systems included in that unit transmit a signal.

(3) For the purpose of subsection (2), a cable transmission system is included in the same unit as one or more other cable transmission systems where

(*a*)   they are owned or directly or indirectly controlled by the same person or

---

* Heading preceding section 1 repealed by SOR/2005-148, s. 2.

group of persons; and

(*b*) their service areas are each less than 5km distant, at some point, from at least one other among them, and those service areas would constitute a series of contiguous service areas, in a linear or non-linear configuration, were it not for that distance.

(4) Subsection (2) does not apply to a cable transmission system that was included in a unit on December 31, 1993.

[SOR/2005-148, s. 4; SOR/2014-80, s. 2(F).]

4. The definition set out in subsection 3(1) does not include a cable transmission system that is a master antenna system if it is located within the service area of another cable transmission system that transmits a signal, with or without a fee, to more than 2,000 premises in that service area.

[SOR/2005-148, s. 5.]

DEFINITION OF "SMALL RETRANSMISSION SYSTEMS" REGULATIONS

(SOR/89-255)

Amendments: SOR/94-754 filed December 6/94, gazetted December 28/94, effective January 1/95; SOR/2005-147 filed May 17/05, gazetted June 1/05, in force May 17/05.

1. [Repealed by SOR/2005-147, s. 2.]*

DEFINITIONS

2. In these Regulations,

licence [Repealed by SOR/2005-147, s. 3(1).]

licensed area [Repealed by SOR/2005-147, s. 3(1).]

premises means

(*a*) a dwelling, including a single-unit residence or a single unit within a multiple-unit residence, or

(*b*) a room in a commercial or institutional building.

service area means an area in which premises served in accordance with the laws and regulations of Canada by a retransmission system are located.
[SOR/94-754, s. 1; SOR/2005-147, s. 3.]

SMALL RETRANSMISSION SYSTEM

3. (1) Subject to subsections (2) to (4) and section 4, *small retransmission system* means a cable retransmission system, or a terrestrial retransmission system utilizing Hertzian waves, that retransmits a signal, with or without a fee, to not more than 2,000 premises in the same service area.

(2) For the purpose of subsection (1), where a cable retransmission system is included in the same unit as one or more other cable retransmission systems, the number of premises to which the cable retransmission system retransmits a signal is deemed to be equal to the total number of premises to which all cable retransmission systems included in that unit retransmit a signal.

(3) For the purpose of subsection (2), a cable retransmission system is included

---

* Heading preceding s. 1 repealed by SOR/2005-147, s. 2.

in the same unit as one or more other cable retransmission systems where

(a) they are owned or directly or indirectly controlled by the same person or group of persons; and

(b) their service areas are each less than 5 km distant, service at some point, from at least one other among them, and those service areas would constitute a series of contiguous service areas, in a linear or non-linear configuration, were it not for that distance.

(4) Subsection (2) does not apply to a cable retransmission system that was included in a unit on December 31, 1993.

[SOR/94-754, s. 1; SOR/2005-147, s. 4.]

4. The definition set out in subsection 3(1) does not include a cable retransmission system that is a master antenna system if it is located within the service area of another cable retransmission system that retransmits a signal, with or without a fee, to more than 2,000 premises in that service area.

[SOR/94-754, s. 1; SOR/2005-147, s. 5.]

DEFINITION OF "WIRELESS TRANSMISSION SYSTEM" REGULATIONS

(SOR/98-307)

Note: SOR/98-307 filed May 28/98, gazetted June 10/98, in force May 28/98.

EXPRESSION DEFINED

1. For the purposes of section 68.1 of the *Copyright Act*, **wireless transmission system** means a system operated by a terrestrial radio station that transmits in analog or digital mode a signal containing performers' performances of musical works or sound recordings embodying the performers' performances, in analog or digital form, whether in the A.M. or F.M. frequency band or in any other range assigned by the Minister under section 5 of the *Radiocommunication Act*, without artificial guide for free reception by the public.

COMING INTO FORCE

2. These Regulations come into force on May 28, 1998.

EDUCATIONAL PROGRAM, WORK AND OTHER SUBJECT-MATTER RECORD-KEEPING REGULATIONS

(SOR/2001-296)

Note: SOR/2001-296 filed August 1/01, gazetted August 15/01, in force August 31/01.

INTERPRETATION

1. The definitions in this section apply in these Regulations.

Act means the *Copyright Act*.

collective society means a collective society that carries on the business of collecting the royalties referred to in subsection 29.6(2) or 29.7(2) or (3) of the Act under a tariff that has been certified as an approved tariff pursuant to paragraph 73(1)(*d*) of the Act.

copy identifier means the number or other reference code assigned to the copy of a program, work or subject-matter in accordance with section 3.

educational institution identifier means the number or other reference code assigned to an educational institution in accordance with section 4.

institution means an educational institution or a person acting under its authority.

APPLICATION

2. These Regulations apply in respect of

(*a*) copies of news programs and news commentary programs that are made pursuant to paragraph 29.6(1)(*a*) of the Act; and

(*b*) copies of works and other subject-matter that are made pursuant to paragraph 29.7(1)(*a*) of the Act.

GENERAL PROVISIONS

3. An institution shall assign a number or other reference code to every copy of a program, work or subject-matter that it makes.

4. A collective society may assign a number or other reference code to an educational institution.

MARKING OF COPY

5. An institution that makes a copy of a program, work or subject-matter shall mark

367

on the copy, or on its container, the copy identifier and, if applicable, the educational institution identifier.

RECORDING OF INFORMATION

6. (1) Subject to subsection (2), an institution that makes a copy of a program, work or subject-matter shall complete, in a legible manner, an information record in the form set out in the schedule regarding

    (*a*)   the copying of the program, work or subject-matter;

    (*b*)   all performances in public of the copy for which royalties are payable under subsection 29.6(2) or 29.7(2) or (3) of the Act; and

    (*c*)   the destruction of the copy.

(2) Subsection (1) does not apply to the copy of a program made pursuant to paragraph 29.6(1)(*a*) of the Act if the copy is destroyed, in a manner that complies with section 7, within 72 hours after the making of the copy.

DESTRUCTION OF COPY

7. Destruction of a copy of a program, work or subject-matter shall be accomplished by

    (*a*)   destroying the medium onto which the program, work or subject-matter was copied; or

    (*b*)   erasing the copy of the program, work or subject-matter from the medium.

SENDING OF INFORMATION RECORD

8. (1) Subject to subsection (2), an institution shall send to each collective society

    (*a*)   within 30 days after the date on which the Board first certifies a tariff as an approved tariff pursuant to paragraph 73(1)(*d*) of the Act, a copy of every information record on which entries have been made during the period between the date on which these Regulations come into force and the date on which the tariff was certified; and

    (*b*)   after that, on or before January 31, May 31 and September 30 in each year, a copy of every information record on which entries have been made during the four months preceding the month in which the record is sent.

(2) Once a copy of a program, work or subject-matter has been destroyed, the institution may send the original information record in respect of the copy to a collective society.

RETENTION OF INFORMATION RECORD

9. An institution shall retain the original information record in respect of a copy of a program, work or subject-matter until two years after the copy is destroyed unless, during that time, the institution sends the original information record to a collective society.

COMING INTO FORCE

10. These Regulations come into force on the 30th day after the day on which they are registered.

SCHEDULE

(Subsection 6(1))

INFORMATION RECORD

Educational Institution
identifier
(if assigned): _____

Name and address of
institution: _____

_____

_____

Contact name: _____

Telephone: _____ Facsimile: _____ E-mail: _____

Details of Program, Work or Subject-Matter

Copy identifier: _____

Title of program, work or subject-
matter: _____

Other identifying information: _____
[e.g. episode title, subject, segment
description, song title(s)]

Duration of seg-
ment copied: _____ minutes

Date of broadcast _____ Time of broadcast: _____
(yy/mm/dd):

Name, network, call sign or other
identifier of the broadcaster: _____

Record of Public Performances

(List only performances for which royalties are payable)

yy/mm/dd   yy/mm/dd

_____   _____

_____   _____

_____   _____

_____   _____

(Use separate sheet to list additional performances)

Record of Destruction

I certify that the copy of the program, work or subject-matter identified above has been destroyed.

Name: _____ Title: _____

Signature: _____ Date of Destruction (yy/mm/dd): _____

EXCEPTIONS FOR EDUCATIONAL INSTITUTIONS, LIBRARIES, ARCHIVES AND MUSEUMS REGULATIONS

(SOR/99-325)

Note: SOR/99-325 filed July 28/99, gazetted August 18/99, in force September 1/99.

Amendments: SOR/2008-169 filed May 15/08, gazetted May 28/08, in force May 15/08.

INTERPRETATION

1. (1) In these Regulations, *Act* means the *Copyright Act*.

(2) In these Regulations, a reference to a copy of a work is a reference to a copy of all or any substantial part of a work.

NEWSPAPER OR PERIODICAL

2. For the purpose of subsection 30.2(6) of the Act, *newspaper or periodical* means a newspaper or a periodical, other than a scholarly, scientific or technical periodical, that was published more than one year before the copy is made.

RECORDS KEPT UNDER SECTION 30.2 OF THE ACT

3. In respect of activities undertaken by a library, an archive or a museum under subsection 30.2(1) of the Act, section 4 applies only to the reproduction of works.

4. (1) Subject to subsection (2), a library, an archive or a museum, or a person acting under the authority of one, shall record the following information with respect to a copy of a work that is made under section 30.2 of the Act:

(*a*) the name of the library, archive or museum making the copy;

(*b*) if the request for a copy is made by a library, archive or museum on behalf of a person who is a patron of the library, archive or museum, the name of the library, archive or museum making the request;

(*c*) the date of the request; and

(*d*) information that is sufficient to identify the work, such as

(i) the title,

(ii)   the International Standard Book Number,

(iii)   the International Standard Serial Number,

(iv)   the name of the newspaper, the periodical or the scholarly, scientific or technical periodical in which the work is found, if the work was published in a newspaper, a periodical or a scholarly, scientific or technical periodical,

(v)   the date or volume and number of the newspaper or periodical, if the work was published in a newspaper or periodical,

(vi)   the date or volume and number of the scholarly, scientific or technical periodical, if the work was published in a scholarly, scientific or technical periodical, and

(vii) the numbers of the copied pages.

(2) A library, an archive or a museum, or a person acting under the authority of one, does not have to record the information referred to in subsection (1) if the copy of the work is made under subsection 30.2(1) of the Act after December 31, 2003.

(3) A library, an archive or a museum, or a person acting under the authority of one, shall keep the information referred to in subsection (1)

(*a*)   by retaining the copy request form; or

(*b*)   in any other manner that is capable of reproducing the information in intelligible written form within a reasonable time.

(4) A library, an archive or a museum, or a person acting under the authority of one, shall keep the information referred to in subsection (1) with respect to copies made of a work for at least three years.

(5) A library, an archive or a museum, or a person acting under the authority of one, shall make the information referred to in subsection (1), with respect to copies made of a work, available once a year to one of the following persons, on request made by the person in accordance with subsection (7):

(*a*)   the owner of copyright in the work;

(*b*)   the representative of the owner of copyright in the work; or

(*c*)   a collective society that is authorized by the owner of copyright in the work to grant licences on their behalf.

(6) A library, an archive or a museum, or a person acting under the authority of one, shall make the information referred to in subsection (1) available to the person making the request, within 28 days after the receipt of the request or any longer period that may be agreed to by both of them.

(7) A request referred to in subsection (5) must be made in writing, indicate the

name of the author of the work and the title of the work, and be signed by the person making the request and include a statement by that person indicating that the request is made under paragraph (5)(*a*), (*b*) or (*c*).

[Editor's note: The heading, "RECORDS KEPT UNDER SUBSECTION 30.21(6) OF THE ACT", before s. 5 was repealed by SOR/2008-169, s. 5, in force May 15, 2008.]

5. [Repealed, SOR/2008-169, s. 5.]

PATRONS OF ARCHIVES

6. (1) If a person registers as a patron of an archive, the archive shall inform the patron in writing at the time of registration that

(*a*)   any copy of a work under section 30.21 of the Act is to be used solely for the purpose of research or private study; and

(*b*)   any use of that copy for any other purpose may require the authorization of the copyright owner of the work.

(2) If a person requests a copy of a work from an archive under section 30.21 of the Act and the person has not registered as a patron of the archive, the archive shall inform the person in writing at the time of the request

(*a*)   that any copy is to be used solely for the purpose of research or private study; and

(*b*)   that any use of a copy for a purpose other than research or private study may require the authorization of the copyright owner of the work in question.

[SOR/2008-169, s. 5.]

STAMPING OF COPIED WORKS

7. A library, archive or museum, or a person acting under the authority of one, that makes a copy of a work under section 30.2 or 30.21 of the Act shall inform the person requesting the copy, by means of text printed on the copy or a stamp applied to the copy, if the copy is in printed format, or by other appropriate means, if the copy is made in another format,

(*a*)   that the copy is to be used solely for the purpose of research or private study; and

(*b*)   that any use of the copy for a purpose other than research or private study may require the authorization of the copyright owner of the work in question.

NOTICE

8. An educational institution, a library, an archive or a museum in respect of which subsection 30.3(2), (3) or (4) of the Act applies shall ensure that a notice that contains at least the following information is affixed to, or within the immediate vicinity of, every photocopier in a place and manner that is readily visible and legible to persons using the photocopier:

"WARNING!

WORKS PROTECTED BY COPYRIGHT MAY BE COPIED ON THIS PHOTOCOPIER ONLY IF AUTHORIZED BY

(*a*)   the *Copyright Act* for the purpose of fair dealing or under specific exceptions set out in that Act;

(*b*)   the copyright owner; or

(*c*)   a licence agreement between this institution and a collective society or a tariff, if any.

For details of authorized copying, please consult the licence agreement or the applicable tariff, if any, and other relevant information available from a staff member.

The Copyright Act provides for civil and criminal remedies for infringement of copyright."

COMING INTO FORCE

9. These Regulations come into force on September 1, 1999.

MICROSD CARDS EXCLUSION REGULATIONS (COPYRIGHT ACT)

(SOR/2012-226)

Note: SOR/2012-226 gazetted November 7, 2012, registered and in force October 18, 2012.

His Excellency the Governor General in Council, on the recommendation of the Minister of Industry, pursuant to sections 79[a] and 87[b] of the *Copyright Act*,[c] makes the annexed *MicroSD Cards Exclusion Regulations (Copyright Act)*.

[a] S.C. 2001, c. 27, s. 240

[b] S.C. 1997, c. 24, s. 50

[c] R.S., c. C-42

MICROSD CARDS

1. Memory cards in microSD form factor, including microSD, microSDHC and microSDXC cards, are excluded from the definition *audio recording medium* in section 79 of the *Copyright Act*.

COMING INTO FORCE

2. These Regulations come into force on the day on which they are registered.

PROGRAMMING UNDERTAKING REGULATIONS

(SOR/93-436)

REGULATIONS DEFINING PROGRAMMING UNDERTAKING

SHORT TITLE

1. These Regulations may be cited as the *Programming Undertaking Regulations.*

PROGRAMMING UNDERTAKING

2. For the purpose of subsection 3(1.4) of the *Copyright Act,* **programming undertaking** means a network, other than a network within the meaning of the *Broadcasting Act,* consisting of

(*a*) a person who transmits by telecommunication all or part of the person's programs or programming directly or indirectly to the person referred to in paragraph (*b*); and

(*b*) a person who communicates all or part of the programs or programming referred to in paragraph (*a*) to the public by telecommunication.

REGULATIONS DEFINING "ADVERTISING REVENUES"

(SOR/98-447)

Note: SOR/98-447 filed August 31/98, gazetted September 16/98, in force August 31/98.

INTERPRETATION

1. In these Regulations, *system* means a wireless transmission system.

ADVERTISING REVENUES

2. (1) For the purposes of subsection 68.1(1) of the *Copyright Act*, *advertising revenues* means the total compensation in money, goods or services, net of taxes and of commissions paid to advertising agencies, received by a system to advertise goods, services, activities or events, for broadcasting public interest messages or for any sponsorship.

(2) For the purpose of calculating advertising revenues, goods and services shall be valued of fair market value.

(3) For purposes of subsection (1), when a system acts on behalf of a group of systems which broadcast a single event, simultaneously or on a delayed basis,

(*a*) any compensation paid by the system acting on behalf of the group of systems to a system that is part of the group is part of the advertising revenues of that system; and

(*b*) the difference between the compensation received by the system acting on behalf of the group of systems and any compensation referred to in paragraph (*a*), is part of the advertising revenue of the system which acts on behalf of the group.

COMING INTO FORCE

3. These Regulations come into force on August 31, 1998.

REGULATIONS ESTABLISHING THE PERIOD WITHIN WHICH OWNERS OF COPYRIGHT NOT REPRESENTED BY COLLECTIVE SOCIETIES CAN CLAIM RETRANSMISSION ROYALTIES

(SOR/97-164)

Note: SOR/97-164 filed March 19/97, gazetted April 2/97, in force March 19/97. Title amended by SOR/2004-152, s. 1.

Amendments: SOR/2004-152 filed June 9/04, gazetted June 30/04, in force June 9/04.

1. The owner of copyright who does not authorize a collective society to collect, for that person's benefit, the royalties referred to in paragraph 31(2)(*d*) of the *Copyright Act* and whose work is so retransmitted has a period of two years following the end of the calendar year in which the retransmission occurred to claim the royalties payable under subsection 76(1) of that Act.

[SOR/2004-152, s. 2.]

2. These Regulations come into force on March 19, 1997.

REGULATIONS ESTABLISHING THE PERIODS WITHIN WHICH ELIGIBLE AUTHORS, ELIGIBLE PERFORMERS AND ELIGIBLE MAKERS NOT REPRESENTED BY COLLECTIVE SOCIETIES CAN CLAIM PRIVATE COPYING REMUNERATION

(SOR/2013-143)

Note: SOR/2013-143 gazetted July 17, 2013, registered and in force June 27, 2013.

The Copyright Board, pursuant to paragraph 83(13)(*b*)[a] of the *Copyright Act*,[b] makes the annexed *Regulations Establishing the Periods Within Which Eligible Authors, Eligible Performers and Eligible Makers not Represented by Collective Societies Can Claim Private Copying Remuneration*.

[a] S.C. 1997, c. 24, s. 50

[b] R.S., c. C-42

DEFINITION OF *ACT*

1. In these Regulations, *Act* means the *Copyright Act*.

ELIGIBLE AUTHORS

2. The period within which an eligible author must exercise the entitlement referred to in subsection 83(11) of the Act is

(*a*) in respect of the *Private Copying Tariff, 1999-2000*, from December 31, 2000 to December 31, 2013;

(*b*) in respect of the *Private Copying Tariff, 2001-2002*, from December 31, 2002 to December 31, 2013;

(*c*) in respect of the *Private Copying Tariff, 2003-2004*, from December 31, 2004 to December 31, 2013; and

(*d*) in respect of any other tariff certified by the Board under paragraph 83(8)(*c*) of the Act, from the day on which the tariff ceases to be effective to December 31 of the seventh year after the year in which the tariff ceases to be effective.

ELIGIBLE PERFORMERS

3. The period within which an eligible performer must exercise the entitlement referred to in subsection 83(11) of the Act is

(*a*) in respect of the *Private Copying Tariff, 1999-2000*, from December 31, 2000 to December 31, 2016;

(*b*) in respect of the *Private Copying Tariff, 2001-2002*, from December 31, 2002 to December 31, 2016;

(*c*) in respect of the *Private Copying Tariff, 2003-2004*, from December 31, 2004 to December 31, 2016;

(*d*) in respect of the *Private Copying Tariff, 2005-2007*, from December 31, 2007 to December 31, 2016;

(*e*) in respect of the *Private Copying Tariff, 2008-2009*, from December 31, 2009 to December 31, 2016; and

(*f*) in respect of any other tariff certified by the Board under paragraph 83(8)(*c*) of the Act, from the day on which the tariff ceases to be effective to December 31 of the seventh year after the year in which the tariff ceases to be effective.

ELIGIBLE MAKERS

4. The period within which an eligible maker must exercise the entitlement referred to in subsection 83(11) of the Act is

(*a*) in respect of the *Private Copying Tariff, 1999-2000*, from December 31, 2000 to December 31, 2013;

(*b*) in respect of the *Private Copying Tariff, 2001-2002*, from December 31, 2002 to December 31, 2013;

(*c*) in respect of the *Private Copying Tariff, 2003-2004*, from December 31, 2004 to December 31, 2013;

(*d*) in respect of the *Private Copying Tariff, 2005-2007*, from December 31, 2007 to December 31, 2013; and

(*e*) in respect of any other tariff certified by the Board under paragraph 83(8)(*c*) of the Act, from the day on which the tariff ceases to be effective to December 31 of the fifth year after the year in which the tariff ceases to be effective.

COMING INTO FORCE

Registration

5. These Regulations come into force on the day on which they are registered.

REGULATIONS PRESCRIBING NETWORKS (COPYRIGHT ACT)

(SOR/99-348)

Note: SOR/99-348 filed August 26/99, gazetted September 15/99, in force October 1/99.

NETWORK

1. For the purpose of subsection 30.8(9) of the *Copyright Act*, the following are prescribed networks:

(*a*) networks that are networks within the meaning of the definition *network* in subsection 2(1) of the *Broadcasting Act*; and

(*b*) networks that consist of two or more programming undertakings that are owned by the same person or group of persons and that have a practice of common programming or an arrangement by which they share programs, as the case may be.

COMING INTO FORCE

2. These Regulations come into force on October 1, 1999.

RETRANSMISSION ROYALTIES CRITERIA REGULATIONS

(SOR/91-690)

REGULATIONS RESPECTING CRITERIA FOR ESTABLISHING A MANNER OF DETERMINING ROYALTIES FOR THE RETRANSMISSION OF DISTANT SIGNALS

SHORT TITLE

1. These Regulations may be cited as the *Retransmission Royalties Criteria Regulations*.

CRITERIA

2. The criteria to which the Board must have regard in establishing under paragraph 70.63(1)(*a*) of the *Copyright Act* a manner of determining royalties that are fair and equitable are the following:

(*a*) royalties paid for the retransmission of distant signals in the United States under the retransmission regime in the United States;

(*b*) the effects on the retransmission of distant signals in Canada of the application of the *Broadcasting Act* and regulations made thereunder; and

(*c*) royalties and related terms and conditions stipulated in written agreements in respect of royalties for the retransmission of distant signals in Canada that have been reached between collecting bodies and retransmitters and that are submitted to the Board in their entirety.

STATEMENT LIMITING THE RIGHT TO EQUITABLE REMUNERATION OF CERTAIN ROME CONVENTION OR WPPT COUNTRIES

(SOR/2014-181)

Note: SOR/2014-182 filed July 14, 2014, gazetted July 30, 2014, in force August 13, 2014.

Whereas the Minister of Industry is of the opinion that the Rome Convention or WPPT countries referred to in the annexed Statement do not grant a right of remuneration, similar in scope and duration to that provided by subsections 19(1.1)[a] and (1.2)[b] of the *Copyright Act*,[c] for the performance in public or the communication to the public by telecommunication of a sound recording whose maker, at the date of its first fixation, was a Canadian citizen or a permanent resident within the meaning of subsection 2(1) of the *Immigration and Refugee Protection Act*[d] or was a corporation that had its headquarters in Canada;

[a] S.C. 2012, c. 20, s. 12(1).
[b] S.C. 2012, c. 20, s. 12(2).
[c] R.S., c. C-42.
[d] S.C. 2001, c. 27.

Therefore, the Minister of Industry, pursuant to subsections 20(2)[e] and (2.1)[f] of the *Copyright Act*,[g] makes the annexed *Statement Limiting the Right to Equitable Remuneration of Certain Rome Convention or WPPT Countries*.

[e] S.C. 2012, c. 20, s. 15(3).
[f] S.C. 2012, c. 20, s. 15(4).
[g] R.S., c. C-42.

LIMITATIONS

BOLIVIA AND LESOTHO

1. A right to equitable remuneration applies only for a duration of 20 years to the performance in public or the communication to the public by telecommunication of a sound recording whose maker, at the date of its first fixation, was a citizen or permanent resident of Bolivia or Lesotho or was a corporation that had its headquarters in either of those countries.

JAPAN AND SINGAPORE

2. (1) Subject to subsections (2) and (7), a right to equitable remuneration applies only to the communication to the public by telecommunication of a sound recording whose maker, at the date of its first fixation, was a citizen or permanent resident of Japan or Singapore or was a corporation that had its headquarters in either of those countries.

EXCEPTION – BROADCASTS AND BACKGROUND MUSIC

(2) In the case of a sound recording whose maker, at the date of its first fixation, was a citizen or permanent resident of Singapore or was a corporation that had its headquarters in that country, a right to equitable remuneration does not apply to

(*a*)   a broadcast that is lawful under the *Broadcasting Act*, by a terrestrial radio station, of a signal that carries the sound recording for reception that is free and does not require a subscription; or

(*b*)   the communication to the public by telecommunication of the sound recording to a business for performance as background music on its premises in the ordinary course of its business.

APPLICATION OF PAR. (2)(A)

(3) For greater certainty, paragraph (2)(*a*) does not apply to broadcasts

(*a*)   through the Internet;

(*b*)   by satellite; or

(*c*)   by point-to-point technology that are received by way of mobile devices.

(4) [Repealed: SOR/2020-82, s. 1]

(5) [Repealed: SOR/2020-82, s. 1]

(6) [Repealed: SOR/2020-82, s. 1]

EXCEPTION – NON-INTERACTIVE INTERNET TRANSMISSION

(7) In the case of a sound recording that has not been published but is deemed to have been published under section 19.2 of the *Copyright Act* and whose maker, at the date of its first fixation, was a citizen or permanent resident of Japan or was a corporation that had its headquarters in that country, a right to equitable remuneration applies only to the communication of the sound recording to the public by non-interactive Internet transmission.

[SOR/2020-82, s. 1]

LEBANON

3. A right to equitable remuneration applies only to the performance in public of a sound recording whose maker, at the date of its first fixation, was a citizen or permanent resident of Lebanon or was a corporation that had its headquarters in that country.

VIETNAM

4. In the case of a sound recording whose maker, at the date of its first fixation, was a citizen or permanent resident of Vietnam or was a corporation that had its headquarters in that country, a right to equitable remuneration does not apply to the performance of the sound recording in public as part of a non-commercial activity.

BARBADOS, CABO VERDE, CONGO AND MONACO

5. A right to equitable remuneration does not apply to the performance in public or the communication to the public by telecommunication of a sound recording whose maker, at the date of its first fixation, was a citizen or permanent resident of Barbados, Cabo Verde, Congo or Monaco or was a corporation that had its headquarters in any of those countries.

PEOPLE'S REPUBLIC OF CHINA

6. (1) Subject to subsections (2) and (3), a right to equitable remuneration does not apply to a sound recording whose maker, at the date of its first fixation, was a citizen or permanent resident of the People's Republic of China or was a corporation that had its headquarters in that country.

MACAO

(2) The performer of a sound recording whose maker, at the date of its first fixation, was a permanent resident of the Macao Special Administrative Region of the People's Republic of China or was a corporation that had its headquarters in the Macao Special Administrative Region of the People's Republic of China is entitled to be paid equitable remuneration in respect of the sound recording.

HONG KONG

(3) The maker of a sound recording who, at the date of its first fixation, was a permanent resident of the Hong Kong Special Administrative Region of the People's Republic of China or was a corporation that had its headquarters in the Hong Kong Special Administrative Region of the People's Republic of China is entitled to be paid equitable remuneration in respect of the sound recording.

COSTA RICA

7. (1) In the case of a sound recording whose maker, at the date of its first fixation, was a citizen or permanent resident of Costa Rica or was a corporation that had its headquarters in that country, a right to equitable remuneration does not apply to

(a)   a broadcast that is lawful under the *Broadcasting Act*, by a terrestrial radio station, of a signal that carries the sound recording for reception that is free and does not require a subscription; or

(*b*) the performance of the sound recording in public as part of a non-commercial activity.

APPLICATION OF PAR. (1)(A)

(2) For greater certainty, paragraph (1)(*a*) does not apply to broadcasts

(*a*) through the Internet;

(*b*) by satellite; or

(*c*) by point-to-point technology that are received by way of mobile devices.

REPEAL

8. [Repeal]

COMING INTO FORCE

PUBLICATION OR COMING INTO FORCE OF WPPT

9. This Statement comes into force on the later of the day on which it is published in the *Canada Gazette*, Part II and the day on which the WIPO Performances and Phonograms Treaty (WPPT), adopted in Geneva on December 20, 1996, comes into force for Canada.

[Note: Statement in force August 13, 2014.]

TIME LIMITS IN RESPECT OF MATTERS BEFORE THE COPYRIGHT BOARD REGULATIONS

(SOR/2020-264)

COPYRIGHT ACT

Registration 2020-12-04

P.C. 2020-982 2020-12-04

Her Excellency the Governor General in Council, on the recommendation of the Minister of Industry and the Minister of Canadian Heritage, pursuant to paragraphs 66.91(2)(a)**ᵃ** and (d)**ᵇ** of the *Copyright Act***ᶜ**, makes the annexed *Time Limits in Respect of Matters Before the Copyright Board Regulations*.

ᵃ S.C. 2018, c. 27, s. 295.

ᵇ S.C. 2018, c. 27, s. 295.

ᶜ R.S., c. C-42.

DEFINITION

1. Definition of *Act* — In these Regulations, *Act* means the *Copyright Act*.

TIME LIMITS

2. Proposed tariff — The Board must make a decision with respect to the approval of a proposed tariff under subsection 70(1) or 83(8) of the Act

(*a*) if the Board holds any written or oral hearings in respect of the proposed tariff, within the period of 12 months after the day that is fixed by the Board or a case manager as the final day on which any party may present their written or oral submissions to the Board; and

(*b*) in any other case, before the day on which the effective period of the proposed tariff begins.

3. Royalty rates or terms and conditions — The Board must make a decision with respect to the fixing of royalty rates or their related terms and conditions, or both, under subsection 71(2) of the Act within the period of 12 months after the day that is fixed by the Board or a case manager as the final day on which any party may present their written or oral submissions to the Board.

4. Final day for submissions — If, on or after the day fixed by the Board or a case manager as the final day on which any party may present their written or oral submissions to the Board, the Board or a case manager fixes another day as the final day on which any party may present their written or oral submissions to the Board, that later day is not considered to be the final day for the purpose of determining the 12-month period referred to in paragraph 2(a) or section 3.

5. Notice to parties — The Board or a case manager must, within the period of three months after the day on which the Board publishes a proposed tariff under section 68.2 or subsection 83(5) of the Act, notify the collective society that filed the proposed tariff and any person or entity that filed an objection to the proposed tariff as to whether the Board will hold a written or oral hearing in respect of the proposed tariff.

6. Extension of time limit — (1) The Board or a case manager may, in exceptional circumstances, give a direction or make an order that extends a period referred to in section 2 or 3 and sets out the extended period and the exceptional circumstances that justify the extension.

(2) **Notice** — After a direction is given or an order is made, the Board must publish, in the manner that it sees fit, a notice of the direction or order.

TRANSITIONAL PROVISIONS

7. Conformity with these Regulations — Subject to sections 8 to 11, every matter that is pending before the Board on the day on which these Regulations come into force must be continued under and in conformity with sections 1 to 6 in so far as it may be done consistently with those provisions.

8. Notice not provided — If, in respect of a matter pending before the Board, on the day on which these Regulations come into force, the Board or a case manager has not notified the collective society that filed a proposed tariff and any person or entity that filed an objection to the proposed tariff as to whether the Board will hold a written or oral hearing in respect of the proposed tariff and the three-month period referred to in section 5 has ended, the Board or a case manager must provide the notice within two months after the day on which these Regulations come into force.

9. No hearing — If, in respect of a proposed tariff, on the day on which these Regulations come into force, the effective period of the proposed tariff has begun and if, at any time before the end of two months after the day on which these Regulations come into force, the Board or a case manager notifies the collective society that filed the proposed tariff and any person or entity that filed an objection to the proposed tariff that the Board will not hold any written or oral hearings in respect of the proposed tariff, the Board must make a decision with respect to the approval of the proposed tariff, under subsection 70(1) or 83(8) of the Act, within 12 months after the day on which these Regulations come into force.

10. Hearing held — If, in respect of a matter pending before the Board, on the day on which these Regulations come into force, the Board has already held a hearing in respect of the matter and the 12-month period referred to in paragraph 2(a) or section 3 has ended or will end in less than six months, the Board must make a decision referred to in that paragraph or section within six months after the day on which these Regulations come into force.

11. No extension — The period within which the Board must make its decision under section 9 or 10 may not be extended under section 6.

COMING INTO FORCE

12. Registration — These Regulations come into force on the day on which they are registered.

COMMENTARY: INDUSTRIAL DESIGN ACT

INTRODUCTION

These notes are intended to be a brief overview of the *Industrial Design Act*. Readers should take caution that there are many details omitted and circumstances not considered. Other resources include the following:

- For a detailed legal text, see *Hughes on Copyright & Industrial Design*, Second Edition (LexisNexis Canada Inc.).

- For forms and precedents, see *Canadian Forms & Precedents, Intellectual Property* (LexisNexis Canada Inc.).

- For commentary and case digests respecting the *Federal Courts Act* and Rules, see *Canadian Federal Courts Practice* (annual publication) (LexisNexis Canada Inc.).

- For encyclopedic treatment of the law, see *Halsbury's Laws of Canada–Patents, Trade Secrets and Industrial Designs* (LexisNexis Canada Inc.).

THE INDUSTRIAL DESIGN ACT

Until 2018, the *Industrial Design Act* (R.S.C. 1985, c. I-9) had remained almost unchanged since the 1928 consolidation of Canadian Statutes. Minor amendments to the Act and substantial amendments to the Rules were made in the 1980s. Substantial changes, effective as of November 5, 2018, are intended to bring Canada into compliance with the Hague Agreement Concerning the International Registration of Industrial Designs. It provides, in effect, for two different types of design registrations: those made in accordance with the Hague Agreement and all others. A registration under the Hague Agreement can be effective in a number of countries, on payment of the applicable fees.

The Act is intended to give effect to Canada's obligations as a member of the Paris Convention as amended, which states that member countries should afford reciprocal protection for "designs" although, as subsequently discussed, the concept of "design" is not easily defined. Where an application to register a design has been filed in a Convention country, a similar application filed in Canada within six months can claim the priority date of the earlier filing.

ADMINISTRATION OF THE INDUSTRIAL DESIGN ACT

The *Industrial Design Act* is administered by the Canadian Patent Office. The Commissioner of Patents is the person ultimately in charge and disputes as to registrability are decided by the Patent Appeal Board. Communications are addressed to:

Canadian Intellectual Property Office
Place du Portage I
50 Victoria Street, room C-114
Gatineau, Quebec
K1A 0C9
Tel: 1-866-997-1936
Fax: (819) 953-2476

WHAT IS AN INDUSTRIAL DESIGN?

An Industrial Design registered in accordance with the *Industrial Design Act* in Canada is a rather strange piece of industrial property. Section 2 of the Act defines "design" to mean "features of shape, configuration, pattern or ornament and any combination of those features that, in a finished article, appeal to and are judged solely by the eye". It has been held that while part of the article can be functional, the design cannot be wholly or only functional. Bill C-43, section 7(*d*) makes it clear that protection does not extend to features of the design that are purely functional.

An Industrial Design is not registrable unless it is original (section 7(3)), it must not be identical to nor closely resemble a design already registered (section 6(1)), and it must not have been published in Canada or elsewhere more than one year before application for registration has been filed in Canada or in Geneva, if a Hague Agreement application (section 6(3)(*a*)).

A problem arises since other countries have the concept of "utility model" or "petit patent", which is a more limited form of patent protection directed to a specific, functional design or article, and which is probably not patentable in the larger, more conceptional sense, but can obtain a lesser form of protection for the specific design or article. Thus, in seeking some form of intellectual property protection in Canada similar to that obtained elsewhere for something that did not quite qualify for patent protection, it is tempting to seek the only Canadian alternative — Industrial Design registration. The conundrum is, therefore, whether a design is sufficiently "ornamental" to qualify as a properly registrable design. While numerous examples of what may appear as simply functional designs are registered in the Industrial Design Office, so few cases make it to the courts in this area that it is difficult to establish clearly where the line between function and ornament exists.

INDUSTRIAL DESIGN VS. COPYRIGHT VS. TRADEMARK

Industrial Designs are specifically addressed and differentiated in the *Copyright Act* (R.S.C. 1985, c. C-42). Section 64 of the *Copyright Act* states that it is not an infringement of copyright to reproduce a "design applied to a useful article", where that article is reproduced (in Canada or anywhere else) in a quantity of more than 50 or, where the article is a mould, to mould more than 50 articles. Although certain exemptions exist, however, the intent is that, if you are going to make over 50 of those articles, an Industrial Design registration is necessary (which you must procure within one year), otherwise any form of protection is lost. The intent is obvious when it comes to industrial articles and "must fit" parts; however, toys, novelties, dinnerware and numerous other articles produced in quantity will have no protection at all unless an Industrial Design is properly registered.

On occasion, someone asserts that a design is a trademark or at least is entitled to protection under the common law respecting unfair competition. If a design has been registered and the registration has expired (they last 10 years), in some instances it has been asserted that the design has acquired distinctive trademark significance. For these arguments to succeed, it must be shown that, in the mind of the appropriate sector of the consuming public, the design indicates the particular source of the product, and is not merely decorative. A counter-argument is that, given the period of exclusivity enjoyed by a registered design, this public recognition should be discounted, as the monopoly period should not be used to create a separate and as of yet "unearned" monopoly. No clear jurisprudence exists in Canada on this point.

APPLICATION FOR REGISTRATION OF A DESIGN

An application for registration of an Industrial Design must be filed within one year from the date it was first published (*i.e.*, displayed in public or in a published picture, *etc.*) whether in Canada or elsewhere. If an application has previously been filed in another Convention country within the previous six months, a Canadian application can be filed claiming priority from the earlier filing date. If the application is filed under the Hague Agreement, and then in Canada, registration in Canada will automatically follow 12 months after the Canadian filing date, unless it has been refused by the Minister.

An application must contain both a picture, whether a photograph or drawing, of the design and a verbal description. The verbal description may be brief, provided that it highlights the particular design feature which is said to be unique. Similarly, where the design relates only to a portion of an article, the picture should show the rest of the article in broken line or the like.

Examiners will, upon receipt of the application and review of formalities, check previously registered designs for similar articles as well as books, publications and even web databases, for similar designs. If a similar previously published design appears, a dialogue will occur between the examiner and applicant as to registrability. If the Minister refuses to register a design (other than one filed under the Hague Agreement), an appeal may be taken to the Patent Appeal Board, which is an informal internal procedure. The Act provides that a refusal may be reviewed by the federal cabinet, which is impractical. Probably the best way to seek relief is by way of judicial review in the Federal Court of Canada under section 18 of the *Federal Courts Act* (R.S.C. 1985, c. F-7). If the application has been filed under the Hague Agreement and refused by the Minister, an appeal lies to the Federal Court.

Unlike filing a patent or trademark application, no special "agent" is required. Anyone can do it, although usually a patent agent handles the application.

WHO IS THE PROPER APPLICANT?

The Act uses the archaic term "proprietor" in section 4, stating that the proprietor or subsequent proprietor can apply to register a design. Section 12 of the Act states that the "author" is the first proprietor of a design unless the author has previously contracted with somebody else to create the design. Neither "proprietor" nor "author" are defined terms under the Act. An "author" appears to be someone who, as in a copyright context, is the creator or "hands on" person as opposed to a person giving instructions or coordinating the project. A "proprietor" appears to be an "owner" such as an employer of an author, or someone who has acquired the rights from the author by assignment.

An application for registration and the registration can be assigned.

REGISTRATION — TERM — EFFECT

Until November 5, 2018, the term of exclusive rights in an Industrial Design is 10 years, beginning on the date of registration, subject to payment of maintenance fees for the second five years. As of November 5, 2018, the term begins on the later of (a) the date of registration and (b) the date on which the application is made available to the public, and ends on the later of (a) 10 years after the date of registration of the design and (b) 15 years after the filing date of the application.

The date of registration of a design that is not registered under the Hague Agreement is stated on the certificate of registration. The date of registration of a design registered under the Hague Agreement is the earlier of (a) the date of the statement of grant of protections sent by the Minister to the International Bureau and (b) the day that is 12 months after the date of publication of the international registration by the International Bureau, unless the Minister has sent a notice of refusal to the International Bureau.

A registration gives to the proprietor the exclusive right in Canada to apply the design to the article for the purpose of importation, rent or sale.

MARKING

Until 1993, it was a mandatory requirement in order to preserve the validity of a design registration, to mark all products bearing the design with the caption "**D** 19 _____" (year of registration). This is no longer a requirement. In order to obtain a remedy other than an injunction, it must be shown that the infringer knew or ought to have known of the registration. Sufficient marking will give rise to a presumption that such knowledge existed.

EXPUNGING OR AMENDING A REGISTRATION

Amendments to a registration of a design, strangely, must be made by way of an application to the Federal Court, whether by the registered owner or an interested third party. The third party may also apply to the Federal Court to expunge the registration entirely.

ASSIGNMENT AND LICENSING

An assignment of a registered design or application and an exclusive licence must be registered on the Industrial Design register; a non-exclusive licence need not be registered. If a product contains a notice such as **D**, the name of the registered owner, if it appears, should coincide with what is reflected on the register.

INFRINGEMENT

An action for infringement can be taken in the Federal Court or an appropriate provincial court. The proprietor and/or an exclusive licensee can bring the action and claim damages, however, damages can only be recovered from a person who "applies" the infringing design and not a re-seller. An injunction is available against anyone handling the products.

There has been some controversy over whether the verbal description or the picture or some combination is to be considered in determining whether there has been an infringement. It appears, however, that the court will look principally at the alleged infringing product and the drawing or photograph of the design, as registered, to determine if "to the eye" they are sufficiently similar. A threefold test had been proposed[1] which cumulatively may assist in determining infringement:

(1)   Would one design be confused with the other?

(2)   Would the alleged infringement have existed were it not for the registered design?

(3)   Is the alleged infringement closer to the design than anything that previously existed?

Intention appears to be irrelevant.

More recently, the Federal Court has adopted a four-step approach:[2]

(1)   examination of the prior art;

(2)   an assessment of the utilitarian function and any method or principles of manufacture or construction;

(3)   an analysis of the scope of protection outlined in the language and figures of the registered design itself; and

(4)   in light of all the above, a comparative analysis of the registered design and the allegedly infringing product.

The prior art is to be considered so as to arrive at the scope of protection afforded to the registered design; in a crowded field the scope of protection may be very narrow.

---

[1] *R. v. Premier Cutlery Ltd.*, [1980] O.J. No. 3913, 55 C.P.R. (2d) 134 at 143-50 (Ont. Prov. Ct.), citing *Cartwright v. Coventry Radiator Co.* (1925), 42 R.P.C. 351 at 357 (Ch. D.); *Mainetti SPA v. ERA Display Co.*, [1984] F.C.J. No. 230, 80 C.P.R. (2d) 206 at 222

(F.C.T.D.); *House of Faces Inc. v. Leblanc*, [1984] O.J. No. 604, 2 C.P.R. (3d) 177 at 181 (Ont. H.C.J.).

² *AFX Licensing Corp. v. HJC America, Inc.*, [2016] F.C.J. No. 463, 2016 FC 435 at paras. 55-61 (F.C.).

INDUSTRIAL DESIGN ACT

408

INDUSTRIAL DESIGN ACT

(R.S.C. 1985, c. I-9)

Amendments: R.S.C. 1985, c. 10 (4th Supp.), ss. 20, 21; S.C. 1992, c. 1, ss. 79-82, s. 143, Sch. VI, ss. 15-16; S.C. 1993, c. 15, ss. 12-24 proclaimed in force June 9, 1993; S.C. 1993, c. 44, ss. 161-173 proclaimed in force January 1, 1994; S.C. 1994, c. 47, s. 118 proclaimed in force January 1, 1996; S.C. 2001, c. 34, s. 52 in force December 18, 2001; S.C. 2014, c. 39, ss. 102-112 proclaimed in force November 5, 2018; S.C. 2015, c. 36, ss. 44-49 proclaimed in force November 5, 2018; S.C. 2017, c. 26, ss. 60-61 proclaimed in force December 12, 2017.

SHORT TITLE

1. Short Title — This Act may be cited as the *Industrial Design Act*.

INTERPRETATION

2. Definitions — In this Act,

article means any thing that is made by hand, tool or machine;

Convention means the Convention of the Union of Paris made on March 20, 1883, including any amendments and revisions made from time to time to which Canada is a party;

[S.C. 2014, c. 39, s. 102.]

country of the Union means

(*a*) a country that is a member of the Union for the Protection of Industrial Property constituted under the Convention, or

(*b*) a member of the World Trade Organization as defined in subsection 2(1) of the *World Trade Organization Agreement Implementation Act*;

[S.C. 2014, c. 39, s. 102.]

design or *industrial design* means features of shape, configuration, pattern or ornament and any combination of those features that, in a finished article, appeal to and are judged solely by the eye;

kit means a complete or substantially complete number of parts that can be assembled to construct a finished article;

[S.C. 1993, c. 44, s. 161(1).]

Minister means such member of the Queen's Privy Council for Canada as is designated by the Governor in Council as the Minister for the purposes of this Act;

prescribed means prescribed by the regulations and, in relation to fees, includes

determined in the manner prescribed by the regulations;
[S.C. 1993, c. 15, s. 12.]

set means a number of articles of the same general character ordinarily on sale together or intended to be used together, to each of which the same design or variants thereof are applied;
[S.C. 1993, c. 44, s. 161(1).]

useful article means an article that has a utilitarian function and includes a model of any such article;

utilitarian function, in respect of an article, means a function other than merely serving as a substrate or carrier for artistic or literary matter.
[R.S.C. 1985, c. 10 (4th Supp.), s. 20.]

variants means designs applied to the same article or set and not differing substantially from one another.
[S.C. 1993, c. 44, s. 161(1).]

PART I
INDUSTRIAL DESIGNS

REGISTRATION

3. Register — (1) The Minister shall cause to be kept a register called the Register of Industrial Designs, which shall contain the prescribed information and statements in respect of designs that are registered under this Act.

(2) *Evidence* — The Register of Industrial Designs is evidence of its contents, and a copy of an entry in the Register is evidence of the particulars of the entry if the copy is certified as a true copy by the Minister, by the Commissioner of Patents or by an officer, clerk or employee of the Commissioner's office.

(3) *Admissibility* — A copy appearing to have been certified under subsection (2) is admissible in evidence in any court.
[S.C. 1992, c. 1, s. 79; S.C. 2014, c. 39, s. 103.]

3.1 Obvious error — The Minister may, within six months after an entry is made in the Register of Industrial Designs, correct any error in the entry that is obvious from the documents relating to the registered design in question that are, at the time that the entry is made, in the Minister's possession.
[S.C. 2015, c. 36, s. 44.]

4. Application to register design — (1) The proprietor of a design, whether the first proprietor or a subsequent proprietor, may apply to register the design by paying the prescribed fees and filing with the Minister an application that contains

(*a*) the name of the finished article in respect of which the design is to be registered;

(*b*) a representation of the design that complies with any prescribed requirements; and

(*c*) any prescribed information or statement.

(2) *Substituted applicants* — The application shall, subject to any prescribed terms and conditions, be considered to have been filed by a person other than the person who filed it if, before the design is registered, it is established to the satisfaction of the Minister that the other person was the proprietor when the application was filed.

(3) *Filing date* — The filing date of an application in Canada is the date on which the Minister receives the prescribed documents, information and statements or, if they are received on different dates, the latest of those dates.

[S.C. 1992, c. 1, s. 79; S.C. 1993, c. 15, s. 13; S.C. 2014, c. 39, s. 104.]

5. Examination of application for registration — The Minister shall examine, in accordance with the regulations, each application for the registration of a design.

[S.C. 1992, c. 1, s. 143; S.C. 1993, c. 15, s. 13; S.C. 2014, c. 39, s. 105.]

5.1. [Repealed by S.C. 2014, c. 39, s. 105.]

6. Refusal of application — (1) The Minister shall refuse an application for the registration of a design and notify the applicant of the refusal if the Minister is satisfied that the design is not registrable.

(2) *Registration of design* — If the Minister is not so satisfied, the Minister shall register the design and notify the applicant of the registration.

[S.C. 1992, c. 1, s. 80; S.C. 1993, c. 15, s. 14; S.C. 1993, c. 44, s. 162; S.C. 2014, c. 39, s. 105.]

7. Registrable design — A design is registrable if

(*a*) the application is filed in accordance with this Act;

(*b*) the design is novel, within the meaning of section 8.2;

(*c*) the design was created by the applicant or the applicant's predecessor in title;

(*d*) the design does not consist only of features that are dictated solely by a utilitarian function of the finished article; and

(*e*) the design is not contrary to public morality or order.

[S.C. 1992, c. 1, ss. 81, 143; S.C. 1993, c. 15, s. 15; S.C. 2014, c. 39, s. 105.]

8. Priority date — (1) The priority date of a design in an application for the registration of a design (in this section and section 8.1 referred to as the "pending application") is the filing date of the application, unless

(*a*) the pending application is filed by a person

413

(i) who, on the filing date of the pending application, is a citizen or national of, or is domiciled in, a country of the Union or has a real and effective industrial or commercial establishment in a country of the Union, and

(ii) who has, or whose predecessor in title has, previously regularly filed an application for the registration of a design disclosing the same design in or for a country of the Union;

(b) the filing date of the pending application is within six months after the filing date of the previously regularly filed application; and

(c) the applicant has made a request for priority in respect of the pending application on the basis of the previously regularly filed application.

(2) *Filing date of previously regularly filed application*—In the circumstances set out in paragraphs (1)(a) to (c), the priority date of the design is the filing date of the previously regularly filed application.

[S.C. 1993, c. 15, s. 16; S.C. 2014, c. 39, s. 105.]

8.1 Request for priority — (1) For the purposes of section 8, an applicant for the registration of a design may submit to the Minister a request for priority in respect of the pending application on the basis of one or more previously regularly filed applications.

(2) *Requirements* — The request for priority shall be made in accordance with the regulations, and the applicant shall submit to the Minister the filing date, the name of the country or office of filing and the number of each previously regularly filed application on which that request is based.

(3) *Request deemed never filed* — A request for priority is deemed never to have been filed if the request is not made in accordance with the regulations or if the applicant does not submit the information, other than the number of each previously regularly filed application, that is required under subsection (2).

(4) *Withdrawal of request* — An applicant may, in accordance with the regulations, withdraw a request for priority, either entirely or with respect to one or more previously regularly filed applications.

(5) *Multiple previously regularly filed applications* — If more than one application has been previously regularly filed either in or for the same country or in or for different countries,

(a) paragraph 8(1)(b) shall be applied using the earliest filing date of the previously regularly filed applications; and

(b) subsection 8(2) shall be applied using the earliest filing date of the previously regularly filed applications on which the request for priority is based.

(6) *Previously regularly filed application deemed never filed* — For the purposes of section 8, a previously regularly filed application shall be deemed never to have been filed if

(*a*)   on the filing date of the pending application, more than six months have elapsed since the filing date of the previously regularly filed application;

(*b*)   before the filing date of the pending application, another application for the registration of a design, disclosing the design in the pending application applied to the same finished article,

(i)   is filed by the person who filed the previously regularly filed application or by that person's successor in title or predecessor in title, and

(ii)   is filed in or for the country where the previously regularly filed application was filed; and

(*c*)   on the filing date of the other application referred to in paragraph (*b*) or, if there is more than one such other application, on the earliest of their filing dates, the previously regularly filed application

(i)   has been withdrawn, abandoned or refused without having been made available to the public and without leaving any rights outstanding, and

(ii)   has not served as a basis for a request for priority in any country, including Canada.

[S.C. 2014, c. 39, s. 105.]

8.2 Novel design — (1) A design in an application for the registration of a design is novel if the same design, or a design not differing substantially from it, applied to a finished article that is the same as or analogous to the finished article in respect of which the design is to be registered,

(*a*)   has not been disclosed, more than 12 months before the priority date of the design in the application, in such a manner that it became available to the public in Canada or elsewhere, by

(i)   the person who filed the application,

(ii)   that person's predecessor in title, or

(iii)   a person who obtained knowledge of the design in the application, directly or indirectly, from the person who filed the application or their predecessor in title;

(*b*)   has not been disclosed by any other person, before the priority date referred to in paragraph (*a*), in such a manner that it became available to the public in Canada or elsewhere; and

415

(c) subject to the regulations, has not been disclosed in an application filed in Canada for the registration of a design whose priority date is before the priority date referred to in paragraph (a).

(2) *Application deemed never filed*—For the purposes of paragraph (1)(c), an application referred to in that paragraph is deemed never to have been filed if it is withdrawn before the earlier of the date on which it is made available to the public under section 8.3 and the date on which a design in it is registered.

[S.C. 2014, c. 39, s. 105.]

8.3 Application and documents made available to public — (1) The Minister shall make available to the public, on the prescribed date, an application for the registration of a design and all documents in the Minister's possession relating to the application and to the design's registration.

(2) *Non-disclosure* — Except with the approval of the applicant or the registered proprietor, the Minister shall, before the prescribed date referred to in subsection (1), refuse to disclose the application for the registration of the design and any information or document relating to the application or to the design's registration.

(3) *Limitation* — The prescribed date referred to in subsection (1) may not be later than the later of the date of registration of the design and 30 months after the filing date of the application for registration or, if a request for priority is made in respect of the application, the earliest filing date of a previously regularly filed application on which the request for priority is based.

(4) *Withdrawal of request* — If a request for priority is withdrawn on or before the prescribed date, it shall, for the purposes of subsection (3) and to the extent that it is withdrawn, be deemed never to have been made.

(5) *Withdrawn applications* — If an application for the registration of a design is withdrawn in accordance with the regulations on or before the prescribed date, the Minister shall not make the application and documents referred to in subsection (1) available to the public and shall refuse to disclose the application and documents, as well as any information relating to them.

(6) *Prescribed date* — A prescribed date referred to in subsection (4) or (5) is to be no later than the prescribed date referred to in subsection (1).

[S.C. 2014, c. 39, s. 105; S.C. 2017, c. 26, s. 60.]

EXCLUSIVE RIGHT

9. Exclusive right — The registration of a design, unless shown to be invalid, gives to the proprietor an exclusive right in relation to the design.

[S.C. 2014, c. 39, s. 105.]

10. Duration of exclusive right — (1) Subject to subsection (3), the term limited for the duration of an exclusive right

(a) begins on the later of the date of registration of the design and the prescribed date, referred to in subsection 8.3(1), on which the application for the registration of the design is made available to the public; and

(b) ends on the later of the end of 10 years after the date of registration of the design and the end of 15 years after the filing date of the application.

(2) *Maintenance fees* — The proprietor of a design shall, to maintain the exclusive right accorded by the registration of the design, pay to the Commissioner of Patents such fees, in respect of such periods, as may be prescribed.

(3) *Expiration of term* — Where the fees payable under subsection (2) are not paid within the time provided for by the regulations, the term limited for the duration of the exclusive right shall be deemed to have expired at the end of that time. [S.C. 1993, c. 15, s. 17; S.C. 1993, c. 44, s. 163; S.C. 2014, c. 39, s. 106.]

11. Using design without licence — (1) During the existence of an exclusive right, no person shall, without the licence of the proprietor of the design,

(a) make, import for the purpose of trade or business, or sell, rent, or offer or expose for sale or rent, any article in respect of which the design is registered and to which the design or a design not differing substantially therefrom has been applied; or

(b) do, in relation to a kit, anything specified in paragraph (a) that would constitute an infringement if done in relation to an article assembled from the kit.

(2) *Substantial differences* — For the purposes of subsection (1), in considering whether differences are substantial, the extent to which the registered design differs from any previously published design may be taken into account. [S.C. 1993, c. 44, s. 164.]

11.1. Restriction on protection — No protection afforded by this Act shall extend to features applied to a useful article that are dictated solely by a utilitarian function of the article or to any method or principle of manufacture or construction. [S.C. 2014, c. 39, s. 107.]

PROPRIETORSHIP

12. First proprietor — (1) The author of a design is the first proprietor of the design, unless the author has executed the design for another person for a good and valuable consideration, in which case the other person is the first proprietor.

(2) *Acquired right* — The right of another person to the property shall only be co-extensive with the right that the other person has acquired. [S.C. 1993, c. 15, s. 18.]

TRANSFERS

13. Design transferable — (1) Every design, whether registered or unregistered, is transferable in whole or in part.

(2) *Recording of transfer of application* — The Minister shall, subject to the regulations, record the transfer of an application for the registration of a design on the request of the applicant or, on receipt of evidence satisfactory to the Minister of the transfer, on the request of a transferee of the application.

(3) *Registration of transfer of design* — The Minister shall, subject to the regulations, register the transfer of any registered design on the request of the registered proprietor or, on receipt of evidence satisfactory to the Minister of the transfer, on the request of a transferee of the design.

(4) *Transfer void* — A transfer of a registered design that has not been registered is void against a subsequent transferee if the transfer to the subsequent transferee has been registered.

(5) *Removal of recording or registration* — The Minister shall remove the recording or registration of the transfer of an application for the registration of a design or the transfer of a registered design on receipt of evidence satisfactory to the Minister that the transfer should not have been recorded or registered.

(6) *Limitation* — The Minister is not authorized to remove the registration of a transfer of a registered design for the reason only that the transferor had previously transferred the registered design to another person.
[S.C. 1993, c. 15, s. 19; S.C. 2014, c. 39, s. 108.]

14. [Repealed by S.C. 1993, c. 15, s. 20.]

ACTION FOR INFRINGEMENT

15. Action by proprietor or licensee — (1) An action for infringement of an exclusive right may be brought in any court of competent jurisdiction by the proprietor of the design or by an exclusive licensee of any right therein, subject to any agreement between the proprietor and the licensee.

(2) *Proprietor to be a party* — The proprietor of the design shall be or be made a party to any action for infringement of the exclusive right.
[S.C. 1993, c. 44, s. 166.]

15.1. Power of court to grant relief — In any proceedings under section 15, the court may make such orders as the circumstances require, including orders for relief by way of injunction and the recovery of damages or profits, for punitive damages, and for the disposal of any infringing article or kit.
[S.C. 1993, c. 44, s. 166.]

15.2. Concurrent jurisdiction — The Federal Court has concurrent jurisdiction to hear and determine

(*a*) any action for the infringement of an exclusive right; and

(*b*) any question relating to the proprietorship of a design or any right in a design.
[S.C. 1993, c. 44, s. 166.]

16. [Repealed by S.C. 1993, c. 44, s. 167.]

17. Defence — (1) In any proceedings under section 15, a court shall not award a remedy, other than an injunction, if the defendant establishes that, at the time of the act that is the subject of the proceedings, the defendant was not aware, and had no reasonable grounds to suspect, that the design was registered.

(2) *Exception* — Subsection (1) does not apply if the plaintiff establishes that the capital letter "D" in a circle and the name, or the usual abbreviation of the name, of the proprietor of the design were marked on

(*a*) all, or substantially all, of the articles to which the registration pertains and that were distributed in Canada by or with the consent of the proprietor before the act complained of; or

(*b*) the labels or packaging associated with those articles.

(3) *Proprietor* — For the purposes of subsection (2), the proprietor is the proprietor at the time the articles, labels or packaging were marked.
[S.C. 1993, c. 15, s. 21; S.C. 1993, c. 44, s. 168.]

18. Limitation — No remedy may be awarded for an act of infringement committed more than three years before the commencement of the action for infringement.
[S.C. 1993, c. 44, s. 169.]

PART II
GENERAL

19. [Repealed by S.C. 2001, c. 34, s. 52.]

[Note: The heading preceding section 20 was repealed by S.C. 2015, c. 36, s. 45.]

20. [Repealed by S.C. 2015, c. 36, s. 45.]

EXTENSION OF TIME
[S.C. 2015, c. 36, s. 46.]

21. Time period extended — (1) If a time period fixed under this Act for doing anything ends on a prescribed day or a day that is designated by the Minister, that time period is extended to the next day that is not a prescribed day or a designated day.

(2) *Power to designate day* — The Minister may, on account of unforeseen circumstances and if the Minister is satisfied that it is in the public interest to do so,

419

designate any day for the purposes of subsection (1). If a day is designated, the Minister shall inform the public of that fact on the website of the Canadian Intellectual Property Office.

[S.C. 1993, c. 15, s. 22; S.C. 2015, c. 36, s. 46.]

PROCEDURE AS TO RECTIFICATION AND ALTERATION

22. Federal Court may rectify entries — (1) The Federal Court may, on the information of the Attorney General or at the suit of any person aggrieved by any omission without sufficient cause to make any entry in the Register of Industrial Designs, or by any entry made without sufficient cause in the Register, make such order for making, expunging or varying any entry in the Register as the Court thinks fit, or the Court may refuse the application.

(2) *Costs* — In either case, the Federal Court may make such order with respect to the costs of the proceedings as the Court thinks fit.

(3) *Questions to be decided* — The Federal Court may in any proceedings under this section decide any question that may be necessary or expedient to decide for the rectification of the Register.

(4) *Jurisdiction* — The Federal Court has exclusive jurisdiction to hear and determine proceedings under this section.

23. Application to alter design — (1) The registered proprietor of any registered industrial design may apply to the Federal Court for leave to add to or alter any industrial design in any particular not being an essential particular, and the Court may refuse or grant leave on such terms as it may think fit.

(2) *Notice to Minister* — Notice of any intended application to the Federal Court under this section for leave to add to or alter any industrial design shall be given to the Minister, and the Minister is entitled to be heard on the application.

24. Consequent rectification of register — A certified copy of any order of the Federal Court for the making, expunging or varying of any entry in the Register of Industrial Designs, or for adding to or altering any registered industrial design, shall be transmitted to the Minister by an officer of the Registry of the Court, and the Register shall thereupon be rectified or altered in conformity with the order, or the purport of the order otherwise duly entered therein, as the case may be.

ELECTRONIC FORM AND MEANS

24.1 Electronic form and means — (1) Subject to the regulations, any document, information or fee that is submitted to the Minister or the Commissioner of Patents under this Act may be submitted in any electronic form, and by any electronic means, that is specified by the Minister or the Commissioner of Patents.

(2) *Collection, storage, etc.* — Subject to the regulations, the Minister and the Commissioner of Patents may use electronic means to create, collect, receive, store,

transfer, distribute, publish, certify or otherwise deal with documents or information.

(3) *Definition of electronic* — In this section, ***electronic***, in reference to a form or means, includes optical, magnetic and other similar forms or means.
[S.C. 2014, c. 39, s. 110.]

REGULATIONS

25. Regulations — The Governor in Council may make regulations

(*a*)   governing titles of designs;

(*b*)   respecting the form and contents of applications for the registration of designs, including

    (i)   the manner of naming finished articles,

    (ii)   the manner of identifying features of shape, configuration, pattern or ornament of all or part of a finished article, and

    (iii)   the manner of identifying that an application relates to only some of the features of shape, configuration, pattern or ornament that, in a finished article, appeal to and are judged solely by the eye, or to only some or all of those features of a part of a finished article;

(*b*.1)   respecting the processing and examination of applications for the registration of designs, including the circumstances in which applications shall be deemed to be abandoned and the circumstances in which they shall be reinstated;

(*b*.2)   respecting the circumstances in which paragraph 8.2(1)(*c*) does not apply in respect of a design that has been disclosed in an application for the registration of a design that was filed in Canada by a person referred to in subparagraph 8.2(1)(*a*)(i) or (ii);

(*b*.3)   respecting the withdrawal of an application for the registration of a design and, for the purposes of subsections 8.3(4) and (5), prescribing the date, or the manner of determining the date, on or before which a request for priority or an application for the registration of a design shall be withdrawn;

(*c*)   respecting the payment of fees and the amount of those fees;

(*d*)   respecting the return of any fees paid under this Act;

(*d*.1)   authorizing the Minister to waive, subject to any prescribed terms and conditions, the payment of a fee if the minister is satisfied that the circumstances justify it;

(*e*)   respecting the registration of sets and of variants of a design;

(*e*.1)   respecting the correction of obvious errors in documents submitted to the

INDUSTRIAL DESIGN ACT

Minister or the Commissioner of Patents, including

    (i)   the determination of what constitutes an obvious error, and

    (ii) the effect of the correction;

  (f)   respecting requests for priority, including

    (i)   the period within which priority shall be requested,

    (ii) the information and documentation that shall be submitted in support of requests for priority,

    (iii) the period within which that information and documentation shall be submitted,

    (iv) the withdrawal of requests for priority, and

    (v) the correction of requests for priority or of information or documentation submitted in support of them and the effect of corrections on the application of section 8.3;

  (g) respecting certificates of registration;

  (g.1) respecting the recording of documents relating to a design;

  (g.2) respecting the recording or registration of transfers of applications for the registration of designs or transfers of registered designs;

  (g.3) respecting the provision, including in electronic form and by electronic means, of documents and information to the Minister or the Commissioner of Patents, including the time at which they are deemed to be received by the Minister or the Commissioner of Patents;

  (g.4) respecting the use of electronic means for the purposes of subsection 24.1(2);

  (g.5) respecting communications between the Minister or the Commissioner of Patents and any other person;

  (g.6) for carrying into effect, despite anything in this Act, the Geneva (1999) Act of the Hague Agreement Concerning the International Registration of Industrial Designs, adopted at Geneva on July 2, 1999, including any amendments and revisions made from time to time to which Canada is a party; and

  (h) prescribing anything else that is to be prescribed under this Act and generally for carrying out the purposes and provisions of this Act.

[S.C. 1993, c. 15, s. 23; S.C. 1993, c. 44, s. 170; S.C. 2014, c. 39, s. 111; S.C. 2015, c. 36, s. 47; S.C. 2017, c. 26, s. 61.]

26. [Repealed by S.C. 1993, c. 15, s. 23.]

27. [Repealed by S.C. 1993, c. 15, s. 23.]

28. [Repealed by S.C. 1993, c. 15, s. 23.]

TRANSITIONAL PROVISIONS

29. Definition of *coming-into-force date* — In sections 30 to 32, *coming-into-force date* means the day on which subsection 104(2) of the *Economic Action Plan 2014 Act, No. 2* comes into force.
[S.C. 1993, c. 44, s. 171; S.C. 1994, c. 47, s. 118; S.C. 2014, c. 39, s. 112.]

29.1. [Repealed by S.C. 2014, c. 39, s. 112.]

30. Prior applications – filing date — An application for the registration of a design whose filing date, determined under this Act as it read immediately before the coming-into-force date, is before the coming-into-force date, shall be dealt with and disposed of in accordance with

(*a*)   the provisions of this Act, as they read immediately before the coming-into-force date, other than sections 5, 13 and 20; and

(*b*)   sections 5, 13, 21 and 24.1.
[S.C. 1993, c. 14, s. 24; S.C. 2014, c. 39, s. 112; S.C. 2015, c. 36, s. 48.]

31. Prior application – no filing date — An application for the registration of a design that is filed before the coming-into-force date and that does not, on that date, have a filing date, determined under this Act as it read immediately before the coming-into-force date, shall be deemed never to have been filed.
[S.C. 2014, c. 39, s. 112.]

32. Registered designs — Any matter arising on or after the coming-into-force date, in respect of a design registered before that date or a design registered on or after that date on the basis of an application whose filing date, determined under this Act as it read immediately before the coming-into-force date, is before the coming-into-force date, shall be dealt with and disposed of in accordance with

(*a*)   the provisions of this Act, as they read immediately before the coming-into-force date, other than sections 3, 13 and 20; and

(*b*)   sections 3, 3.1, 13, 21 and 24.1.
[S.C. 2014, c. 39, s. 112; S.C. 2015, c. 36, s. 49.]

33. Regulations — For greater certainty, a regulation made under section 25 applies to an application referred to in section 30 and to a design referred to in section 32, unless the regulation provides otherwise.
[S.C. 2014, c. 39, s. 112.]

INDUSTRIAL DESIGN REGULATIONS

(SOR/2018-120)

Note: SOR/2018-120 filed June 11, 2018, gazetted June 27, 2018, in force November 5, 2018.

P.C. 2018-715 2018-06-11

Her Excellency the Governor General in Council, on the recommendation of the Minister of Industry, pursuant to section 25[a] of the *Industrial Design Act*[b], makes the annexed *Industrial Design Regulations*.

[a] S.C. 2015, c. 36, s. 47

[b] R.S., c. I-9

INTERPRETATION

1. Definitions — The following definitions apply in these Regulations.

Act means the *Industrial Design Act*.

application means an application for the registration of a design.

Commissioner means the Commissioner of Patents.

Common Regulations means the Common Regulations Under the 1999 Act and the 1960 Act of the Hague Agreement, including any amendments made from time to time.

date of registration means, in relation to a design that is the subject of a Hague registration, the date of registration as determined under subsection 44(4).

divisional application means an application filed in accordance with subsection 20(2).

Hague Agreement means the Geneva (1999) Act of the Hague Agreement Concerning the International Registration of Industrial Designs, adopted at Geneva on July 2, 1999, including any amendments and revisions made from time to time to which Canada is a party.

Hague application means an application referred to in subsection 41(1).

Hague registration means a registration referred to in subsection 44(3).

holder means the person in whose name an international registration is recorded in the International Register.

International Bureau means the International Bureau of the World Intellectual Property Organization.

International Designs Bulletin means the periodical bulletin in which the International Bureau effects the publications provided for in the Hague Agreement or the Common Regulations.

International Register means the official collection of data concerning international registrations maintained by the International Bureau.

international registration means the international registration of a design effected according to the Hague Agreement.

international registration designating Canada means an international registration resulting from an international application that contains an indication under Article 5(1)(*v*) of the Hague Agreement that Canada is a designated Contracting Party.

Office means the Canadian Intellectual Property Office.

PART 1
RULES OF GENERAL APPLICATION

COMMUNICATIONS

2. Written communications — Written communications that are intended for the Minister or Commissioner must be addressed to the "Industrial Design Office".

3. Communications not submitted in writing — Neither the Minister nor the Commissioner is required to have regard to communications that are not submitted in writing.

4. Submission of documents, information or fees — Unless submitted by electronic means under subsection 24.1(1) of the Act, any document, information or fee that is submitted to the Minister or Commissioner must be submitted by physical delivery to the Office or to an establishment that is designated by the Minister or Commissioner as being accepted for that purpose.

5. Deemed receipt — Office — (1) Documents, information or fees that are submitted by physical delivery to the Office are deemed to have been received by the Minister or Commissioner

(*a*) if they are delivered when the Office is open to the public, on the day on which they are delivered to the Office; and

(*b*) if they are delivered when the Office is closed to the public, on the first day on which the Office is next open to the public.

(2) *Deemed receipt — designated establishment* — Documents, information or fees that are submitted by physical delivery to a designated establishment are deemed to have been received by the Minister or Commissioner

(*a*) if they are delivered when the establishment is open to the public,

(i) in the case where the Office is open to the public for all or part of the day on which they are delivered, on that day, and

(ii)   in any other case, on the first day on which the Office is next open to the public; and

(*b*)   if they are delivered when the establishment is closed to the public, on the first day on which the Office is next open to the public that falls on or after the day on which the establishment is next open to the public.

(3) *Deemed receipt — electronic means —* Documents, information or fees that are submitted by electronic means under subsection 24.1(1) of the Act are deemed to have been received on the day on which the Office receives them, according to the local time of the place where the Office is located.

6. Electronic communications — If the Minister or Commissioner makes a communication available by a particular electronic means to a person who has consented to receiving communications by that means, the communication is deemed to have been sent to that person.

7. Postal address — A person doing business before the Office must provide the Minister with their postal address.

8. Written communications in respect of application — (1) Written communications submitted to the Minister or Commissioner in respect of an application must contain the name of the applicant and, if known, the application number.

(2) *Written communications in respect of registered design —* Written communications submitted to the Minister or Commissioner in respect of a registered design must contain the name of the registered proprietor and the registration number.

9. Manner of presentation of documents — Documents submitted to the Minister or Commissioner must be

(*a*)   clear and legible and permit direct reproduction; and

(*b*)   in a form that is specified by the Minister or Commissioner as being accepted for that purpose.

10. Material not in English or French — The Minister and Commissioner must not have regard to any part of a document submitted in a language other than English or French, except for a representation of a design filed under paragraph 4(1)(*b*) of the Act or a document referred to in paragraph 27(1)(*a*).

11. Acknowledgment of protest — Communications received by the Minister before the registration of a design with the stated or apparent intention of protesting against the registration of that design must be acknowledged but, subject to section 8.3 of the Act, information must not be given as to the action taken.

REPRESENTATION BEFORE THE OFFICE

12. Power to appoint agent — (1) A person may appoint an agent to represent them in business before the Office.

(2) *Effect of act by agent* — An act by or in relation to an agent in respect of business before the Office has the effect of an act by or in relation to the person who appointed the agent.

(3) *Business before Office* — Subject to subsection (4), in business before the Office for the purpose of prosecuting an application,

(*a*)   if an agent is appointed by a person, the person must be represented by that agent; or

(*b*)   if a person has not appointed an agent, the person must represent themselves.

(4) *Exception* — A person may represent themselves or be represented by any person authorized by them for the purpose of filing an application, paying a fee, giving notice under subsection (5) or making a request or providing evidence under section 13 of the Act.

(5) *Effective date* — The appointment of an agent or the revocation of such an appointment is effective starting on the day on which the Minister receives notice of the appointment or revocation.

(6) *Postal address* — In the case of an appointment, the notice must contain the postal address of the agent.

REGISTER

13. Prescribed information and statements — For the purpose of subsection 3(1) of the Act, the prescribed information and statements that must be contained in the Register of Industrial Designs are

(*a*)   the date of registration;

(*b*)   the filing date of the application;

(*c*)   particulars of any request for priority submitted under section 8.1 of the Act;

(*d*)   the registration number;

(*e*)   the name and address of the registered proprietor of the design on the date of registration;

(*f*)   particulars of any change in the name or address of a registered proprietor recorded under section 35;

(*g*)   particulars of any transfer that is registered under section 13 of the Act that relates to a registered design;

(*h*)   the date prescribed under subsection 8.3(1) of the Act;

(*i*)   the name of the finished article in respect of which the design is registered;

(*j*)   the representation of the design contained in the application on the date of registration;

(*k*)   if the application contains a statement under section 17 or 18, that statement;

(*l*)   particulars of the payment of maintenance fees; and

(*m*)   particulars of any correction made under section 3.1 of the Act.

APPLICATIONS

14. Requirements for representation of design — The prescribed requirements for the purpose of paragraph 4(1)(*b*) of the Act are that a representation of the design must

(*a*)   be sufficient to disclose the design fully, taking into account the name of the finished article and any statement under section 17 or 18;

(*b*)   be in the form of one or more of the following:

　　(i)   photographs,

　　(ii)   graphic reproductions, or

　　(iii)   any other visual reproduction specified by the Minister or Commissioner as being accepted for that purpose;

(*c*)   be of sufficient quality to permit the features of the design to be identified clearly and accurately; and

(*d*)   include at least one photograph or reproduction that shows the design in isolation or the finished article in isolation.

15. Presentation of photographs or reproductions — Photographs or reproductions contained in an application must be presented in the manner specified by the Minister or Commissioner as being accepted for that purpose.

16. Name and postal address — For the purpose of paragraph 4(1)(*c*) of the Act, an application must contain the applicant's name and postal address.

17. Features of shape, configuration, pattern and ornament — (1) Subject to subsections (2) to (4), an application is deemed to relate to all of the features of shape, configuration, pattern and ornament shown in the representation of the design that, in the finished article, appeal to and are judged solely by the eye.

(2) *Exception — statement of limitation* — If the application contains a statement clearly indicating that it relates only to some of the features of shape, configuration, pattern or ornament that, in the finished article, appeal to and are judged solely by the eye, or only to some or all of those features of a part of the finished article, then the application relates only to those features.

(3) *Exception — features in dotted or broken lines* — An application is deemed

429

not to relate to a feature that is shown in the representation of the design in dotted or broken lines, unless the application contains a statement to the contrary.

(4) *Exception — blurring or colouring —* An application is deemed not to relate to a feature that is shown in the representation of the design by means of blurring or colouring if it is evident that the purpose of the blurring or colouring is to indicate that the application does not relate to that feature.

18. Optional description — An application may contain a brief statement describing the representation or the features of the design, but the statement must not describe a utilitarian function or a method or principle of manufacture or construction.

19. Hague applications— The contents of a Hague application on its filing date are deemed to comply with paragraphs 14(*b*) to (*d*) and sections 15, 16 and 18.

20. One design per application — (1) An application must be limited to one design applied to a single finished article or set or variants applied to a single finished article or set.

(2) *Divisional applications —* The applicant, in the case of a pending application (the "original application"), may file with the Minister a divisional application for the registration of a design applied to a finished article if that design applied to that finished article

(*a*)   in respect of an original application that is not a divisional application, was disclosed in the original application on its filing date; and

(*b*)   in respect of an original application that is a divisional application,

(i)   was disclosed in the original application on the day on which the Minister received the original application, and

(ii)   was disclosed, in the earliest original application in the series of applications from which the divisional application results, on the filing date of the earliest original application.

(3) *Required statement —* An application is a divisional application only if a statement to that effect that identifies the corresponding original application is contained in the application or in a separate document that is submitted to the Minister no later than three months after the day on which the Minister received the application.

(4) *Separate application —* A divisional application is a separate application, including with respect to the payment of any fees.

(5) *Time period —* A divisional application must not be filed later than two years after the filing date of the original application or, if the original application is itself a divisional application, two years after the filing date of the earliest original application in the series of applications from which the divisional application

results.

(6) *Exception* — Subsection (5) does not apply to a divisional application for the registration of a design applied to a finished article if

(*a*) the Minister sends to the applicant, in the case of an original application, a report under subsection 22(2) setting out an objection to registration on the basis that the original application does not comply with subsection (1);

(*b*) on or after the date of the report under subsection 22(2), the applicant amends the original application so that it is no longer for the registration of that design applied to that finished article; and

(*c*) the divisional application is filed no later than six months after the day of the amendment.

FILING DATE

21. Non-application to Hague application — (1) This section does not apply to a Hague application or to a divisional application resulting from a Hague application.

(2) *Required documents, information and statements* — The documents, information and statements prescribed for the purpose of subsection 4(3) of the Act are

(*a*) in respect of an application other than a divisional application,

  (i) an explicit or implicit indication that the registration of a design is sought,

  (ii) information allowing the identity of the applicant to be established,

  (iii) information allowing the Minister to contact the applicant, and

  (iv) a representation of the design; and

(*b*) in respect of a divisional application, those documents, information and statements received by the Minister under paragraph (*a*) in respect of the earliest original application in the series of applications from which the divisional application results.

(3) *Notice* — In respect of an application other than a divisional application, the Minister must by notice inform an applicant whose application does not contain all the documents, information and statements referred to in paragraph (2)(*a*) of which documents, information and statements are outstanding and require that the applicant submit them no later than two months after the date of the notice.

(4) *Application deemed never filed* — If the Minister does not receive those documents, information and statements before the end of that period, the application is deemed never to have been filed. However, the applicant is not entitled to a refund of any fees paid in respect of the application.

EXAMINATION

22. Registrability — (1) The Minister must examine an application to determine if the design is registrable under section 7 of the Act.

(2) *Objections* — Subject to subsection (3), if the Minister has reasonable grounds to believe that the design is not registrable, the Minister must send to the applicant a report setting out the objections to registration and inviting the applicant to reply to the objections no later than three months after the date of the report.

(3) *Objections to Hague application* — In respect of a Hague application, the first report under subsection (2) must be sent by the Minister to the International Bureau in the form of a notification of refusal referred to in Article 12(2) of the Hague Agreement and the Minister is not required to send a copy of the report directly to the applicant.

(4) *Extension of time period* — The time period to reply referred to in subsection (2) is extended by six months if, before it ends, the applicant submits a request to the Minister.

(5) *Limitation on extensions* — Only one request under subsection (4) may be submitted in respect of a particular report.

(6) *Deemed abandonment* — If the applicant does not reply in good faith to a report within the time period set out in subsection (2), or within the time period that has been extended under subsection (4), the application is deemed to be abandoned.

(7) *Reinstatement* — An application that is deemed to be abandoned is reinstated if the applicant, within six months after the day on which the application is deemed to be abandoned,

(*a*) submits a request for reinstatement to the Minister;

(*b*) replies in good faith to the report; and

(*c*) pays the fee set out in item 9 of the schedule.

23. Advanced examination — The Minister must advance the examination of an application out of its routine order on the request of the applicant and on payment of the fee set out in item 10 of the schedule.

24. Delayed registration — In respect of an application other than a Hague application, on the request of the applicant and on payment of the fee set out in item 11 of the schedule, the Minister, if it is technically feasible, must not register a design until the day that is 30 months after the filing date of the application or, if a request for priority is made in respect of the application, after the earliest filing date of a previously regularly filed application on which the request for priority is based.

AMENDMENTS

25. Time limit to amend application — (1) Subject to subsections (2) and (3), an application may be amended before the design is registered.

(2) *Limitations on amendment* — An application must not be amended

(*a*) to change the identity of the applicant, except, in respect of an application other than a Hague application, to record a transfer of the application under section 13 of the Act or to substitute an applicant under subsection 4(2) of the Act;

(*b*) to add a representation of a design;

(*c*) to change a representation of a design if the amendment would result in the application being for a design that differs substantially from the design that was the subject of the application on its filing date or, in the case of a divisional application, on the day on which the Minister received the divisional application;

(*d*) to add or amend a statement under section 17 or 18 if the addition or amendment would result in the application being for a design that differs substantially from the design that was the subject of the application on its filing date or, in the case of a divisional application, on the day on which the Minister received the divisional application; or

(*e*) to add an indication that it is a divisional application, if more than three months have passed since the day on which the Minister received the application.

(3) *Limitation — application made available to public* — If the application contains the name of a finished article in respect of which the design is to be registered, that application must not be amended, on or after the date prescribed under subsection 8.3(1) of the Act for making an application available to the public, to change that name to the name of a substantially different finished article.

PRIORITY

26. Non-application to Hague application — (1) This section does not apply to a Hague application or to a divisional application resulting from a Hague application.

(2) *Requirements* — For the purpose of subsection 8.1(2) of the Act, a request for priority must

(*a*) be made in the application or in a separate document;

(*b*) indicate the filing date and the name of the country or office of filing of each previously regularly filed application on which that request is based; and

(*c*) be made no later than the earlier of the day that is six months after the earliest filing date of those previously regularly filed applications and the date of registration of the design that is the subject of the pending application.

(3) *Corrections* — Subject to subsections (4) and (5), an error in the filing date, the name of the country or office of filing or the number of a previously regularly filed application submitted under subsection 8.1(2) of the Act may be corrected by the applicant before the design is registered.

(4) *Exception* — After the date prescribed under subsection 8.3(1) of the Act for making the pending application available to the public, an error in the name of the country or office of filing submitted under subsection 8.1(2) of the Act may be corrected only if, on the day the application is made available to the public, it would have been obvious from the documents in the Minister's possession relating to the application that the name of another particular country or office of filing was intended by the applicant.

(5) *Exception* — An error in the filing date submitted under subsection 8.1(2) of the Act must not be corrected if more than six months have passed since the filing date of the pending application.

27. Copy of previously filed application — (1) If an applicant requests priority in respect of a pending application on the basis of one or more previously regularly filed applications — other than an application previously regularly filed in or for Canada — the Minister may by notice request that the applicant of the pending application, no later than three months after the date of the notice,

(*a*) at the option of the applicant, either

 (i) submit to the Minister a copy of the previously regularly filed application certified as correct by the office in which it was filed and a certificate from that office showing its filing date, or

 (ii) make a copy of the previously regularly filed application available to the Minister from a digital library that is specified by the Minister or Commissioner as being accepted for that purpose and inform the Minister that it is so available; and

(*b*) if the previously regularly filed application is in a language other than English or French, submit to the Minister an English or French translation of the whole or a specified part of the previously regularly filed application.

(2) *Translation not accurate* — If the Minister has reasonable grounds to believe that a translation submitted under subsection (1) is not accurate, the Minister may by notice request that the applicant, in the case of the pending application, submit to the Minister, no later than three months after the date of the notice,

(*a*) a statement by the translator to the effect that, to the best of their knowledge, the translation is accurate; or

(*b*) a new translation together with a statement by its translator to the effect that, to the best of their knowledge, the new translation is accurate.

434

(3) *Notice included in report* — If the Minister issues a report under subsection 22(2), a notice under subsection (1) or (2) may be given by including the request in that report.

(4) *Extension* — The time period for complying with a request under subsection (1) or (2) is extended by six months if, within that time period, the applicant submits to the Minister a request for an extension.

(5) *Limitation on extensions* — Only one request under subsection (4) may be submitted in respect of a particular request under subsection (1) or (2).

(6) *Non-compliance with request* — If the applicant of a pending application does not comply with a request under subsection (1) or (2) in respect of a particular previously regularly filed application before the end of the time period set out in those subsections or of the time period that has been extended under subsection (4), the request for priority is deemed to have been withdrawn with respect to that previously regularly filed application at the end of that time period.

28. Withdrawal of request for priority — (1) For the purpose of subsection 8.1(4) of the Act, a request for priority may be withdrawn by submitting a request to the Minister before the design is registered.

(2) *Effective date* — The effective date of the withdrawal of a request for priority is the day on which the request for withdrawal is received by the Minister.

29. Deemed action — divisional application — If, on or before the day on which a divisional application is received by the Minister, one of the following actions has been taken in respect of the original application, the same action is deemed to have been taken on the same day in respect of the divisional application:

(*a*)   a request for priority has been made and has not been withdrawn;

(*b*)   information required under subsection 8.1(2) of the Act has been submitted to the Minister in respect of a request for priority;

(*c*)   a copy or a translation of a previously regularly filed application, or a certificate showing its filing date, has been submitted to the Minister; or

(*d*)   a copy of a previously regularly filed application has been made available to the Minister from a digital library that is specified by the Minister or Commissioner as being accepted for that purpose.

30. Priority effect of international registration — For the purpose of sections 8 and 8.1 of the Act and of sections 26 to 29 and 45 of these Regulations, an application for international registration is, from its filing date as determined under Article 9 of the Hague Agreement, equivalent to a regular filing of an application in or for a country of the Union.

NOVEL DESIGN

31. Non-application of paragraph 8.2(1)(c) of Act — In respect of a particular application, paragraph 8.2(1)(*c*) of the Act does not apply in respect of a design that has been disclosed in another application that was filed in Canada by a person referred to in subparagraph 8.2(1)(*a*)(i) or (ii) of the Act if the filing date of that particular application is no later than 12 months after the filing date of the other application.

APPLICATIONS AND DOCUMENTS MADE AVAILABLE TO PUBLIC

32. Prescribed date — (1) Subject to subsection (2), for the purpose of subsection 8.3(1) of the Act, the prescribed date is

(*a*) in respect of an application, other than a Hague application or a divisional application resulting from a Hague application, and in respect of all documents in the Minister's possession relating to the application and the design's registration, the earlier of

    (i) the date of registration of the design, and

    (ii) the day that is 30 months after the filing date of that application or of the application that resulted in that registration or, if a request for priority is made in respect of that application or of the application that resulted in that registration, the earliest filing date of a previously regularly filed application on which the request for priority is based; or

(*b*) in respect of a Hague application or a divisional application resulting from a Hague application, and in respect of all documents in the Minister's possession relating to the application and the design's registration, the date of publication of the international registration by the International Bureau.

(2) *Exception* — If a document relates to more than one application or registration, for the purpose of subsection 8.3(1) of the Act, the prescribed date for that document is the earliest date prescribed under subsection 8.3(1) of the Act for an application or registration referred to in that document.

(3) *Withdrawal of request for priority* — For the purpose of subsection (1), a request for priority with respect to a particular previously regularly filed application is deemed never to have been made if the request is withdrawn more than two months before the day referred to in subparagraph (1)(*a*)(ii), without taking the withdrawal into account.

(4) *Prescribed date regarding withdrawn application* — For the purpose of subsection 8.3(5) of the Act, the prescribed date is the earlier of the date of registration and the day that is two months before the day referred to in subparagraph (1)(*a*)(ii).

MAINTENANCE OF EXCLUSIVE RIGHT

33. Prescribed period — (1) For the purpose of subsection 10(2) of the Act, the prescribed period begins five years after the date of registration of the design and ends on the later of the end of 10 years after the date of registration and the end of 15 years after the filing date of the application.

(2) *Deadline for payment* — Subject to subsection (3), the fee for the maintenance of the exclusive right accorded by the registration of a design set out in item 2 of the schedule must be paid no later than five years after the date of registration of the design.

(3) *Exception* — The fee for the maintenance of the exclusive right accorded by the registration of a design set out in item 2 of the schedule may be paid within six months after the end of that five-year period if the proprietor makes a request to the Commissioner within those six months and pays both the maintenance fee and the late fee set out in item 3 of the schedule.

TRANSFERS AND CHANGES OF NAME OR ADDRESS

34. Request to record or register transfer — A request to record or register a transfer under subsection 13(2) or (3) of the Act must include the name and postal address of the transferee and the fee set out in item 4 of the schedule.

35. Change of name or address — If a registered proprietor changes their name or address, the Minister must register the change on the request of the registered proprietor.

TIME PERIOD EXTENDED

36. Prescribed days — The following days are prescribed for the purpose of subsection 21(1) of the Act:

(*a*) Saturday;

(*b*) Sunday;

(*c*) January 1 or, if January 1 falls on a Saturday or a Sunday, the following Monday;

(*d*) Good Friday;

(*e*) Easter Monday;

(*f*) the Monday preceding May 25;

(*g*) June 24 or, if June 24 falls on a Saturday or a Sunday, the following Monday;

(*h*) July 1 or, if July 1 falls on a Saturday or a Sunday, the following Monday;

(*i*) the first Monday in August;

(*j*)   the first Monday in September;

(*k*)   the second Monday in October;

(*l*)   November 11 or, if November 11 falls on a Saturday or a Sunday, the following Monday;

(*m*)   December 25 and 26 or, if December 25 falls on

      (i)   a Friday, that Friday and the following Monday, or

      (ii)   a Saturday or a Sunday, the following Monday and Tuesday; and

(*n*)   any day on which the Office is closed to the public for all or part of that day during ordinary business hours.

FEES

37. Fees for services — The fee prescribed for a purpose described in column 1 of an item of the schedule is the fee set out in column 2 of that item.

38. Refund excess fees —   (1) Subject to subsection (2), the Minister or Commissioner must refund any amount paid in excess of the fee prescribed.

(2) *Exception* — A refund must not be made unless a request for the refund is received no later than three years after the day on which the fee was paid.

39. Waiver of fee — The Minister is authorized to waive the payment of a fee if the Minister is satisfied that the circumstances justify it.

PART 2
IMPLEMENTATION OF THE HAGUE AGREEMENT

REGISTER

40. Non-application of section 3 of Act — (1) Section 3 of the Act does not apply to a Hague registration.

(2) *Evidence* — The International Register and items in the file of an international registration are evidence of their contents, and a copy of a recording in the International Register or of an item in the file of an international registration is evidence of the particulars of the recording or item if the copy is certified by the International Bureau.

(3) *Admissibility* — A copy appearing to have been certified by the International Bureau is admissible in evidence in any court.

HAGUE APPLICATION

41. Application —   (1) An application is deemed to have been filed under subsection 4(1) of the Act in respect of each design that is the subject of an international registration designating Canada.

(2) *Contents* — On the filing date of a Hague application,

(*a*) for the purpose of paragraph 4(1)(*a*) of the Act, the name of the product that is indicated in the corresponding international registration as the product that constitutes the design or in relation to which the design is to be used is deemed to be the name of the finished article in respect of which the design is to be registered; and

(*b*) the Hague application is deemed to contain the same representation of the design and the same information and statements in respect of the design as in the corresponding international registration.

(3) *Fees not applicable* — The requirement in subsection 4(1) of the Act for the payment of prescribed fees does not apply in respect of a Hague application.

(4) *Applicant* — The holder of the corresponding international registration is deemed to be the applicant in respect of a Hague application.

(5) *Non-application of subsection 4(2) of Act* — Subsection 4(2) of the Act does not apply to a Hague application or to a divisional application resulting from a Hague application.

(6) *Deemed withdrawal of Hague application* — A Hague application is deemed to be withdrawn if

(*a*) the corresponding international registration is cancelled;

(*b*) the International Bureau records in the International Register the renunciation of the corresponding international registration in respect of Canada; or

(*c*) the International Bureau records in the International Register, in respect of Canada, a limitation of the corresponding international registration to one or more designs other than the design that is the subject of the Hague application.

(7) *Effective date* — A withdrawal of a Hague application under subsection (6) is deemed to take effect on the date of the cancellation or the date of the recording of the renunciation or limitation in the International Register.

FILING DATE

42. Non-application of subsection 4(3) of Act — (1) Subsection 4(3) of the Act does not apply to a Hague application or to a divisional application resulting from a Hague application.

(2) *Filing date* — The filing date of a Hague application or a divisional application resulting from a Hague application is the date of the corresponding international registration as determined under Article 10(2) of the Hague Agreement.

REFUSAL

43. Notification of refusal — The Minister must not refuse a Hague application under subsection 6(1) of the Act without first sending the International Bureau a notification of refusal referred to in Article 12(2) of the Hague Agreement within 12 months after the date of publication of the international registration by the International Bureau.

HAGUE REGISTRATION

44. Non-application of subsection 6(2) of Act — (1) Subsection 6(2) of the Act does not apply to a Hague application.

(2) *Statement of grant of protection* — If the Minister is not satisfied that a design that is the subject of a Hague application is not registrable, the Minister must send a statement of grant of protection in respect of the design to the International Bureau.

(3) *Registration of design* — A design that is the subject of a Hague application is deemed to have been registered by the Minister under subsection 6(2) of the Act if

    (*a*)   the Minister sends a statement of grant of protection in respect of the design to the International Bureau; or

    (*b*)   the Minister does not, on or before the day that is 12 months after the date of publication of the international registration by the International Bureau, send to the International Bureau a notification of refusal referred to in Article 12(2) of the Hague Agreement.

(4) *Date of registration* — The date of registration of a design that is the subject of a Hague registration is the earlier of

    (*a*)   if the Minister sends a statement of grant of protection in respect of the design to the International Bureau, the date of the statement; and

    (*b*)   if the Minister does not, on or before the day that is 12 months after the date of publication of the international registration by the International Bureau, send to the International Bureau a notification of refusal referred to in Article 12(2) of the Hague Agreement, the first day after the end of that period.

(5) *Registered proprietor* — The holder of an international registration is deemed to be the registered proprietor of the corresponding Hague registration.

(6) *Deemed cancellation of Hague registration* — A Hague registration is deemed to be cancelled if the International Bureau records in the International Register

    (*a*)   a renunciation of the corresponding international registration in respect of

Canada; or

(*b*) a limitation of the corresponding international registration, in respect of Canada, to one or more designs other than the design that is the subject of the Hague registration.

(7) *Effective date* — A cancellation of a Hague registration under subsection (6) is deemed to take effect on the date of the recording of the renunciation or limitation in the International Register.

PRIORITY

45. Non-application of subsections 8.1(1) to (3) of Act — (1) Subsections 8.1(1) to (3) of the Act do not apply to a Hague application or to a divisional application resulting from a Hague application.

(2) *Request for priority* — For the purpose of paragraph 8(1)(*c*) of the Act, the applicant must not submit a request for priority to the Minister in respect of a Hague application or a divisional application resulting from a Hague application.

(3) *Deemed request for priority* — For the purpose of paragraph 8(1)(*c*) of the Act, the applicant is deemed to have made a request for priority in respect of a Hague application or a divisional application resulting from a Hague application on the basis of a previously regularly filed application if the corresponding international registration contains

(*a*) a declaration claiming the priority of the previously regularly filed application in respect of the design that is the subject of the Hague application; and

(*b*) an indication of the filing date and the name of the country or office of filing of the previously regularly filed application.

APPLICATIONS AND DOCUMENTS MADE AVAILABLE TO PUBLIC

46. Article 10(5) of Hague Agreement — (1) Despite subsection 8.3(1) of the Act, the Minister must not make available to the public a copy of an international registration or any statement, document or specimen sent by the International Bureau to the Minister under Article 10(5) of the Hague Agreement except in accordance with that Article.

(2) *Non-application of subsections 8.3(3) to (6) of Act* — Subsections 8.3(3) to (6) of the Act do not apply to a Hague application or to a divisional application resulting from a Hague application.

DURATION OF EXCLUSIVE RIGHT

47. Non-application of section 10 of Act — (1) Section 10 of the Act does not apply to a Hague registration.

(2) *Term* — The term limited for the duration of an exclusive right in relation to a design that is the subject of a Hague registration

(*a*) begins on the date of registration of the design; and

(*b*) ends on the earlier of

    (i) the later of the end of 10 years after the date of registration of the design and the end of 15 years after the filing date of the corresponding Hague application, and

    (ii) the date of the expiry, in respect of Canada, of the international registration in respect of that design.

TRANSFERS

48. Non-application of subsections 13(2) to (6) of Act — Subsections 13(2) to (6) of the Act do not apply to a Hague application or to a Hague registration.

49. Attestation — The Minister must, on request, provide to the transferee of an international registration an attestation that the transferee appears to be the successor in title of the holder if

(*a*) the holder is a national of Canada or has a domicile, a habitual residence or a real and effective industrial or commercial establishment in Canada; and

(*b*) the transferee submits to the Minister

    (i) evidence satisfactory to the Minister that the transferee appears to be the successor in title of the holder, and

    (ii) a statement to the effect that the transferee made efforts to obtain the signature of the holder or their representative on a request to record the change in ownership and that their efforts were not successful.

APPEAL OR INVALIDATION

50. Non-application of sections 22 to 24 of Act — (1) Sections 22 to 24 of the Act do not apply to a Hague registration.

(2) *Appeal to Federal Court* — An appeal lies to the Federal Court from a refusal by the Minister under subsection 6(1) of the Act of a Hague application no later than two months after the day on which notice of the refusal was sent by the Minister.

(3) *Refusal reversed* — If, in the final judgment given in the appeal, the refusal by the Minister is reversed, the Minister must send a statement of grant of protection in respect of the design to the International Bureau.

(4) *Jurisdiction* — The Federal Court has exclusive jurisdiction, on application of the Minister or any interested person, to make an order invalidating a Hague registration on the ground that the design was not registrable on the date of registration.

(5) *Notification to International Bureau* — If, in the final judgment given in a proceeding under subsection (4), a Hague registration is invalidated, the Minister must notify the International Bureau of the invalidation.

(6) *Certified copy* — An officer of the Registry of the Federal Court must send to the Minister a certified copy of every judgment or order of the Supreme Court of Canada, the Federal Court of Appeal or the Federal Court relating to a Hague registration.

CORRECTIONS

51. Notification of refusal of correction — (1) If the International Bureau modifies the International Register to correct an error concerning an international registration designating Canada and the Minister considers that the effects of the correction cannot be recognized, the Minister must so declare in a notification of refusal of the effects of the correction sent to the International Bureau no later than 12 months after the day on which the correction is published by the International Bureau in the International Designs Bulletin.

(2) *Opportunity to reply* — The holder may reply to the notification within the time specified in the notification.

(3) *Notification of withdrawal of refusal* — If, after considering a reply provided under subsection (2), the Minister considers that the effects of the correction can be recognized, the Minister must send to the International Bureau a notification of withdrawal of refusal of the effects of the correction.

(4) *Amendment — Hague application or Hague registration* — If the International Bureau modifies the International Register to correct an error concerning an international registration designating Canada and one of the circumstances set out in subsection (7) applies, the correction is effective in Canada and any corresponding Hague application or Hague registration is deemed to be amended accordingly.

(5) *Effective date* — For the purpose of paragraphs 25(2)(*c*) and (*d*), a correction under subsection (4) is deemed to take effect on the filing date of the corresponding Hague application.

(6) *No effect* — If the International Bureau modifies the International Register to correct an error concerning an international registration designating Canada that corresponds to a Hague application or a Hague registration and neither of the circumstances set out in subsection (7) applies, the correction has no effect in Canada.

(7) *Circumstances* — For the purpose of subsections (4) and (6), the circumstances are as follows:

(*a*)   the Minister does not, on or before the day that is 12 months after the day on which a correction of an error concerning an international registration designating Canada is published by the International Bureau in the International Designs Bulletin, send a notification of refusal under subsection (1) to the International Bureau; and

(*b*) the Minister sends a notification of withdrawal of refusal of the effects of the correction under subsection (3) to the International Bureau.

EXTENSION OF TIME

52. Non-application of section 21 of Act — Rule 4(4) of the Common Regulations applies, and section 21 of the Act does not apply, to the time periods referred to in sections 43, 44 and 51 of these Regulations.

TRANSITIONAL PROVISIONS

53. Definition of *former Regulations* — (1) In this section, *former Regulations* means the *Industrial Design Regulations* as they read immediately before the day on which these Regulations come into force.

(2) *Filing date* — In respect of an application whose filing date, determined under the Act as it read immediately before the day on which these Regulations come into force, is before the day on which these Regulations come into force, or in respect of a design registered on the basis of such an application,

(*a*) the requirements of subsections 8(2) and 9(1), paragraphs 9(2)(*a*) to (*d*) and sections 9.1 to 13, 16 and 20 of the former Regulations are substituted for the requirements of sections 10, 11, 14 to 21 and 24 to 32 of these Regulations;

(*b*) for the purpose of subsection 10(2) of the Act as it read immediately before the day on which these Regulations come into force, the prescribed period begins five years after the date of registration of the design and ends 10 years after the date of registration of the design; and

(*c*) subsection 22(1) of these Regulations does not apply to that application, and the Minister must examine it to determine if the design meets the requirements for registration under the Act as it read immediately before the day on which these Regulations come into force.

REPEAL

54. The *Industrial Design Regulations*[1] are repealed.

COMING INTO FORCE

*55. S.C. 2014, c. 39 — These Regulations come into force on the day on which section 102 of the *Economic Action Plan 2014 Act, No. 2*, comes into force.

*[Note: Regulations in force November 5, 2018, *see* SI/2018-45.]

---

[1] SOR/99-460

SCHEDULE

(Paragraph 22(7)(c), sections 23 and 24, subsections 33(2) and (3) and sections 34 and 37)

TARIFF OF FEES

Item	Column 1 Description	Column 2 Fee ($)
1.	Examination of an application	
	(*a*) basic fee	400.00
	(*b*) additional fee, for each page of the representation in excess of 10 pages	10.00
2.	Maintenance of the exclusive right accorded by the registration of a design under subsection 33(2) or (3) ...	350.00
3.	Late fee for the maintenance of the exclusive right accorded by the registration of a design under subsection 33(3)	50.00
4.	Recording or registering of a transfer under section 13 of the Act, for each application or registration to which the transfer relates	100.00
5.	Provision of a paper copy of a document, for each page,	
	(*a*) if the user of the service makes the copy using Office equipment	0.50
	(*b*) if the Office makes the copy	1.00
6.	Provision of an electronic copy of a document	
	(*a*) for each request	10.00
	(*b*) for each application or registration to which the request relates	10.00
	(*c*) if the copy is requested on a physical medium, for each physical medium provided other than the first	10.00
7.	Provision of a certified paper copy of a document, other than a certified copy made under Rule 318 or 350 of the *Federal Courts Rules*	
	(*a*) for each certification	35.00
	(*b*) for each page	1.00
8.	Provision of a certified electronic copy of a document, other than a certified copy made under Rule 318 or 350 of the *Federal Courts Rules*	
	(*a*) for each certification	35.00
	(*b*) for each application or registration to which the request relates	10.00
9.	Reinstatement of an abandoned application	200.00
10.	Processing of a request to advance the examination of an application	500.00
11.	Delaying of registration	100.00

ORDER DESIGNATING MINISTERS UNDER CERTAIN FEDERAL ACTS

(SI/2015-112)

P.C. 2015-1260 2015-11-04

His Excellency the Governor General in Council, on the recommendation of the Prime Minister,

(a) pursuant to section 8 of the *Agreement on Internal Trade Implementation Act*[a], designates the Minister of Industry, a member of the Queen's Privy Council for Canada, as the Minister for the purposes of any provision of that Act;

(b) pursuant to the definition **Minister** in section 2 of the *Canada Travelling Exhibitions Indemnification Act*[b], designates the Minister of Canadian Heritage, a member of the Queen's Privy Council for Canada, as the Minister for the purposes of that Act;

(c) pursuant to paragraph (d) of the definition **appropriate Minister** in section 2 of the *Financial Administration Act*[c] and subparagraph (a)(ii) of the definition **appropriate Minister** in subsection 83(1) of that Act,

  (i) repeals paragraph (b) of Order in Council P.C. 1993-1450 of June 25, 1993[d], and

  (ii) repeals paragraph (b) of Order in Council P.C. 1993-1982 of December 2, 1993[e];

(d) pursuant to the definition **Minister**[f] in section 2 of the *Industrial Design Act*[g], designates the Minister of Industry, a member of the Queen's Privy Council for Canada, as the Minister for the purposes of that Act;

(e) pursuant to section 3 of the *Mackenzie Gas Project Impacts Fund Act*[h], designates the Minister of the Canadian Northern Economic Development Agency, a member of the Queen's Privy Council for Canada, to be the Minister for the purposes of that Act;

(f) pursuant to the definition **Minister**[i] in section 2 of the *Museums Act*[j], designates the Minister of Canadian Heritage, a member of the Queen's Privy Council for Canada, as the Minister responsible for the National Gallery of Canada, the Canadian Museum of History, the Canadian Museum of Nature, the National Museum of Science and Technology, the Canadian Museum for Human Rights and the Canadian Museum of Immigration at Pier 21 for the purposes of that Act; and

447

(g)   pursuant to section 4 of the *Nuclear Liability and Compensation Act*[k], designates the Minister of Natural Resources, a minister of the Crown, to be the Minister referred to in that Act.

This Order is effective November 4, 2015.

[a]   S.C. 1996, c. 17.

[b]   S.C. 1999, c. 29.

[c]   R.S., c. F-11.

[d]   SI/93-104.

[e]   SOR/93-536.

[f]   R.S., c. 10 (4th Supp.), s. 20(2).

[g]   R.S., c. I-9.

[h]   S.C. 2013, c. 40, s. 282.

[i]   S.C. 2014, c. 20, s. 194.

[j]   S.C. 1990, c. 3.

[k]   S.C. 2015, c. 4, s. 120.

CANADA–UNITED STATES–MEXICO AGREEMENT

CHAPTER 20:
INTELLECTUAL PROPERTY RIGHTS

* * *

Section G: Industrial Designs

Article 20.52: Protection

1. Each Party shall ensure adequate and effective protection of industrial designs consistent with Articles 25 and 26 of the TRIPS Agreement.

2. Consistent with paragraph 1, each Party confirms that protection is available for designs embodied in a part of an article.

Article 20.53: Non-Prejudicial Disclosures/Grace Period[51]

Each Party shall disregard at least information contained in public disclosures used to determine if an industrial design is new, original, or, where applicable, non-obvious, if the public disclosure:[52]

(a)   was made by the design applicant or by a person that obtained the information directly or indirectly from the design applicant; and

(b)   occurred within 12 months prior to the filing date in the territory of the Party.

Article 20.54: Electronic Industrial Design System

Each Party shall provide a:

(a)   system for the electronic application for industrial design rights; and

(b)   publicly available electronic information system, which must include an online database of protected industrial designs.

---

[51] Articles 20.53 (Non-Prejudicial Disclosures/Grace Period) and 20.54 (Electronic Industrial Design System) apply with respect to industrial design patent systems or industrial design registration systems.

[52] For greater certainty, a Party may limit the application of this Article to disclosures made by, or obtained directly or indirectly from, the creator or co-creator and provide that, for the purposes of this Article, information obtained directly or indirectly from the design applicant may be information contained in the public disclosure that was authorized by, or derived from, the design applicant.

Article 20.55: Term of Protection

Each Party shall provide a term of protection for industrial designs of at least 15 years from either: (a) the date of filing, or (b) the date of grant or registration.

COMMENTARY: INTEGRATED CIRCUIT TOPOGRAPHY ACT

INTRODUCTION

These notes are intended to be a brief overview of the *Integrated Circuit Topography Act*. Readers should take caution that there are many details omitted and circumstances not considered. Other resources include the following:

- For a detailed legal text, see *Hughes on Copyright & Industrial Design*, Second Edition (LexisNexis Canada Inc.).

- For forms and precedents, see *Canadian Forms & Precedents, Intellectual Property* (LexisNexis Canada Inc.).

- For commentary and case digests respecting the *Federal Courts Act* and Rules, see *Canadian Federal Courts Practice* (annual publication) (LexisNexis Canada Inc.).

THE INTEGRATED CIRCUIT TOPOGRAPHY ACT

The *Integrated Circuit Topography Act* (S.C. 1990, c. 37) came into force May 1, 1993, and is designed to provide a limited form of monopoly protection for the three-dimensional integrated circuits used to perform electronic functions and the like. The Act provides protection to Canadians and, on a reciprocal basis, to nationals of other countries who are members of the World Treaty Organization.

In practice, there has been only a very limited number of registrations of such circuits made in Canada under the Act and no jurisprudence in respect of any such registration.

ADMINISTRATION OF THE INTEGRATED CIRCUIT TOPOGRAPHY ACT

The *Integrated Circuit Topography Act* is administered by the Canadian Intellectual Property Office, Registrar of Topographies.

WHAT IS AN INTEGRATED CIRCUIT TOPOGRAPHY?

Integrated circuit topography, which is the subject of the Act, includes a design, however expressed, of the disposition of interconnected elements for the making of a layer or layers added to the platform housing an electronic function. To be registered it must be original, the application must be filed within two years of first commercial exploitation (presumably anywhere) and must have been created by a Canadian or national of a reciprocating World Treaty Organization country.

An original design is one that is not merely a reproduction of the whole or substantial part of a previous topography and exhibits effort beyond the commonplace.

APPLICATION FOR REGISTRATION OF INTEGRATED CIRCUIT TOPOGRAPHY

An application to register Integrated Circuit Topography can be made by the creator, creator's assignee, or agent of such persons. That agent need not be a patent agent or trademark agent, simply an agent. Where the creator creates the topography in the course of employment by another, the employer is considered to be the creator. The term "creator" is not defined by the Act but it would appear that such person is a natural person, that it could be more than one person, and that such person or persons should have been the intellectual source of the finished circuit design.

The application shall give the circuit design a name and shall give the date of first commercial exploitation, if any, since no application should be filed after two years following such exploitation. A description of the circuit, visible to the naked eye, layer by layer, and a description of its function, must be given. Applications are open for public inspection.

REGISTRATION — TERM EFFECT AND VALIDITY

The registration of topography gives to the owner the exclusive right (a) to reproduce the topography; (b) to manufacture circuitry incorporating the topography; and (c) to import or commercially exploit circuitry incorporating the topography. No idea or concept, system, process, technique or information embodied in the topography is protected, just the circuitry itself.

Rights last until the end of the tenth calendar year after the earlier of the year of commercial exploitation or year of filing the application. The rights are registered and may be assigned or licensed, in whole or in part. A person whose application is refused may appeal to the Federal Court.

The Federal Court may expunge or amend a registration on the grounds of invalidity and may amend ownership of a registration. Validity may be challenged on the basis that the topography was not registrable that is, not new, or merely a commonplace variant, or that there was commercial exploitation more than two years before the application was filed or that incorrect information as to a material matter was wilfully included in the application.

INFRINGEMENT AND REMEDIES

Infringement occurs where any of the rights granted to the registered owner have been used without consent. There are exemptions provided for analysis and evaluation purposes, to deal in products of a previous owner, to make private non-commercial use of the circuitry, and for vessels and aircraft temporarily in Canada. Independent creations are exempted.

The Federal Court or appropriate court of an appropriate province has jurisdiction in respect of infringement actions. Relief including an injunction, damages or profits, punitive damages and dispositions of infringing articles may be made. There is a three-year limitation period. Interim determination of imported goods may be sought.

INTEGRATED CIRCUIT TOPOGRAPHY ACT

454

INTEGRATED CIRCUIT TOPOGRAPHY ACT

INTEGRATED CIRCUIT TOPOGRAPHY ACT

(S.C. 1990, c. 37)

Amendments: S.C. 1992, c. 1, s. 145 (Sched. VIII, s. 19) proclaimed in force February 28, 1992; S.C. 1993, c. 15, s. 25 proclaimed in force June 9, 1993; S.C. 1994, c. 47, ss. 129-131 proclaimed in force January 1, 1996; S.C. 1995, c. 1, ss. 62 and 63 proclaimed in force March 29, 1995; S.C. 2001, c. 4, s. 90 proclaimed in force June 1, 2001.

SHORT TITLE

1. This Act may be cited as the *Integrated Circuit Topography Act.*

INTERPRETATION

2. Definitions — (1) In this Act,

commercially exploit means to sell, lease, offer or exhibit for sale or lease, or otherwise distribute for a commercial purpose;

filing date, in respect of an application for registration of a topography, means the filing date of the application as determined in accordance with section 17;

integrated circuit product means a product in a final or intermediate form, that is intended to perform an electronic function and in which the elements, at least one of which is an active element, and some or all of the interconnections, are integrally formed in or on, or both in and on, a piece of material;

Minister means the Minister of Industry;
[S.C. 1995, c. 1, s. 62.]

national, in respect of a country, includes an individual who is a citizen or resident of, or is domiciled in, that country;

prescribed means prescribed by regulations;

register means the register kept pursuant to section 15;

registered topography means a topography that is registered under this Act;

Registrar means the Registrar of Topographies designated pursuant to section 25;

topography means the design, however expressed, of the disposition of

(a) the interconnections, if any, and the elements for the making of an integrated circuit product, or

(b) the elements, if any, and the interconnections for the making of a customization layer or layers to be added to an integrated circuit product in

457

an intermediate form.

(2) *Deemed importation or commercial exploitation* — For the purposes of this Act, where an integrated circuit product forms part of an article that is imported or commercially exploited, the integrated circuit products shall be deemed to be imported or commercially exploited, as the case may be.

(3) *First commercial exploitation of topography* — For the purposes of this Act, a topography is first commercially exploited when the topography or a substantial part thereof, or an integrated circuit product that incorporates the topography or a substantial part thereof, is commercially exploited for the first time in any place in the world by or with the consent of the person who owns the right to so commercially exploit the topography at that time and in that place.

(4) *Deemed creator of topography* — For the purposes of this Act, where a topography is created in the course of employment or pursuant to a contract, the employer or party to the contract for whom the topography was created shall be deemed to be the creator of the topography unless the employer and employee or the parties to the contract, as the case may be, otherwise agree.

HER MAJESTY

2.1. Binding on Her Majesty — This Act is binding on Her Majesty in right of Canada or a province.
[S.C. 1994, c. 47, s. 129.]

EXCLUSIVE RIGHT

3. Exclusive right on registration — (1) Subject to this Act, the registration of a topography under this Act, unless shown to be invalid, gives to the creator of the topography or, where the topography has been transferred, the successor in title thereto, an exclusive right in the topography for the duration of the period referred to in section 5.

(2) *Scope of exclusive right* — The exclusive right in a registered topography consists of the exclusive right to

(*a*) reproduce the topography or any substantial part thereof;

(*b*) manufacture an integrated circuit product incorporating the topography or any substantial part thereof; and

(*c*) import or commercially exploit the topography or any substantial part thereof or an integrated circuit product that incorporates the topography or any substantial part thereof.

(3) *Rights not conferred* — Nothing in this section confers any rights in relation to any idea, concept, process, system, technique or information that may be embodied in a topography or an integrated circuit product.

4. Conditions of registration — (1) Subject to subsection (4), a topography is registrable under this Act only if the following conditions are met:

(*a*) the topography is original;

(*b*) an application for registration of the topography, containing the information and material required by subsection 16(2) and accompanied by the fee required by subsection 16(3), is filed with the Registrar before the topography is first commercially exploited or within two years thereafter; and

(*c*) the creator of the topography is, at the time of its creation or on the filing date of the application,

    (i) a national of Canada or an individual or legal entity that has in Canada a real and effective establishment for the creation of topographies or the manufacture of integrated circuit products.

    (ii) a national of a country that, either directly or through its membership in an intergovernmental organization, affords protection for topographies in accordance with a convention or treaty to which that country or inter governmental organization and Canada are contracting parties, or an individual or legal entity that has in such a country or in the territory of a member state of such an intergovernmental organization an establishment of the kind referred to in subparagraph (i),

    (iii) a national of a country or of a member state of an intergovernmental organization that the Minister has certified by notice published in the *Canada Gazette* to be a country or intergovernmental organization that confers protection on nationals of Canada or legal entities that have an establishment of the kind referred to in subparagraph (i) that is substantially equal to the protection conferred by this Act, or an individual or legal entity that has in such a country or in the territory of a member state of such an intergovernmental organization an establishment of that kind, or

[S.C. 1993, c. 15, s. 25.]

    (iv) a national of a WTO Member.

[S.C. 1994, c. 47, s. 130(1).]

(2) *Originality* — For the purposes of subsection (1), a topography is original if the following conditions are met:

(*a*) it has not been produced by the mere reproduction of another topography or of any substantial part thereof; and

(*b*) it is the result of an intellectual effort and is not, at the time of its creation, commonplace among creators of topographies or manufacturers of integrated circuit products.

(3) *Combinations of elements or interconnections* — Where a topography consists of a combination of elements of interconnections that are commonplace among creators of topographies or manufacturers of integrated circuit products, the topography shall be considered to be original only if the combination, considered as a whole, meets the conditions referred to in subsection (2).

(4) *Exception* — A topography that is not registrable by reason that the condition set out in paragraph (1)(*c*) cannot be met is registrable if the topography is first commercially exploited in Canada.

(5) *Definitions* — In this section,

Commissioner means the Commissioner of Patents;

WTO Agreement has the meaning given to the word "Agreement" by subsection 2(1) of the *World Trade Organization Agreement Implementation Act*;

WTO Member means a Member of the World Trade Organization established by Article I of the WTO Agreement.

[S.C. 1994, c. 47, s. 130(2).]

5. Duration of exclusive right — The exclusive right in a registered topography shall subsists for a period

(*a*)　commencing on the filing date of the application for registration of the topography; and

(*b*)　terminating at the end of the tenth calendar year after the earlier of the calendar year in which the topography is first commercially exploited and the calendar year of the filing date of the application.

6. Infringement — (1) The exclusive right in a registered topography is infringed by any person who does any act referred to in subsection 3(2) without the consent of the owner of the registered topography.

(2) *No infringement* — Notwithstanding subsection (1), it is not an infringement of the exclusive right in a registered topography for any person

(*a*)　to do any act referred to in paragraph 3(2)(*a*) or (*b*) in relation to that registered topography for the sole purpose of analysis or evaluation or of research or teaching with respect to topographies;

(*b*)　to do any act referred to in subsection 3(2) in relation to another topography that is created on the basis of the analysis, evaluation or research referred to in paragraph (*a*) and that is original within the meaning of subsection 4(2) or (3);

(*c*)　to do any act referred to in paragraph 3(2)(*c*) in relation to a particular integrated circuit product that incorporates that registered topography or a substantial part thereof, at any time after the time at which that particular integrated circuit product is sold in any place by or with the consent of the person who owned the right to sell that registered topography at that time and in that place;

(*d*) to do any act referred to in subsection 3(2) where that act is done for a private and non-commercial purpose; or

(*e*) to bring an integrated circuit product that incorporates that registered topography or a substantial part thereof temporarily into Canada if that integrated circuit product forms part of a vehicle, vessel, aircraft or spacecraft registered in a country other than Canada that enters Canada temporarily or accidentally and is used for a purpose that is necessary or ancillary to that vehicle, vessel, aircraft or spacecraft.

(3) *No infringement* — For greater certainty, it is not an infringement of the exclusive right in a registered topography for any person to do any act referred to in subsection 3(2) in relation to another topography that is independently created.

7. Transfer of topography — (1) A topography, whether registered or unregistered, is transfer able, either as to the whole interest therein or as to any undivided portion thereof.

(2) *Licence* — A topography, whether registered or unregistered and either as to the whole interest therein or as to any portion thereof, may constitute the subject-matter of a licence.

7.1. Government may apply to use registered topograph — (1) Subject to section 7.2, the Commissioner may, on application by the Government of Canada or the government of a province, authorize the public non-commercial use of a registered topography by that government.

(2) *Terms of use* — Subject to section 7.2, the use of the registered topography may be authorized for such purpose, for such period and on such other terms as the Commissioner considers expedient, but the Commissioner shall settle those terms in accordance with the following principles:

(*a*) the scope and duration of the use shall be limited to the purpose for which the use is authorized;

(*b*) the use authorized shall be non-exclusive; and

(*c*) any use shall be authorized predominantly to supply the domestic market.

(3) *Notice* — The Commissioner shall notify the owner of the registered topography of any use of the registered topography that is authorized under this section.

(4) *Payment of remuneration* — Where the use of the registered topography is authorized, the authorized user shall pay to the owner of the registered topography

such amount as the Commissioner considers to be adequate remuneration in the circumstances, taking into account the economic value of the authorization.

(5) *Termination of authorization* — The Commissioner may, on application by the owner of the registered topography and after giving all concerned parties an opportunity to be heard, terminate the authorization if the Commissioner is satisfied that the circumstances that led to the granting of the authorization have ceased to exist and are unlikely to recur, subject to such conditions as the Commissioner deems appropriate to protect the legitimate interests of the authorized user.

(6) *Authorization not transferable* — An authorization granted under this section is not transferable.

[S.C. 1994, c. 47, s. 131.]

7.2. Prescribed uses — The Commissioner may not, under section 7.1, authorize any use that is a prescribed use unless the proposed user complies with the prescribed conditions.

[S.C. 1994, c. 47, s. 131.]

7.3. Appeal — Any decision made by the Commissioner under section 7.1 or 7.2 is subject to appeal to the Federal Court under the *Patent Act.*

[S.C. 1994, c. 47, s. 131.]

7.4. Regulations — (1) The Governor in Council may make regulations for the purpose of implementing, in relation to registered topographies, paragraph 2 of Article 37 of the Agreement on Trade-related Aspects of Intellectual Property Rights set out in Annex 1C to the WTO Agreement.

(2) *Definition of WTO Agreement* — In subsection (1), *WTO Agreement* has the same meaning as in subsection 4(5).

[S.C. 1994, c. 47, s. 131.]

LEGAL PROCEEDINGS

ACTION FOR INFRINGEMENT

8. Action for infringement — (1) An action for infringement of the exclusive right in a registered topography may be brought in any court of competent jurisdiction by the owner of the registered topography or by a licensee of any right therein, subject to any agreement between the licensee and the owner.

(2) *Each owner to be party* — Each owner of a registered topography shall be or be made a party to any action for infringement of the exclusive right therein.

9. Power of court to grant relief — In an action for infringement of the exclusive right in a registered topography, a court of competent jurisdiction may make such orders as the circumstances require, including orders providing for relief by way of injunction, the payment of royalties and the recovery of dam ages or profits, for punitive damages, and for the disposal of any infringing integrated circuit product or any article of which an infringing integrated circuit product forms a part.

10. Innocent infringement — Where the exclusive right in a registered topography is infringed by reason of the commercial exploitation or importation of an integrated circuit product that incorporates the registered topography or a substantial part thereof and the defendant in an action for infringement establishes that, at the time the defendant acquired the integrated circuit product, the defendant did not know and had no reasonable grounds to believe that the integrated circuit product was manufactured and sold for the first time without the consent of the owner of the registered topography, the defendant

(*a*) is not liable for royalties, damages, profits or punitive damages in respect of any dealings with the integrated circuit product prior to the time when the defendant had actual knowledge that the product was manufactured and sold for the first time without the consent of the owner; and

(*b*) shall have the right to dispose of any inventory of the integrated circuit product or of the article of which the integrated circuit product forms a part that was acquired before the defendant had that knowledge, subject to the condition that the defendant pay a reasonable royalty in respect of that inventory in such amount and at such time as the court may determine.

11. Infringement after commercial exploitation in Canada — (1) Where an integrated circuit product that incorporates a registered topography or a substantial part thereof is commercially exploited in Canada by or with the consent of the owner of the registered topography and an action for infringement is commenced in respect of an act of infringement committed after that commercial exploitation, the plaintiff is not entitled to any relief under section 9 other than by way of an injunction if the defendant establishes that, at the time of the infringement, the defendant was not aware and had no reasonable grounds to suspect that the topography was registered.

(2) *Exception* — Subsection (1) does not apply if the plaintiff establishes that all or substantially all of the integrated circuit products that were commercially exploited in Canada by or with the consent of the owner of the registered topography before the infringement, or all or substantially all of the containers housing those integrated circuit products, were visibly marked with a title of the topography that is substantially the same as a title there of that, at the time of the infringement, appeared on the register.

12. Limitation period — (1) Subject to subsection (2), no royalties, damages, profits or punitive damages may be awarded for any act of infringement committed more than three years before the commencement of the action for infringement.

(2) *Exception* — The limitation period described in subsection (1) does not apply if

(*a*) the infringement is of such a nature that, at the time of its commission, it would not have come to the attention of a reasonably diligent owner or licensee of any right in the registered topography; and

(*b*)   the action for infringement is commenced within three years after the infringement came or should have come to the attention of the plaintiff.

13. Changes in register not applicable — If any person has relied to the detriment of that person on any entry in the register as it read before being expunged or amended pursuant to this Act or any other Act of Parliament, a court of competent jurisdiction may order that the expungement or amendment not apply in any action for infringement of the exclusive right in a registered topography taken against that person or against any other person who has acquired from that person an integrated circuit product that incorporates the topography or a substantial part thereof.

OTHER PROCEEDINGS

14. Detention of infringing integrated circuit products — (1) Where it is made to appear to a court of competent jurisdiction that an integrated circuit product has been imported into Canada or is about to be commercially exploited in Canada contrary to this Act, the court may make an order for the interim detention of the integrated circuit product or any article of which the integrated circuit product forms a part, pending a final determination of the legality of the importation or commercial exploitation in an action commenced within such time as is specified in the order.

(2) *Security* — Before an order is made under subsection (1), the plaintiff or petitioner may be required to furnish security, in such form and in such amount as the court may determine, to answer any damages that may by reason of the order be sustained by the owner or consignee of the integrated circuit product or article and for any costs of storage or amount that may become chargeable against the integrated circuit product or article while it remains in detention under the order.

(3) *Indemnity* — Subject to paragraph (4)(*c*), the plaintiff or petitioner in an action referred to in subsection (1) shall be liable to indemnify Her Majesty in right of Canada against any liability or expense that may result from the detention of an integrated circuit product or article pursuant to any order made under subsection (1), whether or not security is furnished pursuant to subsection (2).

(4) *Lien, disposal and indemnity* — Where, by the judgment in an action referred to in subsection (1) that finally determines the legality of the importation or commercial exploitation of the integrated circuit product, the court finds that the importation is or the commercial exploitation would be contrary to this Act.

(*a*)   any lien for charges against the integrated circuit product or article, or any hypothecs, prior claims or rights of retention within the meaning of the Civil Code of Québec or any other statute of the Province of Québec with respect to the integrated circuit product or article, that existed prior to the date of an order made under subsection (1) has effect only so far as may be consistent with the due execution of the judgment;

(b) the court may make any order for the disposal of the integrated circuit product or article, including by way of exportation, distribution or destruction, after payment has been made of any taxes or duties owing in respect thereof under any Act of Parliament; and

(c) the owner or consignee of the integrated circuit product or article thereupon becomes jointly and severally liable, with the plaintiff or petitioner, to indemnify Her Majesty in right of Canada under subsection (3).

(5) *Who may make applications* — Any order under subsection (1) may be made on the application of any interested person either in an action or otherwise and either on notice or *ex parte*.
[S.C. 2001, c. 4, s. 90.]

GENERAL

REGISTRATION

15. Register — (1) There shall be kept under the supervision of the Registrar a register for the registration of topographies and of information and material relating to each registered topography.

(2) *Register to be evidence*— The register is evidence of the particulars entered therein and documents purporting to be copies of entries therein or extracts therefrom, that are certified by the Registrar, are admissible in evidence in any court without further proof or production of the originals.

16. Application for registration of topography — (1) The creator of a topography or, where the topography has been transferred, the successor in title thereto may apply to the Registrar for registration of the topography.

(2) *Content of application* — An application for registration of a topography shall contain the following information and material:

(a) one or more titles to identify the topography that conform to the prescribed requirements;

(b) the date on which, and place at which, the topography was first commercially exploited or, if the topography has not been commercially exploited, a statement to that effect;

(c) the name and address of the applicant;

(d) a statement describing the interest that the applicant holds in the topography; and

(e) such other information or material as may be prescribed.

(3) *Fee* — An application for registration of a topography shall be accompanied by the prescribed fee or a fee determined in the prescribed manner.

17. Filing date — (1) Subject to subsection (2), the filing date of an application for registration of a topography is the date on which the Registrar has received, in respect of the application, the information and material required by subsection 16(2) and the fee required by subsection 16(3).

(2) *Exception* — The Registrar may, in such circumstances as are prescribed, assign a filing date to an application for registration of a topography notwithstanding that the requirements of subsection (1) have not been met.

(3) *Notice to applicant* — Where the Registrar assigns a filing date to an application for registration of a topography pursuant to subsection (2), the Registrar shall notify the applicant of that date, of any information or material that is required to complete the application and the amount of the fee, if any, that remains unpaid.

(4) *Obligations of applicant* — An applicant to whom notice is given in accordance with subsection (3) shall, within the prescribed period, file with the Registrar the information or material, if any, that is required to complete the application and the amount of the fee, if any, that remains unpaid and, in default thereof, shall be deemed to have abandoned the application.

18. Registration of topography — (1) Subject to subsection (3), where the Registrar has received the information and material required by subsection 16(2) and the fee required by subsection 16(3) in respect of an application for registration of a topography, the Registrar shall register the topography by entering in the register the following:

(*a*)   the filing date of the application;

(*b*)   the title or titles of the topography that are contained in the application and that conform to the prescribed requirements; and

(*c*)   such other information or material as may be prescribed.

(2) *No inquiry* — The Registrar shall not inquire as to the accuracy of any information or material contained in an application for registration of a topography.

(3) *Registrar may refuse to register* — The Registrar may refuse to register a topography if it appears to the Registrar, on the basis of any information or material contained in the application for registration, that the application was filed more than two years after the topography was first commercially exploited or that neither the condition set out in paragraph 4(1)(*c*) nor the condition set out in subsection 4(4) has been met.

19. Certificate of registration — (1) The Registrar shall issue a certificate of registration in respect of each topography registered under this Act.

(2) *Contents of certificate* — A certificate of registration issued in respect of a topography shall include the filing date of the application for registration of the topography, the date of expiration of the exclusive right therein and such other

particulars as may be prescribed.

(3) *Presumptions* — A certificate of registration issued in respect of a topography that purports to be signed by the Registrar is, with out proof of the signature, admissible in any court as evidence of the facts therein alleged and is, in the absence of evidence to the contrary, proof that

(*a*) the topography was registrable under this Act at the time of the registration; and

(*b*) the application for registration of the topography was correct in all material particulars and did not omit any material information.

(4) *Correction of errors* — The Registrar may, for the purpose of correcting any typographical or clerical error in a certificate of registration, amend the certificate or issue a new certificate in substitution therefor.

20. Invalidity of registration — The registration of a topography is invalid if

(*a*) the topography was not registrable under this Act at the time of the registration; or

(*b*) the application for registration of the topography was incorrect in a material particular or omitted any material information, unless the incorrectness or omission occurred by mistake.

21. Registration of other particulars — (1) The Registrar shall enter in the register particulars of any transfer of an interest or grant of a licence affecting a registered topography on being furnished with evidence of the transfer or grant that is satisfactory to the Registrar.

(2) *Changes in information* — The Registrar may amend any entry in the register, or make new entries, for any of the following purposes:

(*a*) to reflect any change in the name or address of an owner of a registered topography;

(*b*) to reflect any change in a registered title of a topography or the use of a new title;

(*c*) to reflect any prescribed change of information; and

(*d*) to correct any typographical or clerical error.

22. Public inspection — Subject to the regulations, the register, applications for registration of topographies and material filed with the Registrar in relation to any registered topography shall be made available for public inspection during regular business hours.

JURISDICTION OF FEDERAL COURT

23. Concurrent jurisdiction — The Federal Court has concurrent jurisdiction to hear and determine

(*a*) any action for the infringement of the exclusive right in a registered topography; and

(*b*) any question relating to the ownership of a topography or any right in a topography.

24. Exclusive jurisdiction — (1) The Federal Court has exclusive original jurisdiction, on application of any interested person, to order that the registration of a topography or any other entry in the register be expunged or amended on the ground that the registration is invalid or that, at the date of the application, the entry as it appears does not accurately express or define the existing rights of any person appearing on the register as the owner of the topography.

(2) *Application* — An application under subsection (1) may be made by the filing of an originating notice of motion, by counterclaim in an action for infringement or by statement of claim in an action claiming additional relief under this Act.

(3) *Definition of **interested person*** — In subsection (1), ***interested person*** includes the Registrar, the Attorney General of Canada and persons who are affected or who reasonably apprehend that they may be affected by any entry in the register.

REGISTRAR

25. Appointment of Registrar — (1) There shall be a Registrar of Topographies who shall be designated by the Minister from among persons employed in the Department of Industry.
[S.C. 1995, c. 1, s. 63.]

(2) *Duties* — The Registrar shall perform the duties assigned to the Registrar by this Act and such duties as may be assigned to the Registrar by the regulations or by the Minister.

(3) *Acting Registrar* — Where the Registrar is absent or unable to act or the office of Registrar is vacant, the Minister may designate any other person employed in the Department of Industry to perform the duties and exercise the powers of the Registrar for the time being.

OTHER RIGHTS

26. Relationship to other law — Except as provided in this Act, nothing in this Act shall affect any right granted by or under any other law.

REGULATIONS

27. Regulations — The Governor in Council may make regulations (*a*) governing the form of the register, including any indexes thereto, and the entries to be made therein;

(*b*) governing the filing of copies of documents in the register;

(*c*) governing public inspection of the register, of applications for registration of topographies and of material filed with the Registrar in relation to any registered topography;

(*d*) governing, restricting or prohibiting the making or providing of copies of applications for registration of topographies and of material filed with the Registrar in relation to any registered topography;

(*e*) assigning duties to the Registrar;

(*f*) prescribing fees, or the manner of determining the fees, to be paid for any act or service rendered by the Registrar;

(*g*) prescribing any other matter or thing that by this Act is to be or may be prescribed; and

(*h*) generally for carrying out the purposes and provisions of this Act.

MINISTERIAL REVIEW

28. Review of Act — (1) Five years after the coming into force of this Act, the Minister shall undertake a review of the provisions and operation of this Act.

(2) *Report to Parliament*— The Minister shall, within one year after undertaking the review referred to in subsection (1), submit a report on the review to each House of Parliament.

. . .

RELATED PROVISION OF S.C. 1994, C. 47

131. (2) *No liability* — Her Majesty in right of Canada or a province is not, by reason only of the enactment of subsection (1), liable for any use of a registered topography before the day on which subsection (1) comes into force.

REGULATIONS RESPECTING THE PROTECTION OF INTEGRATED CIRCUIT TOPOGRAPHIES

(SOR/93-212)

Amendments: SOR/2007-94 filed May 3, 2007, gazetted May 16, 2007, in force June 2, 2007.

SHORT TITLE

1. These Regulations may be cited as the *Integrated Circuit Topography Regulations*.

INTERPRETATION

2. In these Regulations,

Act means the *Integrated Circuit Topography Act*;

agent means a person or firm appointed by an applicant pursuant to section 10;

applicant means the creator of a topography or, where the topography has been transferred, the successor in title thereto who applies for registration of a topography pursuant to section 16 of the Act;

application means an application for registration of a topography made pursuant to section 16 of the Act;

drawing includes a plot;

Office means the Office of the Registrar of Topographies;

representative for service means a person or firm in Canada appointed by an applicant or the owner of a registered topography pursuant to section 11.

COMMUNICATIONS

3. (1) Correspondence intended for the Registrar or the Office shall be addressed to the "Registrar of Topographies".

(2) Correspondence addressed to the Registrar may be physically delivered to the Office during ordinary business hours of the Office and is considered to be received by the Registrar on the day of the delivery.

(3) For the purposes of subsection (2), if the correspondence is physically delivered to the Office outside of its ordinary business hours, it is considered to have been delivered to the Office during ordinary business hours on the day when the Office is next open for business.

(4) Correspondence addressed to the Registrar may be physically delivered to an establishment that is designated by the Registrar in the *Canadian Patent Office Record* as an establishment to which correspondence addressed to the Registrar may be delivered, during ordinary business hours of that establishment, and

(*a*)   if the delivery is made to the establishment on a day that the Office is open for business, the correspondence is considered to be received by the Registrar on that day; and

(*b*)   if the delivery is made to the establishment on a day that the Office is closed for business, the correspondence is considered to be received by the Registrar on the day when the Office is next open for business.

(5) For the purposes of subsection (4), if the correspondence is physically delivered to an establishment outside of ordinary business hours of the establishment, it is considered to have been delivered to that establishment during ordinary business hours on the day when the establishment is next open for business.

(6) Correspondence addressed to the Registrar may be sent at any time by electronic or other means of transmission specified by the Registrar in the *Canadian Patent Office Record*.

(7) For the purposes of subsection (6), if, according to the local time of the place where the Office is located, the correspondence is delivered on a day when the Office is open for business, it is considered to be received by the Registrar on that day.

(8) For the purposes of subsection (6), if, according to the local time of the place where the Office is located, the correspondence is delivered on a day when the Office is closed for business, it is considered to be received by the Registrar on the day when the Office is next open for business.
[SOR/2007-94, s. 1.]

4. (1) Subject to subsection (2), all communications relating to an application or a registered topography shall be made in writing or by electronic transmission.

(2) The Registrar may, where the circumstances require, have regard to an oral communication made in relation to an application or a registered topography.

5. (1) Subject to subsection (2), all correspondence addressed to the Registrar shall deal with only one application or registered topography.

(2) Subsection (1) does not apply in respect of correspondence relating to

(*a*)   a transfer of an interest or grant of a licence affecting a registered topography, referred to in subsection 21(1) of the Act;

(*b*)   a change in the name or address of an owner of more than one registered topography;

(c) a change in the name or address of an applicant for the registration of more than one topography;

(d) a change in the name or address of the representative for service of an owner of more than one registered topography; or

(e) a change in the name or address of the representative for service or the agent of an applicant for the registration of more than one topography.

6. (1) Subject to subsection (2), every person who is required by the Act or these Regulations to furnish an address shall furnish a complete postal address, including a street name and number where applicable.

(2) A person referred to in subsection (1) may furnish, in addition to the required postal address, another address to which correspondence may be mailed.

7. (1) Correspondence relating to an application shall include

(a) the application number, if one has been assigned;

(b) the name of the applicant; and

(c) the title or titles of the topography.

(2) Correspondence relating to a registered topography shall include

(a) the registration number of the topography;

(b) the name of the owner of the topography; and

(c) the title or titles of the topography.

8. (1) Subject to subsection (2), correspondence relating to an application shall be conducted with

(a) the applicant, where there is only one applicant; or

(b) where there is more than one applicant,

    (i) the applicant authorized by the other applicant or applicants to act on their behalf, or

    (ii) the first applicant named in the application, where no applicant has been authorized in accordance with subparagraph (i).

(2) Correspondence relating to an application shall be conducted with an agent where the agent

(a) has signed the application;

(b) has transmitted the application to the Office; or

(c) has notified the Office of the agent's appointment.

9. No regard shall be had to any correspondence relating to an application that is received from any person or firm other than the person or firm with whom correspondence on the subject of the application is being conducted.

APPOINTMENT OF AGENT

10. (1) An applicant may appoint a person or firm as an agent to act on behalf of the applicant.

(2) Subject to subsection (3), the appointment of an agent need not be made in writing.

(3) The Registrar may, where the circumstances require, request that an agent file a written appointment within a period that the Registrar deems appropriate in the circumstances.

(4) Where an agent fails to file a written appointment as requested pursuant to subsection (3), the Registrar shall give notice to the agent that any further correspondence will be conducted with the applicant until a written appointment is filed.

APPOINTMENT OF REPRESENTATIVE FOR SERVICE

11. (1) An applicant or the owner of a registered topography may appoint a person or firm in Canada as a representative for service.

(2) A notice sent to or a proceeding served on a representative for service has the same effect as if the notice were sent to or the proceeding were served on the applicant or the owner of the registered topography, as the case may be.

APPLICATION

12. (1) An application and any amendment thereto shall be in one of the official languages and shall bear the signature of the applicant or the applicant's agent.

(2) A separate application shall be made for each topography.

13. An application shall contain, in addition to the information and material required by paragraphs 16(2)(*a*) to (*d*) of the Act, the following information:

(*a*) where the applicant has no office or place of business in Canada, the name and address of a representative for service;

(*b*) where an agent has been appointed, the name and address of the agent;

(*c*) a description of the material filed, including, where the topography consists of layers and contains confidential information, the number of layers and the number of layers in relation to which section 15 or 16 has been relied on; and

(*d*) a description of the nature or function of the topography.

14. (1) Subject to these Regulations, an application shall contain, in addition to the information and material required by paragraphs 16(2)(*a*) to (*d*) of the Act, a complete set of overlay sheets, drawings or photographs of the topography.

(2) The material referred to in subsection (1) shall be sufficiently magnified so that the design of the topography is clearly visible to the naked eye.

(3) Where the material referred to in subsection (1) consists of more than one sheet, drawing or photograph, the sheets, drawings or photographs shall be numbered consecutively.

15. Where a topography that consists of more than two layers contains confidential information, an application may contain, instead of a complete set of overlay sheets, drawings or photographs as required by section 14, a set that contains the same total number of sheets, drawings or photographs, but that includes a selected number of sheets, drawings or photographs on which is blocked out up to 50 per cent of the total area covered by those sheets, drawings or photographs, if

(*a*)   the selected sheets, drawings or photographs are clearly indicated in the application;

(*b*)   the number of sheets, drawings or photographs selected does not exceed 50 per cent of the total number of sheets, drawings or photographs, said total number having been reduced by one where it is an odd number; and

(*c*)   the application contains topography design data in printed form for the areas that are blocked out; however, up to 50 per cent of these data may be blocked out, if the application contains four or more integrated circuit products incorporating the topography.

16. Where a topography contains confidential information and has not been commercially exploited at the filing date of an application, the application may contain, instead of the material referred to in section 14,

(*a*)   the topography design data in printed form, of which up to 50 per cent may be blocked out; and

(*b*)   a composite drawing or photograph of the topography, on which up to 50 per cent of each layer of the topography is blocked out.

17. Any topography design data in printed form or integrated circuit products shall be filed at the time of or subsequent to the filing of the other material referred to in section 14, 15 or 16 and on or before the date of registration of the topography.

18. All material filed pursuant to section 14, 15, 16 or 17 shall be identified by a title consisting of letters of the Roman alphabet, Arabic numerals or a combination thereof.

19. All material filed pursuant to section 14, 15 or 16 and all topography design data in printed form referred to in section 17 shall be in a storable size, either folded or otherwise, and shall be (*a*)   not more than 21.5 cm × 28 cm (8½ inches × 11 inches); or

(*b*)   in A4 format.

AMENDMENT OF APPLICATION

20. (1) Subject to subsection (2), an applicant may, at any time prior to the registration of a topography, on submitting any necessary information and material and on payment of the applicable fee set out in the schedule, request that the Registrar amend the applicant's application.

(2) The Registrar shall not make any amendment to an application that would substantially alter the topography to which the application relates.

REGISTER

21. In addition to the information required by the Act to be entered in the register, the Registrar shall enter in the register

(*a*)   all information filed pursuant to section 13; and

(*b*)   all material filed pursuant to section 14, 15, 16 or 17.

AMENDMENT OF REGISTER

22. For the purposes of paragraph 21(2)(*c*) of the Act, the Registrar may amend the register to reflect any change in the name or address of a representative for service.

CERTIFICATE OF REGISTRATION

23. A certificate of registration issued in respect of a topography shall include, in addition to the particulars required by subsection 19(2) of the Act, the following particulars;

(*a*)   the name and address of the registered owner of the topography;

(*b*)   the title of the topography;

(*c*)   where the topography has been commercially exploited, the date on which and place at which the topography was first commercially exploited;

(*e*)   the date of registration of the topography; and

(*f*)   the registration number of the topography.

TRANSFER OF INTEREST

24. A person to whom an application or an interest affecting a registered topography is transferred shall, if the person has no office or place of business in Canada, provide the Registrar with the name and address of a representative for service.

PUBLIC INSPECTION AND COPIES

25. An application shall not be available for public inspection until it has been assigned an application number.

26. Except with the written consent of the applicant or the owner of a registered topography, as the case may be, no person shall, by any means, make or provide a copy of any material filed pursuant to section 14, 15, 16 or 17.

TRANSMISSION TO COURT

27. If an application has been made to the Federal Court under subsection 24(1) of the Act, the Registrar shall, at the request of any of the parties, transmit to that Court all material on file in the Office relating to the application.
[SOR/2007-94, s. 2.]

FEES

28. The fees to be paid for acts or services rendered by the Registrar are as set out in the schedule and the appropriate fees shall be paid in Canadian funds to the Receiver General at the time any act or service is requested.

SCHEDULE

(Subsection 20(1) and sections 27 and 28)

TARIFF OF FEES

1.	Filing an application	$200.00
2.	Amending an application in accordance with a request made pursuant to subsection 20(1) of these Regulations	75.00
3.	Entering in the register particulars of a transfer of an interest or grant of a licence affecting a registered topography pursuant to subsection 21(1) of the Act	75.00
4.	Amending an entry in the register or making a new entry therein pursuant to subsection 21(2) of the Act	75.00
5.	Amending a certificate of registration or issuing a new certificate, pursuant to subsection 19(4) of the Act, for the purpose of correcting a typographical or clerical error made as a result of incorrect information provided by the applicant	75.00
6.	[Repealed, SOR/2007-94, s. 3]	
7.	Providing a copy of a document, of entries in or extracts from the register or of any material referred to in section 26 of these Regulations, for each page measuring 21.5 cm × 28 cm (8½ inches × 11 inches) or less	5.00
8.	Providing a certified copy of a document referred to in subsection 15(2) of the Act, other than a certified copy made under Rule 318 or 350 of the *Federal Courts Rules*	50.00

[SOR/2007-94, ss. 3, 4.]

LIST OF COUNTRIES TO WHICH CANADA ACCORDS RECIPROCAL PROTECTION UNDER THE ACT

(SOR/93-282)

Note: SOR/93-282 filed May 28, 1993, gazetted June 16, 1993, in force May 28, 1993.

Amendments: SOR/94-677.

The Minister of Consumer and Corporate Affairs pursuant to subparagraph 4(1)(c)(iii) of the *Integrated Circuit Topography Act,** hereby certifies that the countries listed in the schedule hereto are countries that confer protection that is substantially equal to the protection conferred by that Act on nationals of Canada and individuals or legal entities that have in Canada a real and effective establishment for the creation of topographies or the manufacture of integrated circuit products.

* S.C. 1990, c. 37

SCHEDULE

Australia

Austria

Belgium

Denmark

Finland

France

Germany

Greece

Iceland

Ireland

Italy

Japan

Luxembourg

Netherlands

Norway

Portugal

Spain

Sweden

United Kingdom of Great Britain and Northern Ireland

United States of America

[SOR/94-677.]

ORDER ACCORDING RECIPROCAL PROTECTION TO SWITZERLAND UNDER THE ACT

(SOR/94-27)

Note: SOR/94-27 filed January 11, 1994, gazetted January 26, 1994, in force January 11, 1994.

The Minister of Industry, Science and Technology, pursuant to subparagraph 4(1)(*c*)(iii)* of the *Integrated Circuit Topography Act***, hereby certifies that Switzerland is a country that confers protection that is substantially equal to the protection conferred by that Act on nationals of Canada and individuals or legal entities that have in Canada a real and effective establishment for the creation of topographies or the manufacture of integrated circuit products.

---

* S.C. 1993, c. 15, s. 25
** S.C. 1990, c. 37

INDEX LEGEND

BCPLAW	Berne Convention for Protection of Literary and Artistic Works
BIR	Book Importation Regulations
Ch.	transitional provisions of the *Copyright Act*
CN	Certification of Countries Granting Equal Copyright Protection Notice
CR	Copyright Regulations
CUSMA	Canada–United States–Mexico Agreement
CWR	Cinematographic Works (Right to Remuneration) Regulations
ELAMR	Exceptions for Educational Institutions, Libraries, Archives and Museums Regulations
EPCR	Regulations Establishing the Periods Within which Eligible Authors, Eligible Performers and Eligible Makers not Represented by Collective Societies Can Claim Private Copying Remuneration
EPWOR	Educational Program, Work and Other Subject-matter Record-keeping Regulations
ICA	*Integrated Circuit Topography Act*
ICR	Integrated Circuit Topography Regulations
IDA	*Industrial Design Act*
IDR	Industrial Design Regulations
LCCA	List of Countries to Which Canada Accords Reciprocal Protection under the Act
LSDSR	Definition of Local Signal and Distant Signal Regulations
MSDR	MicroSD Cards Exclusion Regulations
MT	Marrakesh Treaty to Facilitate Access to Published Works for Persons Who Are Blind, Visually Impaired, or Otherwise Print Disabled
OARPS	Order According Reciprocal Protection to Switzerland under the Act
OCRR	Regulations Establishing the Period Within which Owners of Copyright not Represented by Collective Societies Can Claim Retransmission Royalties
ODMUCFA	Order Designating Ministers under Certain Federal Acts
PUR	Programming Undertaking Regulations
RDAR	Regulations Defining Advertising Revenues
RPN	Regulations Prescribing Networks
RRCR	Retransmission Royalties Criteria Regulations
SCTSR	Definition of Small Cable Transmission System Regulations
SLRER	Statement Limiting the Right to Equitable Remuneration of Certain Rome Convention or WPPT Countries
SRSR	Definition of Small Retransmission Systems Regulations
TLBCBR	Time Limits on Related Matters Before the Copyright Board Regulations

INDEX LEGEND

TRIPS	Agreement on Trade-Related Aspects of Intellectual Property Rights
UCC	Universal Copyright Convention
WCT	WIPO Copyright Treaty
WPPT	WIPO Performances and Phonograms Treaty
WTSR	Definition of Wireless Transmission System Regulations

INDEX

COPYRIGHT—Cont.
Non-commercial user generated content
. . . 29.21
Non-profit organization, definition . . . 32.02
Ownership
  Assignment of . . . 13(4), 13(6), 25
  Author, by . . . 13(1)
  Employment, work made in course of
  . . . 13(3)
  Licence . . . 13(4), 13(7)
  Limitations re . . . 14
  Presumption re . . . 34.1
Print disability outside Canada . . . 32.01
Registration
  Application, defects in . . . CR7
  Application, fee . . . 54, CR5, 8–9, Sch.
  Assignment or licence, of . . . 57
    Request for . . . CR6-9, Sch.
Remedies . . . 34
Remuneration
  Cinematographic works . . . CWR1–2
  Equitable
    Limitations on . . . SLRER1–7
Reproduction
  For later listening or viewing . . . 29.23
  For private purposes . . . 29.22
Restoration
  Compensation for . . . 33(2), 78
  Rights protected . . . 32.4–33
Review of Act . . . 92
Term
  Generally . . . 6
  Crown publications . . . 12
  Death of author, after . . . 8
  Joint authorship . . . 9
    Posthumous works, for . . . 7
Works subject to . . . 5

COPYRIGHT ACT
Application . . . 89
Interpretation . . . 2–2.7, 90
Regulations . . . CR1–11
Review . . . 92
Short title . . . 1
Time limits in respect of matters before Board
  regulations . . . TLBCBR1-12

COPYRIGHT BOARD
Case manager, assignment of . . . 66.504
Chairman of, duties of . . . 66.1
Conflict of interest prohibited . . . 66.3
Decisions, variation of . . . 66.52
Establishment of . . . 66
Fair and equitable . . . 66.501
Greater certainty, for . . . 66.503
Informal and expeditious handling of matters
  . . . 66.502

COPYRIGHT BOARD—Cont.
Interim decisions . . . 66.51
Membership expiration of . . . 66.5
Notice, powers . . . 66.71
Powers of . . . 66.7
Regulations made by . . . 66.6, 66.91
Remuneration and expenses . . . 66.2
Report by . . . 66.9
Staff of . . . 66.4
Studies . . . 66.8
Time limits in respect of matters before
  . . . TLBCBR1-12

COPYRIGHT OFFICE . . . 46; CR2, 9

COPYRIGHT PROTECTION, EQUAL
Certification of countries granting equal copyright protection . . . CN2, Sch.

**CROWN PUBLICATIONS, TERM OF
COPYRIGHT** . . . 12

D

DEFINITIONS
Generally . . . 2, 2.11, 3, 31, 64, 79
Article, design . . . 64
Collective society . . . EPWOR1
Copy identifier . . . EPWOR1
Copyright, of . . . 3
Educational institution . . . 2
  Identifier . . . EPWOR1
Exclusive distributor . . . 2
Institution . . . EPWOR1
Library, archive or museum . . . 2
Maker . . . 2.11
Publication . . . 2.2

DESIGNS . . . 64

**DISABILITIES, PERCEPTUAL, PERSONS
WITH**
Definition . . . 2
Infringement, exceptions . . . 32, 86

DISTANT SIGNAL (See also LOCAL SIG-
  NAL)
Definition . . . LSDSR2

DISTRIBUTOR
Exclusive . . . 2, 2.6, 27.1
Regulations . . . 2.6

**DRAMATIC, OPERATIC OR MUSICAL
WORK** . . . 43